Lecture Notes in Computer Science 12328

More information about this subseries at http://www.springer.com/series/7407

Santiago Escobar · Narciso Martí-Oliet (Eds.)

Rewriting Logic and Its Applications

13th International Workshop, WRLA 2020
Virtual Event, October 20–22, 2020
Revised Selected Papers

Springer

Editors
Santiago Escobar
Valencian Research Institute for Artificial Intelligence
Universitat Politècnica de València
Valencia, Spain

Narciso Martí-Oliet
Facultad de Informática
Universidad Complutense de Madrid
Madrid, Spain

ISSN 0302-9743 ISSN 1611-3349 (electronic)
Lecture Notes in Computer Science
ISBN 978-3-030-63594-7 ISBN 978-3-030-63595-4 (eBook)
https://doi.org/10.1007/978-3-030-63595-4

LNCS Sublibrary: SL1 – Theoretical Computer Science and General Issues

This Springer imprint is published by the registered company Springer Nature Switzerland AG
The registered company address is: Gewerbestrasse 11, 6330 Cham, Switzerland

Preface

This volume contains the formal proceedings of the 13th International Workshop on Rewriting Logic and its Applications (WRLA 2020).

Rewriting logic is a natural model of computation and an expressive semantic framework for concurrency, parallelism, communication, and interaction. It can be used for specifying a wide range of systems and languages in various application fields. It also has good properties as a metalogical framework for representing logics. Over the years, several languages based on rewriting logic have been designed and implemented. The aim of the workshop is to bring together researchers with a common interest in rewriting logic and its applications, and to give them the opportunity to present their recent works, discuss future research directions, and exchange ideas. The previous meetings were held in Asilomar (USA) 1996, Pont-à-Mousson (France) 1998, Kanazawa (Japan) 2000, Pisa (Italy) 2002, Barcelona (Spain) 2004, Vienna (Austria) 2006, Budapest (Hungary) 2008, Paphos (Cyprus) 2010, Tallinn (Estonia) 2012, Grenoble (France) 2014, Eindhoven (The Netherlands) 2016, and Thessaloniki (Greece) 2018.

WRLA 2020 should have been held during April 25–26, 2020, in Dublin, Ireland, as a satellite event of the European Joint Conferences on Theory & Practice of Software (ETAPS). Unfortunately, the COVID-19 pandemic reached us, forcing the organizers first to postpone ETAPS 2020 and later to cancel it, similarly to other events around the world. Due to this, our preparations for having invited speakers and tutorials at the workshop were also canceled. After discussing this matter with the Steering and the Program Committees, we decided to organize an online event that took place during October 20–22, 2020.

We received 16 submissions; each one of them was reviewed by at least three Program Committee members. After an extensive discussion, the Program Committee decided to accept 15 papers for presentation at the workshop, and 11 for inclusion in these formal proceedings.

We sincerely thank all the authors of papers submitted to the workshop, as well as the members of the Program Committee and the referees for their careful work in the review process. This time we cannot thank the ETAPS organizers because we did not reach the celebration stage. Hopefully, the COVID-19 pandemic will soon be over and then we will be able to recover our meetings on rewriting logic and everything else.

October 2020

Santiago Escobar
Narciso Martí-Oliet

Organization

Program Committee

Erika Abraham	RWTH Aachen University, Germany
María Alpuente	Universitat Politècnica de València, Spain
Irina Mariuca Asavoae	Trusted Labs, Thales Group, France
Kyungmin Bae	Pohang University of Science and Technology, South Korea
Clara Bertolissi	Aix-Marseille Université, France
Artur Boronat	University of Leicester, UK
Roberto Bruni	Università di Pisa, Italy
Francisco Durán	University of Málaga, Spain
Santiago Escobar	Universitat Politècnica de València, Spain
Maribel Fernandez	King's College London, UK
Thomas Genet	IRISA, France
Raúl Gutiérrez	Universitat Politècnica de València, Spain
Nao Hirokawa	JAIST, Japan
Alexander Knapp	Universität Augsburg, Germany
Alberto Lluch Lafuente	Technical University of Denmark, Denmark
Dorel Lucanu	Alexandru Ioan Cuza University, Romania
Narciso Martí-Oliet	Universidad Complutense de Madrid, Spain
Aart Middeldorp	University of Innsbruck, Austria
César Muñoz	NASA, USA
Vivek Nigam	fortiss GmbH, Germany
Kazuhiro Ogata	JAIST, Japan
Etienne Payet	LIM, Université de La Réunion, Reunion, France
Adrián Riesco	Universidad Complutense de Madrid, Spain
Christophe Ringeissen	Inria, France
Camilo Rocha	Pontificia Universidad Javeriana Cali, Colombia
Grigore Roşu	University of Illinois at Urbana-Champaign, USA
Vlad Rusu	Inria, France
Ralf Sasse	ETH Zurich, Switzerland
Traian Florin Serbanuta	University of Bucharest, Romania
Carolyn Talcott	SRI International, USA

Additional Reviewers

Abd Alrahman, Yehia
Kremer, Gereon
Marshall, Andrew M.
Van Oostrom, Vincent
Winkler, Sarah

Contents

Combining Parallel Graph Rewriting and Quotient Graphs

Thierry Boy de la Tour(✉) and Rachid Echahed

CNRS and University Grenoble Alpes, LIG Lab., Grenoble, France
{thierry.boy-de-la-tour,rachid.echahed}@imag.fr

Abstract. We define two graph transformations, one by parallelizing graph rewrite rules, the other by taking quotients of graphs. The former consists in the exhaustive application of local transformations defined by graph rewrite rules expressed in a set-theoretic framework. Compared with other approaches to parallel rewriting, we allow a substantial amount of overlapping only restricted by a condition called the *effective deletion property.* This transformation can be reduced by factoring out possibly many equivalent matchings by the automorphism groups of the rules. The second transformation is based on the use of equivalence relations over graph items and offers a new way of performing simultaneous merging operations. The relevance of combining the two transformations is illustrated on a running example.

1 Introduction

Graph structures play an important role in the modeling and construction of complex systems in various disciplines including computer science, biology, chemistry or physics, as they provide natural and concise representation of many data structures. Computing with graphs as first-class citizens requires the use of advanced graph-based computational models. In contrast to term rewriting [2], there are different ways, in the literature, to define graphs (e.g., simple or multiple graphs, hyper-graphs, attributed graphs, etc.) as well as their transformations, see, e.g., [4,13,15].

In this paper, we are interested in parallel transformations of graphs which yield deterministic computations. There are many situations where simultaneous graph transformations occur in practice such as social networks dynamics, cell-phones connections, cellular automata or biological processes such as plant growth. The need of using parallel graph transformations has been pointed out since the 70's, see e.g., [14,17]. The main novelty of our proposal is twofold: first, overlapping transformations can be handled in parallel under a suitable condition called the *effective deletion property.* This new condition makes it possible to fire simultaneously two (or more) rules with a mild form of disagreement in the sense that one rule can delete an item (i.e., node, arrow or attribute) while this is not required by another rule. The second novelty of the paper consists in proposing graph equivalences to formally describe parallel merging of graph items or

S. Escobar and N. Martí-Oliet (Eds.): WRLA 2020, LNCS 12328, pp. 1–18, 2020.
https://doi.org/10.1007/978-3-030-63595-4_1

attributes' expression evaluations. Furthermore, we introduce the notion of automorphism groups associated to graph rewrite rules which induce a substantial improvement of simultaneous graph transformations.

To motivate our purpose and to illustrate the introduced notions, we consider a running example borrowed from the rules defining mesh refinements [1]. In the following rule $\mathrm{r_m}$, a triangle is refined into four smaller triangles. Notice that this example does not show all the expressiveness of the rules we consider but illustrates sufficiently the investigated concepts.

$\mathrm{r_m}$:

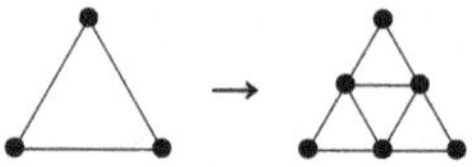

This geometric rule specifies a sequence of mesh refinements as depicted below:

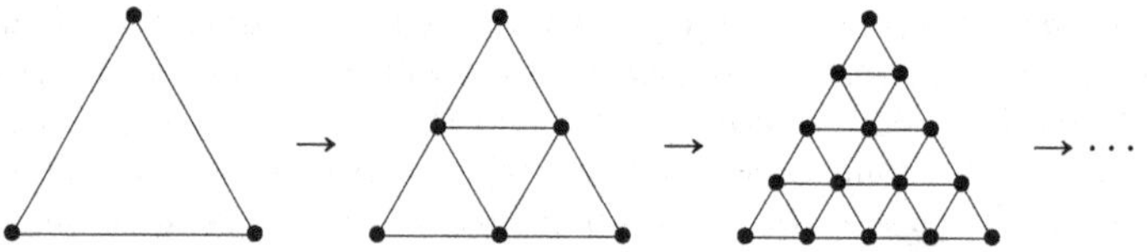

G_0 G_1 G_2

In this paper, we wish to view mesh refinement as a transformation of graphs, and to propose methods that could achieve this purpose. One obvious point is that $\mathrm{r_m}$ has to be applied simultaneously to every triangle subgraph of G_i to obtain G_{i+1}. However, if rule $\mathrm{r_m}$ is applied sequentially, say, at the center triangle subgraph of G_1, we get:

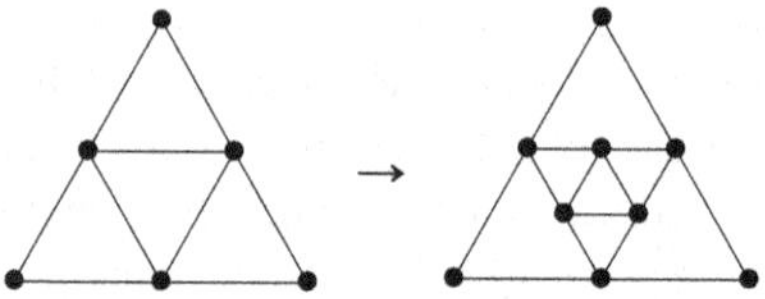

G_1 G_2'

then it is no longer possible to obtain G_2 from G_2' since the side subgraph triangles of G_1 have been modified and cannot be matched anymore by the left-hand side of the rule $\mathrm{r_m}$. In other words, the matchings of $\mathrm{r_m}$ in G_1 are not parallel independent. We therefore need to define a general parallel transformation that may yield a result unreachable by sequential rewriting. This will be achieved in Sects. 5 and 6.

Before that, we start by introducing the considered definition of attributed graphs in Sect. 2, together with convenient notations. A set-theoretic framework is developed starting from Sect. 3 that will enable us to define graph transformations by an algebraic expression (Definition 6). Section 4 is dedicated to defining the notion of rewrite rules, together with their matchings. In Sect. 5, the general parallel graph transformations are defined and a central notion of *effective deletion property* of sets of matchings is exposed, which guarantees that graph objects are consistently deleted during the transformation. Section 6 is dedicated to a particular parallel rewrite relation where parallel matchings are considered up to automorphisms, based on a notion of automorphism groups of the considered rules. This section uses notions borrowed from group theory. In Sect. 7, we introduce the notion of graph transformation as quotient graphs. This is not rule-based but allows one to write fancy definitions of merge actions over graphs that cannot be expressed with the rules above. Finally, related work and concluding remarks are given in Sect. 8. These transformations are all illustrated on the example of rule $\mathrm{r_m}$ in quite some detail. The missing proofs can be found in [5].

2 Preliminaries

We assume a many-sorted signature Σ and a set $\mathscr{V}$ of *variables*, disjoint from Σ, such that every variable has a Σ-sort. For any finite $X \subseteq \mathscr{V}$, $\mathscr{T}(\Sigma, X)$ denotes the algebra of Σ-terms over X.

An *attributed graph* (or *graph* for short) G is a tuple $(\dot{G}, \vec{G}, \acute{G}, \grave{G}, \mathscr{A}_G, \mathring{G})$ where $\dot{G}, \vec{G}$ are sets, $\acute{G}, \grave{G}$ are the *source* and *target* functions from $\vec{G}$ to $\dot{G}$, $\mathscr{A}_G$ is a Σ-algebra and $\mathring{G}$ is an *attribution of* G, i.e., a function from $\dot{G} \cup \vec{G}$ to $\mathscr{P}(\lfloor \mathscr{A}_G \rfloor)$ (the carrier set $\lfloor \mathscr{A}_G \rfloor$ of $\mathscr{A}_G$ is the disjoint union of the carrier sets of the sorts in $\mathscr{A}_G$). We assume that $\dot{G}$, $\vec{G}$ and $\lfloor \mathscr{A}_G \rfloor$ are pairwise disjoint; their elements are respectively called *vertices*, *arrows* and *attributes*. G is *unlabelled* if $\mathring{G}(x) = \varnothing$ for all $x \in \dot{G} \cup \vec{G}$, it is *finite* if the sets $\dot{G}$, $\vec{G}$ and $\mathring{G}(x)$ are finite. The *carrier* of G is the set $\lfloor G \rfloor \stackrel{\text{def}}{=} \dot{G} \cup \vec{G} \cup \lfloor \mathscr{A}_G \rfloor$.

A graph H is a *subgraph* of G, written $H \lhd G$, if the *underlying graph* $(\dot{H}, \vec{H}, \acute{H}, \grave{H})$ of H is a subgraph of G's underlying graph (in the usual sense), $\mathscr{A}_H = \mathscr{A}_G$ and $\forall x \in \dot{H} \cup \vec{H}, \mathring{H}(x) \subseteq \mathring{G}(x)$.

A morphism α from graph H to graph G is a function from $\lfloor H \rfloor$ to $\lfloor G \rfloor$ such that the restriction of α to $\dot{H} \cup \vec{H}$ is a morphism from H's to G's underlying graphs (that is, $\acute{G} \circ \alpha = \alpha \circ \acute{H}$ and $\grave{G} \circ \alpha = \alpha \circ \grave{H}$, this restriction of α is called the *underlying graph morphism of* α), the restriction of α to $\lfloor \mathscr{A}_H \rfloor$ is a Σ-homomorphism from $\mathscr{A}_H$ to $\mathscr{A}_G$, denoted $\mathring{\alpha}$, and $\forall x \in \dot{H} \cup \vec{H}$, $\mathring{\alpha} \circ \mathring{H}(x) \subseteq \mathring{G} \circ \alpha(x)$. This means that α is an isomorphism if and only if α is a bijective morphism *and* α^{-1} is a morphism, hence if and only if the underlying graph morphism of α is an isomorphism, $\mathring{\alpha}$ is a Σ-isomorphism *and* $\mathring{\alpha} \circ \mathring{H} = \mathring{G} \circ \alpha$. We write $H \simeq G$ if there exists an isomorphism from H to G. For all $F \lhd H$, the *image* $\alpha(F)$ is the smallest subgraph of G w.r.t. the order $\lhd$ such that $\alpha|_{\lfloor F \rfloor}$ is a morphism from F to $\alpha(F)$.

If the underlying graph morphism of α is injective then α is called a *matching*. Note that the Σ-homomorphism $\mathring{\alpha}$ need not be injective.

Given two attributions l and l' of G we define $l \setminus l'$ (resp. $l \cap l'$, $l \cup l'$) as the attribution of G that maps any x to $l(x) \setminus l'(x)$ (resp. $l(x) \cap l'(x)$, $l(x) \cup l'(x)$). If l is an attribution of a subgraph $H \lhd G$, we extend it implicitly to the attribution of G that is identical to l on $\dot{H} \cup \vec{H}$ and maps any other x to $\varnothing$.

3 Joinable Graphs

In order to define parallel rewrite relations on graphs, it is convenient to join possibly many different graphs that have a common part, i.e., that are *joinable.* As a matter of fact, this notion also allows a simple definition of graph rewrite rules, and is crucial in defining the automorphism groups of these rules. We start with a simpler notion of joinable functions.

Definition 1 (joinable functions). *Two functions $f : D \to C$ and $g : D' \to C'$ are* joinable *if $\forall x \in D \cap D'$, $f(x) = g(x)$. Then, the* meet *of f and g is the function $f \curlywedge g : D \cap D' \to C \cap C'$ that is the restriction of f (or g) to $D \cap D'$. The* join *$f \curlyvee g$ is the unique function from $D \cup D'$ to $C \cup C'$ such that $f = (f \curlyvee g)|_D$ and $g = (f \curlyvee g)|_{D'}$.*

For any set I and any I-indexed family $(f_i : D_i \to C_i)_{i \in I}$ of pairwise joinable functions, let $\bigcurlyvee_{i \in I} f_i$ be the only function from $\bigcup_{i \in I} D_i$ to $\bigcup_{i \in I} C_i$ such that $f_i = (\bigcurlyvee_{i \in I} f_i)|_{D_i}$ for all $i \in I$.

If S and T are sets of functions, let $S \curlyvee T \stackrel{\text{def}}{=} \{f \curlyvee g \mid f \in S, g \in T\}$ and $S \circ T \stackrel{\text{def}}{=} \{f \circ g \mid f \in S, g \in T\}$, provided these operations can be applied. If f is a function, let $f \circ T \stackrel{\text{def}}{=} \{f\} \circ T$.

In particular, functions with disjoint domains are joinable (e.g. $\dot{\alpha}$ and $\vec{\alpha}$), and every function is joinable with itself: $f \curlyvee f = f \curlywedge f = f$. More generally, any two restrictions $f|_A$ and $f|_B$ of the same function f are joinable, $f|_A \curlywedge f|_B = f|_{A \cap B}$ and $f|_A \curlyvee f|_B = f|_{A \cup B}$. Conversely, if f and g are joinable then each is a restriction of $f \curlyvee g$.

It is obvious that these operations are commutative. On triples of pairwise joinable functions, they are also associative and distributive over each other.

Definition 2 (joinable graphs). *Two graphs H and G are* joinable *if $\mathscr{A}_H = \mathscr{A}_G$, $\dot{H} \cap \vec{G} = \vec{H} \cap \dot{G} = \varnothing$, and the functions $\acute{H}$ and $\acute{G}$ (and similarly $\grave{H}$ and $\grave{G}$) are joinable. We can then define the graphs*

$$H \sqcap G \stackrel{\text{def}}{=} (\, \dot{H} \cap \dot{G},\ \vec{H} \cap \vec{G},\ \acute{H} \curlywedge \acute{G},\ \grave{H} \curlywedge \grave{G},\ \mathscr{A}_H,\ \mathring{H} \cap \mathring{G} \,),$$
$$H \sqcup G \stackrel{\text{def}}{=} (\, \dot{H} \cup \dot{G},\ \vec{H} \cup \vec{G},\ \acute{H} \curlyvee \acute{G},\ \grave{H} \curlyvee \grave{G},\ \mathscr{A}_H,\ \mathring{H} \cup \mathring{G} \,).$$

Similarly, for any set I, any I-indexed family of graphs $(G_i)_{i \in I}$ that are pairwise joinable, and any Σ-algebra $\mathcal{A}$ such that $\mathcal{A} = \mathscr{A}_{G_i}$ for all $i \in I$, let

$$\bigsqcup_{i \in I} G_i \stackrel{\text{def}}{=} (\, \bigcup_{i \in I} \dot{G}_i,\ \bigcup_{i \in I} \vec{G}_i,\ \bigcurlyvee_{i \in I} \acute{G}_i,\ \bigcurlyvee_{i \in I} \grave{G}_i,\ \mathcal{A},\ \bigcup_{i \in I} \mathring{G}_i \,).$$

It is easy to see that these structures are graphs: the sets of vertices and arrows are disjoint and the adjacency functions have the correct domains and codomains. If $I = \varnothing$ the chosen algebra $\mathcal{A}$ is generally obvious from the context. Note that if H and G are joinable then $H \sqcap G = G \sqcap H \lhd H \lhd H \sqcup G = G \sqcup H$. Similarly, if the G_i's are pairwise joinable then $\forall j \in I$, $G_j \lhd \bigsqcup_{i \in I} G_i$. We also see that any two subgraphs of G are joinable, and that $H \lhd G$ iff $H \sqcap G = H$ iff $H \sqcup G = G$. As above, on triples of pairwise joinable $\mathcal{A}$-graphs, these operations are associative and distributive over each other.

Definition 3. *For any graph G, sets V, A and attribution l, we say that G is* disjoint from *V, A, l if $\dot{G} \cap V = \varnothing$, $\vec{G} \cap A = \varnothing$ and $\mathring{G}(x) \cap l(x) = \varnothing$ for all $x \in \dot{G} \cup \vec{G}$.*

We write $G \setminus [V, A, l]$ for the largest subgraph of G (w.r.t. $\lhd$) that is disjoint from V, A, l.

This provides a natural way of removing objects from an attributed graph. It is easy to see that $G \setminus [V, A, l]$ always exists (it is the union of all subgraphs of G disjoint from V, A, l), hence rewriting steps will not be restricted by a *gluing condition* as in the Double-Pushout approach (see [13]).

4 Rules

We consider rules with three joinable graphs L, K and R as depicted below.

The semantics of such rules is defined in Sect. 5. Informally, L shall be matched in the input graph G, the region $L \setminus K$ (the items matched by L but not by K) shall be removed from G, and the region $R \setminus L$ shall be added in order to obtain an image of R in the output graph.

Definition 4 (rules, matchings). *For any finite $X \subseteq \mathscr{V}$, we call (Σ, X)-*graph *a finite graph G such that $\mathscr{A}_G = \mathscr{T}(\Sigma, X)$. We define the set of variables occurring in a (Σ, X)-graph G as*

$$\mathrm{Var}(G) \stackrel{\mathrm{def}}{=} \bigcup_{x \in \dot{G} \cup \vec{G}} \left(\bigcup_{t \in \mathring{G}(x)} \mathrm{Var}(t) \right),$$

where $\mathrm{Var}(t)$ *is the set of variables occurring in t.*

A rule *r is a triple (L, K, R) of (Σ, X)-graphs such that L and R are joinable, $L \sqcap R \lhd K \lhd L$ and $\mathrm{Var}(L) = X$ (see Remark 1 below). The rule r is* standard *if $L \sqcap R = K$.*

A matching *μ of r* in *a graph G is a matching from L to G such that*

$$\mathring{\mu}(\mathring{L}(x) \setminus \mathring{K}(x)) \cap \mathring{\mu}(\mathring{K}(x)) = \varnothing \tag{1}$$

(or equivalently $\mathring{\mu}(\mathring{L}(x) \setminus \mathring{K}(x)) = \mathring{\mu}(\mathring{L}(x)) \setminus \mathring{\mu}(\mathring{K}(x))$) for all $x \in \dot{K} \cup \vec{K}$. We denote $\mathscr{M}(r, G)$ the set of all matchings of r in G (they all have domain $\lfloor L \rfloor$).

We consider finite sets $\mathcal{R}$ of rules such that $\forall r, r' \in \mathcal{R}$, if $(L, K, R) = r \neq r' = (L', K', R')$ then $\dot{L} \cup \vec{L} \neq \dot{L}' \cup \vec{L}'$, so that $\lfloor L \rfloor \neq \lfloor L' \rfloor$ hence $\mathscr{M}(r, G) \cap$

$\mathscr{M}(\mathrm{r}', G) = \varnothing$ for any graph G; we then write $\mathscr{M}(\mathcal{R}, G)$ for $\biguplus_{r \in \mathcal{R}} \mathscr{M}(r, G)$. For any $\mu \in \mathscr{M}(\mathcal{R}, G)$ there is a unique rule $\mathrm{r}_\mu \in \mathcal{R}$ such that $\mu \in \mathscr{M}(\mathrm{r}_\mu, G)$, and its components are denoted $\mathrm{r}_\mu = (\mathrm{L}_\mu, \mathrm{K}_\mu, \mathrm{R}_\mu)$.

Remark 1. If X were allowed to contain a variable v not occurring in L, then v would freely match any element of $\mathscr{A}_G$ and the set $\mathscr{M}(r, G)$ would contain as many matchings with essentially the same effect. Note that matchings are only injective on graph items (vertices and arrows), so that distinct variables may match the same attribute, as is the case in term rewriting. However, condition (1) restricts the possible matchings in order to distinguish the attributes intended for deletion (those matched by $\mathring{L}(x) \setminus \mathring{K}(x)$) from those that are not (matched by $\mathring{K}(x)$).

Also note that $\mathrm{Var}(R) \subseteq \mathrm{Var}(L)$, R and K are joinable and $R \sqcap K = L \sqcap R$. The fact that K is not required to be a subgraph of R allows the possible deletion by other rules of data matched by K but not by R, see Sect. 5.

Example 1. Let us consider the rule given in the introduction. It could be defined as the standard rule $\mathrm{r_m} = (\mathrm{L_m}, \mathrm{K_m}, \mathrm{R_m})$ with

$\mathrm{L_m} =$ 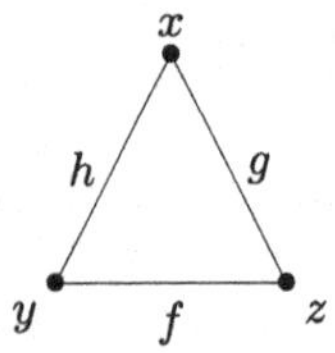

$\mathrm{K_m} =$ 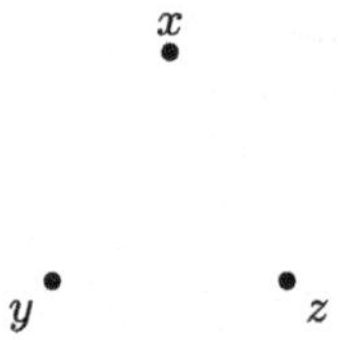

$\mathrm{R_m} =$ 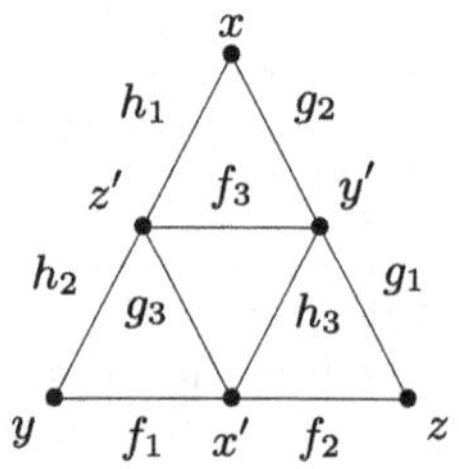

We assume, for the rule above, that all attributes are empty, hence $\mathrm{L_m}$, $\mathrm{K_m}$ and $\mathrm{R_m}$ are $(\Sigma, \varnothing)$-graphs. Each edge f, g, h represents a pair of opposite arrows; for sake of simplicity they will be treated as single objects. Note that $\mathrm{r_m}$ is a standard rule. A matching μ of $\mathrm{r_m}$ in the graph

$G_0 =$ 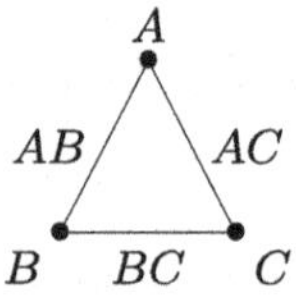

is given by $\mu = \{(x, A), (y, B), (z, C), (f, BC), (g, AC), (h, AB)\}$. The Σ-algebra $\mathscr{A}_{G_0}$ and the Σ-morphism $\mathring{\mu}$ are not relevant here, we can choose $\mathscr{T}(\Sigma, \varnothing)$ and its identity morphism (though other algebras and attributes will be adopted later).

A rewrite step may involve the creation of new vertices in a graph, corresponding to the vertices of a rule that have no match in the input graph, i.e., those in $\dot{R} \setminus \dot{L}$ (or similarly may create new arrows). These vertices should really be new, not only different from the vertices of the original graph but also different from the vertices created by other transformations (corresponding to other matchings in the graph). This is computationally easy to do but not that easy to formalize in an abstract way. We simply reuse the vertices x from $\dot{R}\setminus\dot{L}$ by *indexing* them with any relevant matching μ, each time yielding a new vertex (x,μ) which is obviously different from any new vertex (x,ν) for any other matching $\nu \neq \mu$, and also from any vertex of G since μ depends on G.

Definition 5 (graph $G{\uparrow_\mu}$ and matching $\mu{\uparrow}$). *For any rule $r = (L, K, R)$, graph G and $\mu \in \mathscr{M}(r, G)$ we define a graph $G{\uparrow_\mu}$ together with a matching $\mu{\uparrow}$ of R in $G{\uparrow_\mu}$. We first define the sets*

$$\dot{G}{\uparrow_\mu} \stackrel{\text{def}}{=} \mu(\dot{R}\cap\dot{K}) \uplus ((\dot{R}\setminus\dot{K})\times\{\mu\}) \text{ and } \vec{G}{\uparrow_\mu} \stackrel{\text{def}}{=} \mu(\vec{R}\cap\vec{K}) \uplus ((\vec{R}\setminus\vec{K})\times\{\mu\}).$$

Next we define $\mu{\uparrow}$ by: $\mathring{\mu}{\uparrow} \stackrel{\text{def}}{=} \mathring{\mu}$ and for all $x \in \dot{R}\cup\vec{R}$, if $x \in \dot{K}\cup\vec{K}$ then $\mu{\uparrow}(x) \stackrel{\text{def}}{=} \mu(x)$ else $\mu{\uparrow}(x) \stackrel{\text{def}}{=} (x,\mu)$. Since the restriction of $\mu{\uparrow}$ to $\dot{R}\cup\vec{R}$ is bijective, then $\mu{\uparrow}$ is a matching from R to the graph

$$G{\uparrow_\mu} \stackrel{\text{def}}{=} (\dot{G}{\uparrow_\mu}, \vec{G}{\uparrow_\mu}, \mu{\uparrow}\circ\acute{R}\circ\mu{\uparrow}^{-1}, \mu{\uparrow}\circ\grave{R}\circ\mu{\uparrow}^{-1}, \mathscr{A}_G, \mathring{\mu}{\uparrow}\circ\mathring{R}\circ\mu{\uparrow}^{-1}).$$

Example 2. Following Example 1, we get $\dot{G}_0{\uparrow_\mu} = \{A, B, C, (x',\mu), (y',\mu), (z',\mu)\}$, $\vec{G}_0{\uparrow_\mu} = \{(f_1,\mu),\ldots,(h_3,\mu)\}$, $\mu{\uparrow} = \{(x,A),(y,B),(z,C),(x',(x',\mu)),(y',(y',\mu)),(z',(z',\mu)),(f_1,(f_1,\mu)),\ldots,(h_3,(h_3,\mu))\}$. The graph $G_0{\uparrow_\mu}$ is obtained as $\mu{\uparrow}(\mathrm{R_m})$.

By construction μ and $\mu{\uparrow}$ are joinable and $\mu \curlywedge \mu{\uparrow}$ is a matching from $R\sqcap K$ to $\mu(R\sqcap K)$. It is easy to see that the graph G and the graphs $G{\uparrow_\mu}$ are pairwise joinable.

5 Parallel Rewriting

For any set $M \subseteq \mathscr{M}(\mathcal{R}, G)$ of matchings in a graph G we define below how to rewrite G by applying simultaneously the rules associated with matches in M.

Definition 6 (graph $G\|_M$). *For any graph G, set $M \subseteq \mathscr{M}(\mathcal{R}, G)$ and matching $\mu \in \mathscr{M}(\mathcal{R}, G)$, let*

$$G\|_M \stackrel{\text{def}}{=} G\setminus[\mathrm{V}_M, \mathrm{A}_M, \ell_M] \sqcup \bigsqcup_{\mu\in M} G{\uparrow_\mu} \quad \textit{where}$$

$$\mathrm{V}_M \stackrel{\text{def}}{=} \bigcup_{\mu\in M} \mu(\dot{\mathrm{L}}_\mu\setminus\dot{\mathrm{K}}_\mu),\ \mathrm{A}_M \stackrel{\text{def}}{=} \bigcup_{\mu\in M} \mu(\vec{\mathrm{L}}_\mu\setminus\vec{\mathrm{K}}_\mu) \text{ and } \ell_M \stackrel{\text{def}}{=} \bigcup_{\mu\in M} \mathring{\mu}\circ(\mathring{\mathrm{L}}_\mu\setminus\mathring{\mathrm{K}}_\mu)\circ\mu^{-1}.$$

If M is a singleton $\{\mu\}$ we write $G\|_\mu$ for $G\|_M$, V_μ for V_M, etc.

Note that ℓ_M is only defined on $\bigsqcup_{\mu\in M}\mu(\mathrm{K}_\mu)$; so ℓ_M is implicitly extended to the suitable domain by mapping other vertices and arrows to $\varnothing$. $G\|_M$ is guaranteed to be a graph since the $\sqcup$ operation is only applied on joinable graphs.

The definition of $G\|_M$ bears some similarity with the double pushout diagram (see [13]), where $G \setminus [\mathrm{V}_M, \mathrm{A}_M, \ell_M]$ replaces the pushout complement of G and $\bigsqcup_{\mu\in M} G\!\uparrow_\mu$ its pushout with the right hand side of the rule. But we are not restricted by the gluing condition, and since we use a set of matchings the pushout is actually a colimit. The case where M is a singleton defines the classical semantics of one sequential rewrite step.

It is obvious that $G\|_M$ contains images of the right hand sides of all the rules involved (through the elements M). However it may be the case that some elements of V_M, A_M or ℓ_M occur in $\bigsqcup_{\mu\in M} G\!\uparrow_\mu$, hence also in the result $G\|_M$, since any two matchings may conflict as one retains what another removes as illustrated in the following example.

Example 3. Let us consider the (non standard) rule $r_\mathrm{c} = (L_\mathrm{c}, K_\mathrm{c}, R_\mathrm{c})$ with

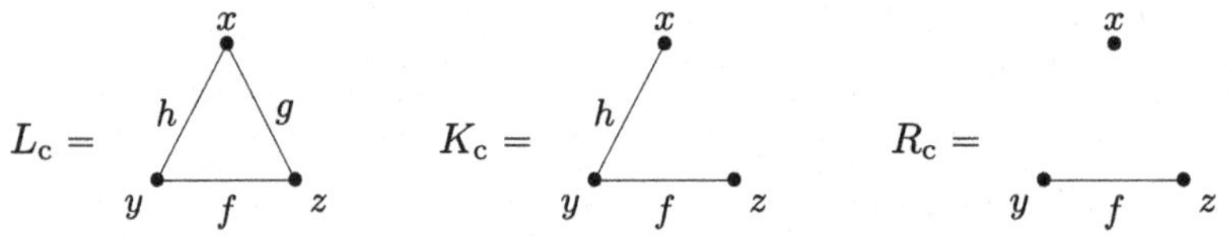

This rule removes g since g is in L_c but not in K_c, retains f (and all vertices) since f is in $K_\mathrm{c} \sqcap R_\mathrm{c}$, and does not care about h since h is in K_c but not in R_c. Nothing is added since $K_\mathrm{c} \sqcap R_\mathrm{c} = R_\mathrm{c}$. We consider the same graph G_0 and matching μ as in Example 1. Let $\nu = \mu \circ (x\ y)(f\ g)$ (in cyclic notation), this is obviously a matching of r_c in G_0. By μ we must remove AC and retain BC, while ν asks exactly the opposite which means there is a conflict between the application of the two matches. We easily see that the graph $G_0\!\uparrow_\mu$ contains BC and that $G_0\!\uparrow_\nu$ contains AC, so that $G_0\|_{\{\mu,\nu\}} = G_0$, hence the instructions of removing AC and BC have not been fulfilled. The reader may check that no such conflict occurs between μ and $\mu \circ (y\ z)(g\ h)$; they remove AC and AB.

Since the semantics of individual rules have to be preserved under parallelization, we must avoid such conflicts by stating that any item deleted by any rule should not occur in the result. We can however allow attributes to be removed and yet restored: this is a situation similar to an assignment $a := 1$, where the former value of a is deleted unless it is 1.

Definition 7 (effective deletion property). *For any graph G, a set $M \subseteq \mathscr{M}(\mathcal{R}, G)$ is said to satisfy the* effective deletion property *if $G\|_M$ is disjoint from $\mathrm{V}_M, \mathrm{A}_M, \ell_M \setminus \ell^{\uparrow}_M$, where*

$$\ell^{\uparrow}_M \stackrel{\mathrm{def}}{=} \bigcup_{\mu\in M} \mathring{\mu} \circ (\mathring{\mathrm{R}}_\mu \setminus \mathring{\mathrm{K}}_\mu) \circ \mu^{-1}.$$

We thus see in Example 3 that $\{\mu, \nu\}$ does not have the effective deletion property, since $G_0\|_{\{\mu,\nu\}}$ (i.e., G_0) is not disjoint from $\mathrm{A}_{\{\mu,\nu\}} = \{AC, BC\}$. The following example illustrates the special treatment of attributes.

Example 4. Consider the assignment $a := b$ where a and b are identifiers of type `nat`. This expression can be represented as a graph transformation rule in the following way. We assume a signature Σ with two sorts `idtf` and `nat`, and two constants a, b of sort `idtf`. Let $X = \{u, v\}$ where u, v are two variables of sort `nat`. A placeholder is represented as a vertex attributed by a set containing both its identifier and its value. Thus the environment where, say, a has value 1 and b has value 2 can be represented by the graph $G = (\{x, y\}, \varnothing, \varnothing, \varnothing, \mathscr{A}_G, \mathring{G})$ where $\mathscr{A}_G$ interprets the sort `idtf` by $\{a, b\}$ (the terms of sort `idtf`) and the sort `nat` by $\mathbb{N}$, and where $\mathring{G}(x) = \{a, 1\}$, $\mathring{G}(y) = \{b, 2\}$. For the sake of conciseness this graph can be represented by

$$G = x, \{a, 1\}\ y, \{b, 2\}.$$

With these conventions the assignment $a := b$ can be represented by the rule $r_1 = (L_1, K_1, R_1)$ with

$$L_1 = x_1, \{a, u\}\ y_1, \{b, v\} \qquad K_1 = x_1, \{a\}\ y_1, \{b, v\} \qquad R_1 = x_1, \{a, v\}$$

that removes the value u of a before replacing it by the value v of b. Similarly the assignment $b := a$ is represented by the rule $r_2 = (L_2, K_2, R_2)$ with

$$L_2 = x_2, \{a, u\}\ y_2, \{b, v\} \qquad K_2 = x_2, \{a, u\}\ y_2, \{b\} \qquad R_2 = y_2, \{b, u\}.$$

Note that these rules are non standard. There is exactly one matching μ_1 of r_1 in G, and one matching μ_2 of r_2 in G, as given below.

	x_1	y_1	a	b	u	v
μ_1	x	y	a	b	1	2

	x_2	y_2	a	b	u	v
μ_2	x	y	a	b	1	2

These two matchings perfectly overlap since $\mu_1(L_1) = \mu_2(L_2) = G$. Let $M = \{\mu_1, \mu_2\}$, hence $\mathrm{V}_M = \mathrm{A}_M = \varnothing$ (no vertex and no arrow is deleted), $\ell_M(x) = \{1\}$ and $\ell_M(y) = \{2\}$ (the values 1 and 2 are removed from $\mathring{G}(x)$ and $\mathring{G}(y)$ respectively), hence $G \setminus [\mathrm{V}_M, \mathrm{A}_M, \ell_M] = x, \{a\}\ y, \{b\}$. We also have $G\!\uparrow_{\mu_1} = \mu_1(R_1) = x, \{a, 2\}$ and $G\!\uparrow_{\mu_2} = \mu_2(R_2) = y, \{b, 1\}$, so that

$$G\|_M = (x, \{a\}\ y, \{b\}) \sqcup (x, \{a, 2\}) \sqcup (y, \{b, 1\}) = x, \{a, 2\}\ y, \{b, 1\}.$$

Hence the parallel transformation of G by r_1 and r_2 yields the same result as the simultaneous assignment $a, b := b, a$ in Python: it swaps the values of a and b. Besides, this transformation preserves the semantics of r_1 and r_2 since the initial values of a and b have effectively been deleted from $\mathring{G}(x)$ and $\mathring{G}(y)$ respectively. Indeed, $\ell_M(x) \setminus \ell_M^{\uparrow}(x) = \{1\} \setminus \{2\} = \{1\}$ and $\ell_M(x) \setminus \ell_M^{\uparrow}(y) = \{2\} \setminus \{1\} = \{2\}$, hence $G\|_M$ is disjoint from $\mathrm{V}_M, \mathrm{A}_M, \ell_M \setminus \ell_M^{\uparrow}$, and M therefore has the effective deletion property.

Assume now that this transformation is applied to an environment where a and b have the same value, say 1. This is represented by $G' = x', \{a, 1\}\ y', \{b, 1\}$, and there are two obvious matchings μ_1', μ_2' of r_1, r_2 respectively in G' (the variables u and v are both matched to 1). Let $M' = \{\mu_1', \mu_2'\}$,, we see that

$$G'\|_{M'} = (x', \{a\}\ y', \{b\}) \sqcup (x', \{a, 1\}) \sqcup (y', \{b, 1\}) = x', \{a, 1\}\ y', \{b, 1\} = G'$$

as expected. But the initial values of a and b have not been deleted from $\mathring{G}(x)$ and $\mathring{G}(y)$ respectively. Yet we have

$$\ell_{M'}(x') \setminus \ell^{\uparrow}_{M'}(x') = \ell_{M'}(y') \setminus \ell^{\uparrow}_{M'}(y') = \{1\} \setminus \{1\} = \varnothing,$$

hence $G\|_M$ is trivially disjoint from $\mathrm{V}_{M'}, \mathrm{A}_{M'}, \ell_{M'} \setminus \ell^{\uparrow}_{M'}$, and M' therefore has the effective deletion property. Even in this case we agree that the semantics of r_1 and r_2 has been respected by the parallel transformation, since 1 has been deleted before it was restored.

We may ask wether it is possible to ensure from particular properties of $\mathcal{R}$ that effective deletion holds for all G and M. It is however easy to see that, given a rule that removes an object, say a vertex, and another (or the same) rule that retains some vertex, there always exists a graph G and two matchings in G that conflict on the same vertex, hence that do not have the effective deletion property. The effective deletion property should therefore be checked for every input G and M.

This naturally leads to the following definition.

Definition 8 (full parallel rewriting). *For any finite set of rules $\mathcal{R}$, we define the relation $\rightrightarrows_{\mathcal{R}}$ of* full parallel rewriting *between graphs by stating that, for all G such that $\mathscr{M}(\mathcal{R}, G)$ has the effective deletion property, $G \rightrightarrows_{\mathcal{R}} G\|_{\mathscr{M}(\mathcal{R},G)}$.*

It can be shown that $\rightrightarrows_{\mathcal{R}}$ is *deterministic up to isomorphism*, that is, if $G \rightrightarrows_{\mathcal{R}} H$, $G' \rightrightarrows_{\mathcal{R}} H'$ and $G \simeq G'$ then $H \simeq H'$.

6 Parallel Rewriting Modulo Automorphisms

Using the full set of matchings exceeds the needs of mesh refinement, see below.

Example 5. Following Example 1, we see that there are 6 matchings of $\mathrm{r_m}$ in G_0, hence the relation $\rightrightarrows_{\mathrm{r_m}}$ does not create 3 but 18 new vertices, not 9 but 54 new edges, which is illustrated as gray areas below.

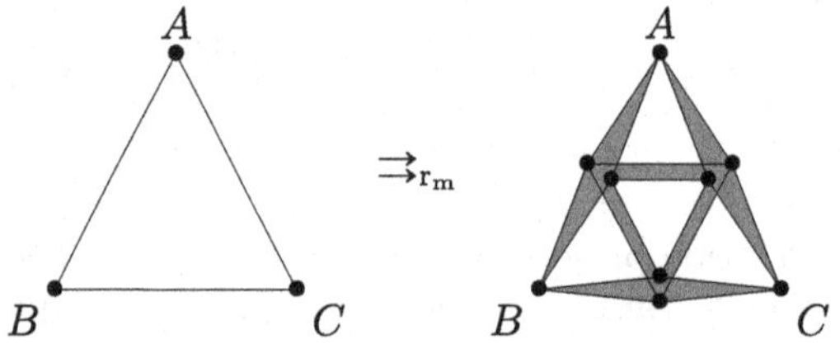

We therefore wish to select a subset M of $\mathscr{M}(\mathcal{R}, G)$ for defining a rewrite relation that yields more natural and concise graphs.

In Example 5, the similarities between the 6 matchings clearly come from the symmetries of rule $\mathrm{r_m}$. These depend on the automorphisms of the graphs $\mathrm{L_m}$, $\mathrm{K_m}$ and $\mathrm{R_m}$, i.e., on the groups commonly denoted $\mathrm{Aut}(\mathrm{L_m})$, $\mathrm{Aut}(\mathrm{K_m})$ and $\mathrm{Aut}(\mathrm{R_m})$. We need to build a notion of rule automorphisms that properly accounts for the interactions between these 3 groups. We first extend the notion of automorphism groups of graphs to their subgraphs.

Definition 9 (groups $\mathrm{Aut}_G(H_1,\ldots,H_n)$ and $\mathcal{S}|_H$). *For all $n \geq 1$, graph G and subgraphs $H, H_1, \ldots, H_n \lhd G$, let*

$$\mathrm{Aut}_G(H) \stackrel{\mathrm{def}}{=} \{\alpha \in \mathrm{Sym}(\dot{G}) \curlyvee \mathrm{Sym}(\vec{G}) \curlyvee \mathrm{Aut}(\mathscr{A}_G) \mid \alpha(H) = H\},$$

$$\mathrm{Aut}_G(H_1,\ldots,H_n) \stackrel{\mathrm{def}}{=} \bigcap_{i=1}^{n} \mathrm{Aut}_G(H_i).$$

For any $\alpha \in \mathrm{Aut}_G(H)$, we write $\alpha|_H$ for $\alpha|_{\lfloor H \rfloor}$, and for any subgroup $\mathcal{S}$ of $\mathrm{Aut}_G(H)$, let $\mathcal{S}|_H = \{\alpha|_H \mid \alpha \in \mathcal{S}\}$; this is a subgroup of $\mathrm{Aut}(H)$.

It is obvious that $\mathrm{Aut}_G(G) = \mathrm{Aut}(G)$. We see that $\mathrm{Aut}_G(H)$ is a permutation group on $\lfloor G \rfloor$, but only the graph structure of H is involved in the constraint $\alpha(H) = H$, not the structure of G.

Example 6. Take for instance

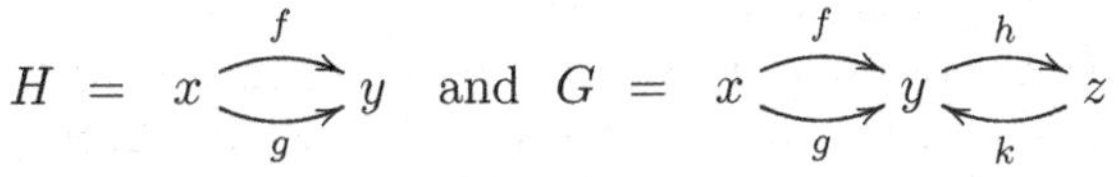

with empty attributes. We have

$$\mathrm{Aut}(H) = \{1_H,\ (x)(y)(f\ g)\} \text{ and } \mathrm{Aut}(G) = \{1_G,\ (x)(y)(z)(f\ g)(h)(k)\}$$

We write non permuted points such as (x) in order to make the domains explicit. However, in $\mathrm{Aut}_G(H)$ the permutations of objects that do not belong to H are free, hence

$$\begin{aligned}\mathrm{Aut}_G(H) &= \{1_G,\ (x)(y)(z)(f\ g)(h)(k),\ (x)(y)(z)(f)(g)(h\ k),\\ &\qquad (x)(y)(z)(f\ g)(h\ k)\}\\ &= \mathrm{Aut}(H) \curlyvee \{(z)(h)(k),\ (z)(h\ k)\}\\ &= \mathrm{Aut}(H) \curlyvee \{(z)\} \curlyvee \{(h)(k),\ (h\ k)\}\\ &= \mathrm{Aut}(H) \curlyvee \mathrm{Sym}\{z\} \curlyvee \mathrm{Sym}\{h,\ k\}.\end{aligned}$$

Since $\mathscr{A}_H = \mathscr{A}_G$, it is easy to see that $\mathrm{Aut}_G(H) = \mathrm{Aut}(H) \curlyvee \mathrm{Sym}(\dot{G} \setminus \dot{H}) \curlyvee \mathrm{Sym}(\vec{G} \setminus \vec{H})$ always holds and thus $\mathrm{Aut}_G(H)|_H = \mathrm{Aut}(H)$. This means that, compared to the elements of $\mathrm{Aut}(H)$ which are only permutations of $\lfloor H \rfloor$, the elements of $\mathrm{Aut}_G(H)$ are *all* possible extensions of the elements of $\mathrm{Aut}(H)$ to permutations of $\lfloor G \rfloor$. This allows us to conveniently intersect the automorphism groups of joinable graphs.

Definition 10 (group $\mathrm{Aut}(r)$, relation $\approx$). *For any rule $r = (L, K, R)$, the* automorphism group *of r is $\mathrm{Aut}(r) \stackrel{\mathrm{def}}{=} \mathrm{Aut}_{L \sqcup R}(L, K, R)|_L$. For any graph G, let $\approx$ be the equivalence relation on $\mathscr{M}(\mathcal{R}, G)$ defined by $\mu \approx \nu$ iff $\mu \circ \mathrm{Aut}(\mathrm{r}_\mu) = \nu \circ \mathrm{Aut}(\mathrm{r}_\nu)$. The equivalence class of μ is denoted $\bar{\mu}$. For any subset $M \subseteq \mathscr{M}(\mathcal{R}, G)$ we write $\bar{M}$ for the set $\bigcup_{\mu \in M} \bar{\mu}$.*

Lemma 1. $\forall \mu \in \mathscr{M}(\mathcal{R}, G),\ \bar{\mu} = \mu \circ \mathrm{Aut}(\mathrm{r}_\mu)$.

Note that $|\bar{\mu}| \leq |\mathrm{Aut}(\mathrm{r}_\mu)|$ and that the equality holds if μ is injective. The more symmetric a rule is, the more matchings are likely to occur in the equivalence classes of matchings of this rule. The definition of the automorphism groups of rules has been crafted so that the isomorphism classes of the output graphs do not depend on the choice of elements in the equivalence classes of matchings.

Theorem 1. *For any graph G, any $\mathcal{M} \subseteq \mathscr{M}(\mathcal{R}, G)$ and any minimal sets M, N such that $\mathcal{M} = \bar{M} = \bar{N}$, the graphs $G\|_M$ and $G\|_N$ are isomorphic.*

This means that the following graph rewrite relation is deterministic up to isomorphism.

Definition 11 (parallel rewriting modulo automorphisms). *For any finite set of rules $\mathcal{R}$, we define the relation $\Rightarrow_{\mathcal{R}}$ of* parallel rewriting modulo automorphisms *between graphs by stating that, for all G and minimal set M such that $\bar{M} = \mathscr{M}(\mathcal{R}, G)$ and M has the effective deletion property, $G \Rightarrow_{\mathcal{R}} G\|_M$.*

Example 7. Following Example 1, we see that the group $\mathrm{Aut}(\mathrm{K_m})$ is generated by $\{(x\ y), (x\ z)\}$ (this is $\mathrm{Sym}\{x, y, z\}$), the group $\mathrm{Aut}(\mathrm{L_m})$ is generated by $\{(x\ y)(f\ g), (x\ z)(f\ h)\}$, and $\mathrm{Aut}(\mathrm{R_m})$ is generated by $\{\rho_1, \rho_2\}$ where $\rho_1 = (x\ y)(x'\ y')(h_1\ h_2)(f_1\ g_2)(f_2\ g_1)(f_3\ g_3)$ and $\rho_2 = (x\ z)(x'\ z')(g_1\ g_2)(f_1\ h_2)(f_2\ h_1)(f_3\ h_3)$. We then use the facts that

$$\mathrm{Aut}_{\mathrm{L_m} \sqcup \mathrm{R_m}}(\mathrm{L_m}) = \mathrm{Aut}(\mathrm{L_m}) \curlyvee \mathrm{Sym}\{x', y', z'\} \curlyvee \mathrm{Sym}\{f_1, g_1, h_1, f_2, g_2, h_2, f_3, g_3, h_3\}$$
$$\mathrm{Aut}_{\mathrm{L_m} \sqcup \mathrm{R_m}}(\mathrm{K_m}) = \mathrm{Aut}(\mathrm{K_m}) \curlyvee \mathrm{Sym}\{x', y', z'\} \curlyvee \mathrm{Sym}\{f, g, h, f_1, \ldots, h_3\}$$
$$\mathrm{Aut}_{\mathrm{L_m} \sqcup \mathrm{R_m}}(\mathrm{R_m}) = \mathrm{Aut}(\mathrm{R_m}) \curlyvee \mathrm{Sym}\{f, g, h\}$$

to see that $\mathrm{Aut}_{\mathrm{L_m} \sqcup \mathrm{R_m}}(\mathrm{L_m})$ is a subgroup of $\mathrm{Aut}_{\mathrm{L_m} \sqcup \mathrm{R_m}}(\mathrm{K_m})$, and then we easily see that $\mathrm{Aut}_{\mathrm{L_m} \sqcup \mathrm{R_m}}(\mathrm{L_m}, \mathrm{K_m}, \mathrm{R_m}) = \mathrm{Aut}_{\mathrm{L_m} \sqcup \mathrm{R_m}}(\mathrm{L_m}, \mathrm{R_m})$ is generated by $\{\rho_1 \curlyvee (f\ g), \rho_2 \curlyvee (f\ h)\}$. We thus obtain that $\mathrm{Aut}(\mathrm{r_m})$ is the group generated by $\{(\rho_1 \curlyvee (f\ g))|_{\mathrm{L_m}}, (\rho_2 \curlyvee (f\ h))|_{\mathrm{L_m}}\} = \{(x\ y)(f\ g), (x\ z)(f\ h)\}$, i.e., $\mathrm{Aut}(\mathrm{r_m}) = \mathrm{Aut}(\mathrm{L_m})$ and this group has 6 elements. The 6 matchings of $\mathrm{L_m}$ in G_0 are therefore all equivalent by $\approx$. Similarly, the 24 matchings of $\mathrm{L_m}$ in G_1 form 4 equivalence classes modulo $\approx$. This yields the following parallel rewrite steps modulo automorphisms.

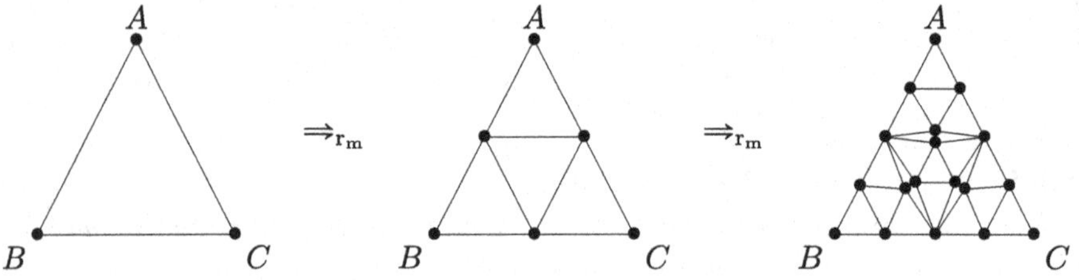

7 Graph Transformations as Quotients

The last example shows that we still need to be able to merge graph items. In this section, we propose to use equivalence relations to merge graph vertices or edges as well as their possible attributes.

Definition 12 (Congruence on a Graph, quotient graph). *For any graph G, a* congruence $\mathcal{C}$ on G *is a tuple $(\sim, \simeq, \cong)$ where $\cong$ is a congruence on $\mathscr{A}_G$ (see [2, p. 45]) and $\sim$, $\simeq$ are equivalence relations on $\dot{G}$, $\vec{G}$ respectively, such that*

$$\forall f, g \in \vec{G},\ \textit{if } f \simeq g \textit{ then } \acute{G}(f) \sim \acute{G}(g) \textit{ and } \grave{G}(f) \sim \grave{G}(g). \tag{2}$$

$\mathcal{C}$ is neutral *if $\cong$ is the identity relation on $\mathscr{A}_G$.*

The quotient of G by $\mathcal{C}$ *is the graph $G/\mathcal{C} = (\dot{G}/\!\sim, \vec{G}/\!\simeq, s, t, \mathscr{A}_G/\!\cong, l)$ where $\dot{G}/\!\sim$ and $\vec{G}/\!\simeq$ are the standard quotients (the sets of equivalence classes), $\mathscr{A}_G/\!\cong$ is the quotient algebra (see [2, p. 45]), and*

- *for any $F \in \vec{G}/\!\simeq$ and any $f \in F$, $s(F)$ (resp. $t(F)$) is the class of $\acute{G}(f)$ (resp. $\grave{G}(f)$) modulo $\sim$ (which by (2) depends only on the class F of f modulo $\simeq$),*
- *for any $C \in (\dot{G}/\!\sim) \cup (\vec{G}/\!\simeq)$, $l(C) \stackrel{\text{def}}{=} \bigcup_{x \in C}\{\bar{t} \mid t \in \mathring{G}(x)\}$, where $\bar{t}$ is the equivalence class of $t \in \lfloor \mathscr{A}_G \rfloor$ modulo $\cong$.*

Note that if $\mathcal{C}$ is neutral then $\mathscr{A}_{G/\mathcal{C}}$ is identified with $\mathscr{A}_G$.

Example 8. Let us consider the following graph Z consisting of six sticks. These sticks could be thought, for example, as a furniture kit. Every stick can be considered as a pair of two opposite arrows attributed by its length (not depicted), with $\lfloor \mathscr{A}_Z \rfloor = \mathbb{R}$. Each end of a stick is a vertex whose attribute is $\varnothing$.

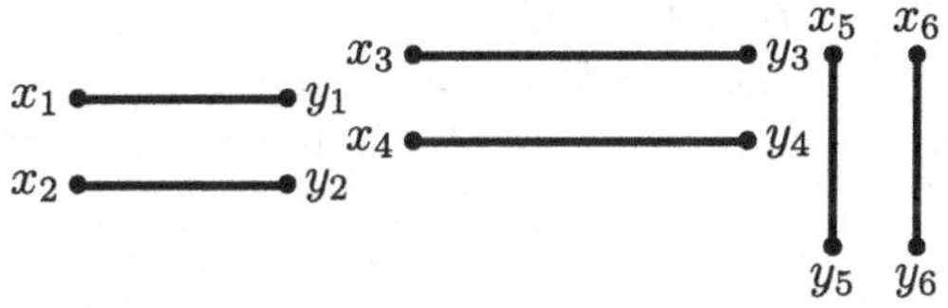

The instructions for assembling the kit can be given as the following equivalence relation on vertices: $x_1 \sim x_3$, $x_2 \sim y_3$, $y_1 \sim x_4 \sim x_5$, $y_2 \sim y_4 \sim x_6$ and $y_5 \sim y_6$. We now consider the neutral congruence $\mathcal{Z} = (\sim, =_{\vec{Z}}, =_{\mathscr{A}_G})$, where $=_{\vec{Z}}$ is the identity relation on $\vec{G}$ (so that condition (2) is obviously satisfied). The reader can easily check that the quotient graph $Z/\mathcal{Z}$ is the following one.

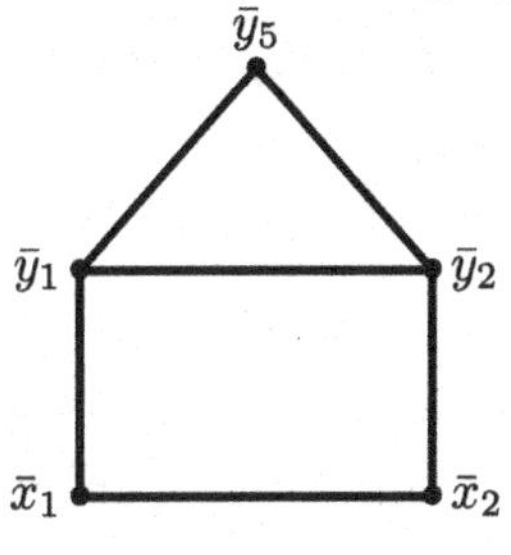

By definition, a congruence is specific to a particular graph, hence we need a way to define a congruence from a graph in order to define a universal transformation by taking quotients of graphs. There are many ways this could be done, and we only propose a solution relevant to mesh refinement.

Definition 13 (The localizing congruence). *For any graph* G, *the* localizing congruence $\mathscr{L}_G$ *on* G *is the tuple* $(\sim, \simeq, =_{\mathscr{A}_G})$ *where*

- *for all* $x, y \in \dot{G}$, $x \sim y$ *iff* $\mathring{G}(x) = \mathring{G}(y)$,
- *for all* $f, g \in \vec{G}$, $f \simeq g$ *iff* $\acute{G}(f) \sim \acute{G}(g)$ *and* $\grave{G}(f) \sim \grave{G}(g)$,
- $=_{\mathscr{A}_G}$ *is the identity relation on* $\mathscr{A}_G$.

We write $\gtrsim_{\mathscr{L}}$ *for the binary relation on graphs defined by* $G \gtrsim_{\mathscr{L}} (G/\mathscr{L}_G)$ *for all graphs* G.

In this transformation, the attributes of the vertices act as coordinates in the sense that there can be only one vertex (or point) at each coordinate, and only one arrow from one point to another. Note that, since $\mathscr{L}_G$ is neutral, then obviously $\mathscr{A}_G = \mathscr{A}_H$ whenever $G \gtrsim_{\mathscr{L}} H$.

Example 9. In Example 1, it was not necessary to define precisely which algebra was considered since all attributes were empty. We now give more substance to the mesh graphs by assuming that every vertex is attributed with its coordinates in the affine plane, i.e., by a singleton containing an element of $\mathbb{R}^2$. The only operation we need is the function that returns the coordinates of the middle of two points, hence we take Σ with a function symbol `mid` of arity 2, and we consider the Σ-algebra $\mathcal{P}$ with carrier set $\mathbb{R}^2$ where `mid` is interpreted as the function that to any $(x, y) \in \mathbb{R}^2$ and $(x', y') \in \mathbb{R}^2$ maps $(\frac{x+x'}{2}, \frac{y+y'}{2}) \in \mathbb{R}^2$. We start with the graph G_0 as in Example 1, but with $\mathscr{A}_{G_0} = \mathcal{P}$, $\mathring{G}_0(A)$ is a singleton that contains the coordinates of A (an element of $\mathbb{R}^2$), and similarly for vertices B and C.

In order to match these coordinates we also need to use variables in the rule $\mathrm{r_m}$, hence we consider 3 distinct variables $u, v, w \in \mathscr{V}$ and let $X = \{u, v, w\}$. We consider the graphs $\mathrm{L_m}$, $\mathrm{K_m}$, $\mathrm{R_m}$ of Example 1 but with the algebra $\mathscr{T}(\Sigma, X)$ and with the following attributes on vertices:

- $\mathring{\mathrm{L}}_\mathrm{m}(x) = \mathring{\mathrm{K}}_\mathrm{m}(x) = \mathring{\mathrm{R}}_\mathrm{m}(x) = \{u\}$, $\mathring{\mathrm{L}}_\mathrm{m}(y) = \mathring{\mathrm{K}}_\mathrm{m}(y) = \mathring{\mathrm{R}}_\mathrm{m}(y) = \{v\}$ and $\mathring{\mathrm{L}}_\mathrm{m}(z) = \mathring{\mathrm{K}}_\mathrm{m}(z) = \mathring{\mathrm{R}}_\mathrm{m}(z) = \{w\}$. These attributes are therefore not modified by the rule.
- We must also compute the coordinates of the new vertices x', y', z' created by $\mathrm{R_m}$. One difficulty is that in the algebra of terms $\mathtt{mid}(u, v)$ is different from $\mathtt{mid}(v, u)$, and if we choose one then we necessarily loose some automorphisms of the rule. The solution is to take both, that is

$$\mathring{\mathrm{R}}_\mathrm{m}(x') = \{\mathtt{mid}(v, w), \mathtt{mid}(w, v)\},$$
$$\mathring{\mathrm{R}}_\mathrm{m}(y') = \{\mathtt{mid}(u, w), \mathtt{mid}(w, u)\},$$
$$\mathring{\mathrm{R}}_\mathrm{m}(z') = \{\mathtt{mid}(v, u), \mathtt{mid}(u, v)\}.$$

With these attributes it is easy to see that $\mathrm{Aut}(\mathrm{r_m})$ is generated by the two permutations $(x\ y)(f\ g)(u\ v)$ and $(x\ z)(f\ h)(u\ w)$, and has 6 elements. The 6 matchings of $\mathrm{L_m}$ in G_0 are all $\approx$-equivalent to the matching $\mu \in \mathscr{M}(\mathrm{r_m}, G_0)$ with the same images of vertices and arrows as in Example 1, and where $\mathring{\mu}(x)$ is the coordinate of A, and similarly for y and z. Hence we have $G_0 \Rrightarrow_{\mathrm{r_m}} G_1$, where to every vertex is attributed the coordinate of the corresponding point of $\mathcal{P}$. Applying $\Rrightarrow_{\mathrm{r_m}}$ still yields a graph with too many vertices and edges, though with correct coordinates, hence quotienting this graph with its localizing congruence yields the graph G_2. We thus see that

 $\Rrightarrow_{\mathrm{r_m}} \circ \gtrsim_{\mathscr{L}}$ 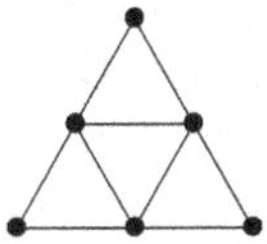 $\Rrightarrow_{\mathrm{r_m}} \circ \gtrsim_{\mathscr{L}}$ 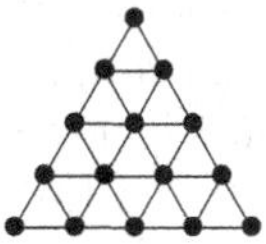 $\Rrightarrow_{\mathrm{r_m}} \circ \gtrsim_{\mathscr{L}} \cdots$

ad infinitum, as we expected (though these graphs contain attributes that are not depicted). Note that $\rightrightarrows_{\mathrm{r_m}} \circ \gtrsim_{\mathscr{L}}$ yields the same result as $\Rrightarrow_{\mathrm{r_m}} \circ \gtrsim_{\mathscr{L}}$, though in a less efficient way since $\mathrm{Aut}(\mathrm{r_m})$ needs only be computed once.

8 Related Work and Concluding Remarks

Parallel graph rewriting has already been considered in the literature. In the mid-seventies, H. Ehrig and H.-J. Kreowski [14] tackled the problem of parallel graph transformations and proposed conditions under which parallel graph transformations could be sequentialized and how sequential independent graph transformations could be parallelized. This pioneering work has been considered for several algebraic graph transformation approaches, see, e.g., the most recent contributions [9,21,22] or Volume 3 of the Handbook of Graph Grammars and Computing by Graph Transformation [12]. However, this stream of work departs drastically from our goal where parallel graph transformations are not aimed to be sequentialized.

Non independent parallel graph transformations has been considered in the Double-Pushout setting, see e.g. [24] where rules can be amalgamated by agreeing on common deletions and preservations. However, the amalgamation technique does not allow the amount of overlaps achieved in the present framework. Indeed, the effective deletion property makes it possible for one rule to delete an item that is matched but not deleted by another (non standard) rule. This is an essential feature for instance in cellular automata where the state of a cell can be modified by one rule and only consulted by others (see [5]).

In [19], a framework based on the algebraic Single-Pushout approach has been proposed and where parallel transformations consider only matchings provided by a control flow mapping. The users can solve the possible conflicts between the rules by providing the right control flow. More recently, a parallel graph rewrite relation has been defined in [11] for a special kind of graphs called port-graphs. Unfortunately, such graphs are not closed under parallel graph transformation, in the sense that a port-graph can be rewritten in a structure which is not a port-graph. In addition, conditions for avoiding conflicts in parallel transformations have been defined over the considered rewrite rules, which limits drastically the class of the considered systems. The present framework provides more abstract and more general conditions over matchings that ensure a correct definition of parallel graph transformations for a large class of systems.

In [23, chapter 14], parallel graph transformations have been studied in order to improve the operational semantics of the functional programming language CLEAN [16]. In that contribution, the authors do not deal with true parallelism but rather have an interleaving semantics. This particularly entails that their parallel rewrite steps can be simulated by sequential ones. This is also the case for other frameworks where massive parallel graph transformations is defined so that it can be simulated by sequential rewriting e.g., [10,20,21].

Graph equivalence has already been used to encode vertex merging as in [3] where the notion of e-graphs has been proposed. An e-graph is a pair $(G, \sim)$ of a hypergraph and an equivalence over vertices. Contrary to our framework, quotient graphs are not used per se as objects to be transformed. Furthermore, our notion of equivalence over graphs is more general since it can be defined either on vertices, arrows or even attributes.

Transforming a graph by using simultaneously several rules in parallel is not an easy task. As mentioned above, most of the proposals in the literature consider parallel transformations that can be sequentialized. In this paper, we have developed a new framework where true parallel graph transformations are defined following an algorithmic approach. We proposed deterministic parallel rewrite relations, particularly one based on the notion of automorphism groups of rules. Furthermore, we defined the notion of *effective deletion property* of matchings which ensures that these relations are well-behaved, even when the overlappings of matches forbids sequentialization, as illustrated by the mesh refinement rule $\mathrm{r_m}$. The proposed rewrite relations may be used in several contexts such as extensions of L-systems to dynamic graph structures (see, e.g., [17,18,25]). For the sake of simplicity we have not addressed here the problem of the finiteness of the graphs obtained by parallel rewriting, see [5] for a discussion and results on this subject.

The considered rewrite systems could be enriched by means of new features such as vertex and edge cloning as proposed in [7,8]. This is possible in an algebraic framework, see [6]. Future work also includes implementation issues, particularly for the parallel rewrite relation up to automorphisms. The present framework has been designed so that the automorphism groups of rules are finite permutation groups, thus paving the way to efficient implementations through the methods of Algorithmic Group Theory.

References

1. Andrew, R.B., Sherman, A.H., Weiser, A.: Some refinement algorithms and data structures for regular local mesh refinement (1983)

2. Baader, F., Nipkow, T.: Term Rewriting and All That. Cambridge University Press, Cambridge (1998)
3. Baldan, P., Gadducci, F., Montanari, U.: Concurrent rewriting for graphs with equivalences. In: Baier, C., Hermanns, H. (eds.) CONCUR 2006. LNCS, vol. 4137, pp. 279–294. Springer, Heidelberg (2006). https://doi.org/10.1007/11817949_19
4. Boronat, A., Heckel, R., Meseguer, J.: Rewriting logic semantics and verification of model transformations. In: Chechik, M., Wirsing, M. (eds.) FASE 2009. LNCS, vol. 5503, pp. 18–33. Springer, Heidelberg (2009). https://doi.org/10.1007/978-3-642-00593-0_2
5. Boy de la Tour, T., Echahed, R.: A set-theoretic framework for parallel graph rewriting. CoRR (abs/1808.03161) (2018)
6. Boy de la Tour, T., Echahed, R.: True parallel graph transformations: an algebraic approach based on weak spans. CoRR (abs/1904.08850) (2019)
7. Brenas, J.H., Echahed, R., Strecker, M.: Verifying graph transformation systems with description logics. In: Lambers, L., Weber, J. (eds.) ICGT 2018. LNCS, vol. 10887, pp. 155–170. Springer, Cham (2018). https://doi.org/10.1007/978-3-319-92991-0_10
8. Corradini, A., Duval, D., Echahed, R., Prost, F., Ribeiro, L.: AGREE – algebraic graph rewriting with controlled embedding. In: Parisi-Presicce, F., Westfechtel, B. (eds.) ICGT 2015. LNCS, vol. 9151, pp. 35–51. Springer, Cham (2015). https://doi.org/10.1007/978-3-319-21145-9_3
9. Corradini, A., et al.: On the essence of parallel independence for the double-pushout and sesqui-pushout approaches. In: Heckel, R., Taentzer, G. (eds.) Graph Transformation, Specifications, and Nets. LNCS, vol. 10800, pp. 1–18. Springer, Cham (2018). https://doi.org/10.1007/978-3-319-75396-6_1
10. Echahed, R., Janodet, J.-C.: Parallel admissible graph rewriting. In: Fiadeiro, J.L. (ed.) WADT 1998. LNCS, vol. 1589, pp. 122–138. Springer, Heidelberg (1999). https://doi.org/10.1007/3-540-48483-3_9
11. Echahed, R., Maignan, A.: Parallel graph rewriting with overlapping rules. CoRR (abs/1701.06790) (2017)
12. Ehrig, H., Kreowski, H.J., Montanari, U., Rozenberg, G. (eds.): Handbook of Graph Grammars and Computing by Graph Transformations, Volume 3: Concurrency, Parallelism and Distribution. World Scientific, Singapore (1999)
13. Ehrig, H., Ehrig, K., Prange, U., Taentzer, G.: Fundamentals of Algebraic Graph Transformation. Monographs in Theoretical Computer Science. An EATCS Series. Springer, Heidelberg (2006). https://doi.org/10.1007/3-540-31188-2
14. Ehrig, H., Kreowski, H.-J.: Parallelism of manipulations in multidimensional information structures. In: Mazurkiewicz, A. (ed.) MFCS 1976. LNCS, vol. 45, pp. 284–293. Springer, Heidelberg (1976). https://doi.org/10.1007/3-540-07854-1_188
15. Engelfriet, J., Rozenberg, G.: Node replacement graph grammars. In: Handbook of Graph Grammars and Computing by Graph Transformations, Volume 1: Foundations, pp. 1–94 (1997)
16. Software Technology Research Group: The Clean Home Page. Radboud University, Nijmegen
17. Culik II, K., Lindenmayer, A.: Parallel graph generating and recurrence systems for multicellular development. Int. J. Gen. Syst. **3**(1), 53–66 (1976). https://doi.org/10.1080/03081077608934737
18. Janssens, D., Rozenberg, G., Verraedt, R.: On sequential and parallel node-rewriting graph grammars. Comput. Graph. Image Process. **18**(3), 279–304 (1982). https://doi.org/10.1016/0146-664X(82)90036-3

19. Kniemeyer, O., Barczik, G., Hemmerling, R., Kurth, W.: Relational growth grammars – a parallel graph transformation approach with applications in biology and architecture. In: Schürr, A., Nagl, M., Zündorf, A. (eds.) AGTIVE 2007. LNCS, vol. 5088, pp. 152–167. Springer, Heidelberg (2008). https://doi.org/10.1007/978-3-540-89020-1_12
20. Kreowski, H., Kuske, S.: Graph multiset transformation: a new framework for massively parallel computation inspired by DNA computing. Nat. Comput. **10**(2), 961–986 (2011)
21. Kreowski, H.-J., Kuske, S., Lye, A.: A simple notion of parallel graph transformation and its perspectives. In: Heckel, R., Taentzer, G. (eds.) Graph Transformation, Specifications, and Nets. LNCS, vol. 10800, pp. 61–82. Springer, Cham (2018). https://doi.org/10.1007/978-3-319-75396-6_4
22. Löwe, M.: Characterisation of parallel independence in AGREE-rewriting. In: Lambers, L., Weber, J. (eds.) ICGT 2018. LNCS, vol. 10887, pp. 118–133. Springer, Cham (2018). https://doi.org/10.1007/978-3-319-92991-0_8
23. Plasmeijer, R., Eekelen, M.V.: Functional Programming and Parallel Graph Rewriting, 1st edn. Addison-Wesley Longman Publishing Co., Inc., Boston (1993)
24. Taentzer, G.: Parallel high-level replacement systems. TCS Theor. Comput. Sci. **186**, 43–81 (1997)
25. Wolfram, S.: A New Kind of Science. Wolfram-Media, Champaign (2002)

Connecting Constrained Constructor Patterns and Matching Logic

Xiaohong Chen[1(✉)], Dorel Lucanu[2], and Grigore Roșu[1]

[1] University of Illinois at Urbana-Champaign, Champaign, USA
{xc3,grosu}@illinois.edu
[2] Alexandru Ioan Cuza University of Iași, Iași, Romania
dlucanu@info.uaic.ro

Abstract. Constrained constructor patterns are pairs of a constructor term pattern and a quantifier-free first-order logic constraint, built from conjunction and disjunction. They are used to express state predicates for reachability logic defined over rewrite theories. Matching logic has been recently proposed as a unifying foundation for programming languages, specification and verification. It has been shown to capture several logical systems and/or models that are important for programming languages, including first-order logic with fixpoints and order-sorted algebra. In this paper, we investigate the relationship between constrained constructor patterns and matching logic. The comparison result brings us a mutual benefit for the two approaches. Matching logic can borrow computationally efficient proofs for some equivalences, and the language of the constrained constructor patterns can get a more logical flavor and more expressiveness.

1 Introduction

The subject of this paper is inspired by a comment given by José Meseguer in a private message: "I strongly conjecture that there is a deep connection between matching logic and the constrained constructor patterns. It would be great to better understand the details of such a connection".

Constrained constructor patterns are the bricks of the *rewrite-theory-generic* reachability logic framework [11], by which we mean that the reachability logic framework as considered in [11] is parametric in the underlying rewriting theory. The order-sorted specifications $(\Sigma, E \cup B)$, used as support for rewrite theories, consist of an order-sorted signature Σ, a set of particular equations B used to reason modulo B, and a set of equations E that can be turned into a set of rewrite rules $\overrightarrow{E}$ convergent modulo B, assuming that the theory $(\Sigma, E \cup B)$ is sufficiently complete [9]. In this paper, we work under the assumptions that ensure all the properties mentioned below (now we implicitly assume them). The definition of constrained constructor patterns is based on the strong relationship between the initial $(\Sigma, E \cup B)$-algebra $T_{\Sigma/E\cup B}$ and its canonical constructor $(\Omega, E_\Omega \cup B_\Omega)$-algebra $C_{\Omega/E_\Omega, B_\Omega}$. This relationship is briefly explained as follows:

S. Escobar and N. Martí-Oliet (Eds.): WRLA 2020, LNCS 12328, pp. 19–37, 2020.
https://doi.org/10.1007/978-3-030-63595-4_2

1. $T_{\Sigma/E\cup B}$ is isomorphic to the canonical term-algebra $C_{\Sigma/E,B}$, consisting of B-equivalence classes of $\overrightarrow{E}$-irreducible-modulo-B Σ-terms;
2. $\Omega \subseteq \Sigma$ is the subsignature of constructors;
3. $C_{\Sigma/E,B}|_{\Omega} = C_{\Omega/E_{\Omega},B_{\Omega}}$.

A constrained constructor pattern predicate is a pair $u|\varphi$, where u is a constructor term pattern and φ is a quantifier-free first-order logic (FOL) formula. The set of constrained constructor patterns includes the constrained constructor pattern predicates and is closed under conjunction and disjunction. The semantics defined by $u|\varphi$ is given by the subset of states $[\![u|\varphi]\!] \subseteq C_{\Omega/E_{\Omega},B_{\Omega}}$ matching u, i.e., for each $a \in [\![u|\varphi]\!]$ there is a valuation ρ such that φ holds (written $\rho \models \varphi$) and $a = u\rho$.

There are several additional operations over constrained constructor patterns required to express reachability properties and to support their verification in a computational efficient way. These include (parameterized) subsumption, over-approximation of the complements, and parameterized intersections. The definitions of these operations exploits the cases when the matching and unification modulo $E \cup B$ can be efficiently solved, using, e.g., the theory of variants [4,7].

Matching Logic (ML) [2,3,10] is a variant of first-order logic (FOL) with fixpoints that makes no distinction between functions and predicates. It uses instead symbols and application to uniformly build patterns that can represent static structures and logical constraints at the same time. Semantically, ML patterns are interpreted as the sets of elements that match them. The functional interpretation is obtained by adding axioms like $\exists y.\mathtt{s}\,x = y$ that forces the pattern $\mathtt{s}\,x$ to be evaluated to a singleton. The conjunction and disjunction are interpreted as the intersection, respectively union. For instance, the ML pattern $\exists x{:}Nat.\,\mathtt{s}\,x \wedge (x = 2 \vee x = 5)$, when interpreted over the natural numbers, denotes the set $\{3, 6\}$ since $\mathtt{s}\,x$ is matched by the successor of x, constants 2 and 5 are matched by the numbers 2 and 5, respectively, and $x = n$ is a "predicate": it matches either the entire carrier set when x and n are matched by the same elements, or otherwise the empty set.

The **main contribution** of the paper is an insightful comparison of constrained constructor patterns and matching logic. Since order-sorted algebras can be captured in matching logic [2], we were tempted to think that this comparison is a natural one, because a constrained constructor pattern $u|\varphi$ can be seen as a special ML pattern $u \wedge \varphi$. When we started to formalize this intuition, we realized a few interesting challenges that we need to address:

- How to capture the logical reasoning modulo equations in B in ML?
- How to formalize the canonical model containing only constructor terms?
- What properties does the ML model corresponding to an OSA canonical model have?
- Which are the most suitable ML patterns that capture constrained constructor pattern operations?
- How to express the equivalence between a constrained constructor pattern and its ML encoding?

In order to better understand the relationship between the two approaches, we consider a running example, the QLOCK mutual exclusion protocol [5,11], and show how to define it in ML. This example gives us a better view of the specificity of ML axioms and how the OSA canonical model is reflected in ML. In this paper, we only consider the static structure of QLOCK. Since the ML axiomatization includes the complete specifications of natural numbers, (finite) list and (finite) multisets, and it specifies their carrier sets using least fixpoints, we can derive from the specifications an induction proof principle for them.

Structure of the Paper. We define constrained constructor patterns and introduce the QLOCK example in Sect. 2. In Sect. 3, we introduce matching logic (ML) in details, as it was recently proposed. In Sect. 4 we discuss the axiomatization of free constructors and the encoding of OSA in ML, and a complete specification of the QLOCK configurations. In Sect. 5, we show the ML encoding of the constrained constructor patterns and their operations, which is our main contribution. We conclude in Sect. 6.

2 Constrained Constructor Patterns

We assume the readers are familiar with order-sorted equational and first-order logics (see, e.g., [8]). Here we briefly recall the definitions of constructor pattern predicates [11].

Definition 1. *An* order-sorted signature $\Sigma = (S, \leq, F)$ *contains a sort set* S*, a partial ordering* $\leq \subseteq S \times S$ *called* subsorting*, and a function (family) set* $F = \{F_{s_1 \ldots s_n, s}\}_{s_1, \ldots, s_n, s \in S}$. *We allow* subsort overloading*, i.e.,* $f \in F_{s_1 \ldots s_n, s} \cap F_{s'_1 \ldots s'_n, s'}$ *with* $s_1 \leq s'_1, \ldots, s_n \leq s'_n, s \leq s'$. *An* order-sorted algebra $A = (\{A_s\}_{s \in S}, \{f_A\}_{f \in F})$ *contains (1) a nonempty carrier set* A_s *for every* $s \in S$*; we require* $A_s \subseteq A_{s'}$ *whenever* $s \leq s'$*; and (2) a function interpretation* $f\colon M_{s_1} \times \cdots \times M_{s_n} \to M_s$ *for every* $f \in F_{s_1 \ldots s_n, s}$. *Note that overloaded functions must coincide on the overlapped parts.*

A function $f \in F_{s_1 \ldots s_n, s}$ is denoted as $f : s_1 \times \cdots \times s_n \to s$. Let $X = \{X_s\}_{s \in S}$ be an S-indexed set of *sorted variables* denoted $x{:}s, y{:}s$. We use $T_\Sigma(X)$ to denote the Σ*-term algebra on* X, whose elements are (ground and non-ground) terms. We use $T_\Sigma = T_\Sigma(\emptyset)$ to denote the Σ-algebra of ground terms.

An (equational) *order-sorted theory* $(\Sigma, B \cup E)$ consists of an order-sorted signature Σ and a union set $B \cup E$ of (possibly conditional) Σ-equations (explained below). We assume that $F = \Omega \cup \Delta$, where Ω contains *constructors* and Δ contains *defined functions*. We assume that B contains a special class of axioms that usually express properties like associativity, commutativity, and identity of functions in Σ. Let $B_\Omega \cup E_\Omega$ be the axioms (equations) that only contain constructors in Ω. Then, $(B \setminus B_\Omega) \cup (E \setminus E_\Omega)$ is the set of axioms (equations) that specify defined functions in Δ.

Given $(\Sigma, B \cup E)$, its *initial model* is isomorphic to the *canonical term algebra* $C_{\Sigma/E,B}$ that contains $(B_\Omega \cup E_\Omega)$-equivalence classes of ground Ω-terms. For a ground Σ-term t that may contain defined functions, we let $\mathit{canf}(t) = [u]_{B_\Omega \cup E_\Omega}$

denote its *canonical form* in $C_{\Sigma/E,B}$, i.e., $u =_{B \cup E} t$ and $u \in T_\Omega$. Let $\rho\colon X \to T_\Omega$ be a valuation. We define its extension $\_\rho\colon T_\Sigma \to T_\Omega$ in the usual way.

Given $s \in S$, an *s-sorted constrained constructor pattern* is an expression $u|\varphi$, where $u \in T_\Omega(X)$ has sort s and φ is a quantifier-free Σ-formula; see [11, p. 204]. The set of *constrained constructor pattern predicates* $PatPred(\Omega, \Sigma)$, is the smallest set that includes $\bot$ and constrained constructor patterns, and is closed under disjunction and conjunction. The *semantics* of a constrained constructor pattern predicate A is the set $[\![A]\!]_C$ of canonical terms that *satisfies* it:

$$[\![\bot]\!]_C = \emptyset \qquad [\![A \vee B]\!]_C = [\![A]\!]_C \cup [\![B]\!]_C \qquad [\![A \wedge B]\!]_C = [\![A]\!]_C \cap [\![B]\!]_C$$
$$[\![u|\varphi]\!]_C = \{ \mathit{canf}(u\rho) \mid \rho\colon X \to T_\Omega, C_{\Sigma/E,B} \models \varphi\rho \}$$

2.1 A Running Example: QLOCK

QLOCK is a mutual exclusion protocol [5] that allows an unbounded number of (numbered) processes that are in one of the three states: "normal" (doing their own things), "waiting" for a resource, and "critical" when using the resource. A QLOCK state is a tuple $\langle n|w|c|q \rangle$ where n, w, c are multisets of identities of the processes that are in "normal", "waiting", and "critical" states, respectively, and q is the waiting queue, i.e., an associative list. In this paper, we are only interested in understanding how constrained constructor patterns express state predicates, so we only consider the static structure of QLOCK states, whose OSA specification [11] is given below:

$S = \{Nat, List, MSet, NeMSet, Conf, state, Pred\}$
$\leq\, = \{Nat < List, Nat < NeMSet < MSet\} \cup =_S$
Σ_Ω (constructors):
  $\mathbb{0} : \;\to Nat,\ \mathtt{s}\_ : Nat \to Nat$
  $nil : \;\to List,\ \_;\_ : List \times List \to List$
  $empty : \;\to MSet,\ \_\,\_ : MSet \times MSet \to MSet,$
  $\_\,\_ : NeMSet \times NeMSet \to NeMSet$
  $\_|\_|\_|\_ : MSet \times MSet \times MSet \times List \to Conf$
  $\langle\_\rangle : Conf \to state$
  $tt : \;\to Pred, ff : \;\to Pred$
$\Sigma(\text{QLOCK}) = \Sigma_\Omega \cup \{dupl : MSet \to Pred, dupl : NeMSet \to Pred\}$
B_Ω:
  associativity for list concatenation $\_;\_$ with the identity nil
  associativity/commutativity for multiset union $\_;\_$ with the identity $empty$
$E_\Omega = \emptyset$
$E = \{dupl(s\,u\,u) = tt\}$, where s is any multiset (could be empty).

The corresponding canonical model, denoted QLK, is given as:

$\mathsf{QLK}_{Nat} = \{\mathbb{0}, \mathtt{s}\,\mathbb{0}, \mathtt{s}^2\,\mathbb{0}, \ldots\}$
$\mathsf{QLK}_{List} = \mathsf{QLK}_{Nat} \cup \{nil\} \cup \{n_1; \ldots; n_k \mid n_i \in \mathsf{QLK}_{Nat}, 1 \leq i \leq k, k \geq 2\}$
$\mathsf{QLK}_{NeMSet} = Nat \cup \{[n_1, \ldots, n_k] \mid n_i \in \mathsf{QLK}_{Nat}, 1 \leq i \leq k, k \geq 2\}$

$\mathsf{QLK}_{MSet} = \mathsf{QLK}_{NeMSet} \cup \{empty\}$
$\mathsf{QLK}_{Conf} = \{x_1|x_2|x_3|y \mid x_1, x_2, x_3 \in \mathsf{QLK}_{MSet}, y \in \mathsf{QLK}_{List}\}$
$\mathsf{QLK}_{state} = \{\langle x\rangle \mid x \in \mathsf{QLK}_{Conf}\}$
$\mathsf{QLK}_{Pred} = \{tt, \mathit{ff}\}$

An example of a constrained constructor pattern predicate is $\langle n|w|c|q\rangle |$ $dupl(n\, w\, c) \neq tt$, since no process can be waiting and critical at the same time.

3 Matching Logic

We give a compact introduction to matching logic (ML) syntax and semantics, and the important mathematical instruments that can be defined as theories and/or notations. For full details, we refer readers to [2,3,10].

3.1 Matching Logic Syntax and Semantics

ML is an unsorted logic whose formulas, called *patterns*, are constructed from constant symbols, two sets of variables (explained below), propositional constructs $\bot$ and $\to$, a binary application function, the FOL-style existential quantifier $\exists$, and the least fixpoint operator μ. In models, patterns are interpreted as the *sets* of elements that *match* them. Important mathematical instruments and structures, as well as various logical systems can be captured in ML.

Definition 2. *We assume two countably infinite sets of variables EV and SV, where EV is the set of* element variables *denoted $x, y, \ldots$ and SV is the set of* set variables *denoted $X, Y, \ldots$. Given an (at most) countable set of constant symbols Σ, the set of Σ-patterns, written* PATTERN, *is inductively generated by the following grammar for every $\sigma \in \Sigma$, $x \in EV$, and $X \in SV$:*

$$\varphi ::= \sigma \mid x \mid X \mid \varphi_1\, \varphi_2 \mid \bot \mid \varphi_1 \to \varphi_2 \mid \exists x\,.\,\varphi \mid \mu X\,.\,\varphi$$

where in $\mu X\,.\,\varphi$ we require that φ is positive in X, i.e., X is not nested in an odd number of times on the left-hand side of an implication $\varphi_1 \to \varphi_2$. This syntactic requirement is to make sure that φ is monotone with respect to the set X, and thus the least fixpoint denoted by $\mu X\,.\,\varphi$ exists.

Both $\exists$ and μ are binders, and we assume the standard notions of free variables, α-equivalence, and capture-avoiding substitution. Specifically, we use $FV(\varphi)$ to denote the set of (element and set) variables that occur free in φ. We regard α-equivalent patterns as syntactically identical. We write $\varphi[\psi/x]$ (resp. $\varphi[\psi/X]$) for the result of substituting ψ for x (resp. X) in φ, where bound variables are implicitly renamed to prevent variable capturing. We define the following logical constructs as syntactic sugar:

$$\neg\varphi \equiv \varphi \to \bot \quad \varphi_1 \vee \varphi_2 \equiv \neg\varphi_1 \to \varphi_2 \quad \varphi_1 \wedge \varphi_2 \equiv \neg(\neg\varphi_1 \vee \neg\varphi_2)$$
$$\top \equiv \neg\bot \quad \forall x\,.\,\varphi \equiv \neg\exists x\,.\,\neg\varphi \quad \nu X\,.\,\varphi \equiv \neg\mu X\,.\,\neg\varphi[\neg X/X]$$

We assume the standard precedence between logical constructs and that application $\varphi_1\,\varphi_2$ binds the tightest. We abbreviate the sequential application $(\cdots((\varphi_1\,\varphi_2)\,\varphi_3)\cdots\varphi_n)$ as $\varphi_1\,\varphi_2\,\varphi_3\cdots\varphi_n$.

ML has a *pattern matching* semantics where patterns are interpreted in models as the *sets* of elements that *match* them.

Definition 3. *Given a symbol set Σ, a Σ-*model $(M, \_\bullet\_, \{\sigma_M\}_{\sigma\in\Sigma})$ *contains:*

- *M: a nonempty carrier set;*
- *$\_\bullet\_$: $M \times M \to \mathcal{P}(M)$ as the interpretation of application, where $\mathcal{P}(M)$ is the powerset of M;*
- *$\sigma_M \subseteq M$: a subset of M as the* interpretation *of $\sigma \in \Sigma$.*

By abuse of notation, we write M for the above model.

For notational simplicity, we extend $\_\bullet\_$ from over elements to over sets, *pointwisely*, as follows:

$$\_\bullet\_ \colon \mathcal{P}(M) \times \mathcal{P}(M) \to \mathcal{P}(M) \quad A \bullet B = \bigcup_{a\in A, b\in B} a \bullet b \;\text{ for } A, B \subseteq M$$

Note that $\emptyset \bullet A = A \bullet \emptyset = \emptyset$ for any $A \subseteq M$.

Definition 4. *Given a symbol set Σ and a Σ-model M, an M-valuation $\rho\colon (EV \cup SV) \to (M \cup \mathcal{P}(M))$ is a function that maps element variables to elements of M and set variables to subsets of M, i.e., $\rho(x) \in M$ and $\rho(X) \subseteq M$ for every $x \in EV$ and $X \in SV$. We extend ρ from over variables to over patterns, denoted $\bar{\rho}$:* Pattern $\to \mathcal{P}(M)$*, as follows:*

$$\bar{\rho}(x) = \{\rho(x)\} \quad \bar{\rho}(X) = \rho(X) \quad \bar{\rho}(\sigma) = \sigma_M \quad \bar{\rho}(\bot) = \emptyset \quad \bar{\rho}(\varphi_1\,\varphi_2) = \bar{\rho}(\varphi_1) \bullet \bar{\rho}(\varphi_2)$$
$$\bar{\rho}(\varphi_1 \to \varphi_2) = M \setminus (\bar{\rho}(\varphi_1) \setminus \bar{\rho}(\varphi_2)) \quad \bar{\rho}(\exists x.\, \varphi) = \bigcup_{a\in M} \overline{\rho[a/x]}(\varphi) \quad \bar{\rho}(\mu X.\, \varphi) = \mu\mathcal{F}^{\rho}_{X,\varphi}$$

where $\mathcal{F}^{\rho}_{X,\varphi}\colon \mathcal{P}(M) \to \mathcal{P}(M)$ is a monotone function defined as $\mathcal{F}^{\rho}_{X,\varphi}(A) = \overline{\rho[A/X]}(\varphi)$ for $A \subseteq M$, and $\mu\mathcal{F}^{\rho}_{X,\varphi}$ denotes its unique least fixpoint given by the Knaster-Tarski fixpoint theorem [12].

Definition 5. *Given M and φ, we say M* satisfies *φ, written $M \vDash \varphi$, iff $\bar{\rho}(\varphi) = M$ for all ρ. Given $\Gamma \subseteq$* Pattern*, we say M* satisfies *Γ, written $M \vDash \Gamma$, iff $\bar{\rho}(\varphi) = M$ for all ρ and $\varphi \in \Gamma$. We call Γ a* theory *and patterns in Γ* axioms.

3.2 Important Mathematical Instruments

Several mathematical instruments of practical importance, such as definedness, totality, equality, membership, set containment, functions and partial functions, constructors, and sorts can all be defined using patterns. We give a compact summary of their definitions in ML and introduce proper notations for them.

Definedness Symbol and Axiom. ML patterns are interpreted as subsets of M. This is different from the classic FOL, whose formulas evaluate to either true or false. However, it is easy to restore the classic two-value semantics in ML, by using M, the entire carrier set, to represent the logical true, and $\emptyset$, the empty set, to represent the logical false. Since M is nonempty, no confusion is possible. We call φ a *predicate* in M if $\bar{\rho}(\varphi) \in \{\emptyset, M\}$ for all ρ. In the following, we define a set of predicate patterns that represent the important mathematical instruments. These patterns are constructed from a special symbol called *definedness*.

Definition 6. *Let* $\lceil \_ \rceil$ *be a symbol, which we call the* definedness *symbol. We write* $\lceil \varphi \rceil$ *instead of* $\lceil \_ \rceil\ \varphi$. *Let* (Definedness) *be the axiom* $\forall x. \lceil x \rceil$. *We define the following important notations:*

$$\textit{totality}\ \lfloor \varphi \rfloor \equiv \neg \lceil \neg \varphi \rceil \qquad \textit{equality}\ \varphi_1 = \varphi_2 \equiv \lfloor \varphi_1 \leftrightarrow \varphi_2 \rfloor$$
$$\textit{membership}\ x \in \varphi \equiv \lceil x \wedge \varphi \rceil \quad \textit{inclusion}\ \varphi_1 \subseteq \varphi_2 \equiv \lfloor \varphi_1 \rightarrow \varphi_2 \rfloor$$

We also define their negations:

$$\varphi_1 \neq \varphi_2 \equiv \neg(\varphi_1 = \varphi_2) \quad x \notin \varphi \equiv \neg(x \in \varphi) \quad \varphi_1 \not\subseteq \varphi_2 \equiv \neg(\varphi_1 \subseteq \varphi_2)$$

In the following, when we say that we consider a theory Γ that contains certain axioms, we implicitly assume that the symbol set contains all symbols that occur in those axioms.

Sorts. ML is an unsorted logic and has no built-in support for sorts or many-sorted functions. However, we can define sorts as constant symbols and use patterns to axiomatize their properties. Specifically, for every sort s, we define a corresponding constant symbol also denoted s that represents its sort name. For technical convenience, we include the following axiom

$$(\textsc{Sort Name}) \quad \exists x. s = x$$

to specify that s is matched by exactly one element, which is the name of the sort s. To get the carrier set of s, we define a symbol $[\![\_]\!]$, which we call the *inhabitant* symbol, and we write $[\![\varphi]\!]$ instead of $[\![\_]\!]\ \varphi$. The intuition is that $[\![s]\!]$ is matched by exactly the elements that have sort s, i.e., it represents the carrier set of s. We also include a symbol *Sort* that is matched by all sort names, by including an axiom $s \in \mathit{Sort}$.

We can specify properties about sorts by patterns. E.g., the following axiom

$$(\textsc{Nonempty Inhabitant}) \quad [\![s]\!] \neq \bot$$

specifies that the carrier set of s is nonempty. The following axiom

$$(\textsc{Subsort}) \quad [\![s_1]\!] \subseteq [\![s_2]\!]$$

specifies that the carrier set of s_1 is a subset of that of s_2, i.e., s_1 is a *subsort* of s_2. We define *sorted negation* $\neg_s\varphi \equiv (\neg\varphi) \wedge [\![s]\!]$, which is matched by all elements of sort s that do not match φ. We define *sorted quantification* that restricts the ranges of $x, x_1, \ldots, x_n$ in the quantification:

$$\forall x{:}s.\,\varphi \equiv \forall x.\, x \in [\![s]\!] \rightarrow \varphi \quad \forall x_1, \ldots, x_n{:}s.\,\varphi \equiv \forall x_1{:}s.\ \ldots \forall x_n{:}s.\,\varphi$$
$$\exists x{:}s.\,\varphi \equiv \forall x.\, x \in [\![s]\!] \wedge \varphi \quad \exists x_1, \ldots, x_n{:}s.\,\varphi \equiv \exists x_1{:}s.\ \ldots \exists x_n{:}s.\,\varphi$$

We can specify sorting restrictions of symbols. For example:

$$(\textsc{Sorted Symbol}) \quad \sigma\,[\![s_1]\!] \cdots [\![s_n]\!] \subseteq [\![s]\!]$$

requires $\sigma\, x_1 \cdots x_n$ to have sort s, given that $x_1, \ldots, x_n$ have sorts $s_1, \ldots, s_n$, respectively. For notational simplicity, we write $\sigma \in \Sigma_{s_1 \ldots s_n, s}$ to mean that we assume the axiom (Sorted Symbol) for σ.

Functions and Partial Functions. ML symbols are interpreted as relations, when they are applied to arguments. Indeed, $\sigma\, x_1 \cdots x_n$ is a pattern that can be matched zero, one, or more elements. In practice, we often want to specify that σ is a function (or partial function), in the sense that $\sigma\, x_1 \cdots x_n$ can be matched by exactly one (or at most one) element. That can be specified by the following axioms, respectively:

$$(\textsc{Function}) \quad \forall x_1{:}s_1.\ \ldots \forall x_n{:}s_n.\, \exists y{:}s.\, \sigma(x_1, \ldots, x_n) = y$$
$$(\textsc{Partial Function}) \quad \forall x_1{:}s_1.\ \ldots \forall x_n{:}s_n.\, \exists y{:}s.\, \sigma(x_1, \ldots, x_n) \subseteq y$$

Recall that y is an element variable, so it is matched by exactly one element. For notational simplicity, we use the function notation $\sigma\colon s_1 \times \cdots \times s_n \rightarrow s$ to mean that we assume the axiom (Function) for σ. Similarly, we use the partial function notation $\sigma\colon s_1 \times \cdots \times s_n \rightharpoonup s$ to mean that we assume the axiom (Partial Function) for σ.

Constructors. *Constructors* are extensively used in building programs and data, as well as semantic structures to define and reason about languages and programs. They can be characterized in the "no junk, no confusion" spirit [6].[1] Specifically, let *Term* be a sort of *terms* and Σ be a set of constructors denoted c. We associate an arity $n_c \geq 0$ with every c. Consider the following axioms:

[1] This answers a question asked by Jacques Carette on the *mathoverflow* site (https://mathoverflow.net/questions/16180/formalizing-no-junk-no-confusion) ten years ago: Are there logics in which these requirements ("no junk, no confusion") can be internalized?

(FUNCTION, for all c) $c\colon \underbrace{\mathit{Term} \times \cdots \times \mathit{Term}}_{n_c \text{ times}} \to \mathit{Term}$

(NO JUNK) $\bigvee_{c \in C} \exists x_1, \ldots, x_{n_c}{:}\mathit{Term}.\, c\, x_1 \cdots x_{n_c}$

(NO CONFUSION I, for all $c \neq c'$)

$$\forall x_1, \ldots, x_{n_c}{:}\mathit{Term}.\, \forall y_1, \ldots, y_{n_{c'}}{:}\mathit{Term}.\, \neg\left(c\, x_1 \cdots x_{n_c} \wedge c'\, y_1 \cdots y_{n_{c'}}\right)$$

(NO CONFUSION II, for all c)

$$\forall x_1, \ldots, x_{n_c}{:}\mathit{Term}.\, \forall y_1, \ldots, y_{n_c}{:}\mathit{Term}.$$
$$(c\, x_1 \cdots x_{n_c} \wedge c\, y_1 \cdots y_{n_c}) \to c\, (x_1 \wedge y_1) \cdots (x_{n_c} \wedge y_{n_c})$$

(INDUCTIVE DOMAIN) $\mu T.\, \bigvee_{c \in C} c\, \underbrace{T \cdots T}_{n_i \text{ times}}$

Intuitively, (NO CONFUSION I) says different constructs build different things; (NO CONFUSION II) says constructors are injective; and (INDUCTIVE DOMAIN) says the carrier set of *Term* is the smallest set that is closed under all constructors. We refer to the first two axioms as (NO CONFUSION). Technically, (NO JUNK) is not necessary as it is implied by (INDUCTIVE DOMAIN).

4 Encoding Order-Sorted Algebras

As seen in Sect. 3.2, the subset relation between the carrier sets of sorts can be captured in ML by patterns. Therefore, OSA and subsorting can be naturally captured in ML; see [2] for details. Specifically, to capture OSA, we define for every sorts $s \in S$ a corresponding sort, also denoted s, in ML. For every $s \leq s'$, we include a subsorting axiom $[\![s]\!] \subseteq [\![s']\!]$. We define for every OSA function $f \in F_{s_1 \ldots s_n, s}$ a corresponding symbol, also denoted f, and include the (FUNCTION) axiom, i.e., $f\colon s_1 \times \cdots \times s_n \to s$. This is summarized in Fig. 1.

Let $\Sigma = (S, \leq, F)$ be an order-sorted signature and Σ^{ML} be the corresponding ML signature. Let $A = (\{A_s\}_{s \in S}, \{f_A\}_{f \in F})$ be an OSA. We define its derived ML Σ^{ML}-model, denoted A^{ML}, as in [2], which includes the standard interpretations of the definedness and inhabitant symbols, sorts, functions, and elements in A.

Theorem 1 (See [2]). *For every formula φ, we have $A^{\mathsf{ML}} \models \varphi^{\mathsf{ML}}$ iff $A \models \varphi$.*

4.1 QLOCK Example in ML

We have shown the OSA specification of QLOCK's static structures in Sect. 2.1 and the ML encoding of OSA in Sect. 4. Putting them together, we get an ML specification for QLOCK, which we show below in full details.

Notations

- $\bar{x}$: a syntactic sugar for $x_1, \ldots, x_n$
- $\forall \bar{x}{:}\bar{s}$: a syntactic sugar for $\forall x_1{:}s_1. \ldots \forall x_n{:}s_n$, where we assume $\bar{x}$ and $\bar{s}$ have the same length n.

ML Signature $\Sigma(\text{QLOCK})^{\mathsf{ML}}$ contains the following symbols (we remind readers of the mathematical instruments defined in Sect. 3.2):

- a definedness symbol $\lceil \_ \rceil$;
- an inhabitant symbol $[\![\_]\!]$;
- a symbol S for sort names;
- a symbol for each sort: *Nat*, *List*, *MSet*, *NeMSet*, *Conf*, *state*, *Pred*;
- a symbol for each function: *nil*, *conc*, *union*, *conf*, *state*, *dupl*, $\mathbb{0}$, $\mathbb{s}$;

	Order-Sorted Algebra	**Matching Logic**
Signature	$\Sigma = (S, \leq, F)$	$\Sigma^{\mathsf{ML}} = \{\lceil \_ \rceil, [\![\_]\!], Sort\} \cup S \cup F$
Axioms	OSA metalanguage	ML axioms
	$s \in S$	$s \in Sort$ $\exists y.\, s = y$ $[\![s]\!] \neq \bot$
	$s \leq s'$	$[\![s]\!] \subseteq [\![s']\!]$
	$f \in F_{s_1 \ldots s_n, s}$	$f : s_1 \times \cdots \times s_n \to s$
	$x{:}s$ (sorted variable)	$x \in [\![s]\!]$
Terms	t	t^{ML}
	$f(t_1, \ldots, t_n)$	$f\, t_1 \cdots t_n$
Sentences	φ	φ^{ML}
	$\{x_1, \ldots, x_n\}$ = variables in φ	$x_1 \in [\![s_1]\!] \wedge \cdots \wedge x_n \in [\![s_n]\!] \to (\varphi = \top)$
Model	A	$M \equiv A^{\mathsf{ML}}$
	$f_A : A_{s_1} \times \cdots A_{s_n} \to A_s$ $f_A(a_1, \ldots, a_n)$	$f_M\, a_1 \cdots a_n = \{f_A(a_1, \ldots, a_n)\}$

Fig. 1. Given an order-sorted signature $\Sigma = (S, \leq, F)$ and a Σ-OSA A, we derive a ML signature Σ^{ML} and a corresponding Σ^{ML}-model $M \equiv A^{\mathsf{ML}}$.

ML Axioms Γ^{QLOCK} includes the (Definedness) axiom (see Definition 6) and the following axioms:

ML Axioms for Sort Names

- the sort symbols are functional constants:

$$\exists y.\, y = Nat \quad \exists y.\, y = List \quad \exists y.\, y = MSet \quad \exists y.\, y = NeMSet$$
$$\exists y.\, y = Conf \quad \exists y.\, y = state \quad \exists y.\, y = Pred$$

- S is the set of sorts:

$$S = Nat \vee List \vee MSet \vee NeMSet \vee Conf \vee state \vee Pred$$

- for each sort $s \in S$, its carrier set is non-empty:

$$\forall s{:}S.\, [\![s]\!] \neq \bot$$

ML Axioms for the Natural Numbers

- the constructors are functional:

$$\exists y{:}Nat.\, y = \mathbb{0} \qquad \forall x{:}Nat.\, \exists y{:}Nat.\, y = \mathbb{s}\, x$$

- "no confusion" axioms:

$$\forall x{:}Nat.\, \neg(\mathbb{0} \wedge \mathbb{s}\, x) \qquad \forall x, y{:}Nat.\, \mathbb{s}\, x \wedge \mathbb{s}\, y \rightarrow \mathbb{s}(x \wedge y)$$

- the domain of *Nat* is the smallest set that is closed under $\mathbb{0}$ and $\mathbb{s}$:

$$[\![Nat]\!] = \mu X.\, \mathbb{0} \vee \mathbb{s}(X)$$

  There is no need to add the "no junk" axiom $[\![Nat]\!] = \mathbb{0} \vee \mathbb{s}\, [\![Nat]\!]$ as it is a consequence of the above axiom.

Remark. Note that we use the sorted quantification in the above functional axioms. In other words, we only specify that $\mathbb{s}$ is a function when it is within the domain of *Nat*. Its behavior outside the domain of *Nat* is *unspecified*. This way, we allow maximal flexibility in terms of modeling, because each model (i.e., implementation) of the specification Γ can decide the behavior of $\mathbb{s}$ outside *Nat*. An "order-sorted-like" model will make $\mathbb{s}\, x$ return $\bot$, the empty set, whenever x is not in *Nat*, while an "error-algebra-like" model will make $\mathbb{s}\, x$ return *error*, a distinguished error element, to denote the "type error". Note that if we do not use the sorted quantification, but use the unsorted version, $\forall x.\, \exists y.\, y = \mathbb{s}\, x$, then we explicitly *exclude* the order-sorted model, which is not what we want.

Remark. We point out that the sorted quantification axioms do not *restrict* $\mathbb{s}$ to be only applicable within *Nat*. The pattern $\mathbb{s}\, x$ when x is outside the domain of *Nat* is still a well-formed pattern, whose semantics is not specified by the theory of natural numbers, but can be specified by other theories. For example, the theory of real numbers may re-use $\mathbb{s}$ and overload it as the increment-by-one function on reals. The theory of bounded arithmetic may re-use and overload $\mathbb{s}$ as the successor "function", which is actually a partial function and is undefined on the maximum value. The theory of transition systems may re-use and overload $\mathbb{s}$ as the successor "function", which is actually the underlying transition relation, and $\mathbb{s}\, x$ yields the set of all next states of the state x. In the last two cases, $\mathbb{s}$ is no longer a function because it is not true that $\mathbb{s}\, x$ always returns one element. Therefore, if we use not the sorted quantification axiom but the unsorted one, we cannot re-use $\mathbb{s}$ in the theories of bounded arithmetic or transition systems, without introducing inconsistency. Thus, by using sorted quantification for $\mathbb{s}$ in the theory of natural numbers, we do not restrict but actually encourage the re-use and overloading of $\mathbb{s}$ in other theories. On the other hand, ML is expressive enough if one wants to allow a restricted use of a symbol. For instance, if we want to restrict the use of $\mathtt{s}$ only to Nat, then we can add the axiom $\forall x.\, \lceil \mathtt{s}\, x \rceil \to x \in [\![Nat]\!]$.

ML Axioms for Boolean Values ***Pred***

- the constructors are functional:

$$\exists y{:}Pred.\, y = tt \qquad \exists y{:}Pred.\, y = ff$$

- "no confusion" axiom: $\neg(tt \wedge ff)$
- the domain of $Pred$ consists only of ff and tt:

$$[\![Pred]\!] = ff \vee tt$$

ML Axioms for Associative Lists (Over Natural Numbers)

- the constructors are functional:

$$\forall x,y{:}List.\, \exists z{:}List.\, z = conc\, x\, y \qquad \exists x{:}List.\, x = nil$$

- the associativity axiom:

$$\forall x,y,z{:}List.\, conc(conc\, x\, y)\, z = conc\, x\, (conc\, y\, z)$$

- the unity axioms:

$$\forall x{:}List.\, conc\, x\, nil = x \qquad \forall x{:}List.\, conc\, nil\, x = x$$

- the domain of $List$ is the smallest set that includes $[\![Nat]\!]$ and closed under $conc$ and nil:

$$[\![List]\!] = \mu X.\, [\![Nat]\!] \vee nil \vee conc\, X\, X$$

  There is no need to add the subsort axiom $[\![Nat]\!] \subseteq [\![List]\!]$ to Γ since it is a consequence of the above axiom.

ML Axioms for Multisets (Over Natural Numbers)

- the constructors are functional:

$$\exists y{:}MSet.\, y = empty \qquad \forall x,y{:}MSet.\, \exists z{:}MSet.\, z = union\, x\, y$$
$$\forall x,y{:}NeMSet.\, \exists z{:}NeMSet.\, z = union\, x\, y$$

- the associativity axiom:

$$\forall x,y,z{:}MSet.\, union(union\, x\, y)\, z = union\, x\, (union\, y\, z)$$

- the unity and commutativity axioms:

$$\forall x{:}MSet.\, union\, x\, empty = x \qquad \forall x, y{:}MSet.\, union\, x\, y = union\, y\, x$$

– the domain axiom:

$$[\![NeMSet]\!] = \mu X.\, [\![Nat]\!] \vee union\, X\, X \quad [\![MSet]\!] = empty \vee [\![NeMSet]\!]$$

The axioms $[\![Nat]\!] \subseteq [\![NeMSet]\!]$ and $[\![NeMSet]\!] \subseteq [\![MSet]\!]$, corresponding to subsorting relations $Nat < NeMSet$ and respectively $NeMSet < MSet$, are not needed, as they are consequences of the above.

ML Axioms for Configurations

– the constructors are functional:

$$\forall x_1{,}x_2{,}x_3{:}MSet.\, \forall y{:}List.\, \exists z{:}Conf.\, conf\, x_1\, x_2\, x_3\, y = z$$

– "no confusion" axiom:

$$\begin{aligned}&\forall x_1{,}x_2{,}x_3{,}x_1'{,}x_2'{,}x_3'{:}MSet.\, \forall y{,}y'{:}List.\\ &\quad conf\, x_1\, x_2\, x_3\, y \wedge conf\, x_1'\, x_2'\, x_3'\, y' \rightarrow conf\, (x_1 \wedge x_1')(x_2 \wedge x_2')(x_3 \wedge x_3')(y \wedge y')\end{aligned}$$

– the domain of *Conf* is the set that is closed under *conf*:

$$[\![Conf]\!] = conf\, [\![MSet]\!]\, [\![MSet]\!]\, [\![MSet]\!]\, [\![List]\!]$$

ML Axioms for States

– the constructors are functional:

$$\forall x{:}Conf.\, \exists y{:}state.\, state\, x = y$$

– "no confusion" axiom:

$$\forall x{,}x'{:}Conf.\, state\, x \wedge state\, x' \rightarrow state\, x \wedge x'$$

– the domain of *state* is the set that is closed under *state*:

$$[\![state]\!] = state\, [\![Conf]\!]$$

The specification of the carrier set for the sorts *Nat*, *List*, *MSet*, and *NeMSet* as least fix points allows to formalize in ML of their induction proof principles. In what follows, $\varphi(x)$ says that the pattern φ depends on the variable x.

ML Axioms that Define *dupl*

We here give the complete specification of *dupl*:

$$\begin{aligned}&\forall x{:}MSet.\, \exists y{:}Pred.\, dupl\, x = y\\ &\forall s.\, \exists s', u.\, s =_{NeMSet} union\, s'(union\, u\, u) \rightarrow dupl\, s = tt\\ &\forall s.\, \forall s', u.\, s \neq_{MSet} union\, s'(union\, u\, u) \rightarrow dupl\, s = ff\end{aligned}$$

Proposition 1. $\mathsf{QLK}^{\mathsf{ML}} \models \Gamma^{QLOCK}$.

Proof. By construction.

In the following, we show that *inductive reasoning* is available in $\mathsf{QLK}^{\mathsf{ML}}$ for natural numbers, (finite) lists, and (finite) multisets. We write $\varphi(x)$ to mean a pattern φ with a distinguished variable x and write $\varphi(t)$ to mean $\varphi[t/x]$.

Proposition 2 (Peano Induction).

$$\Gamma^{QLOCK} \models \varphi(0) \wedge (\forall y{:}Nat.\, \varphi(y) \to \varphi(\mathtt{s}\, y)) \to \forall x{:}Nat.\, \varphi(x)$$

Proof. See [2].

Since the specifications for lists and multisets do not include "no confusion" axioms (due to the associativity, commutativity and identity axioms), their induction principles are given only for the ML model generated from the canonical OSA. This is sufficient for the purpose of this paper, because our goal is to show a faithful ML representation of constrained constructor patterns, whose semantics are given in the canonical model.

Proposition 3 (List and Multiset Induction).

$$\begin{aligned}
\mathsf{QLK}^{\mathsf{ML}} \models\ & \varphi(nil) \wedge \\
& \forall x{:}Nat.\varphi(x) \wedge (\forall \ell_1{,}\ell_2{:}List.\varphi(\ell_1)\wedge\varphi(\ell_2)\to\varphi(conc\,\ell_1\,\ell_2))) \to \forall \ell{:}List.\, \varphi(\ell)\\
\mathsf{QLK}^{\mathsf{ML}} \models\ & \forall x{:}Nat.\varphi(x) \wedge (\forall m_1{,}m_2{:}NeMSet.\varphi(m_1)\wedge\varphi(m_2)\to\varphi(union\, m_1\, m_2))\to\\
& \forall m{:}NeMSet.\, \varphi(m)\\
\mathsf{QLK}^{\mathsf{ML}} \models\ & \varphi(empty) \wedge \forall x{:}Nat.\, \varphi(x) \wedge\\
& (\forall m_1{,}m_2{:}MSet.\, \varphi(m_1) \wedge \varphi(m_2) \to \varphi(union\, m_1\, m_2)) \to\\
& \forall m{:}MSet.\, \varphi(m)
\end{aligned}$$

Proof. By the inductive principle of the canonical model QLK and Theorem 1.

5 Encoding Constrained Constructor Patterns in ML

Let $(\Sigma, B \cup E)$ be an order-sorted theory with $(\Omega, B_\Omega \cup E_\Omega)$ being its subtheory of constructors. Recall that $C_{\Sigma/E,B}$ denotes the canonical constructor term algebra. Let $(\Sigma^{\mathsf{ML}}, \Gamma^{\Sigma,E,B})$ be the ML translation of $(\Sigma, E \cup B)$ with $\Gamma^{\Sigma,E,B} = B^{\mathsf{ML}} \cup E^{\mathsf{ML}}$, as discussed in Sect. 4.

Definition 7. *For a constrained constructor pattern $u|\varphi$, its ML translation is the pattern $u^{\mathsf{ML}} \wedge \varphi^{\mathsf{ML}}$. The ML translations of constrained constructor pattern predicates are defined in the expected way, where $\bot$ translates to $\bot$, conjunction translates to conjunction, and disjunction translates to disjunction.*

The canonical model $C_{\Sigma/E,B}$ has a corresponding $(\Sigma^{\mathsf{ML}}, \Gamma^{\Sigma,E,B})$-model $C^{\mathsf{ML}}_{\Sigma/E,B}$ by Theorem 1. For $\rho\colon X \to T_\Omega$ and a FOL formula φ, we have $C_{\Sigma/B,E} \models \varphi\rho$ iff $C^{\mathsf{ML}}_{\Sigma/E,B} \models (\varphi\rho)^{\mathsf{ML}}$ by the same theorem. This allows us to define the semantics of a constrained constructor pattern $[\![u|\varphi]\!]$ as the interpretation of the ML pattern $\exists\overline{x}{:}\overline{s}.\,u^{\mathsf{ML}} \wedge \varphi^{\mathsf{ML}}$ in $C^{\mathsf{ML}}_{\Sigma/E,B}$, where $\overline{x}{:}\overline{s} = FV(u \wedge \varphi)$.

Next we explain in ML terms some of the constrained constructor pattern operations discussed in [11]. We regard a substitution $\sigma \triangleq \{x_1 \mapsto t_1, \ldots, x_n \to t_n\}$ as the ML pattern $\sigma^{\mathsf{ML}} \triangleq x_1 = t_1 \wedge \cdots \wedge x_n = t_n$.

Constrained Constructor Pattern Subsumption. In [11], the following question is asked: When is the constrained constructor pattern $u|\psi$ an instance of a finite family $\{(v_i|\psi_i) \mid i \in I\}$, i.e., $[\![u|\varphi]\!] \subseteq \bigcup_{i\in I}[\![v_i|\psi_i]\!]$? Perhaps, at this level of abstraction, the above question is unclear, because we do not know yet what exactly it means by "when". Let us elaborate it. The constrained constructor patterns are evaluated in the canonical model $C_{\Sigma/E,B}$, so the above question asks when there is a computationally efficient way to decide whether[2]

$$C_{\Sigma/E,B} \models [\![u|\varphi]\!] \subseteq \bigcup_{i\in I}[\![v_i|\psi_i]\!]$$

The answer is given by $E_\Omega \cup B_\Omega$-matching. Let $\textsc{match}(u, \{v_i \mid i \in I\})$ denote the set of pairs (i, β) with β a substitution such that $u =_{E_\Omega \cup B_\Omega} v_i\beta$, i.e., β matches v_i on u modulo $E_\Omega \cup B_\Omega$. Assuming that $u|\psi$ and $\{(v_i|\psi_i) \mid i \in I\}$ do not share variables, the constrained constructor pattern subsumption is formally defined as follows:

Definition 8 ([11]). *A family of constrained constructor patterns* $\{(v_i|\psi_i) \mid i \in I\}$ subsumes $u|\varphi$, *denoted* $u|\varphi \sqsubseteq \{(v_i|\psi_i) \mid i \in I\}$, *iff*

$$C_{\Sigma/B,E} \models \varphi \to \bigvee_{(i,\beta)\in\textsc{match}(u,\{v_i|i\in I\})} \psi_i\beta$$

Defined in this way, the constrained constructor pattern subsumption is computationally cheap in some cases; see [11]. One such case for example is when $E = \emptyset$ and Ω consists of associativity or associativity-commutativity and the terms are not too large. Note that $u|\varphi \sqsubseteq \{(v_i|\psi_i) \mid i \in I\}$ implies $[\![u|\varphi]\!] \subseteq \bigcup_{i\in I}[\![v_i|\psi_i]\!]$, but the inverse implication is not always true. The following counterexample is from [11], where a simple "inductive" instantiation of variable m by 0 and $s(k)$ can yield a proof by subsumption for the above set inclusion. Formally, let $\langle \_, \_ \rangle$ denote the pairing of natural numbers. Then we have $[\![\langle n, m\rangle|\top]\!] \subseteq [\![\langle x, 0\rangle|\top \vee \langle y, \mathsf{s}(z)\rangle|\top]\!]$, but $\langle n, m\rangle|\top \not\sqsubseteq \langle x, 0\rangle|\top \vee \langle y, \mathsf{s}(z)\rangle|\top$.

Let us discuss the ML counterpart of the subsumption. The ML pattern that corresponds to $[\![u|\varphi]\!] \subseteq \bigcup_{i\in I}[\![(v_i|\psi_i)]\!]$, is the following:

$$\left(\exists\overline{x}{:}\overline{s}.\,u^{\mathsf{ML}} \wedge \varphi^{\mathsf{ML}}\right) \subseteq \left(\bigvee_{i\in I} \exists\overline{y_i}{:}\overline{s_i}.\,v_i^{\mathsf{ML}} \wedge \psi_i^{\mathsf{ML}}\right)$$

[2] This is an informal notation because $[\![u|\varphi]\!] \subseteq \bigcup_{i\in I}[\![v_i|\psi_i]\!]$ is not exactly a formula.

where $\overline{x}{:}\overline{s} = FV(u|\varphi)$, and $\overline{y_i}{:}\overline{s_i} = FV(v_i|\psi_i)$. Since the two patterns do not share variables by assumption, the above is a well-formed ML pattern (we remind that $\varphi \subseteq \varphi'$ is the sugar-syntax of the ML pattern $\lfloor \varphi \to \varphi' \rfloor$).

The ML translation of the definition for $u|\varphi \sqsubseteq \{(v_i|\psi_i) \mid i \in I\}$ is

$$C^{\mathsf{ML}}_{\Sigma/B,E} \models \varphi^{\mathsf{ML}} \to \bigvee_{(i,\beta)\in \textsc{match}(u,\{v_i|i\in I\})} (\psi_i^{\mathsf{ML}} \wedge \beta^{\mathsf{ML}})$$

where β^{ML} is the pattern describing the substitution β. We can prove now that the two ML patterns are equivalent:

Theorem 2. *The following holds:*

$$C^{\mathsf{ML}}_{\Sigma/E,B} \models (\exists \overline{x}{:}\overline{s}.\, u^{\mathsf{ML}} \wedge \varphi^{\mathsf{ML}}) \subseteq \left(\bigvee_{i\in I} \exists \overline{y_i}{:}\overline{s_i}.\, v_i^{\mathsf{ML}} \wedge \psi_i^{\mathsf{ML}}\right) \leftrightarrow$$
$$\left(\varphi^{\mathsf{ML}} \to \bigvee_{(i,\beta)\in \textsc{match}(u,\{v_i|i\in I\})} (\psi_i^{\mathsf{ML}} \wedge \beta^{\mathsf{ML}})\right)$$

Explanation. The key property is that of the match result (i, β), which satisfies that $u =_{E_\Omega \cup B_\Omega} v_i\beta$. In other words, β is the logical constraint that states that u can be matched by v_i. Thus, the reasoning is as follows. Intuitively, the LHS holds when $u^{\mathsf{ML}} \wedge \varphi^{\mathsf{ML}}$ is $\bot$, i.e., φ^{ML} is $\bot$, or when u^{ML} can be matched by v_i^{ML} for some i. This yields the RHS, which states that if φ^{ML} holds, then there exists i such that u is matched by the constraint term pattern $v_i|\psi_i$. The matching part is equivalent to the logical constraint β given by the matching function MATCH, and ψ_i is the logical constraint in the original constraint term pattern. Both need to be satisfied, and thus we have $\psi_i^{\mathsf{ML}} \wedge \beta^{\mathsf{ML}}$ on the RHS.

Regarding the counterexample, we show that

$$C^{\mathsf{ML}}_{\Sigma/E,B} \models \exists m,n{:}Nat.\, \langle n, m\rangle \subseteq \exists x,y,z{:}Nat.\, \langle x, 0\rangle \vee \langle y, \mathtt{s}(z)\rangle \qquad (*)$$

is proved in ML. Consider $\varphi(m) \triangleq \forall n,x,y,z{:}Nat.\, \langle n, m\rangle \subseteq \langle x, 0\rangle \vee \langle y, \mathtt{s}(z)\rangle$ and applying the induction principle for natural numbers, given by Proposition 2, we obtain

$$C^{\mathsf{ML}}_{\Sigma/E,B} \models \forall m{:}Nat.\, \exists n{:}Nat.\, \langle n, m\rangle \subseteq \exists x,y,z{:}Nat.\, \langle x, 0\rangle \vee \langle y, \mathtt{s}(z)\rangle$$

which implies (*).

Over-Approximating Complements. In [11] it is showed that the complement of a constrained constructor pattern cannot be computed using negation, i.e, $[\![u|\top]\!] \setminus [\![u|\varphi]\!] = [\![u|\neg\varphi]\!]$ does not always hold, but the inclusion $[\![u|\top]\!] \setminus [\![u|\varphi]\!] \subseteq [\![u|\neg\varphi]\!]$ holds. Therefore an over-approximation of the difference is defined as:

$$[\![u|\varphi]\!] \setminus\!\!\setminus [\![u|\psi]\!] \triangleq [\![u|\varphi]\!] \cap [\![u|\neg\psi]\!] \quad (= [\![u|\varphi \wedge \neg\psi]\!])$$

Since ML has negation, the difference $[\![u|\top]\!] \setminus [\![u|\varphi]\!]$ is the same with the interpretation in $C^{\mathsf{ML}}_{\Sigma/E,B}$ of the ML pattern

$$\exists\overline{x}{:}\overline{s}.\, u^{\mathsf{ML}} \wedge \neg(\exists\overline{x}{:}\overline{s}.\,(u^{\mathsf{ML}} \wedge \varphi^{\mathsf{ML}}))$$

The constructor pattern predicate $[\![u|\top]\!]$ is the same with the interpretation in $C^{\mathsf{ML}}_{\Sigma/E,B}$ of the pattern $\exists\overline{x}{:}\overline{s}.\, u^{\mathsf{ML}}$, where $\overline{x}{:}\overline{s}$ is the set of variables occurring in u, and constructor predicate $[\![u|\neg\varphi]\!]$ is the same with the interpretation of $\exists\overline{x}{:}\overline{s}.\,(u^{\mathsf{ML}} \wedge \neg\varphi^{\mathsf{ML}})$.

The counterexample for equality as in [11] is $u \triangleq (x, y, z)$, as a multiset over $\{a, b, c\}$, $\varphi \triangleq x \neq y$. Using ML we may explain why $[\![u|\top]\!] \setminus [\![u|\varphi]\!] = [\![u|\neg\varphi]\!]$ does not hold in a more generic way. We use the notation from the QLOCK example. Apparently, the interpretations of $\exists x,y,z{:}MSet.\,(union\, x\, y\, z) \wedge x \neq y$ and $\exists x,y,z{:}MSet.\,(union\, x\, y\, z) \wedge x = y$ are disjoint because $a \neq b$ and $a = b$ are contradictory. This is not true because Γ includes the axioms ACU for the multisets; let us denote these axioms by ϕ. Then the two patterns are equivalent to $\exists x,y,z{:}MSet.\,(union\, x\, y\, z) \wedge x \neq y \wedge \phi$ and $\exists x,y,z{:}MSet.\,(union\, x\, y\, z) \wedge x = y \wedge \phi$, respectively. Obviously, $x \neq y \wedge \phi$ and $x = y \wedge \phi$ are not contradictory and the two patterns could match common elements.

The difference $[\![u|\varphi]\!] \setminus [\![u|\psi]\!]$ is the same as the interpretation of the pattern

$$\exists\overline{x}{:}\overline{s}.\,(u^{\mathsf{ML}} \wedge \varphi^{\mathsf{ML}}) \wedge \neg(\exists\overline{x}{:}\overline{s}.\,(u^{\mathsf{ML}} \wedge \psi^{\mathsf{ML}}))$$

and $[\![u|\varphi]\!] \setminus\!\!\setminus [\![u|\psi]\!]$ is the same as the interpretation of

$$\exists\overline{x}{:}\overline{s}.\,(u^{\mathsf{ML}} \wedge \varphi^{\mathsf{ML}}) \wedge \exists\overline{x}{:}\overline{s}.\,(u^{\mathsf{ML}} \wedge \neg\psi^{\mathsf{ML}}),$$

which is equivalent to $\exists\overline{x}{:}\overline{s}.\,(u^{\mathsf{ML}} \wedge \varphi^{\mathsf{ML}} \wedge \neg\psi^{\mathsf{ML}})$. We can prove that $[\![u|\varphi]\!] \setminus\!\!\setminus [\![u|\psi]\!]$ is indeed an over-approximation of the difference:

Proposition 4. *The following holds:*

$$C^{\mathsf{ML}}_{\Sigma/E,B} \models \exists\overline{x}{:}\overline{s}.\,(u^{\mathsf{ML}} \wedge \varphi^{\mathsf{ML}}) \wedge \neg(\exists\overline{x}{:}\overline{s}.\,(u^{\mathsf{ML}} \wedge \psi^{\mathsf{ML}})) \subseteq \exists\overline{x}{:}\overline{s}.\,(u^{\mathsf{ML}} \wedge \varphi^{\mathsf{ML}} \wedge \neg\psi^{\mathsf{ML}})$$

Parameterized Intersections. The intersection of two constrained constructor patterns that share a set of variables Y is defined as

$$(u|\varphi) \wedge_Y (v|\psi) \triangleq \bigvee_{\alpha \in Unif_{E_\Omega \cup B_\Omega}(u,v)} (u|\varphi \wedge \psi\alpha)$$

where $Unif_{E_\Omega \cup B_\Omega}(u, v)$ is a complete set of $E_\Omega \cup B_\Omega$-unifiers (the parameterized intersection is defined only when such a set exists). We have

$$[\![(u|\varphi) \wedge_Y (v|\psi)]\!] = \bigcup_{\rho \in [Y \to T_\Omega]} [\![u|\varphi]\!] \cap [\![v|\psi]\!]$$

For the case when $E = B = \emptyset$, it is shown in [1] that

$$\Gamma^{\Sigma} \models u \wedge v \leftrightarrow u \wedge \sigma^{\mathsf{ML}}$$

where σ is the most general unifier of u and v. We obtain as a consequence that $(u \wedge \varphi) \wedge (v \wedge \psi)$ is equivalent to $u \wedge \sigma^{\mathsf{ML}} \wedge \varphi \wedge \psi$, which is the ML translation of the corresponding constrained constructor pattern $(u|\varphi) \wedge_Y (v|\psi)$. We claim that this result can be generalized:

Theorem 3. *If $\{\sigma_1, \ldots, \sigma_k\}$ is a complete set of $B_\Omega \cup E_\Omega$-unifiers for u_1 and u_2, then $C^{\mathsf{ML}}_{\Sigma/E,B} \models (u_1 \wedge u_2) \leftrightarrow (u_i \wedge (\sigma_1^{\mathsf{ML}} \vee \cdots \vee \sigma_k^{\mathsf{ML}}))$, for $i = 1, 2$.*

So, the parameterized intersection of two constrained constructor patterns is encoded in ML by the conjunction of the corresponding ML patterns.

Parameterized Containments. Given the constrained constructor patterns $u|\varphi$ and $\{(v_i|\psi_i) \mid i \in I\}$ with the shared variables Z, their set containment is defined as follows:

$$[\![u|\varphi]\!] \subseteq_Z [\![\bigvee_{i\in I}(v_i|\psi_i)]\!] \quad \text{iff} \quad \forall \rho \in [Z \to T_\Omega] \text{ s.t. } [\![(u|\varphi)\rho]\!] \subseteq [\![\bigvee_{i\in I}(v_i|\psi_i)\rho]\!]$$

The Z-parameterized subsumption of $u|\varphi$ by $\{(v_i|\psi_i) \mid i \in I\}$, denoted $u|\varphi \sqsubseteq_Z \bigvee_{i\in I}(v_i|\psi_i)$, holds iff $C_{\Sigma/E,B} \models \varphi \to \bigvee_{(i,\beta)\in\textsc{match}(u,\{v_i|i\in I\},Z)}(\psi_i\beta)$. The following result holds: if $u|\varphi \sqsubseteq_Z \bigvee_{i\in I}(v_i|\psi_i)$ then $[\![u|\varphi]\!] \subseteq_Z [\![\bigvee_{i\in I}(v_i|\psi_i)]\!]$.

Let us discuss the ML counterpart of the parameterized subsumption. The ML pattern expressing $[\![u|\varphi]\!] \subseteq \bigcup_{i\in I}[\![(v_i|\psi_i)]\!]$ is

$$\forall \overline{z}{:}\overline{s'}.\ \left(\exists \overline{x}{:}\overline{s}.\ u^{\mathsf{ML}} \wedge \varphi^{\mathsf{ML}} \subseteq \bigvee_{i\in I} \exists \overline{y_i}{:}\overline{s_i}.\ v_i^{\mathsf{ML}} \wedge \psi_i^{\mathsf{ML}}\right)$$

where $\overline{z}{:}\overline{s'}$ is the set of shared variables freely occurring in both $u|\varphi$ and $\{(v_i|\psi_i) \mid i \in I\}$, $\overline{x}{:}\overline{s}$ is the set of variables different of $\overline{z}{:}\overline{s'}$ that freely occur in $u|\varphi$, and $\overline{y_i}{:}\overline{s_i}$ is the set of variables different of $\overline{z}{:}\overline{s'}$ that freely occur in $v_i|\psi_i$.

The ML translation of $u|\varphi \sqsubseteq \{(v_i|\psi_i) \mid i \in I\}$ is

$$C^{\mathsf{ML}}_{\Sigma/B,E} \models \varphi^{\mathsf{ML}} \to \bigvee_{(i,\beta)\in\textsc{match}(u,\{v_i|i\in I\},Z)} (\psi_i^{\mathsf{ML}} \wedge \beta^{\mathsf{ML}})$$

where $\textsc{match}(u, \{v_i \mid i \in I\}, Z)$ is a set of substitutions β defined over $var(v_i)\backslash Z$, and β^{ML} is the pattern describing the substitution β. We can prove now that the two ML patterns are equivalent.

Theorem 4.

$$C^{\mathsf{ML}}_{\Sigma/E,B} \models \left(\forall \overline{z}{:}\overline{s'}.\ \left(\exists \overline{x}{:}\overline{s}.\ u^{\mathsf{ML}} \wedge \varphi^{\mathsf{ML}} \subseteq \bigvee_{i\in I} \exists \overline{y_i}{:}\overline{s_i}.\ v_i^{\mathsf{ML}} \wedge \psi_i^{\mathsf{ML}}\right)\right) \leftrightarrow$$
$$\left(\varphi^{\mathsf{ML}} \to \bigvee_{(i,\beta)\in\textsc{match}(u,\{v_i|i\in I\},Z)} (\psi_i^{\mathsf{ML}} \wedge \beta^{\mathsf{ML}})\right)$$

Explanation. The main idea is the same as Theorem 2 and to use the property (i, β); that is, $u =_{E_\Omega \cup B_\Omega} v_i\beta$ for any shared variables $z_i \in Z$, explaining the quantifier $\forall \overline{z}{:}\overline{s'}$ that appear on top of the LHS.

6 Conclusion

The paper establishes the exact relationship between two approaches that formalize state predicates of distributed systems: constrained constructor patterns [11] and matching logic [2]. The main conclusion from this comparison is that there is a mutual benefit. Matching logic can benefit from borrowing the computationally efficient reasoning modulo $E \cup B$. A first step is given in [1], but we think that there is more potential that can be exploited. On the other hand, the theory of constrained constructor patterns can get more expressiveness from its formalization as a fragment of the matching logic.

References

1. Arusoaie, A., Lucanu, D.: Unification in matching logic. In: ter Beek, M.H., McIver, A., Oliveira, J.N. (eds.) FM 2019. LNCS, vol. 11800, pp. 502–518. Springer, Cham (2019). https://doi.org/10.1007/978-3-030-30942-8_30
2. Chen, X., Roşu, G.: Applicative matching logic. Technical report (2019). http://hdl.handle.net/2142/104616. University of Illinois at Urbana-Champaign
3. Chen, X., Rosu, G.: Matching μ-logic. In: Proceedings of the 34th Annual ACM/IEEE Symposium on Logic in Computer Science (LICS 2019), Vancouver, Canada, pp. 1–13. IEEE (2019). https://doi.org/10.1109/LICS.2019.8785675
4. Escobar, S., Sasse, R., Meseguer, J.: Folding variant narrowing and optimal variant termination. J. Log. Algebraic Program. **81**(7–8), 898–928 (2012). https://doi.org/10.1016/j.jlap.2012.01.002
5. Futatsugi, K.: Fostering proof scores in CafeOBJ. In: Dong, J.S., Zhu, H. (eds.) ICFEM 2010. LNCS, vol. 6447, pp. 1–20. Springer, Heidelberg (2010). https://doi.org/10.1007/978-3-642-16901-4_1
6. Goguen, J.A., Thatcher, J.W., Wagner, E.G.: An initial algebra approach to the specification, correctness, and implementation of abstract data types. Technical report. RC 6487, IBM Res. Rep (1976). See also Current Trends in Programming Methodology, vol. 4: Data Structuring, R. T. Yeh, Ed. Englewood Cliffs, NJ: Prentice-Hall **1978**, 80–149 (1976)
7. Meseguer, J.: Variant-based satisfiability in initial algebras. Sci. Comput. Program. **154**, 3–41 (2018). https://doi.org/10.1016/j.scico.2017.09.001
8. Meseguer, J.: Generalized rewrite theories, coherence completion, and symbolic methods. J. Log. Algebraic Methods Program. **110** (2020). https://doi.org/10.1016/j.jlamp.2019.100483
9. Meseguer, J.: Twenty years of rewriting logic. J. Log. Algebraic Program. **81**(7), 721–781 (2012). https://doi.org/10.1016/j.jlap.2012.06.003
10. Roşu, G.: Matching logic. Log. Methods Comput. Sci. **13**(4), 1–61 (2017)
11. Skeirik, S., Stefanescu, A., Meseguer, J.: A constructor-based reachability logic for rewrite theories. In: Fioravanti, F., Gallagher, J.P. (eds.) LOPSTR 2017. LNCS, vol. 10855, pp. 201–217. Springer, Cham (2018). https://doi.org/10.1007/978-3-319-94460-9_12
12. Tarski, A.: A lattice-theoretical fixpoint theorem and its applications. Pac. J. Math. **5**(2), 285–309 (1955)

Analysis of the Runtime Resource Provisioning of BPMN Processes Using Maude

Francisco Durán[1(✉)], Camilo Rocha[2], and Gwen Salaün[3]

[1] ITIS Software, University of Málaga, Málaga, Spain
duran@lcc.uma.es
[2] Pontificia Universidad Javeriana, Cali, Colombia
[3] Univ. Grenoble Alpes, CNRS, Grenoble INP, Inria, LIG, 38000 Grenoble, France

Abstract. Companies are continuously adjusting their resources to their needs following different strategies. However, the dynamic provisioning strategies are hard to compare. This paper proposes an automatic analysis technique to evaluate and compare the execution time and resource occupancy of a business process relative to a workload and a provisioning strategy. Such analysis is performed on models conforming to an extension of BPMN with quantitative information, including resource availability and constraints. Within this framework, the approach is fully mechanized using a formal and executable specification in the rewriting logic framework, which relies on existing techniques and tools for simulating probabilistic and real-time specifications.

1 Introduction

A crucial concern in most organizations is to have explicit and precise models of their business processes. These models may allow organizations to better understand, control, and manage critical activities and, possibly, make improvements to their processes. Indeed, process optimization is at the heart of business process management because of its potential to increase profit margins and reduce operational costs.

A business process is a collection of structured activities or tasks that produce a specific product and fulfil a specific organizational goal for a customer or market. A process aims at modeling activities, and their causal and temporal relationships by defining specific business rules. Process instances then have to comply with such a description once they are deployed. The Business Process Model and Notation (BPMN) [12] is a graphical modeling language for specifying business processes, which has become the common notation for designing business processes. Several industrial platforms have been developed during the last 10 years to support the modeling and management of BPMN processes. Nowadays, organizations are making efforts to use such platforms to define their organizational processes, aiming at achieving better control over the processes when they are deployed.

S. Escobar and N. Martí-Oliet (Eds.): WRLA 2020, LNCS 12328, pp. 38–56, 2020.
https://doi.org/10.1007/978-3-030-63595-4_3

Once a process description has been obtained, a key question to ask—from the business perspective—is the following: can this process be improved to, e.g., save money? Process optimization is becoming a strategic activity in organizations because of its potential to increase profit margins and reduce operational costs. One of the main problems in process optimization is concerned with the task of streamlining resource provisioning, allocation, and sharing. A resource can be a machine, a robot, a tool, or an employee profile, and it may be associated with a cost. Given the strategic importance in saving costs where possible, a collection of resource patterns have been defined in the context of the workflow patterns initiative [1].

Providing automated techniques for analyzing and optimizing BPMN processes is a challenging problem. It requires a model of the process including execution time of tasks and flows, as well as an explicit description of resource usage requirements. A solution to this problem would take such a process as input and compute a set of metrics (e.g., process execution time, waiting times, resource occupancy) as output. These measures would then be used as part of a further analysis stage with the goal of optimizing the process relative to a cost model. All this effort is to have a proposal for, e.g. better allocation of resources and, thus, reducing the overall time and/or costs of the process when it is finally deployed. However, the assignment of resources is seldom static, rendering the optimization problem more interesting. Modern enterprises and systems have access to resource repositories and to the possibility of acquiring/releasing or hiring/firing them with great flexibility. Thus, they can provision and release resource instances as needed. Since the analysis procedure involves complex computations and lengthy simulations, it is highly convenient to be able to perform resource analysis in a fully automated way, especially at design time before the processes are deployed.

This paper presents a solution for the analysis of alternative strategies for the dynamic adaptation of resource assignments in process models. Instead of focusing on the allocation of a fixed set of available resources, alternative strategies are analyzed for the dynamic provisioning of such resources. Once the best strategy is chosen using one of the proposed methods, such adaptation strategy will allow to automatically adjust the number of required instances of resources at runtime, depending on the workload and the behavior of the process. The annotations on the BPMN processes will provide the necessary information on task durations, probabilistic choice, and information regarding resources (e.g., initial number of available resources, resources required per task, maximum number of resources). The approach relies on a formal specification in rewriting logic of BPMN processes. The specification is given in the rewriting-logic based language Maude [5–7] and serves as an executable semantics of the BPMN language under consideration. Since it is *executable*, it has the advantage of enabling the use of Maude's verification tools for computing a number of metrics of processes with a precise mathematical meaning.

The approach presented here is concerned with the analysis of quantitative properties associated to BPMN processes. Although it encompasses a broad selection of quantitative measures, the main focus in this paper is given to execution time (i.e., the time it takes to execute a process) and resource occupancy (i.e., the percentage of usage of any or all replicas of a resource). The final goal is thus to use such analyses to streamline a process by reducing its operational costs in relation to execution time and resources, which can be directly inferred from the estimated execution times and resource usage. Since these measures are computed by significant simulations, and also along the actual executions, they can be used to dynamically adjust the number of resources at runtime. The given formalization and the accompanying tools will enable the comparison of different strategies for resource provisioning in a dynamic environment. More precisely, given a process description, and taking as parameters the workload and the provisioning strategy, the techniques and tools presented here provide detailed information on the evolution of execution times, resources in use, and therefore costs, which altogether will help in deciding on the best fit for the specific needs.

The application of the approach is presented and discussed on a case study with dynamic allocation of resources. It is used to show how the proposed approach can be helpful to effectively reduce the cost and execution time of a process. The current Maude specification builds on the one developed by the same authors in previous related work [8,9] for different forms of analysis of business processes. The reader is referred to http://maude.lcc.uma.es/BPMN-RA for details on the formal specification, experiments, and additional examples.

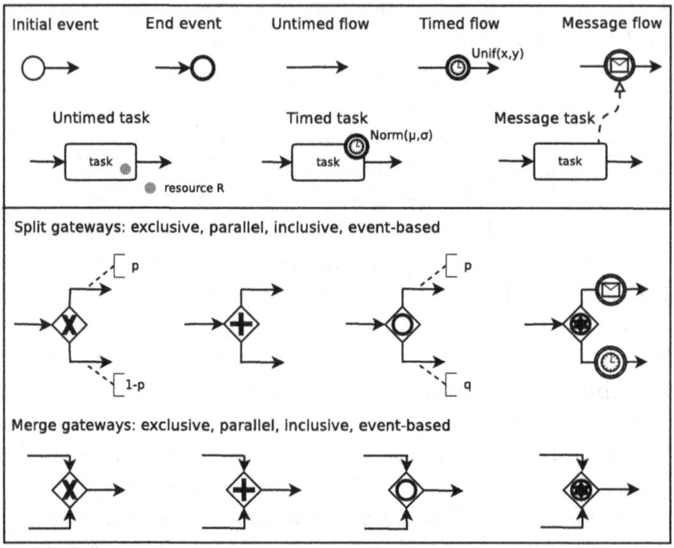

Fig. 1. Supported BPMN syntax.

The organization of the rest of the paper is as follows. Section 2 presents the BPMN notation extended with the annotations supporting the proposed approach. Section 3 introduces Real-Time Maude. Section 4 overviews the specification of the annotated BPMN extension in Maude's rewriting logic, which serves as a semantics for the language and makes automated analysis possible using Maude's tools. Section 5 presents the novel analysis techniques and case studies illustrating how the number of resources evolve, and how costs and time can be reduced in practice without the need for human intervention. Section 6 presents a discussion on related work. Finally, Sect. 7 concludes the paper.

2 Annotated BPMN

Familiarity with the BPMN notation is assumed. In this section the focus is on its extension to support quantitative information. In essence, times are expressed as stochastic expressions and branching alternatives as probabilities associated to branches. These parameters are supposed to be provided by the experts that specify the business process, or are learnt from available execution logs using, for instance, recent contributions on process mining and discovery such as [14, 21]. Figure 1 summarizes the BPMN constructs supported in this work. These elements are used to develop activity and collaboration diagrams of process models. In addition to the description of specific tasks and their sequencing, collaboration diagrams also involve *pools* and *lanes*, which are structuring elements that split processes into pieces.

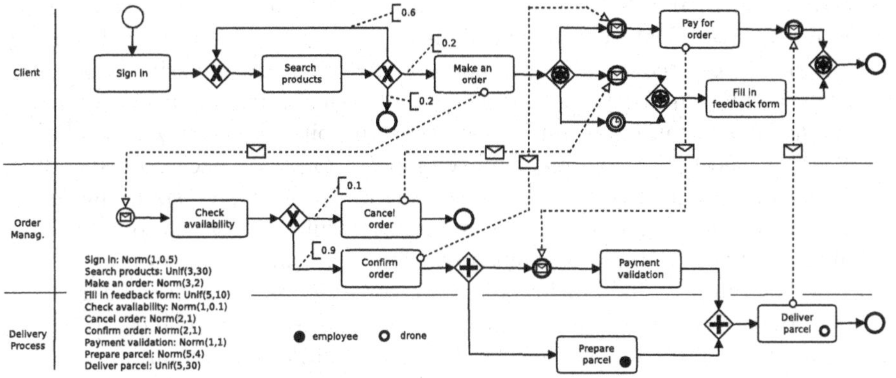

Fig. 2. Running example: parcel delivery by drones.

To introduce and illustrate the use of the BPMN constructs and annotations supported, and the analysis techniques presented in this paper, a process describing a parcel ordering and delivery by drones will be used. Figure 2 presents a collaboration diagram modeling such a process. It consists of three lanes, namely, one for the client, one for the order management, and one for the delivery process. In this process, the client first signs in and then repeatedly looks for products. Eventually, the client can decide to give up (i.e., termination) or to make an order by submitting it to the order management lane. The client then waits for a response (i.e., acceptance or refusal of this order). If the order can be completed, then the parcel is received and the client pays for it. Otherwise (i.e., timeout or order refused), the client fills in a feedback form. As far as the management lane is concerned, the first task aims at verifying whether the goods ordered by the client are available. If they are not available, then the order is canceled; otherwise, the order is confirmed. The order management takes care of the payment of the order whereas the delivery lane is triggered to prepare the parcel to be delivered by a drone. This process exhibits different kinds of gateways, probabilities for choice gateways, stochastic functions for time associated to tasks, and a loop (Search products task).

The timing information associated to tasks and flows (durations or delays) is described either as a literal value (a non-negative real number) or sampled from a probability distribution function according to some meaningful parameters. The probability distribution functions currently available include exponential, normal/Gauss, and uniform (see, e.g., [22]). To simplify the reading of the process in Fig. 2, the delays in all flows are set to 0 and the specification of the task duration has been placed apart from the process description, at the bottom-left corner. In the modelling tool, these parameters would be specified as properties of the corresponding elements. For instance, the duration of the Sign in task follows a normal distribution with mean 1 and variance 0.5, and the Search products task follows a uniform distribution in the interval [3].

Four types of gateways are considered: *exclusive*, *inclusive*, *parallel*, and *event-based*. Both BPMN 1.0 and 2.0 semantics for inclusive gateways are supported in this work. Data-based conditions for split gateways are modeled using probabilities associated to outgoing flows of exclusive and inclusive split gateways. For instance, notice the exclusive split after the Search products task in the Client lane of the running example, which has outgoing branches with probabilities 0.6, 0.2, and 0.2, specifying the likelihood of following each corresponding path. The probabilities of the outgoing flows in an exclusive split must sum up to 1, while each outgoing flow in an inclusive split can be equipped with a probability between 0 and 1 without a restriction on their total sum.

Each lane in a collaboration diagram corresponds to a specific role or resource. However, instead of implicitly associating resources to lanes, resources are explicitly defined at the task level. Thus, a task that requires resources can include, as part of its specification, the number of required instances (or replicas) of a resource. The process in Fig. 2 relies on employees for parcel packing and drones for parcel delivery. The small circles at the bottom-right corner of the Prepare parcel and Deliver parcel tasks indicate that one instance of the employee resource and another one of the drone resource are required, resp., for the tasks completion. Several tasks could compete for the same resources. Furthermore, since *multiple* instances of a same process may be executed concurrently, instances also access and may compete for the shared resources. Notice that resources can refer to humans (e.g., employee, cashier, executive) as well as non-human ones (e.g., drone, virtual machine, paper, money), and we can specify the number of instances or replicas as a natural number. In case of unlimited resources, the number of units of time, length, or volume can also be considered.

As presented in Sect. 4, provisioning strategies are specified in Maude. Although in future work alternative mechanisms to specify them can be developed, in the present work the interest is in their comparative analysis, and therefore a catalog of strategies is presented from which the desired one can be chosen. Independently of the criteria used for the provisioning/releasing of resources, it is assumed that the amount of resources is accounted for periodically (time between checks or TBC), and that in that check the recent history of the process is considered, being the length of the considered history another parameter (history length or HL) of the optimization process. The provisioning and releasing of resource instances is supposed to happen in accordance to some given thresholds, which will also be provided as parameters. Finally, it is assumed that there is a maximum and minimum number of instances available for each resource, which will be given by a range (min, max). Unlimited availability of a resource can then be modeled by just assigning a negative max value.

3 Real-Time and Probabilistic Rewrite Theories

This section provides an overview of real-time and probabilistic features of rewriting logic [15] and Maude [6]. The executable specification of BPMN presented in the following sections is a probabilistic rewrite theory [3] $\mathcal{R} = (\Sigma, E \uplus B, R)$, where $(\Sigma, E \uplus B)$ is a membership equational logic [4] theory with Σ its signature, E a set of conditional equations, B a set of equational axioms so that equational rewriting is performed modulo B, and R is a set of labeled conditional rules. The equational subtheory offers the infrastructure for defining a process in the sublanguage of BPMN described in Sect. 2, including the timing behavior for tasks and flows, resource dynamics, and probabilities for outgoing flows of split gateways. The real-time aspects are modeled using Real-Time Maude [18], which supports the formal specification and analysis of *real-time systems*. Specifically, the probabilistic rewrite rules R axiomatize how time advances and probabilistic choices are made in this infrastructure, in order for a given process to transition from an initial to a final state.

Real-Time Maude provides a sort Time to model the time domain, which can be either discrete or dense. Time advancement is modeled with *tick rules*, e.g.,

$$\texttt{crl}\ [l] : \{t, T\} \texttt{=>} \{t', T + \tau\}\ \texttt{if}\ C.$$

where t and t' are system states (an evolving model in our case), T is the global time and τ is a term of sort Time that denotes the *duration* of the rewrite, affecting the *global time elapse*. Since tick rules affect the global time, in Real-Time Maude time elapse is usually modeled by one single tick rule and the system dynamic behavior by instantaneous transitions. Although there can be many sampling strategies, in this work time elapse is modeled with a single tick rule with the help of two functions: the delta function, that defines the effect of time elapse over every model element, and the mte (maximal time elapse) function, that defines the maximum amount of time that can elapse before any action is performed (see [18] for additional details).

In a standard rewrite theory, the conditions of rewrite rules are assumed to be purely equational. A rewrite rule $l(\overrightarrow{x}) \rightarrow r(\overrightarrow{x})$ if $\phi(\overrightarrow{x})$ specifies a pattern $l(\overrightarrow{x})$ that can match some fragment of the system's state t if there is a substitution θ for the variables $\overrightarrow{x}$ that makes $\theta(l(\overrightarrow{x}))$ equal modulo B to that state fragment, changing it to the term $\theta(r(\overrightarrow{x}))$ in a local transition if the condition $\theta(\phi(\overrightarrow{x}))$ is true. In a probabilistic rewrite theory, rewrite rules can have the more general form $l(\overrightarrow{x}) \rightarrow r(\overrightarrow{x}, \overrightarrow{y})$ if $\phi(\overrightarrow{x})$ with probability $\overrightarrow{y} := \phi(\overrightarrow{x})$, where some new variables $\overrightarrow{y}$ are present in the pattern r on the right-hand side. Because the pattern $r(\overrightarrow{x}, \overrightarrow{y})$ may have new variables $\overrightarrow{y}$, the next state specified by such a rule is not uniquely determined: it depends on the choice of an additional substitution ρ for the variables $\overrightarrow{y}$. In this case, the choice of ρ is made according to the family of probability functions π_θ: one for each matching substitution θ of the variables $\overrightarrow{x}$. Therefore, a probabilistic rewrite theory can express both non-deterministic and probabilistic behavior of a concurrent system.

4 Executable Specification of BPMN

This section presents the Maude representation of the timed and probabilistic extensions of BPMN introduced in Sect. 2. The algebraic semantics of BPMN is provided by a MEL theory $Spec_{\text{BPMN}}$ so that a process model P is an element of the initial algebra $\mathcal{T}_{Spec_{\text{BPMN}}}$. The rewrite theory RT_{BPMN} extends $Spec_{\text{BPMN}}$ and defines the behavior of BPMN processes by providing some additional definitions and rules specifying such a behavior. The Maude specification of BPMN therefore consists of two parts: the process structure as an equational specification and its evolution semantics using rewrite rules.

Process Description. In the Maude specification of BPMN, a process is represented as an object with sets of flows and nodes as attributes. The representation of each node type includes the necessary information to describe its structure and to contribute to the overall process analysis. For instance, a task node involves an identifier, a description, two flow identifiers (input and output), a stochastic function modeling its duration (0 if there is no duration), a set of resources required for its execution, and a set of messages to be delivered after its completion. A split node includes a node identifier, a gateway type (exclusive, parallel, inclusive, or event-based), an input flow identifier, and a set of output flow identifiers. A merge node includes a node identifier, a gateway type, a set of input flow identifiers, and an output flow identifier. The representation of any flow includes a probability distribution function specifying its delay, a message produced by a task that blocks the flow until the message is received, and a timer representing a delay after which the execution can be triggered.

Figure 3 gives an excerpt of the representation for the running example. It shows how a `Process` object has attributes with the definition of its nodes and flows connecting them. For example, the exclusive split `g2` has as incoming flow `cf4` and outgoing flows `cf5`, `cf6`, and `cf7`, with associated probabilities 0.6, 0.2, and 0.2, respectively. As another example, the event-based split gate `g3` has as incoming flow `cf8` and outgoing flows `cf9`, `cf10`, and `cf11`. These flows are defined in the set of flows.

```
< pid : Process |
    nodes : (start(initial, cf1),
             merge(g1, exclusive, (cf2, cf5), cf3),
             split(g2, exclusive, cf4, ((cf5, 0.6) (cf6, 0.2) (cf7, 0.2))),
             split(g3, eventbased, cf8, (cf9, cf10, cf11)),
             task(t10, "Prepare parcel", mf7, df1, Norm(5.0, 4.0), employee, empty),
             task(t11, "Deliver parcel", df1, df2, Unif(5.0, 30.0), drone, parceldelivered),
             ...),
    flows : (flow(cf1, 0),
             flow(cf9, 0, message(orderconfirmed, "Order confirmed")),
             flow(cf10, 0, message(ordercanceled, "Order canceled")),
             flow(cf11, 0, timer(timeout, 60)),
             ...) >
```

Fig. 3. Running example: representation in Maude of the parcel delivery process.

The transformation from the BPMN diagrammatic representation of processes into the corresponding Maude representation is carried out using the VBPMN platform [13].

Execution Semantics. The operational semantics of BPMN is defined using rewrite rules, modeling how *tokens* (see below) evolve through a process, thus defining the execution semantics of BPMN. Each observable action is modeled as a rewrite rule. E.g., when a token arrives at an event-based split gateway, the token is made active with its optional timer. In that rule, if there is an outgoing flow with a timer, an event is added with the corresponding time to the set of available events. Another rule specifies the case where there is an outgoing flow with a message in the set of events. For instance, in that case, that branch is activated and one token is added for that flow. Additional objects of classes Workload and Supervisor are in charge of, respectively, modelling the workload of the process, and provisioning resources depending on the whereabouts of the process execution. In general, rewrite rules operate on systems composed of a Process object, a Simulation object, a Workload object, and a Supervisor object.

Simulation. While the process object represents the BPMN process and does not change during executions, a simulation object keeps information on an execution of the process. It stores a collection of tokens (in a scheduler, see below), a global time (gtime), a set of events (messages and timers), and a set of resources. It also keeps track of the metrics being computed. Fig. 4 presents the attributes of the Simulation class. We can get an intuition of how these values get updated in the rule in Fig. 5.

Tokens. Tokens are used to represent the evolution of the workflow under execution. A token is represented as a term token(TId, Id, T). Since several executions of the process are simultaneously happening, each execution has a unique identifier. Tokens are identified by the execution instance TId they belong to, and the flow or node Id they are attached to. The expression T represents a timer, of sort Time, modeling a delay on the token. Once this timer becomes 0, the token can be consumed.

Scheduling. Tokens are stored in a *scheduler*—see the attribute tokens of the Simulation object in Fig. 4—implemented as a priority queue, so that tokens are

```
class Simulation |
  tokens : List{Token},                ---- scheduler
  gtime : Time,                        ---- global time
  resources : Set{Resource},           ---- resources in the system
  events : Map{Id,Set{Event}},         ---- events in each execution
  process-execs : Map{Id,Time},        ---- execution time of each execution
  sync-times : Map{Id,Map{Id,Time}},   ---- synchronization time of each gate in each execution
  task-times : Map{Id,Map{Id,Time}},   ---- task execution times
  ...
```

Fig. 4. Declaration of the Simulation class (partial, please, note the ellipsis).

stored according to their due time. However, even with its timer set to 0, the token at the front may be not enough to fire some action. Consider for example a task that requires some resource that is not available or a parallel merge for which some incoming flow is not yet active. To avoid blocking situations, the scheduler is provided with a *shifting* mechanism, which moves the first active token to the front of the scheduler in case the current head cannot fire the corresponding action. This scheduler is similar to those used in typical discrete event simulations.

Events.[1] A message event may be associated to a flow, which is blocked until the message is received. A timer event may be associated to a flow. When a token arrives at a timer event, its countdown is started: once the countdown is completed, the token moves to the outgoing flow. Both message and timer events are usually associated to event-based gateways, but it is not necessarily the case (see, e.g., the initial flow for the order management lane in the process in Fig. 2). Asynchronous events are modeled using an event set in the Simulation object. When a message is dispatched, a corresponding event is added to the set. Flows and gateways that are waiting for specific messages use this set to check whether the messages have arrived.

Dynamic Resources. Each resource is described with an identifier, the number of available replicas (initially the total number), the total amount of time this resource has been in use, and the intervals of time on which it was used. These two last parameters are required for analysis purposes only. When a task requires several resources, it atomically uses them or waits for them to be available.

Tasks. A task execution is modeled with two rules. The first rule, the initTask rule shown in Fig. 5, represents the task initiation, which is applied when a token with zero time is available at the incoming flow (Line 05). If all the resources required by this task are available, which is checked with the allResourcesAvailable function (Line 08), then a new token is generated with the task identifier and the task duration (Line 12). Otherwise, the scheduler's token shifting mechanism is invoked (Line 19—note the ellipsis). If available, all required resources are removed from the resource set and the time those resources have been in use is updated (grabResources&updateTime function, Line 17). Note also that rules

[1] Only inter-lane events are considered; to consider environment events, the environment may be added to the simulation model.

update the information on execution times, task durations, etc. (see, e.g., the update of the task-tstamps attribute, Lines 13–15).

```
01 rl [initTask] :
02    < PId : Process |
03       nodes : (task(NId, TaskName, FId1, FId2, SE, RIds, SEI), Nodes), Atts >
04    < SId : Simulation |
05       tokens : (token(TId, FId1, 0) Tks),
06       task-tstamps : TTSs, gtime : T, resources : Rs, Atts1 >
07    < CId : Counter | counter : N >
08 => if allResourcesAvailable(RIds, Rs)
09    then < PId : Process |
10             nodes : (task(NId, TaskName, FId1, FId2, SE, RIds, SEI), Nodes), Atts >
11         < SId : Simulation |
12            tokens : insert(Tks, token(TId, NId, time(eval(SE, N)))),
13            task-tstamps : if TTSs[TId][NId] == undefined
14                           then insert(TId, insert(NId, T, TTSs[TId]), TTSs)
15                           else TTSs fi,  ---- for loops, stamps get overwritten
16            gtime : T,
17            resources : grabResources&updateTime(RIds, Rs, time(eval(SE, N)), T), Atts1 >
18         < CId : Counter | counter : int(eval(SE, N)) >
19    else ... fi .                          ---- if necessary, the scheduler is updated
```

Fig. 5. Task initiation rule.

Merge Gateways. When a merge gateway is triggered, the incoming tokens are removed, a new token is added to the scheduler for the outgoing flow, and simulation information is updated with synchronization times. For inclusive gateways, the semantics of BPMN 1.0 and 2.0 are both supported in this research.

Supervisor. A Simulation object collects all data relevant for the analysis, which is then used by a supervisor object to decide on the number of resource instances. Intuitively, the supervisor object is in charge of collecting the data on the chosen metric for the specified window of time (history length) and then decides in accordance. It takes into account ranges and thresholds for each resource to change, every TBC time units, the total amount of resources available to the process. Figure 6 represents the resource check action. Every TBC time units, the supervisor object updates the number of resource instances (Line 06) according to the state of the resources (Rs), the thresholds (Thds), the interval to consider (CI), and the current global time (T).

```
01 rl [supervisor] :
02    < SId : Simulation | resources : Rs, gtime : T, Atts1 >
03    < Sup : SupervisorUsage | TBC : TBC, time-to-next-check : 0,
04                              CI : CI, thresholds : Thds, Atts2 >
05 => < SId : Simulation | gtime : T,
06         resources : update(Rs, Thds, CI, T), Atts1 >
07    < Sup : SupervisorUsage | TBC : TBC, time-to-next-check : TBC,
08                              CI : CI, thresholds : Thds, Atts2 >
```

Fig. 6. Usage-based strategy supervisor rule.

Workloads. Simulation-based analysis techniques are typically parameterized by the workload. They define the rate at which new instances of a given process are executed. The rule in Fig. 7 specifies the behavior of closed workloads. Given a number of works, or times the process is to be executed (attribute works), and a stochastic expression SE describing the inter-arrival time (kept in the rate attribute), the rule generates a new work after the specified amount of time until all works have been created. Notice that the timer attribute of the Workload object is initialized with the result of evaluating the stochastic expression (Line 05). The rule is applicable when the timer becomes 0 and then a new token in the initial node is inserted in the scheduler (Line 07). The evaluation of stochastic expressions is carried out by the eval operation. Random numbers are generated using a pseudo-random number algorithm, which takes a number that indicate the position in the sequence (the Counter object is in charge of appropriately increasing these numbers).

```
01 rl [Workload] :
02     < WId : Workload | timer : 0, rate : SE, works : s W >
03     < SId : Simulation | tokens : Tks, events : ME, Atts1 >
04     < CId : Counter | counter : N >
05 =>  < WId : Workload | timer : time(eval(SE, N)), rate : SE, works : W >
06     < SId : Simulation |
07         tokens : insert(Tks, token(token(s W), initial, 0)),
08         events : (token(s W) |-> empty, ME),
09         Atts1 >
10     < CId : Counter | counter : int(eval(SE, N)) >
```

Fig. 7. Workload rule.

5 Dynamic Resource Allocation

This section presents automated techniques for analyzing dynamic adjustment of resource allocation. The provisioning of resources may be carried out using different criteria. These adaptation strategies present trade-offs between the difficulty of use—mainly due to the amount of parameters that need to be specified or the difficulty to estimate them—and the benefits of an adaptive provisioning in terms of resource costs and response time. In this section, two alternative strategies are presented: one based on the observed resource usage (*usage-based* strategy) and another one based on the demand on the resources (*queue-based* strategy). Although only these two strategies are used here, other metrics could have been used instead. That is, the resource adaptation strategy presented is a parameter of the generic analysis techniques proposed here. It is fair to say that the selected strategies cover two alternative and complementary approaches: while the usage-based one is based on the observation of the behavior of the system, the queue-based one relies on the prediction of the resource demand. As behavioral observations, other typical metrics could have been considered, including the observed response time or its average or variance. As predictive indicators, synchronization times, bottlenecks, or other observations on the internals of processes could also be used.

Whatever the metric used to adapt the processes is, it is assumed that each of them is driven by a recommended range of values: If the observed value goes over some maximum threshold, then the number of instances of a resource is increased; if it goes below some minimum value, then the number is decreased. In trying to avoid under- or over-provisioning, it is assumed that the minimum and maximum number of instances are also bounded. E.g., due to office space limitations, a process cannot have more than ten employees, independently of its cost or productivity. It is also assumed that the strategy proceeds by checking on some given metrics periodically, and considering the latest values of such metrics in order to make a decision on the provisioning or releasing of resources.

Table 1 summarizes the parameters for the analysis of the process and a possible instantiation of them. TBC and HL stand for the Time Between Checks and the History Length or window of values considered in the check, respectively. Every TBC time units, the state of the system is evaluated and the amount of resource instances correspondingly updated. The evaluation takes into account the given metric for HL time units. Although these strategies consider the average value for the samples in the window, other strategies could also check that all values in the window were over/under a given threshold or any other check considered useful.

Notice that each resource has its own range and threshold. Table 1 specifies a possible selection of values with which the simulations of the delivery running example may be executed, as well as the threshold values for the usage-driven strategy. Specifically, the average usage of each resource replica is expected to be in the range [50%, 70%] for employees and [50%, 75%] for drones.

Table 1. Sample set of parameters for the delivery process.

	TBC	HL	Range		Initial number of instances	Thresholds	
			Min	Max		Min	Max
Employee	5	10	1	3	1	50	70
Drone			1	6	1	50	75

Given a process description, a specification of resources (i.e., specific values for the above parameters), and a workload, the experiments discussed in what follows illustrate how information on execution times and resource usage is collected. This information can then be used to find the best strategy or best fit of its parameters. All simulations were performed assuming a closed workload with 1000 instances and an exponentially distributed inter-arrival time ($\lambda = 0.5$).

Figure 8 shows the evolution of the total amount of resources provisioned along the execution of the delivery process using the usage-guided strategy. The evolution of the number of instances is shown on the left for employees and on the right for drones. In this case, the parameters are: unlimited availability, thresholds (50, 70) for employee and (50, 75) for drone, TBC 1, and HL 0. Notice, first, that the variability is very high; since the TBC is set to 1, the amount of resources is almost continuously re-evaluated. A HL value of 0 increases this continuous adaptation, since decisions are taken by considering the values at the given time, even if that value is not maintained for some time. Also, note that employees, an expensive resource, move between 1 and 14, although most of the time it ranges between 2 and 6–7. For drones, although the most frequent values are in the range 10–20, it moves between 1 and 38. However, there are other values to take into consideration before changing the process parameters. The average execution time for the process is 55.01, with variance 0.61. The usage percentage was rather low, 42.86% for employees and 34.34% for drones. This results in a total cost, assuming the cost per hour for employee is 50€ and 20€ per drone, of 991, 613.3€. A comparative study of these values will be presented later to better understand what these numbers mean for the example (see Table 2). But even with these raw data, a poor use of our resources can be observed, which means a higher cost than possibly required.

Figure 9 shows the evolution of the amounts of resources for a new set of parameters. Specifically, two parameters have been changed: the number of instances is now restricted, so that employee instances are now in the range [1,3] and drone instances in the range [1,6]; the number of instances is now re-evaluated every 10 time units. With these parameters, the execution time has slightly improved (average 57.22 and variance 0.72), and also the usage percentage (52.12% for employees and 67.05% for drones). A bigger TBC is allowing the system to stabilize before attempting a new adaptation. This leads to a significant reduction in the total cost to 454, 713.8€ (assuming the same costs per hour for employee and drone as above).

As it is shown in the comparative study below, these results are quite good, although they are obtained at the expense of a great variability, as Figs. 8 and 9 show. This variability could have been reduced by deciding on the provisioning or release of the resource instances with a larger TBC or a larger window of values, instead of just the latest one. Furthermore, there is also the more realistic

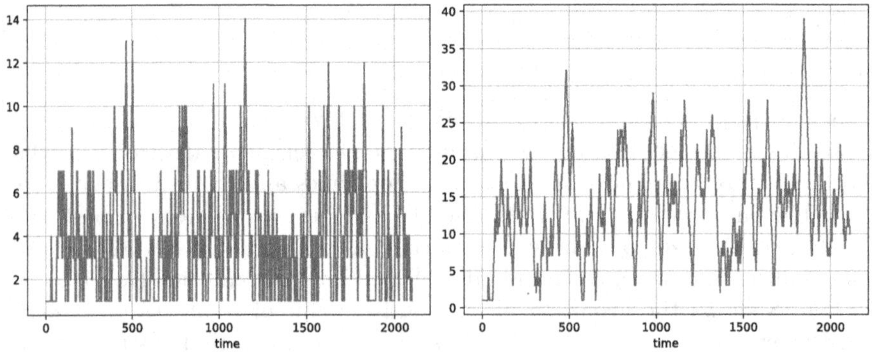

Fig. 8. Number of employee (left) and drone (right) instances along execution with a resource-usage-based strategy (unlimited availability, thresholds: employee (50, 70), drone (50, 75)). TBC: 1, HL: 0.

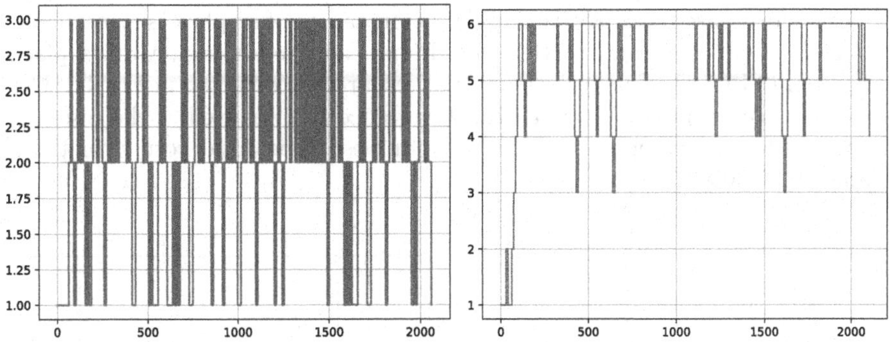

Fig. 9. Number of employee (left) and drone (right) instances along execution with a resource-usage-based strategy (ranges: employee [1,3], drone [1,6], thresholds: employee (50,70), drone (50, 75)). TBC: 10, HL: 0.

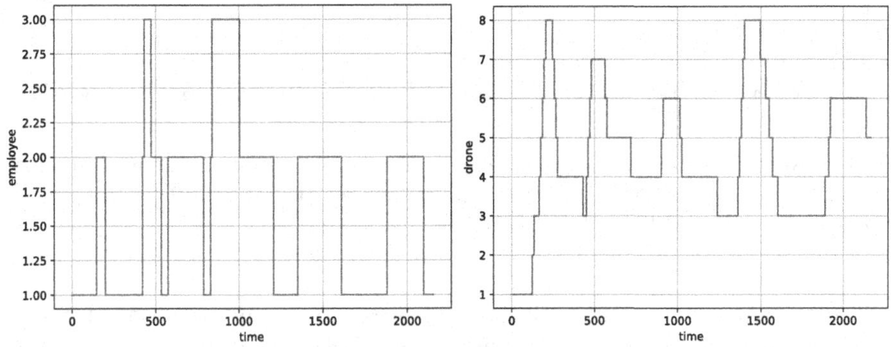

Fig. 10. Number of employee (left) and drone (right) instances along execution with a resource-queue-based strategy (unlimited availability, thresholds: employee (3, 6), drone (2, 8)). TBC: 10, HL: 5.

alternative of deciding on the current demand of resources and not on the history of results, whatever the size of the window one may want to consider.

Figure 10 depicts the evolution of the total number of instances for employees and drones using the queue-based strategy with the following parameters: unlimited availability, thresholds [3, 6] for employee and [2, 8] for drone, TBC 10, and HL 5. It can be observed in the figure that the total number of instances remains much more stable: the number of employees stays between 1 and 3, and the number of drones varies between 1 and 8, going up and down repeatedly depending on the demand. The information observed in these graphs is complemented with the execution times (average 69.09, variance 1.49), and usage percentages (71.37% for employees, 86.38% for drones). Assuming the same costs as above, this results in a total cost of 370, 742.7€.

Although many other values could have been considered for these parameters, the set of graphs we present here is completed by showing what happens if, again with the queue-based strategy, the number of instances of employees is restricted to [1,3] for employees and to [1,6] for drones, and re-evaluation takes place more often (TBC: 1). The evolution of the resources is depicted in Fig. 11. The execution times improved (average 70.04, variance 1.57) as well as the resource usage (82.81% for employees, 93.83% for drones). The total cost with these parameters is 305, 961.9€.

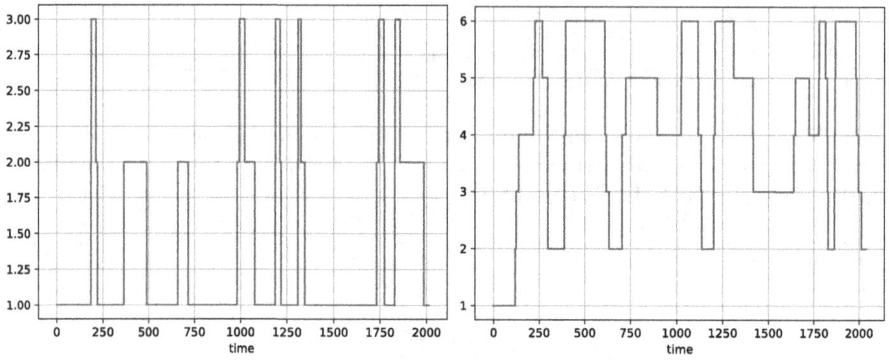

Fig. 11. Number of employee (left) and drone (right) instances along execution with a resource-queue-based strategy (ranges: employee [1,3], drone [1,6], thresholds: employee (3, 6), drone (2, 8)). TBC: 1, HL: 5.

Table 2 shows the execution times, usage percentages and total costs for several simulations using different parameters. Specifically, a combination of TBCs of 1 and 10, HLs of 0 and 5, restricted and unrestricted resource amounts, and different threshold values are considered. As the previous discussion shows, the selection of the right parameters is indeed a multi-objective problem, where the goal is to minimize execution times and total costs. However, it is not only that, restrictions such as the tolerable variability and the maximum amount of resource instances available need to also be taken into account. It can be observed that the minimum cost in the table is obtained for Row 8, which is the result of restricted availability and stability. Unrestricted resource availability results in higher costs. Furthermore, having unrestricted amounts of resources may be unrealistic in practice. Notice, however, that the difference is not that significant with the queue-based strategy, where resource queues are already representing the accumulated demand. This is indeed what makes this strategy better in general terms than the usage-based strategy.

Table 2. Exec. times, resource usage, and total costs for different parameters

	Strat.	TBC	HL	Range	Threshold	Exec. time		Usage (%)		Total cost
				Empl.-drone	Empl.-drone	Avg	Var	Empl.	Drone	(in €)
1	Usage	1	0	Unrestricted	(50, 70)–(50, 75)	55.01	0.61	42.86	34.34	991,613.3
2		10	0	Unrestricted	(50, 70)–(50, 75)	57.06	0.71	36.10	29.87	972,868.4
3		1	0	[1,3]–[1,6]	(50, 70)–(50, 75)	57.30	0.73	62.79	70.69	453,761.4
4		10	0	[1,3]–[1,6]	(50, 70)–(50, 75)	57.22	0.72	52.12	67.05	454,713.8
5	Queue	1	5	Unrestricted	[3,6]–[2,8]	70.10	1.58	85.93	92.94	313,555.1
6		10	5	Unrestricted	[3,6]–[2,8]	69.09	1.49	71.37	86.38	370,742.7
7		1	5	[1,3]–[1,6]	[3,6]–[2,8]	70.04	1.57	82.81	93.83	305,961.9
8		10	5	[1,3]–[1,6]	[3,6]–[2,8]	68.63	1.46	76.02	90.08	303,030.7

6 Related Work

Oliveira *et al.* [17] use generalized stochastic Petri nets for correctness verification and performance evaluation of business processes. In their work, an activity can be associated to multiple roles and the completion of an activity can use a portion of the resources available for a role. They also propose metrics for evaluating process performance such as: the minimum number of resources needed for a role in order to complete a process, the expected number of activity instances when completing a process under the assumption of sufficient resources, and the expected activity response time. Colored Petri Nets are used in [16] for understanding how bounded resources can impact the behavior of a process. They introduce the notion of "flexible resource allocation" as a way to assign resources associated to a given role based on priorities. In their approach, they use alternative strategies to better allocate a fixed number of available resources. Havur *et al.* [11] study the problem of resource allocation in business processes management systems where constraints can be assigned to resources (e.g., time of availability) and have dependencies. Their technique is based on the answer set programming formalism and is capable of deriving optimal schedules. Sperl *et al.* [20] describe a stochastic method for quantifying resource utilization relative to structural properties of processes and historical executions. In [9], Maude is used to model and analyze the resource allocation of business processes. In this work, optimal allocation is presented as a multi-objective optimization problem, where response time and resource usage are minimized. None of the aforementioned works attempts at providing analysis techniques or tools for the dynamic allocation of resources with respect to response time and resource usage, as the proposed approach does.

There are many tools supporting the design and management of business processes (e.g., Arena, ARIS10, iGraphx, Signavio, BPMOne, BIMP, Camunda), of which a subset supports the analysis and optimization of processes. This is the case of, for instance, Signavio [2], which packs tools such as the Signavio Process Intelligence for process optimization. This tool automatically mines process models from currently running systems and monitors those processes with the purpose of collecting data that enables end-users to make decisions for process improvement. Our proposal takes a different approach, since the focus here is on predicting the behavior of designed models given resource provisioning strategies: thus, the approach presented in this work supports the decision making at design time, even before a process is deployed. Then, given a resource allocation strategy, resources are dynamically provisioned and released, respecting the constraints specified as parameters to the process model.

7 Concluding Remarks

This paper focuses on the problem of dynamic resource allocation using BPMN as modeling language for business processes. It presents a version of BPMN extended with annotations for describing the duration of task execution, probabilities in split gateways, and additional information about resources. Given such a process specification, automated techniques are proposed for analyzing its behavior and dynamically adjusting the number of necessary resources following some given adaptation strategy. In this paper, two strategies for resource provisioning (usage-based and queue-based) were presented and illustrated on a concrete example showing how parameters (namely, time between checks, history length, resource ranges, and adaptation thresholds) could be adjusted. The automatic approach was able to handle analyses about the response time and total cost associated to the process. These results were possible thanks to an encoding of the annotated BPMN language into rewriting logic and by using Maude's tools for automating all checks on the concurrent executions of the processes.

Providing mechanisms to automatically finding the best values for given strategies is the first future work direction. This is a multi-objective problem, which is restricted by the concrete nature of the process at hand. The plan is also to investigate on alternative provisioning strategies, with the goal of providing more precise decision criteria. Considering that the provisioning of resources depends on the predictive analysis of the future executions, it is something to also be considered (see, e.g., [10,19]). Another aim would be at designing and implementing more precise modeling support for the provisioning/releasing procedure, by taking into account aspects such as the time to provision, the releasing cost, etc. Finally, the plan is also to consider a broader form of resources, and to cover resource patterns not currently covered such as the chain and pile-based execution patterns (see [1]).

Acknowledgments. The first author was partially supported by projects PGC2018-094905-B-I00 (Spanish MINECO/FEDER) and UMA18-FEDERJA-180 (J. Andalucía/FEDER). The second author was partially supported by CAPES, Colciencias, and INRIA via the STIC AmSud project "EPIC: EPistemic Interactive Concurrency" (Proc. No 88881.117603/2016-01) and by via the Colciencias ECOS-NORD project "FACTS: Foundational Approach to Computation in Today's Society" (Proc. code 63561).

References

1. Workflow resource patterns. BETA Working Paper Series, WP 127 (2004)
2. Signavio (2019). https://www.signavio.com
3. Agha, G., Meseguer, J., Sen, K.: PMaude: rewrite-based specification language for probabilistic object systems. ENTCS **153**(2), 213–239 (2006)
4. Bouhoula, A., Jouannaud, J.-P., Meseguer, J.: Specification and proof in membership equational logic. Theor. Comput. Sci. **236**(1), 35–132 (2000)
5. Clavel, M., et al.: Maude: specification and programming in rewriting logic. Theor. Comput. Sci. **285**(2), 187–243 (2002)
6. Clavel, M., et al.: All About Maude - A High-Performance Logical Framework, How to Specify, Program and Verify Systems in Rewriting Logic. LNCS, vol. 4350. Springer, Heidelberg (2007). https://doi.org/10.1007/978-3-540-71999-1
7. Durán, F., et al.: Programming and symbolic computation in maude. J. Log. Algebraic Methods Program. **110**, 100497 (2020)
8. Durán, F., Rocha, C., Salaün, G.: Stochastic analysis of BPMN with time in rewriting logic. Sci. Comput. Program. **168**, 1–17 (2018)
9. Durán, F., Rocha, C., Salaün, G.: A rewriting logic approach to resource allocation analysis in business process models. Sci. Comput. Program. **183**, 102303 (2019)
10. Di Francescomarino, C., Ghidini, C., Maggi, F.M., Petrucci, G., Yeshchenko, A.: An eye into the future: leveraging a-priori knowledge in predictive business process monitoring. In: Carmona, J., Engels, G., Kumar, A. (eds.) BPM 2017. LNCS, vol. 10445, pp. 252–268. Springer, Cham (2017). https://doi.org/10.1007/978-3-319-65000-5_15
11. Havur, G., Cabanillas, C., Mendling, J., Polleres, A.: Resource allocation with dependencies in business process management systems. In: La Rosa, M., Loos, P., Pastor, O. (eds.) BPM 2016. LNBIP, vol. 260, pp. 3–19. Springer, Cham (2016). https://doi.org/10.1007/978-3-319-45468-9_1
12. ISO/IEC. International Standard 19510, Information technology - Business Process Model and Notation (2013)
13. Krishna, A., Poizat, P., Salaün, G.: VBPMN: automated verification of BPMN processes (tool paper). In: Polikarpova, N., Schneider, S. (eds.) IFM 2017. LNCS, vol. 10510, pp. 323–331. Springer, Cham (2017). https://doi.org/10.1007/978-3-319-66845-1_21
14. Leemans, S.J.J., Fahland, D., van der Aalst, W.M.P.: Scalable process discovery and conformance checking. Softw. Syst. Model. **17**(2), 599–631 (2016). https://doi.org/10.1007/s10270-016-0545-x
15. Meseguer, J.: Conditional rewriting logic as a unified model of concurrency. Theor. Comput. Sci. **96**(1), 73–155 (1992)
16. Netjes, N., van der Aalst, W., Reijers, H.: Analysis of resource-constrained processes with colored Petri Nets. Proceedings of the CPN. DAIMI **576**, 251–266 (2005)
17. Oliveira, C., Lima, R., Reijers, H., Ribeiro, J.: Quantitative analysis of resource-constrained business processes. Trans. Syst. Man Cybern. **42**(3), 669–684 (2012)
18. Ölveczky, P.C., Meseguer, J.: Semantics and pragmatics of real-time maude. High. Order Symb. Comput. **20**(1–2), 161–196 (2007)
19. Polato, M., Sperduti, A., Burattin, A., Leoni, M.: Time and activity sequence prediction of business process instances. Computing **100**(9), 1005–1031 (2018). https://doi.org/10.1007/s00607-018-0593-x

20. Sperl, S., Havur, G., Steyskal, S., Cabanillas, C., Polleres, A., Haselböck, A.: Resource utilization prediction in decision-intensive business processes. In: Proceedings of SIMPDA, CEUR Workshop, pp. 128–141 (2017)
21. van der Aalst, W.M.P., De Masellis, R., Di Francescomarino, C., Ghidini, C.: Learning hybrid process models from events - process discovery without faking confidence. In: Carmona, J., Engels, G., Kumar, A. (eds.) BPM 2017. LNCS, vol. 10445, pp. 59–76. Springer, Cham (2017). https://doi.org/10.1007/978-3-319-65000-5_4
22. Walck, C.: Hand-book on statistical distributions for experimentalists. Technical report SUF-PFY/96-01, Universitet Stockholms, Stockholm, September 2007

A Rule-Based System for Computation and Deduction in Mathematica

Mircea Marin[1(✉)], Besik Dundua[2], and Temur Kutsia[3]

[1] Faculty of Mathematics and Informatics, Department of Computer Science, West University of Timişoara, Timişoara, Romania
mircea.marin@e-uvt.ro

[2] Ilia Vekua Institute of Applied Mathematics, Ivane Javakhishvili Tbilisi State University, Tbilisi, Georgia
bdundua@gmail.com

[3] Research Institute for Symbolic Computation, Johannes Kepler University, Linz, Austria
kutsia@risc.jku.at

Abstract. ρLog is a system for rule-based programming implemented in Mathematica, a state-of-the-art system for computer algebra. It is based on the usage of (1) conditional rewrite rules to express both computation and deduction, and of (2) patterns with sequence variables, context variables, ordinary variables, and function variables, which enable natural and concise specifications beyond the expressive power of first-order logic. Rules can be labeled with various kinds of strategies, which control their application. Our implementation is based on a rewriting-based calculus proposed by us, called ρLog too. We describe the capabilities of our system, the underlying ρLog calculus and its main properties, and indicate some applications.

Keywords: Rewriting-based calculi · Strategies · Constrained rewriting

1 Introduction

In this paper we present our main contributions to the design and implementation of a system for rewriting-based declarative programming with rewriting strategies. The system is called ρLog, and is implemented as an add-on package on top of the rewriting and constraint solving capabilities of Mathematica [16]. It provides (1) a logical framework to reason in theories whose deduction rules can be specified by conditional rewrite rules of a very general kind, and (2) a semantic framework where computations are sequences of state transitions modelled as rewrite steps controlled by strategies.

This work was supported by Shota Rustaveli National Science Foundation of Georgia under the grant no. FR17 439 and by the Austrian Science Fund (FWF) under project 28789-N32.

S. Escobar and N. Martí-Oliet (Eds.): WRLA 2020, LNCS 12328, pp. 57–74, 2020.
https://doi.org/10.1007/978-3-030-63595-4_4

ρLog has some outstanding capabilities:

1. It has a specification language which, in addition to term variables, allows the use of sequence variables, function variables, and context variables. Sequence variables are placeholders for sequences of terms; function variables are placeholders for function symbols; and context variables are placeholders for functions of the form $\lambda x.t$ where t is a term with a single occurrence of the term variable x. These new kinds of variables enable natural and concise specifications beyond the expressive power of first-order logic. For example, solving equations involving sequence variables has applications in AI, knowledge management, rewriting, XML processing, and theorem proving.
2. It is based on a rewrite-based calculus proposed by us [14, 15] which integrates novel matching algorithms for the kinds of variables mentioned above, and is sound and complete if we impose some reasonable syntactic restrictions [12].
3. It is seamlessly integrated with the constraint solving capabilities of Mathematica, a state of the art system with nearly 5000 built-in functions covering all areas of technical computing. As a result, we can use ρLog to tackle a wide range of applications.
4. It can generate human-readable traces of its computations and deductions. In particular, this capability can be turned into a tool to generate human-readable proof certificates for deduction.

The paper is structured as follows. Section 2 contains a brief description of ρLog and its core concepts: programs, strategies and queries. In Sect. 2.1 we present the rewriting calculus implemented by us. Section 3 indicates some applications. Section 4 concludes.

2 The ρLog System

A program consists of rule declarations

$\texttt{DeclareRules}[rule_1, \ldots, rule_m]$

where $rule_1, \ldots, rule_m$ are labeled conditional rewrite rules of the form

$$t \rightarrow_{stg} t' /; cond_1 \wedge \ldots \wedge cond_n \tag{1}$$

with the intended reading "t reduces to t' with strategy stg (notation $t \rightarrow_{stg} t'$) whenever $cond_1$ and ... and $cond_n$ hold." Such a rule is a partial definition for strategy stg. In the special case when $n = 0$, rules become unconditional: $t \rightarrow_{stg} t'$ has the intended reading "t is reducible to t' with strategy stg". Thus, the rewrite rules of ρLog differ from the usual rewrite rules of a rewrite theory because we label them with terms which we call *strategies.*

To illustrate how reduction works, consider the problem of extracting the smallest number from a non-empty list of numbers. We can achieve this by repeated application of the labeled rule

$\{\mathtt{x\_}, \mathtt{a\_\_\_}, \mathtt{y\_}, \mathtt{b\_\_\_}\} \rightarrow_{\text{"swap"}} \{\mathtt{y}, \mathtt{a}, \mathtt{x}, \mathtt{b}\} /; (\mathtt{x} > \mathtt{y})$

until the smallest element is moved at first position in the list, followed by one application of the labeled rule

$\{\mathtt{x\_}, \mathtt{\_\_\_}\} \rightarrow_{\mathtt{"first"}} \mathtt{x}$

We can declare these labeled rewrite rules as follows:

$$\mathtt{DeclareRules}[\{\mathtt{x\_}, \mathtt{a\_\_\_}, \mathtt{y\_}, \mathtt{b\_\_\_}\} \rightarrow_{\mathtt{"swap"}} \{\mathtt{y}, \mathtt{a}, \mathtt{x}, \mathtt{b}\}/; (\mathtt{x} > \mathtt{y}),$$
$$\{\mathtt{x\_}, \mathtt{\_\_\_}\} \rightarrow_{\mathtt{"first"}} \mathtt{x}]$$

If L is a nonempty list of numbers and we pose the query

```
ApplyRule[NF["swap"]∘"first",L]
```

then the interpreter of ρLog returns as answer the term t which satisfies the reducibility formula $\mathtt{L} \rightarrow_{\mathtt{NF["swap"]\circ"first"}} t$, and this term is the smallest number in list L. Note the following peculiarities of our specification language:

1. a, b, x, y are variables. They are identified by suffixing their first occurrences[1] in the rule with _ or ___. The variables suffixed by _ are either term variables or function variables, whereas those suffixed by ___ are sequence variables. Thus, a, b are sequence variables, and x, y are term variables. Like in Prolog, we allow the use of anonymous variables: _ is a nameless placeholder for an element (a function symbol or a term), and ___ is a nameless placeholder for a sequence of terms.
2. (x>y) is a boolean condition that is properly interpreted by the constraint logic programming component (CLP) of ρLog.
3. 'NF' and '∘' are predefined general-purpose strategy combinators: $t \rightarrow_{\mathtt{NF}[stg]} t'$ holds if t' is a normal form produced by repeated applications of $\rightarrow_{stg}$-reduction steps starting from t; and $t \rightarrow_{stg_1 \circ stg_2} t'$ holds if $t \rightarrow_{stg_1} t'' \rightarrow_{stg_2} t'$ holds for some intermediary term t''.

Sequence variables introduce nondeterminism in the reduction process. For example, there are 2 ways to reduce $\{4,1,5,2\}$ with the labeled rule for "swap": $\{4,1,5,2\} \rightarrow_{\mathtt{"swap"}} \{1,4,5,2\}$ with matcher $\{\mathtt{x} \rightarrow 4, \mathtt{a} \rightarrow \ulcorner\urcorner, \mathtt{y} \rightarrow 1, \mathtt{b} \rightarrow \ulcorner 5,2 \urcorner\}$, $\{4,1,5,2\} \rightarrow_{\mathtt{"swap"}} \{2,1,5,4\}$ with matcher $\{\mathtt{x} \rightarrow 4, \mathtt{a} \rightarrow \ulcorner 1,5 \urcorner, \mathtt{y} \rightarrow 2, \mathtt{b} \rightarrow \ulcorner\urcorner\}$. Here, $\ulcorner t_1, \ldots, t_n \urcorner$ represents the sequence of terms $t_1, \ldots, t_n$, in this order.

Sequence variables provide a simple way to traverse and process terms of any width. In contrast, context variables allow to traverse terms of any depth. For example, the parametric strategy "rw" defined by the rule

$\mathtt{C\_}^{\circ}[\mathtt{s\_}] \rightarrow_{\mathtt{"rw"}[\mathtt{r\_}]} \mathtt{C}^{\circ}[\mathtt{t}]/; (\mathtt{s} \rightarrow_{\mathtt{r}} \mathtt{t\_})$

specifies term rewriting with rules corresponding to parameter r. Here, $\mathtt{C}^{\circ}$ is a context variable, and the pattern $\mathtt{C\_}^{\circ}[\mathtt{s\_}]$ matches a term t in all ways which bind s to a subterm t' of t, and $\mathtt{C}^{\circ}$ to the context in which t' occurs. If "r" is the strategy defined by the rule

[1] By 'first occurrence' in (1), we mean first occurrence in the sequence of expressions (stg, t), $cond_1, \ldots, cond_n, t'$.

$\mathtt{f\_[f\_[x\_\_\_]]} \rightarrow_{\text{"r"}} \mathtt{f[x]}$

then there are two ways to reduce the term $\mathtt{t} = \mathtt{a[a[b[b[1,2]]]]}$ with the labeled rule for strategy "rw"["r"]:

- $t \rightarrow_{\text{"rw"["r"]}} t_1 = \mathtt{a[b[b[1,2]]]}$ with matcher $\{\mathtt{C}^\circ \rightarrow \lambda \mathtt{x}.\mathtt{x}, \mathtt{s} \rightarrow t, \mathtt{t} \rightarrow t_1\}$ because $t \rightarrow_{\text{"r"}} t_1$ with matcher $\{\mathtt{f} \rightarrow \mathtt{a}, \mathtt{x} \rightarrow \ulcorner \mathtt{b[b[1,2]]} \urcorner\}$, and
- $t \rightarrow_{\text{"rw"["r"]}} t_2 = \mathtt{a[a[b[1,2]]]}$ with matcher $\{\mathtt{C}^\circ \rightarrow \lambda \mathtt{x}.\mathtt{a[a[x]]}, \mathtt{s} \rightarrow \mathtt{b[b[1,2]]}, \mathtt{t} \rightarrow \mathtt{b[1,2]}\}$ because $\mathtt{b[b[1,2]]} \rightarrow_{\text{"r"}} \mathtt{b[1,2]}$ with matcher $\{\mathtt{f} \rightarrow \mathtt{b}, \mathtt{x} \rightarrow \ulcorner \mathtt{1,2} \urcorner\}$.

This strategy definition illustrates another feature of ρLog: variable f matches a function symbol. In first-order logic, variables are placeholders for terms only, but some functional programming languages, including Mathematica, go beyond this limitation and allow variables to match function symbols too.

Matching with sequence variables and context variables is finitary [8,9]. Algorithms which enumerate all finitely many matchers with terms containing such variables are described in [10,11], and are used by the interpreter of ρLog.

The constraints in the conditional part of a rule are of three kinds: (1) reducibility formulas $t \rightarrow_{stg} t'$, (2) irreducibility formulas $t \nrightarrow_{stg} t'$, (3) any boolean formulas expressed in the host language of Mathematica.

ρLog is designed to work with three kinds of **strategies**:

1. Atomic strategies, designated by a string identifier sId, and defined by one or more labeled rules of the form

$$t \rightarrow_{\mathtt{sId}} t' /; cond_1 \wedge \ldots \wedge cond_n.$$

   The following atomic strategies are predefined:
   "Id": $t \rightarrow_{\text{"Id"}} t'$, abbreviated $t \equiv t'$, holds if and only if t' matches t.
   "elem": $l \rightarrow_{\text{"elem"}} e$ holds if and only if e matches an element of list l.
   "subset": $t \rightarrow_{\text{"subset"}} t'$ holds if and only if t' matches a subset of set t.
2. Parametric strategies, defined by rules of the form

$$t \rightarrow_{sId[s_1,\ldots,s_m]} t' /; cond_1 \wedge \ldots \wedge cond_n$$

   where *sId* is the strategy identifier (a string) and $s_1, \ldots, s_m$ are its parameters. The parameters provide syntactic material to be used in the conditional part and result of the rule application.
3. Composite strategies, built from other strategies with strategy combinators. In ρLog, the following combinators are predefined:
   composition: $t \rightarrow_{stg_1 \circ stg_2} t'$ holds if $t \rightarrow_{stg_1} t'' \rightarrow_{stg_2} t'$ holds for some intermediary term t''
   choice: $t \rightarrow_{stg_1 | stg_2} t'$ holds if either $t \rightarrow_{stg_1} t'$ holds or $t \rightarrow_{stg_2} t'$ holds.
   repetition: $t \rightarrow_{stg^*} t'$ holds if either $t \rightarrow_{\text{"Id"}} t'$ holds or there exist $u_1, \ldots, u_n$ such that $t \rightarrow_{stg} u_1 \rightarrow_{stg} \cdots \rightarrow_{stg} u_n \rightarrow_{stg} t'$ holds.
   first choice: $t \rightarrow_{\mathtt{Fst}[stg_1,\ldots,stg_n]} t'$ holds if there exists $1 \leq i \leq n$ such that $t \rightarrow_{stg_i} t'$ and $t \nrightarrow_{stg_j} t'$ hold for all $1 \leq j < j \leq n$.
   normalization: $t \rightarrow_{\mathtt{NF}[stg]} t'$ holds if $t \rightarrow_{stg^*} t'$ and $t' \nrightarrow_{stg} \_$ hold.

Queries are formulas of the form $cond_1 \land \ldots \land cond_n$ where $cond_i$ must be of the same kind as the formulas from the conditional parts of rules. For $n = 0$ we obtain the vacuously true query, which we denote by $\top$.

We can submit to ρLog requests of the form

$\texttt{Request}[cond_1 \land \ldots \land cond_n]$ or $\texttt{RequestAll}[cond_1 \land \ldots \land cond_n]$

They instruct the system to compute one (resp. all) substitution(s) for the variables in the formula $cond_1 \land \ldots \land cond_n$ for which it holds with respect to the current program. For example, if the current program contains the previous definition of the atomic strategy "swap", then the request

$\texttt{Request}[\{4, 1, 5, 2\} \rightarrow_{\text{"swap"}} \texttt{x\_}]$

computes the substitution $\{\texttt{x} \rightarrow \{1, 4, 5, 2\}\}$, whereas the request

$\texttt{RequestAll}[\{4, 1, 5, 2\} \rightarrow_{\text{"swap"}} \texttt{x\_}]$

computes the set of all substitutions $\{\{\texttt{x} \rightarrow \{1, 4, 5, 2\}\}, \{\texttt{x} \rightarrow \{2, 1, 5, 4\}\}\}$ for which the reducibility formula $\{4, 1, 5, 2\} \rightarrow_{\text{"swap"}} \texttt{x}$ holds.

Another use of ρLog is to compute a reduct of a term with respect to a strategy. The request

$\texttt{ApplyRule}[stg, t]$

instructs ρLog to compute one (if any) reduct of t with respect to strategy stg, that is, a term t' such that the reducibility formula $t \rightarrow_{stg} t'$ holds. ρLog reports "no solution found." if there is no reduct of t with stg. ρLog can also be instructed to find *all* reducts of a term with respect to a strategy, with

$\texttt{ApplyRuleList}[stg, t]$

More information about ρLog can be found at

http://staff.fmi.uvt.ro/~mircea.marin/rholog/

2.1 The ρLog Calculus

The ρLog system is designed to solve problems of the following kind:

Given a rewrite theory represented by a program P, and a query Q,
Find one, or all, substitutions σ for which formula $\sigma(Q)$ holds in the rewrite theory represented by P.

There is no effective method to solve this problem in full generality because syntactic unification of terms with our kinds of variables is infinitary [8]. We can avoid this difficulty by imposing syntactic restrictions on the structure of programs and queries, that guarantee the possibility to use matching instead of unification (we already mentioned that matching with terms containing the kinds of variables recognized by ρLog is finitary). Therefore, the ρLog calculus is designed to solve the following restricted version of the previous problem:

Given a rewrite theory represented by a deterministic program P, and a deterministic query Q,

Find one, or all, substitutions σ for which formula $\sigma(Q)$ holds in the rewrite theory represented by P.

Here, the notion of determinism is defined as follows: if $vars(E)$ denotes the set of variables in a syntactic construct E then

- If X is a set of variables and *cond* is a component formula of a query or of the conditional part of a rule, then *cond* is X-*deterministic* if either
  - *cond* is $t \rightarrow_{stg} t'$ or $t \nrightarrow_{stg} t'$ with $vars(t) \cup vars(stg) \subseteq X$, or
  - *cond* is a formula in which all predicate symbols are predefined in Mathematica, and $vars(cond) \subseteq X$.
- a rule $t \rightarrow_{stg} t'/; cond_1 \wedge \ldots \wedge cond_n$ is *deterministic* if $vars(t') \subseteq vars(t) \cup vars(stg) \cup \bigcup_{i=1}^{n} vars(cond_i)$ and, for all $1 \leq i \leq n$, $cond_i$ is X_i-deterministic where $X_i = vars(t) \cup vars(stg) \cup \bigcup_{j=1}^{i-1} vars(cond_j)$.
- a query $cond_1 \wedge \ldots \wedge cond_n$ is *deterministic* if, for all $1 \leq i \leq n$, $cond_i$ is X_i-deterministic where $X_i = \bigcup_{j=1}^{i-1} vars(cond_j)$.

Our calculus is, in essence, SLDNF-resolution with leftmost literal selection: every rule $t \rightarrow_{stg} t'/; cond_1 \wedge \ldots \wedge cond_n$ is logically equivalent with the clause

$$t \rightarrow_{stg} \mathtt{x}/; cond_1 \wedge \ldots \wedge cond_n \wedge (t' \equiv \mathtt{x\_})$$

where $\mathtt{x}$ is a fresh term variable and we can use resolution with respect to these equivalent clauses. The main difference from resolution in first-order logic is that, instead of using the auxiliary function $mgu(t, t')$ to compute a most general unifier of two terms, we use the auxiliary function $mcsm(t, t')$ which computes the finitely many matchers between a term t and a ground term t'.

Inference Rules. The calculus has inference rules for the judgment $Q \leadsto_{\sigma} Q'$ with intended reading "query Q is reducible to Q' if substitution σ is performed." We use the notation

$$\frac{H_1 \quad \ldots \quad H_n}{Q \leadsto_{\sigma} Q'}$$

for an inference rule that allows us to conclude that $Q \leadsto_{\sigma} Q'$ holds if the assumptions $H_1, \ldots, H_n$ hold. Also, we write

- $Q_0 \leadsto_{\sigma}^{*} Q_n$, or just $Q_0 \leadsto^{*} Q_n$ whenever we succeed to infer a sequence of judgments $Q_0 \leadsto_{\sigma_1} Q_1 \ldots \leadsto_{\sigma_n} Q_n$, and σ is the restriction of substitution $\sigma_1 \ldots \sigma_n$ to $vars(Q_0)$.
- $Q_0 \not\leadsto^{*} Q_n$ whenever we finitely fail to infer that $Q_0 \leadsto^{*} Q_n$ holds.

The inference rules of ρLog are shown in Fig. 1. They differ from those of the initial ρLog calculus in some important ways:

1. The current version allows to have unrestricted Mathematica constraints in the specification of queries and conditional parts of rules. In this way, we achieve full integration of the CLP component of our system with the constraint solving capabilities of Mathematica.
   The inference rule of ρLog for such constraints is the last one from Fig. 1.
2. We introduced parametric strategies, that is, strategies with arguments that get instantiated during the reduction process. They enable natural and concise specifications of many kinds of rules, like those for strict and lazy evaluation. The inference rule of ρLog for this feature is the first one from Fig. 1: it matches both the left side and the strategy of the selected rule with the left side and strategy of the reducibility formula selected from the query.

$$\frac{(t'_1 \rightarrow_{stg'} t'_2/;\bigwedge_{i=1}^{n} cond_i) \in P \quad \sigma \in mcsm((t'_1, stg'), (t_1, stg))}{(t_1 \rightarrow_{stg} t_2) \wedge Q \rightsquigarrow_{\sigma} (\bigwedge_{i=1}^{n} cond_i \wedge (t'_2 \equiv t_2) \wedge Q)}$$

$$\frac{\sigma \in mcsm(t', t)}{(t \equiv t') \wedge Q \rightsquigarrow_{\sigma} \sigma(Q)} \qquad \frac{\sigma \in mcsm(t', t)}{(t \rightarrow_{\texttt{"Id"}} t') \wedge Q \rightsquigarrow_{\sigma} \sigma(Q)}$$

$$\frac{(t \rightarrow_{stg} t') \not\rightsquigarrow^{*} \top}{(t \not\rightarrow_{stg} t') \wedge Q \rightsquigarrow_{\{\}} Q}$$

$$\frac{(t \rightarrow_{stg} t') \rightsquigarrow_{\sigma}^{*} \top}{(t \rightarrow_{\texttt{Fst}[stg,\ldots]} t') \wedge Q \rightsquigarrow_{\sigma} \sigma(Q)}$$

$$\frac{(t \rightarrow_{stg_1} t') \not\rightsquigarrow^{*} \top}{(t \rightarrow_{\texttt{Fst}[stg_1, stg_2 \ldots, stg_n]} t') \wedge Q \rightsquigarrow_{\{\}} (t \rightarrow_{\texttt{Fst}[stg_2,\ldots,stg_n]} t') \wedge Q}$$

$$\frac{(t \rightarrow_{stg} \_) \rightsquigarrow^{*} \top}{(t \rightarrow_{\texttt{NF}[stg]} t') \wedge Q \rightsquigarrow_{\{\}} (t \rightarrow_{stg \circ \texttt{NF}[stg]} t') \wedge Q}$$

$$\frac{(t \rightarrow_{stg} \_) \not\rightsquigarrow^{*} \top \quad \sigma \in mcsm(t', t)}{(t \rightarrow_{\texttt{NF}[stg]} t') \wedge Q \rightsquigarrow_{\sigma} \sigma(Q)}$$

$$\frac{cond \text{ is a valid Mathematica formula}}{cond \wedge Q \rightsquigarrow_{\{\}} Q}$$

Fig. 1. The inference rules of the ρLog calculus

The proper interpretation of the other composite strategies and predefined parametric strategies is guaranteed by assuming that P contains defining rules for them. For example, the rules for the strategy combinators of ρLog are:

$\texttt{x\_} \longrightarrow_{\texttt{s1\_}\circ\texttt{s2\_}} \texttt{z}/; (\texttt{x} \longrightarrow_{\texttt{s1}} \texttt{y\_}) \wedge (\texttt{y} \longrightarrow_{\texttt{s2}} \texttt{z\_}).$
$\texttt{x\_} \longrightarrow_{\texttt{s1\_}|\texttt{s2\_}} \texttt{z}/; (\texttt{x} \longrightarrow_{\texttt{s1}} \texttt{z\_}).$
$\texttt{x\_} \longrightarrow_{\texttt{s1\_}|\texttt{s2\_}} \texttt{z}/; (\texttt{x} \longrightarrow_{\texttt{s2}} \texttt{z\_}).$
$\texttt{x\_} \longrightarrow_{[\texttt{s\_}^*]} \texttt{y}/; (\texttt{x} \longrightarrow_{\texttt{"Id"}|(\texttt{s}\circ\texttt{s}^*)} \texttt{y\_}).$

The set of answers computed by ρLog for Q in a rewrite theory represented by a program P is $Ans_P(Q) := \{\sigma \mid \text{there is an inference derivation } Q \rightsquigarrow_{\sigma}^{*} \top\}$.

Properties. ρLog is a sound calculus: for every $\sigma \in Ans_P(Q)$, the formula $\sigma(Q)$ holds in the rewrite theory presented by P. Unfortunately, ρLog is not complete: some substitutions that satisfy Q w.r.t. P may not be found because the leftmost selection strategy of query components is not fair, and some attempts to compute a derivation $Q \rightsquigarrow^* \top$ may run forever. The same phenomenon happens in most implementations of Prolog: SLDNF resolution with leftmost literal selection is incomplete for the same reason.

Implementations of logic programming languages usually adopt SLDNF resolution with leftmost literal selection, mainly for efficiency reasons; there are other, less efficient literal selection strategies, which preserve completeness. But for ρLog we have no other selection strategies, because this is the only way to avoid the problem of infinitary unification: by preserving determinism of queries.

3 Applications

3.1 Evaluation Strategies

Suppose $P = \{t_i \to t'_i/; cond_{i,1} \wedge \ldots \wedge cond_{i,p_i} \mid 1 \leq i \leq n\}$ is a set of conditional rewrite rules that represent a functional program, and we wish to evaluate a term t with respect to P. A straightforward way to encode the rules of P in ρLog is to assign to all of them a common strategy identifier, say "P", to indicate that they all belong to the same program. Thus, a ρLog program for P could be declared as follows:

DeclareRules["P",
$t_1 \to t'_1/; cond_{1,1} \wedge \ldots \wedge cond_{1,p_1}$,
...
$t_n \to t'_n/; cond_{n,1} \wedge \ldots \wedge cond_{n,p_n}$]

The main evaluation strategies in programming language theory are: eager (or strict) and lazy. When confined to expressions consisting of nested function calls, strict evaluation corresponds to innermost rewriting, and lazy evaluation corresponds to outermost rewriting with the conditional rewrite rules of P. If we adopt the small-step operational style, the value of a term is the normal form produced by derivations consisting of innermost (resp. outermost) rewrite steps.

In ρLog, the small-step operational specification of these evaluation strategies is straightforward:

strict evaluation: $t \to_{\text{"strict"[s]}} t'$ holds if t' is obtained by reducing with s an innermost subterm of t. It can be defined by mutual recursion as follows:

DeclareRules[
$\texttt{x\_} \to_{\text{"strict"[s\_]}} \texttt{y}/; (\texttt{x} \to_{\text{Fst["sAux"[s],s]}} \texttt{y\_})$,
$\texttt{f\_[as\_\_\_, x\_, bs\_\_\_]} \to_{\text{"sAux"[s\_]}} \texttt{f[as, y, bs]}/; (\texttt{x} \to_{\text{"strict"[s]}} \texttt{y\_})$]

lazy evaluation: $t \to_{\text{"lazy"[s]}} t'$ holds if t' is obtained by reducing with s an outermost subterm of t. It can be defined by mutual recursion as follows:

```
DeclareRules[
  x_ →"lazy"[s_] y/; (x →Fst[s,"lAux"[s]] y_),
  f_[as___, x_, bs___] →"lAux"[s_] f[as, y, bs]/; (x →"lazy"[s] y_)]
```

The strict value of a term t is returned by `ApplyRule[`t`,NF["strict"["P"]]]`, and the lazy value of term t is returned by `ApplyRule[`t`,NF["lazy"["P"]]]`.

3.2 Natural Deduction

In logic and proof theory, natural deduction is a proof system whose inference rules are closely related to the "natural" way of reasoning. The general form of an inference rule is

$$\frac{J_1 \quad \ldots \quad J_n}{J}\ (name)$$

where $J_1, \ldots, J_n, J$ are judgments (that is, representations of something that is knowable), and *name* is the name of the inference rule. The judgments above the line are called *premises* and that below the line is called *conclusion*. For example, Gentzen's proof system LK for natural deduction has inference rules for judgments of the form $L \vdash R$ where L and R are finite (possibly empty) sequences of formulas in first-order logic. Such a judgment is called sequent, and its intended reading is "If all formulas in L hold then at least one formula in R holds." For example, the inference rules of system LK that pertain to the propositional fragment of first-order logic are those shown in Fig. 2, where the metavariables L, L_1, L_2, R, R_1, R_2 denote sequences of formulas, and A, B denote formulas.

$$\frac{}{L_1, A, L_2 \vdash R_1, A, R_2}\ (I)$$

$$\frac{L_1, A, B, L_2 \vdash R}{L_1, A \wedge B, L_2 \vdash R}\ (\wedge L) \qquad \frac{L \vdash R_1, A, R_2 \quad L \vdash R_1, B, R_2}{L \vdash R_1, A \wedge B, R_2}\ (\wedge R)$$

$$\frac{L_1, A, L_2 \vdash R \quad L_1, B, L_2 \vdash R}{L_1, A \vee B, L_2 \vdash R}\ (\vee L) \qquad \frac{L \vdash R_1, A, B, R_2}{L \vdash R_1, A \vee B, R_2}\ (\vee R)$$

$$\frac{L_1, L_2 \vdash A, R \quad B, L_1, L_2 \vdash R}{L, A \Rightarrow B, L_2 \vdash R}\ (\Rightarrow L) \qquad \frac{A, L \vdash R_1, B, R_2}{L \vdash R_1, A \Rightarrow B, R_2}\ (\Rightarrow R)$$

$$\frac{L_1, L_2 \vdash A, R}{L_1, \neg A, L_2 \vdash R}\ (\neg L) \qquad \frac{A, L \vdash R_1, R_2}{L \vdash R_1, \neg A, R_2}\ (\neg R)$$

Fig. 2. System LK: inference rules for propositional formulas.

System LK is sound and complete. This implies that $L \vdash R$ holds iff it can be derived from the above rules.

Often, we can translate an inference rule $\frac{J_1 \quad \ldots \quad J_n}{J}$ (*name*) into a corresponding rule of ρLog, as follows:

$J \to_{name}$ `True`/; $(J_1 \to_{stg}$ `True`$) \wedge \ldots \wedge (J_n \to_{stg}$ `True`$)$.

where strategy *stg* can be defined such that

> $J \to_{stg}$ `True` holds iff J can be derived using the inference rules of the proof system under consideration.

This translation technique works well for Gentzen's proof system illustrated in Fig. 2: We obtain the program consisting of the following nine rule declarations:

```
DeclareRules[
    {___, A_, ___} ⊢ {___, A_, ___} →"I" True,
    {L1___, A_ ∧ B_, L2___} ⊢ R_ →"∧L" True/; ({L1, A, B, L2} ⊢ R →s True),
    L_ ⊢ {R1___, A_ ∧ B_, R2___} →"∧R" True/; (L ⊢ {R1, A, R2} →s True)∧
                                              (L ⊢ {R1, B, R2} →s True),
    {L1___, A_ ∨ B_, L2___} ⊢ R_ →"∨L" True/; ({L1, A, L2} ⊢ R →s True)∧
                                              ({L1, B, L2} ⊢ R →s True),
    L_ ⊢ {R1___, A_ ∨ B_, R2___} →"∨R" True/; (L ⊢ {R1, A, B, R2} →s True),
    {L1___, A_ ⇒ B_, L2___} ⊢ {R___} →"⇒L" True/; ({L1, L2} ⊢ {A, R} →s True)∧
                                                  ({B, L1, L2} ⊢ {R} →s True),
    {L___} ⊢ {R1___, A_ ⇒ B_, R2___} →"⇒R" True/; ({A, L} ⊢ {B, R1, R2} →s True),
    {L1___, ¬A_, L2___} ⊢ {R___} →"¬L" True/; ({L1, L2} ⊢ {A, R} →s True),
    {L___} ⊢ {R1___, ¬A_, R2___} →"¬R" True/; ({L, A} ⊢ {R1, R2} →s True)]
```

where `s` is an identifier which should be instantiated with strategy *stg*. It could be the choice

"∧L" | "∧R" | "∨L" | "∨R" | "⇒L" | "⇒R" | "¬L" | "¬R" | "I"

but we can do better than that: We can use heuristics in the definition of `s` to reduce the search space for a proof. For example

`Fst["I", "∧L" | "∧R" | "∨L" | "∨R" | "⇒L" | "⇒R" | "¬L" | "¬R"]`

would be a better specification for `s` because it gives highest priority to rule `"I"` which, if applicable, detects immediately a proof for a sequent.

ρLog can generate a trace of its computation:

`Request[`Q`,Trace→True]`

instructs ρLog to generate and open a Mathematica notebook with human-readable explanations of the rule-based computations that produced an answer or ended with failure. For example

```
s = Fst["I"," ∧ L"|" ∧ R"|" ∨ L"|" ∨ R"|"⇒L"|"⇒R"|"¬L"|"¬R"];
Request[{} ⊢ {(P ⇒ Q) ⇒ ((¬Q) ⇒ ¬P)} →s True,Trace→True]
```

generates a notebook with explanations that certify that the sequent

{} ⊢ {(P ⇒ Q) ⇒ ((¬Q) ⇒ ¬P)

can be derived with the inference rules of system LK. A snapshot of this trace is shown in Fig. 3.

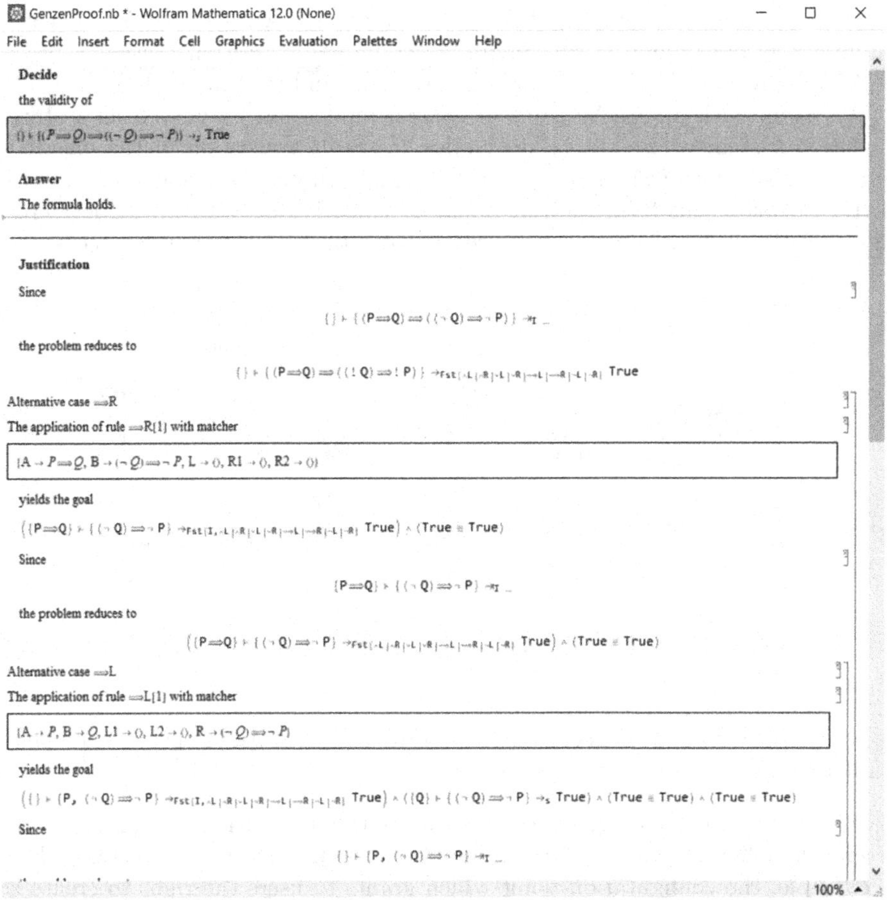

Fig. 3. A human-readable trace of a rule-based deduction.

3.3 Specification and Safety-Check of Access-Control Models

A fundamental security problem in computing environments is to control the access of subjects to system abstractions (e.g., processes, files, or ports) or resources (e.g., printers). Attribute-based access control (ABAC) is the most recent authorization model, where access rights are granted to users through the use of policies which combine together the attributes of the participating entities (user/subject or subject/object), operations, and the environment relevant to a request. To better understand the power and limitations of this logical access control paradigm, several foundational models have been proposed [6,7]: They provide minimal set of capabilities that suffice to configure many access control models of practical interest.

Of particular importance is $ABAC_\alpha$ [7], a foundational model for ABAC with a minimal set of capabilities to configure the dominant traditional access control models: discretionary (DAC), mandatory (MAC), and role-based (RBAC).

A system with an $ABAC_\alpha$ access control model can be viewed as a state transition system whose states are triples $\{U, S, O\}$ consisting of the existing users (U), subjects (S), and objects (O), and whose transitions correspond to the six operations from the functional specification of $ABAC_\alpha$: subject creation/deletion/modification, object creation/deletion, and authorized access.

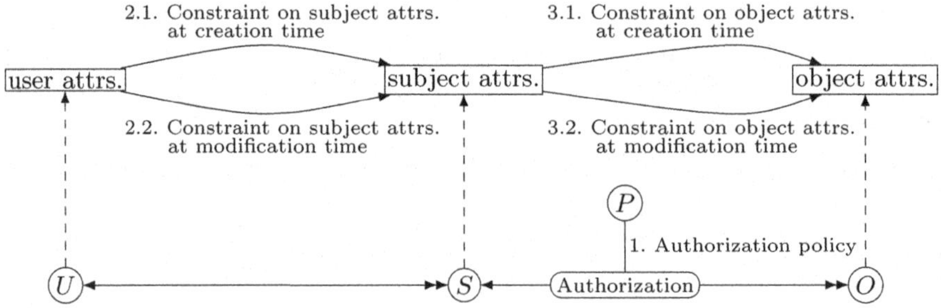

Fig. 4. The structure of $ABAC_\alpha$ model (adapted from [6])

In [13] we have shown that ρLog is a suitable framework to specify the operational model of $ABAC_\alpha$, because:

1. With parametric strategies, we can separate the declaration of configuration-specific policies from the declaration of policies characteristic to $ABAC_\alpha$. For example, the configuration point which grants to users the right to create a subject has a policy which depends on the specific configuration type (e.g., DAC, MAC, or RBAC).
2. The constraint logic programming component of ρLog is based on the constraint solving capabilities of Mathematica and can interpret correctly all boolean constraints expressed in the CPL instances of $ABAC_\alpha$.
3. The transitions of the operational model of $ABAC_\alpha$ can be defined as parametric strategies whose parameters get bound to configuration-specific identifiers, and can be used to enforce the application of the rule-based specifications of the configuration points.

In the remainder of this section, we describe a software tool developed by us in Mathematica, which relies on the rule-based programming capabilities of ρLog to specify any possible configuration of $ABAC_\alpha$ and its operational model, and to check safety properties. The tool can be downloaded from the website of our system:

`http://staff.fmi.uvt.ro/~mircea.marin/rholog/`

Representation of ABAC$_\alpha$ Entitites. The entities of ABAC$_\alpha$ are users, subjects, or objects. Each user, subject, object is associated with a finite set of user attributes (UA), subject attributes (SA) and object attributes (OA) respectively. Every attribute *att* has a type, scope, and finite range of possible values. The sets of attributes specific to each kind of entity, together with their corresponding type, scope, and range, are specified in a *configuration type.*

We represent entities as flat terms of the form

$$E[at_1[\ val_1], \ldots,\ at_n[\ val_n]]$$

where the term constructor $E \in \{\bullet\texttt{U}, \bullet\texttt{S}, \bullet\texttt{O}\}$ indicates the entity type (user, subject, or object), every at_i is a string literal that indicates an attribute name, and val_i is a Mathematica literal that indicates the value of the corresponding attribute.

Configuration Types and Configurations. In ABAC$_\alpha$, every attribute *at* has (1) a scope SCOPE[*at*] which is a finite set of values, and (2) a type which is either <u>atomic</u> or <u>set</u>. The range of values of *at* is SCOPE[*at*] if the type of *at* is <u>atomic</u>, and $2^{\text{SCOPE}[at]}$ if the type of *at* is <u>set</u>. A *configuration type* specifies the admissible attributes for every kind of entity, their scope and their type.

Our tool provides the command `DeclareCfgType` to declare ABAC$_\alpha$ configuration types. The syntax of this command is

```
DeclareCfgType[typeId,
  {UA→ {uAt₁,...,uAtₘ},SA→ {sAt₁,...,sAtₙ},OA→ {oAt₁,...,oAtₚ},
   Scope→ {at₁ → {sId₁,τ₁},...,atᵣ → {sIdᵣ,τᵣ}}}]
```

where ***typeId*** is the newly declared ID of a configuration type; $\{sAt_1, \ldots, sAt_n\}$ is the set of attributes for users; $\{uAt_1, \ldots, uAt_m\}$ is the set of attributes for subjects; $\{oAt_1, \ldots, oAt_p\}$ is the set of attributes for objects; and

> the scope of every attribute at_i is the set bound to identifier sId_i in a particular configuration (see below), and its type is $\tau_i \in \{$`"elem"`,`"subset"`$\}$, where `"elem"` stands for <u>atomic</u> and `"subset"` for <u>set</u>.

A *configuration* is an instance of a configuration type which indicates (1) the sets of values for the identifiers sId_i from the specification of a configuration type, and (3) the sets U, S, and O of entities (users, subjects, objects) in the initial configuration of the system.

Our tool provides the command `DeclareConfiguration` to declare a configuration ***cId*** for a configuration type ***typeId***. It has the syntax

```
DeclareConfiguration[cId, {CfgType→typeId,
  Users→{uId₁→u₁,...,uIdₘ→uₘ},
  Range→{UId→{uId₁,...,uIdₘ},
           sId₂ → SCOPE(at₂),...,sIdᵣ → SCOPE(atᵣ)},
  Subjects→{s₁,...,sₙ},
  Objects→{o₁,...,o_q}}]
```

The side effect of this command is to instantiate some globally visible entries:

> CfgType[*cId*] with ***typeId***,
> Users[*cId*] with the set $\{u_1, \ldots, u_m\}$ of terms for users,
> every User[*cId*,uId$_i$] with the term u_i,
> Subjects[*cId*] with the set $\{s_1, \ldots, s_n\}$ of terms for subjects, and
> Objects[*cId*] with the set $\{o_1, \ldots, o_q\}$ of terms for objects.

To illustrate, consider the mandatory access control model (MAC). Users and subjects have a clearance attribute of type elem, whose value is a number from a finite set of integers $L = \{1, 2, \ldots, N\}$ which indicates the security level of the corresponding entity. Objects have a sensitivity attribute of type "elem" whose value is also from L, and represents the sensitivity degree of the information in that object. When read and write are the only permissions on objects, we can assume the set of permissions P to be {"read","write"}. A configuration type for MAC can be defined as follows:

```
DeclareCfgType["MAC",
 {UA→{"id","clearance"},
  SA→{"id","clearance"},
  OA→{"sensitivity"},
  Scope→{"id"→{"uId","elem"},"clearance"→{"level","elem"},
                        "sensitivity"→{"level","elem"}}}]
```

and a particular MAC configuration can be defined by

```
DeclareConfiguration["MAC-Cfg01",
 {CfgType→"MAC",
  Users→{"u1"→•U["id"["u"],"clearance"[3]],
         "u2"→•U["id"["u2"],"clearance"[4]]},
  Range→{uId→{"u1","u2"},"level"→{1,2,3,4,5}},
  Subjects→{•S["id"["u1"],"clearance"[3]],
            •S["id"["u2"],"clearance"[2]]},
  Objects→{•O["sensitivity"[1],•O["sensitivity"[4]]}}]
```

Specification of the Policy Configuration Points. The operational model depicted in Fig. 4 has five policy configuration points: for subject creation, object creation, modification of the attribute values of a subject, modification of attribute value of an object, and granting a permission to a subject on an object. With our tool, all configuration points of a particular configuration type can be specified by declaring instances of parametric strategies for every kind of operation.

For a configuration type ***cfgTypeId***, the configuration point for subject creation is specified with a declaration

DeclareRules[ConstrSub[*uPatt*, *sPatt*]$\rightarrow_{cfgTypeId}$ True/;⟨*CPL-formula*⟩]

where ⟨*CPL-formula*⟩ is a logical formula written in the CPL-language of $ABAC_\alpha$. For example, subject creation in MAC can be specified by

```
DeclareRules[
  ConstrS[{•U[x_,"clearance"[y_]],•S[x_,"clearance"[z_]]}
        →"MAC" True/;(z≤y)]
```

The other four configuration points are specified in a similar way, with declarations of the form

```
DeclareRules[
   ConstrModS[uPatt, sPatt1, sPatt2] →cfgTypeId True/;⟨CPL-formula2⟩,
   ConstrO[sPatt, oPatt] →cfgTypeId True/;⟨CPL-formula3⟩,
   ConstrModO[sPatt, oPatt1, oPatt2] →cfgTypeId True/;⟨CPL-formula4⟩,
   Auth[p1, sPatt, oPatt] →cfgTypeId True/;⟨CPL-formula5,1⟩,
   ...
   Auth[pn, sPatt, oPatt] →cfgTypeId True/;⟨CPL-formula5,n⟩
]
```

For example, the rule-based specifications of MAC are

```
DeclareRules[
  ConstrModS[_,_,_] →"MAC" False,
  ConstrO[{•S[_,"clearance"[x_]],•O[x_,"sensitivity"[y_]]
        →"MAC" True/;(x≤y),
  ConstrModO[_,_,_] →"MAC" False,
  Auth["read",•S[_,"clearance"[x_],•O["sensitivity"[y_]]
        →"MAC" True/;(y≤x),
  Auth["write",•S[_,"clearance"[x_],•O["sensitivity"[y_]]
        →"MAC" True/;(x≤y)
]
```

Specification of the Operational Model. The state transitions in the operational model of $ABAC_\alpha$ of a particular configuration `cId` of $ABAC_\alpha$ can be specified as instances of parametric strategies:

1. `"createSubj"[cId]`: it acts on a state $\{U, S, O\}$ by extending, if possible, S with a newly created subject,
2. `"deleteSubj"[cId]`: it acts on a state $\{U, S, O\}$ by deleting, if possible, a subject from S,
3. `"createObj"[cId]`: it acts on a state $\{U, S, O\}$ by extending, if possible, O with a newly created object,
4. `"modifySubj"[cId]`: it acts on a state $\{U, S, O\}$ by modifying, if possible, the attributes of a subject from S,
5. `"modifyObj"[cId]`: it acts on a state $\{U, S, O\}$ by modifying, if possible, the attributes of an object from O,

6. `"auth?"`$[p, cfgTypeId]$: it acts on a pair $\{S, O\}$ and yields True if there is a subject $s \in S$ with permission p on an object $o \in O$.

The definition of these strategies in terms of the parametric strategies of the policy configuration points is quite straightforward, and can be found in [13].

Safety Analysis of ABAC$_\alpha$ Configurations. A fundamental problem for any access control model is safety analysis. For ABAC$_\alpha$, the safety problem can be stated as follows:

Given an initial state $St_0 = \{U, S_0, O_0\}$ for a particular configuration of ABAC$_\alpha$, a subject $s \in S_0$, an object $o \in O_0$, and a permission p
Decide if there is a scenario, that is, a sequence of ABAC$_\alpha$ state transitions from St_0 to a state $St_n = \{U, S_n, O_n\}$ where s and o have attribute values that authorize subject s to exercise permission p on object o.

This problem was recently shown to be decidable [1], but no practical algorithm was proposed. In [13], we described a rule-based implementation in ρLog of such an algorithm. Our algorithm decides the safety problem in two steps:

1. First, we compute all possible combinations of attribute values that s may get, if the initial state is St_0. There are finitely many such combinations, which we call descendants of s, and collect them incrementally in a set $sDesc$.
   - We interleave the computation of $sDesc$ with the application of the labeled conditional rewrite rule
     `Auth`$[p, sPatt, oPatt] \rightarrow_{cfgTypeId}$ `True/;`$\langle$*CPL-formula*$\rangle$
     to early detect if any descendant of s can exercise permission p on o. If yes, the configuration of ABAC$_\alpha$ is unsafe.
2. Next, we compute all possible combinations of attribute values that o may get by the operations exercised by all subjects that can be created and can modify their attribute values. There are finitely many such combinations, which we call *descendants* of o, and collect them incrementally in a set $oDesc$.
   - We interleave the computation of $oDesc$ with the application of the labeled conditional rewrite rule
     `Auth`$[p, sPatt, oPatt] \rightarrow_{cfgTypeId}$ `True/;`$\langle$*CPL-formula*$\rangle$
     to early detect if any descendant of s can exercise permission p on and descendant of o. If yes, the configuration of ABAC$_\alpha$ is unsafe. If no such situation is detected, the configuration of ABAC$_\alpha$ is reported to be safe.

To run this algorithm, we provide the method `CheckSafety`$[cfgId, s, o, p]$ where $cfgId$ is the identifier of the initial configuration under consideration. The method returns `"UNSAFE"` as soon as it detects that a descendant of s can get permission p on a descendant of object o, and `"SAFE"` otherwise.

4 Conclusion

ρLog is a system for rule-based programming with strategies and labeled conditional rewrite rules. It is based on a rewriting calculus designed by us, which has the following characteristics:

1. It accepts specifications with term variables, function variables, sequence variables, and context variables. As a result, the specifications are more natural and concise. For instance, sequence variables and context variables permit matching to descend to arbitrary depth and width in a term represented as a tree. The ability to explore terms in two orthogonal directions in a uniform turned out be useful for querying data available as a large term, like XML documents [10].
2. It is based on sound and complete matching algorithms developed by us.
3. Its range of applications is enlarged significantly by its access to the constraint solving capabilities of Mathematica, its host language.

The ρLog calculus was also used to implement PρLog [4], an experimental tool that extends logic programming with strategic conditional transformation rules. PρLog combines Prolog with the ρLog calculus, and is available for free download from

`https://www3.risc.jku.at/people/tkutsia/software/prholog`

We already mentioned that ρLog can trace the computation of a derivation $Q \rightsquigarrow_{\sigma}^{*} \top$ as a human-readable proof that substitution σ satisfies query Q in the rewrite theory represented by a program P [12,14]. Failed proof attempts $Q \not\rightsquigarrow^{*} \top$ can be traced too. This capability was inspired from Theorema [3,5], a theorem prover which influenced the development of ρLog and with which our system shares many features.

We are currently investigating the possibility to extend our calculus with capabilities for approximate reasoning, by solving constraints over several similarity relations [2]. Similarity relations are reflexive, symmetric, and transitive fuzzy relations. They help to make approximate inferences, but pose challenges to constraint solving, since we can not rely on the transitivity property anymore.

References

1. Ahmed, T., Sandhu, R.: Safety of ABAC$_{\alpha}$ is decidable. In: Yan, Z., Molva, R., Mazurczyk, W., Kantola, R. (eds.) NSS 2017. LNCS, vol. 10394, pp. 257–272. Springer, Cham (2017). https://doi.org/10.1007/978-3-319-64701-2_19
2. Aït-Kaci, H., Pasi, G.: Fuzzy unification and generalization of first-order terms over similar signatures. In: Fioravanti, F., Gallagher, J.P. (eds.) LOPSTR 2017. LNCS, vol. 10855, pp. 218–234. Springer, Cham (2018). https://doi.org/10.1007/978-3-319-94460-9_13
3. Buchberger, B., Jebelean, T., Kriftner, F., Marin, M., Tomuţa, E., Văsaru, D.: A survey of the Theorema project. In: Proceedings of ISSAC 1997, Maui, Hawaii, USA, pp. 384–391 (1997)
4. Dundua, B., Kutsia, T., Reisenberger-Hagmayer, K.: An overview of PρLog. In: Lierler, Y., Taha, W. (eds.) PADL 2017. LNCS, vol. 10137, pp. 34–49. Springer, Cham (2017). https://doi.org/10.1007/978-3-319-51676-9_3
5. Jebelean, T., Drămnesc, I.: Synthesis of list algorithms by mechanical proving. JSC **69**, 61–92 (2015)

6. Jin, X., Krishnan, R., Sandhu, R.: A unified attribute-based access control model covering DAC, MAC and RBAC. In: Cuppens-Boulahia, N., Cuppens, F., Garcia-Alfaro, J. (eds.) DBSec 2012. LNCS, vol. 7371, pp. 41–55. Springer, Heidelberg (2012). https://doi.org/10.1007/978-3-642-31540-4_4
7. Jin, X.: Attribute-based access control models and implementation in cloud infrastructure as a service. Ph.D. thesis, University of Texas at San Antonio (2014)
8. Kutsia, T.: Solving equations with sequence variables and sequence functions. JSC **42**(3), 352–388 (2007)
9. Kutsia, T.: Solving equations involving sequence variables and sequence functions. In: Buchberger, B., Campbell, J. (eds.) AISC 2004. LNCS (LNAI), vol. 3249, pp. 157–170. Springer, Heidelberg (2004). https://doi.org/10.1007/978-3-540-30210-0_14
10. Kutsia, T., Marin, M.: Can context sequence matching be used for querying XML? In: Vigneron, L. (ed.) Proceedings of the 19th International Workshop on Unification (UNIF 2005), Nara, Japan, pp. 77–92 (2005)
11. Kutsia, T., Marin, M.: Matching with regular constraints. In: Sutcliffe, G., Voronkov, A. (eds.) LPAR 2005. LNCS (LNAI), vol. 3835, pp. 215–229. Springer, Heidelberg (2005). https://doi.org/10.1007/11591191_16
12. Marin, M., Kutsia, T.: Foundations of the rule-based system ρLog. J. Appl. Non Cl. Log. **16**(1–2), 151–168 (2006)
13. Marin, M., Kutsia, T., Dundua, B.: A rule-based approach to the decidability of safety of $ABAC_\alpha$. In: Proceedings of the 24th ACM Symposium on Access Control Models and Technologies, SACMAT 2019, New York, NY, USA, pp. 173–178. Association for Computing Machinery (2019). https://doi.org/10.1145/3322431.3325416
14. Marin, M., Piroi, F.: Deduction and presentation in ρlog. In: Proceedings of MKM. ENTCS, vol. 93, pp. 161–182 (2004)
15. Marin, M., Piroi, F.: Rule-based programming with mathematica. In: Proceedings of International Mathematica Symposium (IMS 2004), Banff, Canada (2004)
16. Wolfram, S.: The Mathematica Book, 5 edn. Wolfram Media (2003)

Variants in the Infinitary Unification Wonderland

José Meseguer(✉)

Department of Computer Science, University of Illinois at Urbana-Champaign, Urbana, USA
meseguer@illinois.edu

Abstract. So far, results about variants, the finite variant property (FVP), and variant unification have been developed for equational theories $E \cup B$ where B is a set of axioms having a finitary unification algorithm, and the equations E, oriented as rewrite rules $\vec{E}$, are convergent modulo B. The extension to the case when B has an infinitary unification algorithm, for example because of non-commutative symbols having associative axioms, seems undeveloped. This paper takes a first step in developing such an extension. In particular, the relationships between the FVP and the boundedness properties, the identification of conditions on $E \cup B$ ensuring FVP, and the effective computation of variants and variant unifiers are explored in detail. The extension from the finitary to the infinitary case includes both surprises and opportunities.

1 Introduction

The notions of variant and variant unifier, e.g., [7,17], have many applications, for example to cryptographic protocol analysis, e.g., [5,7,16,22], program termination [12], SMT solving, e.g., [26,29], partial evaluation, e.g., [1], program transformation and symbolic model checking, e.g., [2,27], and theorem proving, e.g., [28,30]. There is, however, an important current limitation, namely, that known results about variants, the finite variant property (FVP), and variant unification have been developed for equational theories $E \cup B$ where B is a set of axioms having a finitary unification algorithm, and the equations E, oriented as rewrite rules $\vec{E}$, are convergent modulo B. This leaves out of the picture many applications involving specifications whose axioms B have an infinitary unification algorithm, for example, because of non-commutative symbols having associative axioms. Important rule-based languages such as OBJ [20], ASF+SDF [9], CafeOBJ [18], and Maude [6], all support rewriting modulo associativity without commutativity as well as other axioms, so that proving properties about such rule-based programs with the help of variant-based techniques would be very useful, but is currently out of reach, because the extension of the FVP results and algorithms to the infinitary unification case has not yet been developed and is a *terra incognita*.

In this case, practice has run ahead of theory, since Maude 3 [10] already supports the computation of variants and variant unifiers also in the case of

S. Escobar and N. Martí-Oliet (Eds.): WRLA 2020, LNCS 12328, pp. 75–95, 2020.
https://doi.org/10.1007/978-3-030-63595-4_5

axioms B that can include associativity without commutativity. The problem, however, is that at present we do not have any criteria to know when a theory involving such axioms is FVP. This paper is all about extending all the results and algorithms about variants, the finite variant property (FVP), and variant unification to the infinitary unification case. This includes investigating in the infinitary unification case: (i) adequate criteria for a theory to be FVP; (ii) the exact relationship between FVP and the so-called boundedness property [4,5,7]; (iii) notions weaker than FVP, and (iv) variant unification algorithms for both FVP theories and theories enjoying weaker properties.

As usual in these cases, the extension from the finitary to the infinitary case includes both some interesting surprises (thus, the poetic license of talking about a "Wonderland"), and also some important opportunities. In a usual situation, I would now proceed to spell out in more detail the technical content and contributions of the paper. However, since for me the investigation of these problems has been quite full of surprises, I fear that I would spoil the fun for you, dear reader, by telling you more details at this point. What I have already said is enough to give you the gist of the paper without depriving you of the suspense and fun ahead. Enjoy!

2 Preliminaries

2.1 Background on Order-Sorted Algebra

I summarize the order-sorted algebra notions needed in the paper. The material, adapted from [25], extends ideas in [19]. It assumes the notions of many-sorted signature and many-sorted algebra, e.g., [14], which include unsorted signatures and algebras as a special case.

Definition 1. *An* order-sorted (OS) signature *is a triple* $\Sigma = ((S, \leqslant), \Sigma)$ *with* $(S, \leqslant)$ *a poset and* (S, Σ) *a many-sorted signature.* $\widehat{S} = S/{\equiv_{\leqslant}}$*, the quotient of* S *under the equivalence relation* $\equiv_{\leqslant} = (\leqslant \cup \geqslant)^+$*, is called the set of* connected components *of* $(S, \leqslant)$*. The order* $\leqslant$ *and equivalence* $\equiv_{\leqslant}$ *are extended to sequences of same length in the usual way, e.g.,* $s'_1 \ldots s'_n \leqslant s_1 \ldots s_n$ *iff* $s'_i \leqslant s_i$*,* $1 \leqslant i \leqslant n$*.* Σ *is called* sensible *if for any two* $f : w \to s, f : w' \to s' \in \Sigma$*, with* w *and* w' *of same length, we have* $w \equiv_{\leqslant} w' \;\Rightarrow\; s \equiv_{\leqslant} s'$*. A* many-sorted signature Σ *is the special case where the poset* $(S, \leqslant)$ *is discrete, i.e.,* $s \leqslant s'$ *iff* $s = s'$*.* $\Sigma = ((S, \leqslant), \Sigma)$ *is a* subsignature *of* $\Sigma' = ((S', \leqslant'), \Sigma')$*, denoted* $\Sigma \subseteq \Sigma'$*, iff* $S \subseteq S'$*,* $\leqslant \subseteq \leqslant'$*, and* $\Sigma \subseteq \Sigma'$*.*

For connected components $[s_1], \ldots, [s_n], [s] \in \widehat{S}$

$$f_{[s]}^{[s_1]\ldots[s_n]} = \{f : s'_1 \ldots s'_n \to s' \in \Sigma \mid s'_i \in [s_i],\ \ 1 \leqslant i \leqslant n,\ s' \in [s]\}$$

denotes the family of "subsort polymorphic" operators f*.*

I will always assume that Σ's poset of sorts $(S, \leqslant)$ is *locally finite*, that is, that for any $s \in S$ its connected component $[s]$ is a finite set.

Definition 2. *For $\Sigma = (S, \leqslant, \Sigma)$ an OS signature, an* order-sortedΣ*-algebra A is a many-sorted (S, Σ)-algebra A such that:*

- *whenever $s \leqslant s'$, then we have $A_s \subseteq A_{s'}$, and*
- *whenever $f : w \to s, f : w' \to s' \in f_{[s]}^{[s_1]\ldots[s_n]}$ and $\overline{a} \in A^w \cap A^{w'}$, then we have $A_{f:w\to s}(\overline{a}) = A_{f:w'\to s'}(\overline{a})$, where $A^\epsilon = 1$ (ϵ denotes the empty string and $1 = \{0\}$ is a singleton set), and $A^{s_1\ldots s_n} = A_{s_1} \times \ldots \times A_{s_n}$.*

An order-sorted Σ-homomorphism *$h : A \to B$ is a many-sorted (S, Σ)-homomorphism such that whenever $[s] = [s']$ and $a \in A_s \cap A_{s'}$, then we have $h_s(a) = h_{s'}(a)$. We call h* injective, *resp.* surjective, *resp.* bijective, *iff for each $s \in S$ h_s is injective, resp. surjective, resp. bijective. We call h an* isomorphism *if there is another order-sorted Σ-homomorphism $g : B \to A$ such that for each $s \in S$, $h_s; g_s = 1_{A_s}$, and $g_s; h_s = 1_{B_s}$, with $1_{A_s}, 1_{B_s}$ the identity functions on A_s, B_s. This defines a category $\mathbf{OSAlg}_\Sigma$.*

Theorem 1. *[25] The category $\mathbf{OSAlg}_\Sigma$ has an initial algebra. Furthermore, if Σ is sensible, then the term algebra T_Σ with:*

- *if $a : \epsilon \to s$ then $a \in T_{\Sigma,s}$,*
- *if $t \in T_{\Sigma,s}$ and $s \leqslant s'$ then $t \in T_{\Sigma,s'}$,*
- *if $f : s_1 \ldots s_n \to s$ and $t_i \in T_{\Sigma,s_i}$ $1 \leqslant i \leqslant n$, then $f(t_1, \ldots, t_n) \in T_{\Sigma,s}$, is initial, i.e., there is a unique Σ-homomorphism from T_Σ to each Σ-algebra.*

T_Σ will (ambiguously) denote both the above-defined S-sorted set and the set $T_\Sigma = \bigcup_{s\in S} T_{\Sigma,s}$. For $[s] \in \widehat{S}$, $T_{\Sigma,[s]} = \bigcup_{s'\in[s]} T_{\Sigma,s'}$. An OS signature Σ is said to *have non-empty sorts* iff for each $s \in S$, $T_{\Sigma,s} \neq \varnothing$. Unless explicitly stated otherwise, *I will assume throughout that Σ has non-empty sorts.* An OS signature Σ is called *preregular* [19] iff for each $t \in T_\Sigma$ the set $\{s \in S \mid t \in T_{\Sigma,s}\}$ has a least element, denoted $ls(t)$. *I will assume throughout that Σ is preregular.*

An S-sorted set $X = \{X_s\}_{s\in S}$ of *variables*, satisfies $s \neq s' \Rightarrow X_s \cap X_{s'} = \varnothing$, and the variables in X are always assumed disjoint from all constants in Σ. The *Σ-term algebra* on variables X, $T_\Sigma(X)$, is the *initial algebra* for the signature $\Sigma(X)$ obtained by adding to Σ the variables X *as extra constants.* Since a $\Sigma(X)$-algebra is just a pair (A, α), with A a Σ-algebra, and α an *interpretation of the constants* in X, i.e., an S-sorted function $\alpha \in [X{\to}A]$, the $\Sigma(X)$-initiality of $T_\Sigma(X)$ can be expressed as the following corollary of Theorem 1:

Theorem 2. *(Freeness Theorem). If Σ is sensible, for each $A \in \mathbf{OSAlg}_\Sigma$ and $\alpha \in [X{\to}A]$, there exists a unique Σ-homomorphism, $\_\alpha : T_\Sigma(X) \to A$ extending α, i.e., such that for each $s \in S$ and $x \in X_s$ we have $x\alpha_s = \alpha_s(x)$.*

In particular, when $A = T_\Sigma(X)$, an interpretation of the constants in X, i.e., an S-sorted function $\sigma \in [X{\to}T_\Sigma(X)]$ is called a *substitution*, and its unique homomorphic extension $\_\sigma : T_\Sigma(X) \to T_\Sigma(X)$ is also called a substitution. Define $dom(\sigma) = \{x \in X \mid x \neq x\sigma\}$, and $ran(\sigma) = \bigcup_{x\in dom(\sigma)} vars(x\sigma)$.

The first-order language of *equational Σ-formulas* is defined in the usual way: its atoms are *Σ-equations* $t = t'$, where $t, t' \in T_\Sigma(X)_{[s]}$ for some $[s] \in \widehat{S}$

and each X_s is assumed countably infinite. The set $Form(\Sigma)$ of *equational Σ-formulas* is then inductively built from atoms by: conjunction ($\wedge$), disjunction ($\vee$), negation ($\neg$), and universal ($\forall x{:}s$) and existential ($\exists x{:}s$) quantification with sorted variables $x{:}s \in X_s$ for some $s \in S$. The literal $\neg(t = t')$ is denoted $t \neq t'$.

Given a Σ-algebra A, a formula $\varphi \in Form(\Sigma)$, and an assignment $\alpha \in [Y \rightarrow A]$, with $Y = fvars(\varphi)$ the free variables of φ, the *satisfaction relation* $A, \alpha \models \varphi$ is defined inductively as usual. Likewise, $A \models \varphi$ holds iff $A, \alpha \models \varphi$ holds for each $\alpha \in [Y \rightarrow A]$, where $Y = fvars(\varphi)$. We say that φ is *valid* (or *true*) in A iff $A \models \varphi$. We say that φ is *satisfiable* in A iff $\exists \alpha \in [Y \rightarrow A]$ such that $A, \alpha \models \varphi$, where $Y = fvars(\varphi)$. For a subsignature $\Omega \subseteq \Sigma$ and $A \in \mathbf{OSAlg}_{\Sigma}$, the *reduct* $A|_{\Omega} \in \mathbf{OSAlg}_{\Omega}$ agrees with A in the interpretation of all sorts and operations in Ω and discards everything in $\Sigma - \Omega$. If $\varphi \in Form(\Omega)$ we have the equivalence $A \models \varphi \Leftrightarrow A|_{\Omega} \models \varphi$.

An OS *equational theory* is a pair $T = (\Sigma, E)$, with E a set of Σ-equations. $\mathbf{OSAlg}_{(\Sigma,E)}$ denotes the full subcategory of $\mathbf{OSAlg}_{\Sigma}$ with objects those $A \in \mathbf{OSAlg}_{\Sigma}$ such that $A \models E$, called the *(Σ, E)-algebras.* $\mathbf{OSAlg}_{(\Sigma,E)}$ has an *initial algebra* $T_{\Sigma/E}$ [25]. Given $T = (\Sigma, E)$ and $\varphi \in Form(\Sigma)$, we call φ *T-valid*, written $E \models \varphi$, iff $A \models \varphi$ for each $A \in \mathbf{OSAlg}_{(\Sigma,E)}$. We call φ *T-satisfiable* iff there exists $A \in \mathbf{OSAlg}_{(\Sigma,E)}$ with φ satisfiable in A. Note that φ is *T-valid* iff $\neg\varphi$ is *T-unsatisfiable.*

The inference system in [25] is *sound and complete* for OS equational deduction, i.e., for any OS equational theory (Σ, E), and Σ-equation $u = v$ we have an equivalence $E \vdash u = v \quad \Leftrightarrow \quad E \models u = v$. Deducibility $E \vdash u = v$ is often abbreviated as $u =_E v$ and called *E-equality.* A preregular signature Σ is called *E-preregular* iff for each $u = v \in E$ and variable specialization ρ, $ls(u\rho) = ls(v\rho)$.

An *E-unifier* of a system of Σ-equations, i.e., of a conjunction $\phi = u_1 = v_1 \wedge \ldots \wedge u_n = v_n$ of Σ-equations, is a substitution σ such that $u_i\sigma =_E v_i\sigma$, $1 \leqslant i \leqslant n$. An *$E$-unification algorithm* for (Σ, E) is an algorithm generating a *complete set* of E-unifiers $Unif_E(\phi)$ for any system of Σ equations ϕ, where "complete" means that for any E-unifier σ of ϕ there is a $\tau \in Unif_E(\phi)$ and a substitution ρ such that $\sigma =_E (\tau\rho)|_{dom(\sigma) \cup dom(\tau)}$, where $=_E$ here means that for any variable x we have $x\sigma =_E x(\tau\rho)|_{dom(\sigma) \cup dom(\tau)}$. The algorithm is *finitary* if it always terminates with a *finite set* $Unif_E(\phi)$ for any ϕ.

Given a set of equations B used for deduction modulo B, a preregular OS signature Σ is called *B-preregular*[1] iff for each $u = v \in B$ and substitutions ρ, $ls(u\rho) = ls(v\rho)$.

2.2 Convergent Theories, Constructors and Narrowing

Given an order-sorted equational theory $\mathcal{E} = (\Sigma, E \cup B)$, where B is a collection of associativity and/or commutativity and/or identity axioms and Σ

[1] If $B = B_0 \uplus U$, with B_0 associativity and/or commutativity axioms, and U identity axioms, the B-preregularity notion can be *broadened* by requiring only that: (i) Σ is B_0-preregular in the standard sense that $ls(u\rho) = ls(v\rho)$ for all $u = v \in B_0$ and substitutions ρ; and (ii) the axioms U oriented as rules $\vec{U}$ are *sort-decreasing* in the sense explained in Sect. 2.2.

is B-preregular, we can associate to it a corresponding *rewrite theory* [24] $\vec{\mathcal{E}} = (\Sigma, B, \vec{E})$ by orienting the equations E as left-to right rewrite rules. That is, each $(u = v) \in E$ is transformed into a rewrite rule $u \rightarrow v$. The main purpose of the rewrite theory $\vec{\mathcal{E}}$ is to reduce the complex bidirectional reasoning with equations to the much simpler unidirectional reasoning with rules under suitable assumptions. I assume familiarity with the notion of subterm $t|_p$ of t at a term position p and of term replacement $t[w]_p$ of $t|_p$ by w at position p (see, e.g., [8]). The rewrite relation $t \rightarrow_{\vec{E},B} t'$ (which can be abbreviated to $t \rightarrow_{\vec{\mathcal{E}}} t'$) holds iff there is a subterm $t|_p$ of t, a rule $(u \rightarrow v) \in \vec{E}$ and a substitution θ such that $u\theta =_B t|_p$, and $t' = t[v\theta]_p$. We denote by $\rightarrow^*_{\vec{E},B}$ the reflexive-transitive closure of $\rightarrow_{\vec{E},B}$. The requirements on $\vec{\mathcal{E}}$ allowing us to reduce equational reasoning to rewriting are the following: (i) $vars(v) \subseteq vars(u)$; (ii) *sort-decreasingness*: for each substitution θ we must have $ls(u\theta) \geqslant ls(v\theta)$; (iii) *strict B-coherence*: if $t_1 \rightarrow_{\vec{E},B} t_1'$ and $t_1 =_B t_2$ then there exists $t_2 \rightarrow_{\vec{E},B} t_2'$ with $t_1' =_B t_2'$; (iv) *confluence*: for each term t if $t \rightarrow^*_{\vec{E},B} v_1$ and $t \rightarrow^*_{\vec{E},B} v_2$, then there exist rewrite sequences $v_1 \rightarrow^*_{\vec{E},B} w_1$ and $v_2 \rightarrow^*_{\vec{E},B} w_2$ such that $w_1 =_B w_2$; (v) *termination*: the relation $\rightarrow_{\vec{E},B}$ is well-founded. If $\vec{\mathcal{E}}$ satisfies conditions (i)–(v) then it is called *convergent*. The key point is that then, given a term t, all terminating rewrite sequences $t \rightarrow^*_{\vec{E},B} w$ end in a term w, denoted $t!_{\vec{\mathcal{E}}}$, that is unique up to B-equality, and its called t's *canonical form*. Three major results then follow for the convergent case: (1) (Church-Rosser Theorem) for any terms t, t' we have $t =_{E \cup B} t'$ iff $t!_{\vec{\mathcal{E}}} =_B t'!_{\vec{\mathcal{E}}}$, (2) the B-equivalence classes of canonical forms of ground terms are the elements of the *canonical term algebra* $C_{\Sigma/E,B}$, where for each $f : s_1 \dots s_n \rightarrow s$ in Σ and $[t_i] \in C_{\Sigma/E,B,s_i}$, $1 \leqslant i \leqslant n$, the operation $f_{C_{\Sigma/E,B}}$ is defined by the identity: $f_{C_{\Sigma/E,B}}([t_1] \dots [t_n]) = [f(t_1 \dots t_n)!_{\vec{\mathcal{E}}}]$, and (3) we have an isomorphism $T_{\mathcal{E}} \cong C_{\Sigma/E,B}$.

Given a convergent rewrite theory $\vec{\mathcal{E}} = (\Sigma, B, \vec{E})$ and a subsignature Ω on the same poset of sorts, a *constructor subspecification* is a convergent rewrite subtheory $\vec{\mathcal{E}}_\Omega = (\Omega, B_\Omega, \vec{E}_\Omega)$ of $\vec{\mathcal{E}}$ (i.e., we have an inclusion of convergent theories $(\Omega, B_\Omega, \vec{E}_\Omega) \subseteq (\Sigma, B, \vec{E})$) such that: (i) for each ground term t, $t!_{\vec{\mathcal{E}}} \in T_\Omega$, and (ii) $T_{\mathcal{E}}|_\Omega \cong T_{\mathcal{E}_\Omega}$. Furthermore, if $E_\Omega = \varnothing$, then $T_{\mathcal{E}}|_\Omega \cong T_{\Omega/B_\Omega}$, and Ω is then called a signature of *free constructors modulo axioms* B_Ω. Furthermore, if $\vec{\mathcal{E}}_\Omega \subseteq \vec{\mathcal{E}}$ is a constructor subspecification we say that $\vec{\mathcal{E}}$ is *sufficiently complete* w.r.t. Ω.

Whenever we have an inclusion of convergent theories $\vec{\mathcal{E}} \subseteq \vec{\mathcal{E}}'$, with respective signatures Σ and Σ', such that $T_{\mathcal{E}'}|_\Sigma \cong T_{\mathcal{E}}$, we say that $\vec{\mathcal{E}}'$ *protects* $\vec{\mathcal{E}}$. Therefore, condition (ii) above just states that $\vec{\mathcal{E}}$ protects $\vec{\mathcal{E}}_\Omega$.

2.3 Parameterized Theories

The general semantics and formal reasoning methods for order-sorted parameterized theories have been developed in [23]. In general, and as supported by Maude [6], the parameter theory $\mathcal{P}$ of a parameterized module $\mathcal{E}[\mathcal{P}]$ can be an order-sorted theory and can have *initiality constraints* [13]. However, for our present purposes in this paper a much simpler, yet commonly occurring, special case, namely, parameterized theories of the form $\mathcal{E}[X]$, where X is just a *parameter sort* (specified in Maude by the "trivial theory" `TRIV` [6]) will suffice and will allow a quite simple and self-contained explanation. For example, parameterized data types of lists, **List**$[X]$, sets, **Set**$[X]$, or multisets, **MSet**$[X]$, are all parametric on a parameter sort X. Any parameterized module $\mathcal{E}[X]$ like this, with a parameter sort X can then be*instantiated* to any chosen sort s in any order-sorted equational theory $\mathcal{M}$. We denote such an instantiation as $\mathcal{E}[\mathcal{M}, X \mapsto s]$ For example, $\mathcal{M}$ can be the theory **Nat** of natural numbers with addition and multiplicaiton, and the sort s the subsort *NzNat* of non-zero natural numbers. Then **MSet**[**Nat**, $X \mapsto$ *NzNat*] denotes the instantiation of **MSet**$[X]$ to multisets whose elements are non-zero natural numbers.

In the simple setting of a parameterized theory $\mathcal{E}[X]$ with parameter sort X, its formal parameter X is just a *chosen sort* X in the order-sorted signature $\Sigma_{\mathcal{E}}$ of the order-sorted theory $\mathcal{E}$, i.e., $\mathcal{E}[X]$ just denotes the choice of sort X in $\mathcal{E}$. What is the *semantics* of such instantiations $\mathcal{E}[\mathcal{M}, X \mapsto s]$? This question can be split in two: (i) what *theory* is denoted by $\mathcal{E}[\mathcal{M}, X \mapsto s]$? and (ii) what *algebra* is specified by $\mathcal{E}[\mathcal{M}, X \mapsto s]$? Let us answer question (i). We will *always assume* that X is a *minimal element* in the poset of sorts $(S_{\mathcal{E}}, <)$ of $\mathcal{E}$. The theory $\mathcal{E}[\mathcal{M}, X \mapsto s]$ is defined as the result of a *theory transformation*

$$(\mathcal{M}, s) \mapsto \mathcal{E}[\mathcal{M}, X \mapsto s]$$

where $(\mathcal{M}, s)$ is a pair consisting of an order-sorted equational theory $\mathcal{M}$ and a sort s in the poset of sorts $(S_{\mathcal{M}}, <')$ of its signature $\Sigma_{\mathcal{M}}$. Then, the resulting order-sorted theory $\mathcal{E}[\mathcal{M}, X \mapsto s]$ is defined as follows: (i) its signature is the signature $(\Sigma_{\mathcal{E}} \uplus \Sigma_{\mathcal{M}})/\overline{\{X = s\}}$ obtained by (a) forming the disjoint union of signatures (to ensure disjoint sorts and operations) $\Sigma_{\mathcal{E}} \uplus \Sigma_{\mathcal{M}}$, and (b) identifying the sorts X and s in the disjoint union of posets $(S_{\mathcal{E}}, <) \uplus (S_{\mathcal{M}}, <')$ to get the quotient poset $((S_{\mathcal{E}}, <) \uplus (S_{\mathcal{M}}, <'))/\overline{\{X = s\}}$. Thanks to the assumption that X is a minimal element in $(S_{\mathcal{E}}, <)$, this quotient poset has a very easy description. Its set of sorts is the quotient set $(S_{\mathcal{E}} \uplus S_{\mathcal{M}})/\overline{\{X = s\}}$ under the equivalence relation $\overline{\{X = s\}}$ generated by the pair (X, s), i.e., $\overline{\{X = s\}} = \{(X, s), (s, X), (X, X), (s, s)\}$, so that we just "identify" X and s an leave the other sorts untouched, and its order relation is just $(< \cup <') \cup (<'; <)$, which can be easily shown to be irreflexive and transitive, where we assume $<$ and $<'$ already disjoint. The answer to question (ii) is now straight forward: the *algebra* denoted by the theory instantiation $\mathcal{E}[\mathcal{M}, X \mapsto s]$ is just the *initial algebra*, let us denote is $T_{\mathcal{E}[\mathcal{M}, X \mapsto s]}$, of the theory $\mathcal{E}[\mathcal{M}, X \mapsto s]$. For example, the initial algebra of **MSet**[**Nat**, $X \mapsto$ *NzNat*] has indeed (finite) multisets of non-zero natural numbers as its elements.

Note that, as further discussed in [23] all the notions about convergent theories and sufficient completeness extend to the parameterized case. Therefore, the instantiation $\mathcal{E}[\mathcal{M}, X \mapsto s]$ yields also an instantiation of rewrite theories $\vec{\mathcal{E}}[\vec{\mathcal{M}}, X \mapsto s]$, which under suitable modularity conditions is convergent if both $\vec{\mathcal{E}}$ and $\vec{\mathcal{M}}$ are so, and is sufficiently complete relative to a constructor signature

$(\Omega_{\mathcal{E}} \uplus \Omega_{\mathcal{M}})/\overline{\{X = s\}}$ in a way that can be checked by the methods developed in [23] assuming constructor signatures $\Omega_{\mathcal{E}}$, resp. $\Omega_{\mathcal{M}}$ for $\mathcal{E}$, resp. $\mathcal{M}$.

2.4 Narrowing and Variants in a Nutshell

Narrowing. Given a convergent $\vec{\mathcal{E}} = (\Sigma, B, \vec{E})$ such that B has a (not necessarily finitary) unification algorithm, by replacing B-matching by B-unification, we can generalize the rewrite relation $t \rightarrow_{\vec{\mathcal{E}}} t'$ to the *narrowing relation* $t \rightsquigarrow_{\vec{\mathcal{E}}} t'$, often decorated as $t \overset{\theta}{\rightsquigarrow}_{\vec{\mathcal{E}}} t'$, which holds between Σ-terms t and t' iff there is a *non-variable* position p in t, a rewrite rule $(l \rightarrow r) \in \vec{E}$ (renamed if necessary so as not to share variables with t), and a B-unifier $\theta \in Unif_B(l = t|_p)$, with $ran(\theta)$ all fresh new variables "standardized apart," i.e., never generated before in the same narrowing process, such that $t' = (t[r]_p)\theta$. Likewise, in $t \overset{\theta}{\rightsquigarrow}{}^*_{\vec{\mathcal{E}}} t'$, the relation $\rightsquigarrow^*_{\vec{\mathcal{E}}}$ denotes the reflexive-transtive closure of $\rightsquigarrow_{\vec{\mathcal{E}}}$, and θ denotes the composition $\theta = \theta_1 \ldots \theta_n$ of the substitutions appearing in the n steps of the narrowing sequence, or the identity substitution when the sequence has length 0. What narrowing a term t with $\rightsquigarrow_{\vec{\mathcal{E}}}$, means is to *symbolically execute* t in the theory $\vec{\mathcal{E}}$. That is, even though t may be in $\vec{\mathcal{E}}$-canonical form and therefore not be executable by rewriting with $\rightarrow_{\vec{\mathcal{E}}}$, by instantiating t with $\rightsquigarrow_{\vec{\mathcal{E}}}$ in all possible "most general" ways, these instantiations *become* executable. Specifically, if $t \overset{\theta}{\rightsquigarrow}{}^*_{\vec{\mathcal{E}}} t'$ holds, then $t\theta \rightarrow^*_{\vec{\mathcal{E}}} u =_B t'$ also holds and, conversely, (the so-called "Lifting Lemma" [21]), if γ is an $\vec{\mathcal{E}}$-canonical substitution and $t\gamma \rightarrow^*_{\vec{\mathcal{E}}} v$ holds, then there is a narrowing sequence $t \overset{\theta}{\rightsquigarrow}{}^*_{\vec{\mathcal{E}}} t'$ of same length as $t\gamma \rightarrow^*_{\vec{\mathcal{E}}} u$ and a substitution δ such that $t'\delta =_B v$.

Variants. Given a convergent rewrite theory $\vec{\mathcal{E}} = (\Sigma, B, \vec{E})$ associated to an equational theory $\mathcal{E}$ a *variant* of a term t is a pair (u, θ) such that θ is a substitution in canonical form, i.e., $\theta = \theta!_{\vec{\mathcal{E}}}$, and $u =_B (t\theta)!_{\vec{\mathcal{E}}}$. $\vec{\mathcal{E}}$ has the *finite variant property* (FVP) iff for any term t there is a finite set $[\![t]\!]_{\vec{\mathcal{E}}} = \{(u_1, \theta_1), \ldots, (u_n, \theta_n)\}$ of variants of t that are *most general possible* among all such variants, where the "most general" relation $\sqsupseteq$ between variants is defined by the equivalence: $(v, \alpha) \sqsupseteq (w, \beta) \Leftrightarrow \exists\gamma(\beta =_B \alpha\gamma \wedge v\gamma =_B w)$. Furthermore, if B has a finitary unification algorithm, a finite set of most general variants in $[\![t]\!]_{\vec{\mathcal{E}}}$ can be effectively computed for any t by *folding variant narrowing* [17].

There are two ways to understand variants and FVP. One is in terms of the notion of a *pattern*, i.e., a term u with variables describing *something*. The variants $\{(u_1, \theta_1), \ldots, (u_n, \theta_n)\}$ of a term t in an FVP theory $\vec{\mathcal{E}}$ are clearly patterns $u_1, \ldots, u_n$ (plus the added technical monkeys $\theta_1, \ldots, \theta_n$). But what do they describe? Obviously, up to B-equality, the infinite set of *all* patterns of the form $(t\theta)!_{\vec{\mathcal{E}}}$ for a given term t. But there is a second, equivalent way of understanding the FVP notion. Implicit in the idea that for *any* variant (w, β) of t there is a most general one $(u_1, \theta_1) \in [\![t]\!]_{\vec{\mathcal{E}}}$ lies the property, called the *boundedness property* [7], that *all variants* of a term t can be computed in a finite number of rewriting steps smaller or equal to a *fixed bound* $bd(t)$ depending on t. Why so? Because: (1) we can choose $bd(t)$ to be the maximum of the smallest rewriting depths needed to compute $(t\theta_i)!_{\vec{\mathcal{E}}} = u_i$ for $1 \leqslant i \leqslant n$, and (2) since for each variant (w, β) of t there is a $(u_i, \theta_i) \in [\![t]\!]_{\vec{\mathcal{E}}}$ such that $(u_i, \theta_i) \sqsupseteq (w, \beta) \Leftrightarrow \exists\gamma(\beta =_B \theta_i\gamma \wedge u_i\gamma =_B w)$, by the fact that the rewrite relation is B-coherent, we can obtain a rewrite sequence from $t\beta$ to $(t\beta)!_{\vec{\mathcal{E}}} =_B w$ of length l with $l \leqslant bd(t)$ just by instantiating by γ the sequence of length l from $t\theta_i$ to $(t\theta_i)!_{\vec{\mathcal{E}}} =_B u_i$.

In fact we have the following equivalence (see [7], and for a more precise statement, [4])

Theorem 3. *(FVP iff Boundedness). Give a convergent $\vec{\mathcal{E}} = (\Sigma, B, \vec{E})$ associated to an equational theory $\mathcal{E}$ such that B has a finitary unification algorithm, $\vec{\mathcal{E}}$ is FVP iff $\vec{\mathcal{E}}$ has the boundedness property.*

Furthermore, for *any* convergent $\vec{\mathcal{E}} = (\Sigma, B, \vec{E})$ such that B has a finitary unification algorithm a complete (but not necessarily finite) set of $\vec{\mathcal{E}}$-variants of a term t can be effectively generated by folding variant narrowing [17]. Although FVP is an undecidable property [3], as proved in [4] (and mechanized in Maude) there is a simple semi-decision procedure to check whether such a convergent $\vec{\mathcal{E}}$ is FVP: it is so if and only if for each $f \in \Sigma$ the term $f(x_1, \ldots, x_n)$, with variables $x_1, \ldots, x_n$ having most general possible sorts, has a finite number of most general $\vec{\mathcal{E}}$-variants.

Another key point about $\vec{\mathcal{E}}$ being FVP is that, as proved in [17], if B has a finitary unification algorithm, then $E \cup B$ has also a finitary unification algorithm called *variant unification*. If $\vec{\mathcal{E}}$ is FVP and it furthermore has a constructor subspecification $\vec{\mathcal{E}}_\Omega \subseteq \vec{\mathcal{E}}$, say with $\vec{\mathcal{E}}_\Omega = (\Omega, B_\Omega, \vec{E}_\Omega)$, then several more notions appear: (1) A *constructor variant* of t is a variant (u, θ) of t such that u is an Ω-term. The set of constructor variants of t is denoted $[\![t]\!]^{\Omega}_{\vec{\mathcal{E}}}$. (2) A *constructor unifier* of a system of Σ-equations $u_1 = v_1 \wedge \ldots \wedge u_n = v_n$ is a $E \cup B$-unifier α such that for $1 \leqslant i \leqslant n$, $u_i\alpha!_{\vec{\mathcal{E}}}$ is an Ω-term. As explained in [26,29], under very mild conditions on the constructor subspecification $\vec{\mathcal{E}}_\Omega \subseteq \vec{\mathcal{E}}$, if $\vec{\mathcal{E}}$ is FVP and B and B_Ω have finitary unification algorithms, there is an effectively computable finite subset $\{(u_1, \theta_1), \ldots, (u_n, \theta_n)\}$ of most general constructor variants in $[\![t]\!]^{\Omega}_{\vec{\mathcal{E}}}$. Furthermore, under the same assumptions, for any system of Σ-equations $\phi \equiv u_1 = v_1 \wedge \ldots \wedge u_n = v_n$ there is an algorithm computing a finite set $Unif^{\Omega}_{E \cup B}(\phi)$ of most general constructor unifiers. In particular, since any ground substitution $\rho : Y \to T_\Sigma$ is $E \cup B$-equivalent to the ground constructor substitution $\rho!_{\vec{\mathcal{E}}}$, any ground unifier of ϕ is $E \cup B$-equivalent to a ground constructor unifier that is an instance up to $E \cup B$-equality of a constructor unifier in $Unif^{\Omega}_{E \cup B}(\phi)$.

Note that all the results and algorithms known so far about variants depend crucially on the assumption that the convergent theory $\vec{\mathcal{E}} = (\Sigma, B, \vec{E})$ is such that B has a *finitary* unification algorithm. The notion of variant, however, is more general and has been defined without the finitary unification assumption. But what happens when we weaken this assumption and assume instead that B just *has* a (not necessarily finitary) unification algorithm? For example, B may contain an associativity axiom for some non-commutative symbol f, and then the B-unification algorithm will be infinitary. What happens to variants in such an infinitary wonderland?

3 Variants in the Infinitary Unification Wonderland

To explore variants in the infinitary unification wonderland, let us begin with an example.

Example 1. Consider a 2-sorted equational theory **St** of strings, whose signature Σ has sorts St and $Pred$ and operators: (i) constants a, b of sort St, (ii) a constant tt of sort $Pred$, (iii) a string concatenation operator $\_\ \_ : St\ St \rightarrow St$, and (iv) an equality predicate $\_ \equiv \_ : St\ St \rightarrow Pred$; and with just two equations: the associativity axiom for string concatenation $(x\ y)\ z = x\ (y\ z)$, which we denote by A, and the equality predicate definition $x \equiv x = tt$, denoted E. By orienting the equality definition as a singleton rule set $\vec{E}$, we get an obviously convergent rewrite theory $\vec{\mathbf{St}} = (\Sigma, A, \vec{E})$. Furthermore, $\vec{\mathbf{St}}$ enjoys the following two nice properties: (1) **Boundedness**, since all terms of sort St are in $\vec{\mathbf{St}}$-canonical form, and any term of sort $Pred$ *not* in $\vec{\mathbf{St}}$-canonical form must be of the form $u \equiv v$ with $u =_A v$, and can therefore be put in the canonical form tt in *one* rewrite step. (2) **Finite Variants for all Function Symbols**. Each $f \in \Sigma$ is such that $f(x_1, \ldots, x_n)$ is either a constant (n=0) in canonical form, or the string expression $x_1\ x_2$ which is in canonical form and has the single most general variant $(x_1\ x_2, id)$, with id the identity substitution, or is the equality expression $x_1 \equiv x_2$, and when we request its variants form its Maude specification we get two of them, namely, $(x_1 \equiv x_2, id)$, and $(tt, \{x_1 \mapsto x_3, x_2 \mapsto x_3\})$. *Ergo*, by Theorem 3, $\vec{\mathbf{St}}$ must be FVP! Right? No, this is wrong. Consider the term $a\ x \equiv x\ a$. When we request its variants from Maude (where it is written as `a x ~ x a`) we get:

```
Variant #1
rewrites: 0 in 0ms cpu (3ms real) (0 rewrites/second)
Pred: (a #1:St) ~ #1:St a
x --> #1:St
Warning: Unification modulo the theory of operator __
has encountered an instance for which it may not be complete.

Variant #2
rewrites: 1 in 1ms cpu (8ms real) (660 rewrites/second)
Pred: tt
x --> a

No more variants.
rewrites: 1 in 1ms cpu (8ms real) (647 rewrites/second)
Warning: Some variants may have been missed due to incomplete
unification algorithm(s).
```

That is, up to renaming of variable we get two variants: $(a\ x \equiv x\ a, id)$, and $(tt, \{x \mapsto a\})$, *plus* a warning: since, to cope in a practical manner with the infinitary nature of associative unification, the Maude unification algorithm for associativity is incomplete, for a unification problem having an infinite number of solutions, only a finite number of them are returned. Here, when trying to narrow the term $a\ x \equiv x\ a$ with the rule $x \equiv x \rightarrow tt$, solving the A-unification problem $(a\ x \equiv x\ a) = (y \equiv y)$ reduces to solving the A-unification problem $a\ x = x\ a$. But this problem does *not* have a finite set of solutions. It has instead the infinite set of solutions $\{x = a,\ x = a\ a,\ x = a\ a\ a,\ \ldots,\ x = a \overset{n}{\ldots} a,\ \ldots\}$. Therefore, the term $a\ x \equiv x\ a$ has the following *infinite* set of variants: $(a\ x \equiv x\ a, id)$, $(tt, \{x \mapsto a\}), \ldots, (tt, \{x \mapsto a \overset{n}{\ldots} a,\}), \ldots$, none of which are comparable with each other in the $\sqsupseteq$ relation. *Ergo*, Theorem 3 fails in general for a convergent $\vec{\mathcal{E}} = (\Sigma, B, \vec{E})$ where the B-unification algorithm is not finitary. In particular, $\vec{\mathbf{St}}$ has the boundedness property but is *not* FVP.

Given this, somewhat perplexing situation, we can ask two questions: (a) What do we *know* at this point? (b) How can Properties (1) and (2) hold for $\vec{\mathbf{St}}$ in Example 1 and, yet, $\vec{\mathbf{St}}$ is not FVP? Question (a) can be given two answers. First of all, we know that if $\vec{\mathcal{E}} = (\Sigma, B, \vec{E})$ is FVP, then, as explained in Sect. 2.2, the boundedness property follows from the FVP property, and is therefore enjoyed by $\vec{\mathcal{E}}$. Second, we also know:

Theorem 4. *(Boundedness Sufficient Condition). If a convergent theory $\vec{\mathcal{E}} = (\Sigma, B, \vec{E})$, (1) has a B-unification algorithm, and (2) (Σ-boundedness) for each $f \in \Sigma$ the term $f(x_1, \ldots, x_n)$ with most general possible variables $x_1, \ldots, x_n$ has a finite number of most general $\vec{\mathcal{E}}$-variants, then $\vec{\mathcal{E}}$ has the boundedness property.*

The proof is indeed the same structural induction proof as in Theorem 7 of [4], with Theorem 7 suitably rephrased by means of Theorem 6 in [4].

Question (b) can be generalized to question (b'): How can a convergent theory $\vec{\mathcal{E}}$ have the boundedness property, yet not be FVP? Question (b') can perhaps be best answered in narrowing terms: since for each term t we have a bound $bd(t)$ on the maximum of the minimal-length terminating rewrite sequences starting at all its instances $t\gamma$ for any $\vec{\mathcal{E}}$-canonical γ, by the Lifting Lemma for $\vec{\mathcal{E}}$-narrowing (see Sect. 2.2), we know that we can compute a complete set of most general variants for t by bounding the $\vec{\mathcal{E}}$-narrowing tree of t at depth $bd(t)$, and then obtaining as most general variants the pairs (u, θ) such that $t \overset{\theta}{\leadsto}{}^{n}_{\vec{\mathcal{E}}}\ u$, $n \leqslant bd(t)$, $u = u!_{\vec{\mathcal{E}}}$, and $\theta = \theta!_{\vec{\mathcal{E}}}$. The problem, though, is that, as shown in Example 1, the bounded narrowing tree for t may have *infinite branching* at some of its nodes, so that the finiteness of such a set of most general variants (and therefore the FVP property) cannot be ensured in general. So, what can we do?

3.1 Finitely Branching Theories

To ensure that a convergent $\vec{\mathcal{E}}$ having the boundedness property is FVP, "all" we need to do is to make sure that the $\vec{\mathcal{E}}$-narrowing tree of any term t never has infinite branching. Under suitable conditions this can be ensured in some cases, either for a convergent theory $\vec{\mathcal{E}}$, or for a class of instances of a parameterized theory $\vec{\mathcal{E}}[X]$ with parameter sort X in the sense explained in Sect. 2.3.

Definition 3. *(FB, FB Instance, and Parametric FB). A convergent theory $\vec{\mathcal{E}} = (\Sigma, B, \vec{E})$ having a B-unification algorithm is called* finitely branching *(FB) iff for each $(l \to r) \in \vec{E}$ and any equality $l = w$ such that w is not a variable and $vars(l) \cap vars(w) = \varnothing$, the set $Unif_B(l = w)$ is finite.*

Given a convergent parameterized theory $\vec{\mathcal{E}}[X]$, an, also convergent, instantiation $\vec{\mathcal{E}}[\vec{\mathcal{M}}, X \mapsto s]$ is called a finitely branching *(FB)* instance *of $\vec{\mathcal{E}}[X]$ iff $\vec{\mathcal{E}}[\vec{\mathcal{M}}, X \mapsto s]$ is FB.*

Given a convergent parameterized theory $\vec{\mathcal{E}}[X]$ and a class $\mathcal{C}$ of convergent theories such that for all pairs $(\vec{\mathcal{M}}, s)$ with $\vec{\mathcal{M}} \in \mathcal{C}$ and s a sort in $\mathcal{M}$, $\vec{\mathcal{E}}[\vec{\mathcal{M}}, X \mapsto s]$ is also convergent, we call $\vec{\mathcal{E}}[X]$ parametrically FB *with respect to $\mathcal{C}$ iff each $\vec{\mathcal{E}}[\vec{\mathcal{M}}, X \mapsto s]$, with $\vec{\mathcal{M}} \in \mathcal{C}$ and s a sort in $\mathcal{M}$, is an FB instance of $\vec{\mathcal{E}}[X]$.*

We can apply these notions as follows:

Theorem 5. *(FVP whenever FB + Boundedness). (1) An FB convergent theory $\vec{\mathcal{E}} = (\Sigma, B, \vec{E})$ having a B-unification algorithm is FVP iff it has the boundedness property. (2) If $\vec{\mathcal{E}}[X]$, with $\vec{\mathcal{E}} = (\Sigma, B, \vec{E})$ having a B-unification algorithm and enjoying the boundedness property, is* parametrically FB *with respect to $\mathcal{C}$, and each $\vec{\mathcal{M}} \in \mathcal{C}$ with $\vec{\mathcal{M}} = (\Sigma_{\mathcal{M}}, B_{\mathcal{M}}, \vec{E}_{\mathcal{M}})$ has both a $B_{\mathcal{M}}$-unification algorithm extensible to a $B \uplus B_{\mathcal{M}}$-unification algorithm and the boundedness property, then each $\vec{\mathcal{E}}[\vec{\mathcal{M}}, X \mapsto s]$, with $\vec{\mathcal{M}} \in \mathcal{C}$ and s a sort in $\mathcal{M}$, is FVP.*

Proof. For (1), the proof of the ($\Rightarrow$) part follows from any FVP theory having the boundedness property. The proof of the ($\Leftarrow$) part follows under the boundedness assumption from the already-described narrowing-based method to extract a complete set of most general variants of a term t from its $\vec{\mathcal{E}}$-narrowing tree bounded at depth $bd(t)$, which is a *finite* tree by the FB assumption.

The proof of (2) can be obtained from that of (1) as follows: $\vec{\mathcal{E}}[\vec{\mathcal{M}}, X \mapsto s]$ has the boundedness property since, by the disjointness of $\mathcal{E}$ and $\mathcal{M}$, since both $\mathcal{E}$ and $\mathcal{M}$ have the boundedness property, by Theorem 4 this means that each function symbol in the signature of $\vec{\mathcal{E}}[\vec{\mathcal{M}}, X \mapsto s]$ has also the bounded property (the set of variants for each symbol in either $\mathcal{E}$ or $\mathcal{M}$ remains the same also in $\vec{\mathcal{E}}[\vec{\mathcal{M}}, X \mapsto s]$), which, again by Theorem 4 and (1), yields (2). □

What algorithmic consequences can we derive from part (1) of Theorem 5? The main one is a *business as usual* consequence: under the FB assumption, the *finite variant narrowing algorithm* specified and proved correct in [17] for the case where the axioms B of $\vec{\mathcal{E}}$ have a *finitary* B-unification algorithm applies and is correct *exactly as before* when the B-unification algorithm is infinitary, because in all the folding variant narrowing steps the B-unification problems *are finitary* thanks to the FB property. A second practical consequence, indeed an obvious corollary of Theorem 5, is that, thanks to Theorem 4, to check that a convergent $\vec{\mathcal{E}}$ is FVP we just need three conditions: (i) it has a B-unification algorithm; (ii) satisfies the Σ-boundedness property; and (iii) is FB. Conditions (i) and (ii) are easily checkable. How about condition (iii)?

For the parametric case, we have a similar situation in part (2) of Theorem 5: condition (i) is easily checkable, condition (2) is modular in $\mathcal{E}$ and $\mathcal{M}$, so the key condition that needs to be checked is again condition (iii).

3.2 Checking FB and Parametric FB

How can we *check* that a convergent theory is FB or a parametric theory is FB relative a suitable class of $\mathcal{C}$ of theories? And how *restrictive* are such conditions in practice? The answers will of course depend on the axioms B in question. For many examples, and certainly for any example specifiable in Maude, the source of infinity in B-unification for a set B of associativity and/or commutativity and/or identity axioms will always come from some associative but not commutative symbol in the signature Σ. Let us call any such symbol an A-symbol, and shorten associative unification to A-unification. A useful general observation is that in (order-sorted) A-unification, there are classes of pure A-terms l, i.e., involving at most a single A-symbol, such that any pure A-unification problem $l = w$ where $vars(l) \cap vars(w) = \varnothing$, has always a finite set of A-solutions. For example, one such class is the class of *linear* A-terms (see, e.g., [15]). This class, and other similar such classes, can be exploited to ensure conditions such as FB.[2] For my present purposes, it is not necessary to develop here the technical details of how criteria such as linearity of A-terms can be used for checking FB. It will be enough for me to illustrate in some detail how properties such as linearity of rules involving in some way A-symbols can be used to check FB in a concrete example, namely, a data type of strings:

Example 2. (Strings Data Type). Consider the following parameterized algebraic data type of strings, whose rewrite theory $\mathbf{St}[X] = (\Sigma, A, \vec{E})$ has signature Σ with parameter sorts X, additional sorts $NeSt$ and St, subsort inclusions $X < NeSt < St$, a constant ε of sort St, a subsort-overloaded string concatenation operator $\_\ \_ : St\ St \to St$, $\_\ \_ : NeSt\ NeSt \to NeSt$, two functions $\mathit{first}, \mathit{last} : NeSt \to X$, and two other functions $\mathit{rest}, \mathit{prior} : NeSt \to St$. The only axiom in A is the associativity axiom $(u\ v)\ w = u\ (v\ w)$, were u, v, w are variables of sort St, p, q, r variables of sort $NeSt$, and x is a variable of sort X. The rules $\vec{E}$ are: (i) the identity rules $u\ \varepsilon \to u$ and $\varepsilon\ u \to u$, (ii) the *first* and *rest* rules $\mathit{first}(x) \to x$, $\mathit{first}(x\ q) \to x$, $\mathit{rest}(x) \to \varepsilon$, $\mathit{rest}(x\ q) \to q$, and (iii) the *last* and *prior* rules $\mathit{last}(x) \to x$, $\mathit{last}(q\ x) \to x$, $\mathit{prior}(x) \to \varepsilon$, $\mathit{prior}(q\ x) \to q$. The theory $\mathbf{St}[X]$ is clearly terminating, since the associativity axiom is term-size-preserving, and all the rules are term-size-decreasing. It is also sort-decreasing

[2] Note that this class does not impose very strong restrictions on the rewrite rules of a convergent theory $\vec{\mathcal{E}}$ that we want to check FB: all we would need is something like an "A-linearity" condition on rules $l \to r$ in $\vec{E}$. Call a sort s an *A-sort* (resp. *A-reachable sort*) if it is the sort of an associative but non-commutative symbol (resp. if there is a term t of sort s having a variable whose sort is an A-sort). Call $l \to r$ *A-linear* iff any variable of l having an A-reachable sort appears only once in l.

and strictly A-coherent. The only critical pairs modulo A are those between the rules $u\ \varepsilon \rightarrow u$ and $\varepsilon\ u \rightarrow u$, which are clearly joinable, so $\vec{\mathbf{St}}[X]$ is also confluent and therefore convergent. It satisfies also the Σ-boundedness property: for each non-constant symbol $f \in \Sigma$, the term $f(x_1, \ldots, x_n)$ has exactly 3 most general variants.

The proof of Theorem 6 below is given in Appendix A.

Theorem 6. *($\vec{\mathbf{St}}[X]$ is parametrically FB relative to $\mathcal{C}$). Let $\mathcal{C}$ be the class of convergent order-sorted theories $\mathbf{M} \in \mathcal{C}$ such that: (i) axioms $B_{\mathbf{M}}$ of $\mathbf{M}$ are any combination of associativity and/or commutativity axioms,[3] (ii) have the boundedness property, (iii) are FB, and (iv) for any sort s in $\mathbf{M}$, $\vec{\mathbf{St}}[\vec{\mathbf{M}}, X \mapsto s]$ is convergent. Then, $\vec{\mathbf{St}}[X]$ is parametrically FB relative to $\mathcal{C}$. Therefore, by Theorem 5, $\vec{\mathbf{St}}[\vec{\mathbf{M}}, X \mapsto s]$ is FVP for any $\mathbf{M} \in \mathcal{C}$ and sort s in $\mathbf{M}$.*

Let me also illustrate the breakdown of the FB property due to the presence of non-left-linear rewrite rules. Assume that we add to our $\vec{\mathbf{St}}$ module above the following sort, operator and equations: (1) a new sort *Pred* of predicates, (2) a constant *tt* of sort *Pred* and a string membership predicate $\_ \in \_ : X\ St \rightarrow Pred$, and the definition of that predicate (in the positive case) by the rewrite rules: $x \in x \rightarrow tt$, $x \in x\ u \rightarrow tt$, $x \in u\ x \rightarrow tt$ and $x \in u\ x\ v \rightarrow tt$. The extended module thus obtained, let us denote it $\vec{\mathbf{St}}^{\in}$, is also terminating due to the same term-size decreasing nature of all rules, strictly A-coherent as before, sort decreasing, and also confluent, since all the new critical pairs associated to the string membership rules are joinable to the constant *tt*. Furthermore, since the term $x \in u$ has exactly 5 variants, the module is Σ-bounded and therefore, by Theorem 4 satisfies the Boundedness property. However, $\vec{\mathbf{St}}^{\in}$ is not FVP. Here is a counterexample in Maude, when we ask for the variants of the term $first(q\ q') \in first(q'\ q)$:

```
Variant #1
rewrites: 0 in 0ms cpu (0ms real) (0 rewrites/second)
Pred: first(#1:NeSt #2:NeSt) in first(#2:NeSt #1:NeSt)
q --> #1:NeSt
q' --> #2:NeSt
Warning: Unification modulo the theory of operator __ has encountered an
    instance for which it may not be complete.

Variant #2
rewrites: 5 in 3ms cpu (17ms real) (1516 rewrites/second)
Pred: tt
q --> %1:NeSt
q' --> %1:NeSt
```

[3] I am purposefully avoiding identity axioms because, thanks to the theory transformation $\vec{\mathcal{E}} \mapsto \vec{\mathcal{E}}_U$ in [12] mapping a convergent $\vec{\mathcal{E}}$ with identity axioms U into a semantically equivalent convergent $\vec{\mathcal{E}}_U$ where such axioms have been transformed into rewrite rules, this involves no real loss of generality.

```
Variant #3
rewrites: 5 in 3ms cpu (17ms real) (1492 rewrites/second)
Pred: %1:X in first(%3:NeSt %1:X %2:NeSt)
q --> %1:X %2:NeSt
q' --> %3:NeSt

Variant #4
rewrites: 5 in 3ms cpu (17ms real) (1470 rewrites/second)
Pred: %1:X in first(%2:NeSt %1:X)
q --> %1:X
q' --> %2:NeSt

Variant #5
rewrites: 5 in 3ms cpu (17ms real) (1458 rewrites/second)
Pred: first(%3:NeSt %1:X %2:NeSt) in %1:X
q --> %3:NeSt
q' --> %1:X %2:NeSt

Variant #6
rewrites: 5 in 3ms cpu (17ms real) (1446 rewrites/second)
Pred: first(%2:NeSt %1:X) in %1:X
q --> %2:NeSt
q' --> %1:X

Variant #7
rewrites: 13 in 6ms cpu (23ms real) (1985 rewrites/second)
Pred: #3:X in #1:X
q --> #3:X #4:NeSt
q' --> #1:X #2:NeSt

Variant #8
rewrites: 13 in 6ms cpu (24ms real) (1973 rewrites/second)
Pred: #2:X in #1:X
q --> #2:X #3:NeSt
q' --> #1:X

Variant #9
rewrites: 13 in 6ms cpu (24ms real) (1965 rewrites/second)
Pred: #3:X in #1:X
q --> #3:X
q' --> #1:X #2:NeSt

Variant #10
rewrites: 13 in 6ms cpu (24ms real) (1957 rewrites/second)
Pred: #2:X in #1:X
q --> #2:X
q' --> #1:X
```

```
Variant #11
rewrites: 17 in 7ms cpu (25ms real) (2282 rewrites/second)
Pred: tt
q --> %1:X %2:NeSt
q' --> %1:X %3:NeSt

Variant #12
rewrites: 17 in 7ms cpu (25ms real) (2266 rewrites/second)
Pred: tt
q --> %1:X %2:NeSt
q' --> %1:X

Variant #13
rewrites: 17 in 7ms cpu (25ms real) (2251 rewrites/second)
Pred: tt
q --> %1:X
q' --> %1:X %2:NeSt

No more variants.
rewrites: 17 in 7ms cpu (25ms real) (2232 rewrites/second)
Warning: Some variants may have been missed due to incomplete unification
    algorithm(s).
```

The breakdown of the FB property is manifested in this example by the fact that, when trying to narrow the term $\mathit{first}(q\ q') \in \mathit{first}(q'\ q)$ with the rule $x \in x \to tt$, the unification problem $(x \in x) = (\mathit{first}(q\ q') \in \mathit{first}(q'\ q))$ is equivalent to the system of equations $x = \mathit{first}(q\ q') \wedge x = \mathit{first}(q'\ q)$, which is equivalent to the equation $\mathit{first}(q\ q') = \mathit{first}(q'\ q)$, which, in turn, is equivalent to the A-equation $q\ q' = q'\ q$, which has an infinite number of solutions.

3.3 Variant Unification

Suppose that $\vec{\mathcal{E}} = (\Sigma, B, \vec{E})$ is a convergent FB theory having a B-unification algorithm and that we have checked that it has the boundedness property, for example by checking that it has the Σ-boundedness property. Then, by Theorem 5, $\vec{\mathcal{E}} = (\Sigma, B, \vec{E})$ is FVP. So we should be able to obtain an $E \cup B$-unification algorithm by folding variant narrowing [17], right? Yes, but with a twist. Suppose that the B-unification algorithm is infinitary. Then, $E \cup B$-unification will in general be infinitary. For example, even though the convergent $\vec{\mathbf{St}}$ module enjoys the Σ-boundedness property and is FB and therefore FVP, since the terms $q\ q'$ and $q'\ q$ cannot be narrowed at all by the rules in $\vec{\mathbf{St}}$, folding variant narrowing reduces the $E \cup A$-unification problem to the A-unification problem: $q\ q' = q'\ q$, which has an infinite number of solutions. That is, folding variant narrowing *does* indeed provide an $E \cup B$-unification algorithm for any FVP theory. But when B-unification is infinitary, then $E \cup B$-unification is generally infinitary. The key observation, however, from an algorithmic point of view, is that the *folding variant narrowing* part of the variant $E \cup B$-unification algorithm is *finite* for any unification problem; but in the last step, when each unification problem obtained by exploring the finite $\vec{\mathcal{E}}$-narrowing tree for the problem is transformed into a B-unification problem, we can experience the infinitary nature of the algorithm. Let me further clarify this point by reducing variant $E \cup A$-unification for a single equation in our $\vec{\mathbf{St}}$ module to folding variant narrowing of single terms in the transformed module $\vec{\mathbf{St}}^{\equiv}$ obtained by adding: (1) a new sort *Pred* of predicates, (2) a constant *tt* of sort *Pred* an equality predicate $\_ \equiv \_ : St\ St \rightarrow Pred$, and the equality rewrite rule $u \equiv u \rightarrow tt$. The module $\vec{\mathbf{St}}^{\equiv}$ thus obtained is still convergent. Furthermore, since the term $u \equiv v$ has exactly two variants, it enjoys the boundedness property. Furthermore, any $E \cup A$-unification problem $t = t'$ in $\vec{\mathbf{St}}$ can be reduced to a folding variant narrowing problem in $\vec{\mathbf{St}}^{\equiv}$, namely, the variant $E \cup A$-unifiers of $t = t'$ are exactly the substitutions $\theta = \theta_1 \ldots \theta_{n+1}$ associated to variant narrowing sequences in $\vec{\mathbf{St}}^{\equiv}$ of the term $t \equiv t'$ of the form:

$$t \equiv t' \overset{\theta_1}{\rightsquigarrow}_{\vec{\mathbf{St}}} t_1 \equiv t_1' \ldots t_{n-1} \equiv t_{n-1}' \overset{\theta_n}{\rightsquigarrow}_{\vec{\mathbf{St}}} t_n \equiv t_n' \overset{\theta_{n+1}}{\rightsquigarrow}_{\vec{\mathbf{St}}^{\equiv}} tt.$$

where, the first n steps are actually $\vec{\mathbf{St}}$-narrowing steps in the FB subtheory $\vec{\mathbf{St}}$, and therefore build a *finitely branching* tree. Only the *last* narrowing step, corresponding to narrowing with the rule $u \equiv u \rightarrow tt$, which is *equivalent* to solving the A-unification problem $t_n = t_n'$ with A-unifier θ_{n+1}, is a $\vec{\mathbf{St}}^{\equiv}$-narrowing step. This is exactly the step where the narrowing tree can become *infinitely branching*, due to the infinitary nature of A-unification.

3.4 I Am Feeling Lucky!

But what can we do when our convergent theory $\vec{\mathcal{E}} = (\Sigma, B, \vec{E})$ having an infinitary B-unification algorithm has the boundedness property, but either is not FB (like in our $\vec{\mathbf{St}}^{\in}$ example) or we just do not *know* for sure whether it is FB? Shall we just give up? Not at all! We should just *wing it*! Maybe *we are lucky*, and the failure of FB does not come back and bite us *for the particular problem we need to solve*. Furthermore, if our problem is a *variant unification* problem, there isn't such a drastic difference between the FB case and the case only enjoying the boundedness property, since the transformed theory $\vec{\mathcal{E}}^{\equiv}$ in which we recast a variant $E \cup B$-unification problem into computing $\vec{\mathcal{E}}^{\equiv}$-variants is *not* an FB theory, but only a theory satisfying the boundedness property. Sure, in the folding variant $\vec{\mathcal{E}}^{\equiv}$-narrowing sequences used to compute $E \cup B$-unifiers of a problem $t = t'$ by narrowing $t \equiv t'$, if we are FB, *only* the last step can be infinitely branching. But what practical difference does it make if, by dropping FB, now *all* narrowing steps are *potentially* infinitely branching? Maybe we are just lucky, and actually they are not so for our given problem $t = t'$. For example, our $\vec{\mathbf{St}}^{\in}$ module is a perfectly fine module: there is nothing wrong with it, and if we want to reason formally about the string membership predicate, loss of FB is the price we have to pay. So what? Why should this stop us from reasoning about string memberships?

In the *most common* case of infinitary B-unification that we are likely to encounter in practice, at least using Maude, B is infinitary because of the presence of some associative but not commutative symbol. But the way this infinitary nature of B-unification is handled by Maude should give us strong encouragement and inspiration for not giving up in computing variants and variant unifiers in the non FB case. The reasons for optimism are the following: (1) Although *in principle* A- and a fortiory B-unification, when $A \subseteq B$ (of course, without making A-operators AC in B!), are infinitary, *in practice* the infinitary case is never encountered in many substantial problems. For example, in analyzing some cryptographic protocols involving strings by folding variant narrowing in the Maude-NPA tool [16], many thousands of A-unification problems need to be solved, yet for all protocols for which this has been done, the infinitary case has not showed up: the B-unification algorithm (for $A \subseteq B$) provided by Maude covers a very large class of unification problems for which unification is finitary; and this is greatly helped by the fact that, in narrowing applications, such unification problems always involve terms with *disjoint* sets of variables. (2) Using Maude's *incomplete* B-unification algorithm, we can *know* when the algorithm has found a complete set of unifiers and when it has not. This means that, if Maude does *not* print a warning as the ones shown in earlier examples in this paper, we *know* that we are complete, which can be very important for some verification purposes. For example, if Maude-NPA does not print any such warnings and terminates without having found an specified security attack, we can the know for sure that such an attack is not possible *modulo* the algebraic properties specified for the protocol.

We can put all these brave ideas together in a somewhat more systematic fashion as follows. The incomplete (when $A \subseteq B$) B-unification algorithm that Maude provides can be described as an *incomplete* but *finitary* algorithm of the form $\mathit{IUnif}_B(\phi)$ with respect to the *complete* but *infinitary* algorithm $\mathit{Unif}_B(\phi)$. $\mathit{IUnif}_B(\phi)$ works as follows: for each B-unification system of equations ϕ, *always responds* (up to avoiding the Turing tar pits of high computational complexity of algorithms such as AC-unification) with a *pair* (Θ, f), where Θ is a finite set of B-unifiers of ϕ, and where f is a Boolean flag indicating completeness, so that if $f = \mathit{true}$, then we *know* that $\Theta = \mathit{Unif}_B(\phi)$. Instead, if $f = \mathit{false}$, we only know that $\Theta \subseteq \mathit{Unif}_B(\phi)$. Since, at least in Maude, all we actually have available is the pragmatically useful $\mathit{IUnif}_B(\phi)$, we are *always* in the "I am feeling lucky" mode anyway. So why not live with incompleteness (actually not so different in practice form the claimed completeness of finitary unification algorithms when we fall into a Turing tar pit) and just *pretend* that we have a finitary B-unification algorithm, since this is just what $\mathit{IUnif}_B(\phi)$ gives us, while keeping us honest and informed about whether completeness has been achieved? For some applications, completeness may not even be needed.

4 Conclusions and Related Work

So, what do we know, and what can be concluded, from the somewhat long-winded exhortation in Sect. 3.4 and from all the results in this paper? At least the following:

1. In the infinitary B-unification case, the equivalence $FVP \Leftrightarrow Boundedness$ drops to just an implication $FVP \Rightarrow Boundedness$.
2. The equivalence $FVP \Leftrightarrow Boundedness$ is regained if $\vec{\mathcal{E}}$ is FB, and then:
   - effective computation of a finite set of variants by folding variant narrowing works exactly as in the finitary B-unification case, but
   - variant $E \cup B$-unification also works as before, except that now, it is in general infinitary, since B-unification is so.
3. The practical difference between $\vec{\mathcal{E}}$ being FB and satisfying only the boundedness property is not as drastic as one might fear: we should just wing it and hope for the best (i.e., for no incompleteness warnings from Maude). We can still compute: (i) a possibly knowingly incomplete set of variants of a term; and (ii) a possibly knowingly incomplete set of variant $E \cup B$-unifiers.
4. At the cost of having only a generating algorithm (resp. a semi-decision procedure) we can wing it even further and drop the boundedness property, i.e., assume just that $\vec{\mathcal{E}}$ is convergent. Then we get: (i) the generation of a possibly infinite and possibly knowingly incomplete set of variants of a term; and (ii) a semi-algorithm for computing a possibly infinite and possibly knowingly incomplete set of variant $E \cup B$-unifiers.

Regarding related work, besides all the previous literature on variants and variant computation mentioned in the references (and in the references in those references), perhaps the most important additional paper behind this work is the, sadly as yet unpublished, SRI manuscript on his brilliant order-sorted A- and B-unification algorithms (with $A \subseteq B$) by Steven Eker [15], for which only a summary has appeared in published form in [11].

Last but not least, without the efficient implementation of the $IUnif_B(\phi)$ algorithm and of variants and variant unification modulo B, also when $A \subseteq B$, in Maude 3 [10], all the results in this paper would be still theoretically relevant, but somewhat of a pipe dream. As it is, thanks to Maude 3 they are also of direct and immediate practical relevance for many applications.

Of course, further work on criteria for checking the FB property, as well as further experimentation with the ideas proposed in this paper, are exciting future prospects.

Acknowledgements. My warmest thanks to Santiago Escobar and Steven Eker for many discussions that have helped me arrive at the ideas presented here. I cordially thank the referees for their very helpful suggestions to improve the paper. This work has been partially supported by NRL under contract N00173-17-1-G002.

A Proof of Theorem 6

We just need to show that for each $\mathbf{M} \in \mathcal{C}$ and sort s in $\mathbf{M}$, $\vec{\mathbf{St}}[\vec{\mathbf{M}}, X \mapsto s]$ is FB. But: (i) FB is a rule-local property: it holds iff it does for each rewrite rule; (ii) up to renaming to ensure symbol disjointness, the rewrite rules in $\vec{\mathbf{St}}[\vec{\mathbf{M}}, X \mapsto s]$ are just the disjoint union of those in $\vec{\mathbf{St}}[X]$ and those in $\mathbf{M}$;

(iii) by the construction of $\vec{\mathbf{St}}[\vec{\mathbf{M}}, X \mapsto s]$, the rewrite rules in $\mathbf{M}$ apply to the exact same terms in both $\mathbf{M}$ and in $\vec{\mathbf{St}}[\vec{\mathbf{M}}, X \mapsto s]$, and, since both the rules and the terms they apply to do not involve any operators in $\vec{\mathbf{St}}[X]$, narrowing with those rules modulo the entire set of axioms $A \uplus B_{\mathbf{M}}$, where A is the associativity axiom in $\vec{\mathbf{St}}[X]$, is identical with narrowing with such rules modulo $B_{\mathbf{M}}$ only. Therefore, the rules from $\mathbf{M}$ are FB in $\vec{\mathbf{St}}[\vec{\mathbf{M}}, X \mapsto s]$. Thus, all we need to check is that the rewrite rules in $\vec{\mathbf{St}}[X]$ are FB in $\vec{\mathbf{St}}[\vec{\mathbf{M}}, X \mapsto s]$. First of all, note that the axioms $A \uplus B_{\mathbf{M}}$ in $\vec{\mathbf{St}}[\vec{\mathbf{M}}, X \mapsto s]$ only involve associativity and/or commutativity axioms. Since FB is a property satisfied by each rule, we just reason one rule at a time. I prove the FB property for the rules: (1) $u\ \varepsilon \rightarrow u$ (2) $\mathit{first}(x) \rightarrow x$, (3) $\mathit{first}(x\ q) \rightarrow x$, (4) $\mathit{rest}(x) \rightarrow \varepsilon$, and (5) $\mathit{rest}(x\ q) \rightarrow q$.

Case (1). Up to A-equivalence and disregarding parentheses, the $A \uplus B_{\mathbf{M}}$-unification problem $u\ \varepsilon = w$, where w is a non-variable term in $\vec{\mathbf{St}}[s]$ not sharing any variables with $u\ \varepsilon$ is just the $A \uplus B_{\mathbf{M}}$-unification problem $u\ \varepsilon = w_1\ \dots\ w_n$ with $n \geqslant 1$ where each w_i is either: (i) a variable of sort St or (ii) a so-called *A-alien subterm* or constant of the form $f(t_1, \dots, t_n)$ with f different from $\_\ \_$. When $n = 1$, the only possible $A \uplus B_{\mathbf{M}}$-unifier exists when w_1 is a variable v of sort St and is the unifier $\{v \mapsto u\ \varepsilon\}$. When $n \geqslant 2$, the only possible $A \uplus B_{\mathbf{M}}$-unifiers exist when either: (i) $w_n = \varepsilon$, with unifier $\{u \mapsto w_1\ \dots\ w_{n-1}\}$, or (ii) w_n is a variable v of sort St, with unifier $\{u \mapsto w_1\ \dots\ w_{n-1}, v \mapsto \varepsilon\}$.

Case (2). Up to A-equivalence and disregarding parentheses, the $A \uplus B_{\mathbf{M}}$-unification problem $\mathit{first}(x) = w$ can only be solved if w is a term of the form $\mathit{first}(w_1\ \dots\ w_n)$ with w_y a variable of sort $NeSt$ or less, or an A-alien subterm of sort s or less, and has a solution only when $n = 1$ and either: (i) w_1 is a variable q' of sort $NeSt$, yielding the $A \uplus B_{\mathbf{M}}$-unifier $\{q' \mapsto x\}$, or (ii) w_1 is a variable y of sort s or less or an A-alien subterm of sort s or less, yielding the $A \uplus B_{\mathbf{M}}$-unifier $\{x \mapsto w_1\}$.

Case (3). Up to A-equivalence and disregarding parentheses, the $A \uplus B_{\mathbf{M}}$-unification problem $\mathit{first}(x\ q) = w$ can only be solved if w is a term of the form $\mathit{first}(w_1\ \dots\ w_n)$ with w_y a variable of sort $NeSt$ or less, or an A-alien subterm of sort s or less, and has a solution only when: (i) $n = 1$ and w_1 is a variable q' of sort $NeSt$, yielding the $A \uplus B_{\mathbf{M}}$-unifier $\{q' \mapsto x\ q\}$, or (ii) $n \geqslant 2$ and either (ii).1 w_1 is a variable q' of sort $NeSt$, yielding the $A \uplus B_{\mathbf{M}}$-unifier $\{q' \mapsto x\ q \mapsto w_2\ \dots\ w_n\}$, or (ii).2 w_1 is either a variable of sort s or less, or an A-alien subterm of sort s or less, yielding the $A \uplus B_{\mathbf{M}}$-unifier $\{x \mapsto w_1, q \mapsto w_2\ \dots\ w_n\}$.

Cases (4), resp. (5), have proofs entirely analogous to **Cases** (2), resp. (3). This finishes the proof of Theorem 6. □

References

1. Alpuente, M., Cuenca-Ortega, A., Escobar, S., Meseguer, J.: A partial evaluation framework for order-sorted equational programs modulo axioms. J. Log. Algebraic Methods Program. **110**, 100501 (2020)

2. Bae, K., Escobar, S., Meseguer, J.: Abstract logical model checking of infinite-state systems using narrowing. In: Rewriting Techniques and Applications (RTA 2013), LIPIcs, vol. 21, pp. 81–96. Schloss Dagstuhl-Leibniz-Zentrum fuer Informatik (2013)
3. Bouchard, C., Gero, K.A., Lynch, C., Narendran, P.: On forward closure and the finite variant property. In: Fontaine, P., Ringeissen, C., Schmidt, R.A. (eds.) FroCoS 2013. LNCS (LNAI), vol. 8152, pp. 327–342. Springer, Heidelberg (2013). https://doi.org/10.1007/978-3-642-40885-4_23
4. Cholewa, A., Meseguer, J., Escobar, S.: Variants of variants and the finite variant property. Technical report, CS Department University of Illinois at Urbana-Champaign, February 2014. http://hdl.handle.net/2142/47117
5. Ciobaca., S.: Verification of composition of security protocols with applications to electronic voting. Ph.D. thesis, ENS Cachan (2011)
6. Clavel, M., et al.: All About Maude - A High-Performance Logical Framework. LNCS, vol. 4350. Springer, Heidelberg (2007). https://doi.org/10.1007/978-3-540-71999-1
7. Comon-Lundh, H., Delaune, S.: The finite variant property: how to get rid of some algebraic properties. In: Giesl, J. (ed.) RTA 2005. LNCS, vol. 3467, pp. 294–307. Springer, Heidelberg (2005). https://doi.org/10.1007/978-3-540-32033-3_22
8. Dershowitz, N., Jouannaud, J.P.: Rewrite systems. In: van Leeuwen, J. (ed.) Handbook of Theoretical Computer Science, vol. B, pp. 243–320. North-Holland (1990)
9. van Deursen, A., Heering, J., Klint, P.: Language Prototyping: An Algebraic Specification Approach. World Scientific, Singapore (1996)
10. Durán, F., et al.: Programming and symbolic computation in Maude. J. Log. Algebr. Meth. Program. **110**, 100497 (2020)
11. Durán, F., Eker, S., Escobar, S., Martí-Oliet, N., Meseguer, J., Talcott, C.: Associative unification and symbolic reasoning modulo associativity in Maude. In: Rusu, V. (ed.) WRLA 2018. LNCS, vol. 11152, pp. 98–114. Springer, Cham (2018). https://doi.org/10.1007/978-3-319-99840-4_6
12. Durán, F., Lucas, S., Meseguer, J.: Termination modulo combinations of equational theories. In: Ghilardi, S., Sebastiani, R. (eds.) FroCoS 2009. LNCS (LNAI), vol. 5749, pp. 246–262. Springer, Heidelberg (2009). https://doi.org/10.1007/978-3-642-04222-5_15
13. Durán, F., Meseguer, J.: Structured theories and institutions. Theor. Comput. Sci. **309**(1–3), 357–380 (2003)
14. Ehrig, H., Mahr, B.: Fundamentals of Algebraic Specification 1. Springer, Heidelberg (1985)
15. Eker, S.: A pragmatic approach to implementing associative unification, unpublished manuscript. SRI International, circa (2015)
16. Escobar, S., Meadows, C., Meseguer, J.: Maude-NPA: cryptographic protocol analysis modulo equational properties. In: Aldini, A., Barthe, G., Gorrieri, R. (eds.) FOSAD 2007-2009. LNCS, vol. 5705, pp. 1–50. Springer, Heidelberg (2009). https://doi.org/10.1007/978-3-642-03829-7_1
17. Escobar, S., Sasse, R., Meseguer, J.: Folding variant narrowing and optimal variant termination. J. Algebraic Logic Program. **81**, 898–928 (2012)
18. Futatsugi, K., Diaconescu, R.: CafeOBJ Report. World Scientific, Singapore (1998)
19. Goguen, J., Meseguer, J.: Order-sorted algebra I: equational deduction for multiple inheritance, overloading, exceptions and partial operations. Theoret. Comput. Sci. **105**, 217–273 (1992)

20. Goguen, J., Winkler, T., Meseguer, J., Futatsugi, K., Jouannaud, J.P.: Introducing OBJ. In: Software Engineering with OBJ: Algebraic Specification in Action, pp. 3–167. Kluwer (2000)
21. Jouannaud, J.-P., Kirchner, C., Kirchner, H.: Incremental construction of unification algorithms in equational theories. In: Diaz, J. (ed.) ICALP 1983. LNCS, vol. 154, pp. 361–373. Springer, Heidelberg (1983). https://doi.org/10.1007/BFb0036921
22. Meier, S., Schmidt, B., Cremers, C., Basin, D.: The TAMARIN prover for the symbolic analysis of security protocols. In: Sharygina, N., Veith, H. (eds.) CAV 2013. LNCS, vol. 8044, pp. 696–701. Springer, Heidelberg (2013). https://doi.org/10.1007/978-3-642-39799-8_48
23. Meseguer, J.: Order-sorted parameterization and induction. In: Palsberg, J. (ed.) Semantics and Algebraic Specification. LNCS, vol. 5700, pp. 43–80. Springer, Heidelberg (2009). https://doi.org/10.1007/978-3-642-04164-8_4
24. Meseguer, J.: Conditional rewriting logic as a unified model of concurrency. Theoret. Comput. Sci. **96**(1), 73–155 (1992)
25. Meseguer, J.: Membership algebra as a logical framework for equational specification. In: Presicce, F.P. (ed.) WADT 1997. LNCS, vol. 1376, pp. 18–61. Springer, Heidelberg (1998). https://doi.org/10.1007/3-540-64299-4_26
26. Meseguer, J.: Variant-based satisfiability in initial algebras. Sci. Comput. Program. **154**, 3–41 (2018)
27. Meseguer, J.: Generalized rewrite theories, coherence completion, and symbolic methods. J. Log. Algebr. Meth. Program. **110**, 100483 (2020)
28. Meseguer, J., Skeirik, S.: Inductive reasoning with equality predicates, contextual rewriting and variant-based simplification. In: Escobar, S., Martí-Oliet, N. (eds.) WRLA 2020, LNCS vol. 12328, pp. 114–135 (2020)
29. Skeirik, S., Meseguer, J.: Metalevel algorithms for variant satisfiability. J. Log. Algebr. Meth. Program. **96**, 81–110 (2018)
30. Skeirik, S., Stefanescu, A., Meseguer, J.: A constructor-based reachability logic for rewrite theories. Fundam. Inform. **173**(4), 315–382 (2020)

Variant Satisfiability of Parameterized Strings

José Meseguer(✉)

Department of Computer Science, University of Illinois at Urbana-Champaign, Urbana, USA
meseguer@illinois.edu

Abstract. Two "knowingly incomplete," yet useful, variant-based satisfiability procedures for QF formulas in the instantiations of two, increasingly more expressive, parameterized data types of strings are proposed. The first has four selector functions decomposing a list concatenation into its parts. The second adds a list membership predicate. The meaning of "parametric" here is much more general than is the case for decision procedures for strings in current SMT solvers, which are parametric on a finite alphabet. The parameterized data types presented here are parametric on a (typically infinite) algebraic data type of string elements. The main result is that if an algebraic data type has a variant satisfiability algorithm, then the data type of strings over such elements has a "knowingly incomplete," yet practical, variant satisfiability algorithm, with no need for a Nelson-Oppen combination algorithm relating satisfiability in strings and in the given data type.

1 Introduction

Variant satisfiability [19,20] is a flexible method to develop decision procedures for satisfiability of QF formulas in initial models of *user-definable* algebraic data types. The power and generality of variant satisfiability can be greatly increased by specifying and proving decidable the satisfiability of QF formulas in *parameterized* data types of the form $\mathbf{Q}[X]$, which map another data type $\mathbf{M}$, also with decidable initial satisfiability and a chosen sort s in $\mathbf{M}$, to the instance $\mathbf{Q}[\mathbf{M}, X \mapsto s]$ replacing the formal parameter X by the actual parameter s in $\mathbf{M}$. In fact, a useful collection of such parameterized variant satisfiability procedures was presented in [19]. The procedures presented in this work apply to the instances of a parameterized data type of strings $\mathbf{St}[X]$ with four selector functions decomposing a list concatenation into its parts, which is then extended to a parameterized data type of strings $\mathbf{St}^{\in}[X]$ that adds a list membership predicate.

The procedures rely on the fact that $\mathbf{St}[X]$ has the finite variant property (FVP) in a parametric sense and, under the usual variant satisfiability assumptions, the theory $\mathbf{M}$ in the contemplated instantiations $\mathbf{St}[\mathbf{M}, X \mapsto s]$ is also FVP. The procedures then use the fact that, under such assumptions, $\mathbf{St}[\mathbf{M}, X \mapsto s]$ is FVP and has a variant unification algorithm. But, since $\mathbf{St}[\mathbf{M}, X \mapsto s]$ contains the associativity axiom for strings, whose unification algorithm is infinitary, variant unification in $\mathbf{St}[\mathbf{M}, X \mapsto s]$ is also infinitary. This is the reason why the QF satisfiability algorithms are "knowingly incomplete," since, in general, given a conjunction of literals in $\mathbf{St}[\mathbf{M}, X \mapsto s]$, say, $\bigwedge G \wedge \bigwedge D$, with G equalities and D disequalities, the satisfiability of $\bigwedge G \wedge \bigwedge D$ in

S. Escobar and N. Martí-Oliet (Eds.): WRLA 2020, LNCS 12328, pp. 96–113, 2020.
https://doi.org/10.1007/978-3-030-63595-4_6

the initial algebra of $\mathbf{St}[\mathbf{M}, X \mapsto s]$ is equivalent to that of $\bigwedge D\alpha$ for some unifier α of $\bigwedge G$ modulo $\mathbf{St}[\mathbf{M}, X \mapsto s]$. Since the set of such α may be infinite, in general we would have to decide QF satisfiability for an infinite number of problems $\bigwedge D\alpha$, which makes the problem semi-decidable only. The practical approach taken in the algorithms presented uses the fact that a practical "knowingly incomplete" algorithm for associative unification (and for B-unification, for any combination of associative and/or commutative and/or identity axioms), such as the one currently supported by Maude 3.1, can be optimized to succeed in solving B-unification problems having a *finite* number of solutions, and can then do a "best-effort" work to find a finite set of solutions and either: (i) be able to determine that such a set is complete and return it as such, or (ii) return the found finite set of unifiers with a *warning* that completeness is not assured. The upshot of this is that the *same* "knowingly incomplete" character is now inherited by the variant unification algorithm modulo $\mathbf{St}[\mathbf{M}, X \mapsto s]$ *and* by the parametric variant satisfiability algorithm for QF satisfiability in the initial algebra of $\mathbf{St}[\mathbf{M}, X \mapsto s]$ (resp. of $\mathbf{St}^{\in}[\mathbf{M}, X \mapsto s]$). That is, if a complete finite set of variant unifiers is found for $\bigwedge G$, then satisfiability of $\bigwedge G \wedge \bigwedge D$ is decidable; otherwise, it may still be decidable if some $\bigwedge D\alpha$ among the returned unifiers α is satisfiable; but if for the found α, $\bigwedge D\alpha$ is unsatisfiable, the procedure returns "don't know."

To the best of my knowledge, this is the first variant satisfiability procedure that involves associativity axioms for non-commutative operators: all former variant satisfiability procedures have involved any combination of associativity and/or commutativity and/or identity axioms, *except* associativity without commutativity. The deep reason for this case not having been treated before is that, as summarized in Sect. 2.5 and more fully explained in the companion paper [15], all the variant-based results and algorithms have up to now been developed under the assumption that the data type's equational theory has the form $E \cup B$, with the equations E convergent as rewrite rules modulo axioms B, and B having a *finitary* unification algorithm. Since the associativity axiom needed for strings was outside the class of such axioms B, no theoretical framework existed for it within the known variant-based techniques.

A point worth emphasizing is that the meaning of "parametric" here is much more general than is the case for decision procedures for strings in current SMT solvers, e.g., [1, 14, 21, 22], which are parametric on a *finite alphabet*. The parameterized modules presented here are parametric on any algebraic data type as its (typically infinite) set of string elements. Those SMT-based procedures for strings and the ones presented here complement each other in several ways: (i) the traditional string procedures assume a finite alphabet of string elements, whereas here an infinite set of elements in a user-definable data type is assumed; for example: strings whose elements can be binary trees holding natural numbers as their leaf elements; (ii) in variant satisfiability, the decision procedures for the data type of elements and for the parameterized module, in this case strings, are seamlessly combined: no Nelson-Oppen-like combination procedures are needed at all.

2 Preliminaries

2.1 Background on Order-Sorted First-Order Logic

We assume familiarity with the notions of an order-sorted signature Σ on a poset of sorts $(S, \leqslant)$, an order-sorted Σ-algebra A, and the term Σ-algebras T_Σ and $T_\Sigma(X)$ for X

an S-sorted set of variables. We also assume familiarity with the notions of: (i) order-sorted substitution θ, its domain $dom(\theta)$ and range $ran(\theta)$, and its application $t\theta$ to a term t; (ii) a *preregular* order-sorted signature Σ, where each term t has a least sort, denoted $ls(t)$; (iii) the set $\widehat{S} = S/(\geqslant \cup \leqslant)^+$ of *connected components* of $(S, \leqslant)$; and (iv) for A a Σ-algebra, the set A_s of it elements of sort $s \in S$, and the set $A_{[s]} = \bigcup_{s' \in [s]} A_{s'}$ for $[s] \in \widehat{S}$. All these notions are explained in detail in [12, 18]. The material below is adapted from [15, 19].

The first-order language of *equational Σ-formulas* is defined in the usual way: its atoms are *Σ-equations* $t = t'$, where $t, t' \in T_\Sigma(X)_{[s]}$ for some $[s] \in \widehat{S}$ and each X_s is assumed countably infinite. The set $Form(\Sigma)$ of *equational Σ-formulas* is then inductively built from atoms by: conjunction ($\wedge$), disjunction ($\vee$), negation ($\neg$), and universal ($\forall x_1 : s_1, \ldots, x_n : s_n$) and existential ($\exists x_1 : s_1, \ldots, x_n : s_n$) quantification with distinct sorted variables $x_1 : s_1, \ldots, x_n : s_n$, with $s_1, \ldots, s_n \in S$ (by convention, for $\emptyset$ the empty set of variables and φ a formula, we define $(\forall \emptyset)\ \varphi \equiv (\exists \emptyset)\ \varphi \equiv \varphi$). A literal $\neg(t = t')$ is denoted $t \neq t'$. Given a Σ-algebra A, a formula $\varphi \in Form(\Sigma)$, and an assignment $\alpha \in [Y \rightarrow A]$, where $Y \supseteq fvars(\varphi)$, with $fvars(\varphi)$ the free variables of φ, the *satisfaction relation* $A, \alpha \models \varphi$ is defined inductively as usual: for atoms, $A, \alpha \models t = t'$ iff $t\alpha = t'\alpha$; for Boolean connectives it is the corresponding Boolean combination of the satisfaction relations for subformulas; and for quantifiers: $A, \alpha \models (\forall x_1 : s_1, \ldots, x_n : s_n)\ \varphi$ (resp. $A, \alpha \models (\exists x_1 : s_1, \ldots, x_n : s_n)\ \varphi$) holds iff for all $(a_1, \ldots, a_n) \in A_{s_1} \times \ldots \times A_{s_n}$ (resp. for some $(a_1, \ldots, a_n) \in A_{s_1} \times \ldots \times A_{s_n}$) we have $A, \alpha[x_1 : s_1 := a_1, \ldots, x_n : s_n := a_n] \models \varphi$, where if $\alpha \in [Y \rightarrow A]$, then $\alpha[x_1 : s_1 := a_1, \ldots, x_n : s_n := a_n] \in [(Y \cup \{x_1 : s_1, \ldots, x_n : s_n\}) \rightarrow A]$ and is such that for $y : s \in (Y \setminus \{x_1 : s_1, \ldots, x_n : s_n\})$, $\alpha[x_1 : s_1 := a_1, \ldots, x_n : s_n := a_n](y : s) = \alpha(y : s)$, and $\alpha[x_1 : s_1 := a_1, \ldots, x_n : s_n := a_n](x_i : s_i) = a_i$, $1 \leqslant i \leqslant n$. We say that φ is *valid* in A (resp. is *satisfiable* in A) iff $A, \underline{\emptyset} \models (\forall Y)\ \varphi$ (resp. $A, \underline{\emptyset} \models (\exists Y)\ \varphi$), where $Y = fvars(\varphi)$ and $\underline{\emptyset} \in [\emptyset \rightarrow A]$ denotes the empty S-sorted assignment of values in A to the empty S-sorted family $\emptyset$ of variables. The notation $A \models \varphi$ abbreviates validity of φ in A. More generally, a set of formulas $\Gamma \subseteq Form(\Sigma)$ is called *valid* in A, denoted $A \models \Gamma$, iff $A \models \varphi$ for each $\varphi \in \Gamma$. For a subsignature $\Omega \subseteq \Sigma$ and $A \in \mathbf{OSAlg}_\Sigma$, the *reduct* $A|_\Omega \in \mathbf{OSAlg}_\Omega$ agrees with A in the interpretation of all sorts and operations in Ω and discards everything in $\Sigma \setminus \Omega$. If $\varphi \in Form(\Omega)$ we have the equivalence $A \models \varphi \Leftrightarrow A|_\Omega \models \varphi$.

An OS *equational theory* is a pair $T = (\Sigma, E)$, with E a set of Σ-equations. $\mathbf{OSAlg}_{(\Sigma,E)}$ denotes the full subcategory of $\mathbf{OSAlg}_\Sigma$ with objects those $A \in \mathbf{OSAlg}_\Sigma$ such that $A \models E$, called the *(Σ, E)-algebras*. $\mathbf{OSAlg}_{(\Sigma,E)}$ has an *initial algebra* $T_{\Sigma/E}$ [18]. Given $T = (\Sigma, E)$ and $\varphi \in Form(\Sigma)$, we call φ *T-valid*, written $E \models \varphi$, iff $A \models \varphi$ for all $A \in \mathbf{OSAlg}_{(\Sigma,E)}$. We call φ *T-satisfiable* iff there exists $A \in \mathbf{OSAlg}_{(\Sigma,E)}$ with φ satisfiable in A. Note that φ is *T-valid* iff $\neg\varphi$ is *T-unsatisfiable*. The inference system in [18] is *sound and complete* for OS equational deduction, i.e., for any OS equational theory (Σ, E), and Σ-equation $u = v$ we have an equivalence $E \vdash u = v \Leftrightarrow E \models u = v$. Deducibility $E \vdash u = v$ is abbreviated as $u =_E v$, called *E-equality*. An *E-unifier* of a system of Σ-equations, i.e., of a conjunction $\phi = u_1 = v_1 \wedge \ldots \wedge u_n = v_n$ of Σ-equations, is a substitution σ such that $u_i\sigma =_E v_i\sigma$, $1 \leqslant i \leqslant n$. An *$E$-unification algorithm* for (Σ, E) is an algorithm generating a *complete set* of E-unifiers $Unif_E(\phi)$ for any system of Σ equations ϕ, where "complete" means that for any E-unifier σ of ϕ

there is a $\tau \in Unif_E(\phi)$ and a substitution ρ such that $\sigma =_E (\tau\rho)|_{dom(\sigma)\cup dom(\tau)}$, where $=_E$ here means that for any variable x we have $x\sigma =_E x(\tau\rho)|_{dom(\sigma)\cup dom(\tau)}$. The algorithm is *finitary* if it always terminates with a *finite set* $Unif_E(\phi)$ for any ϕ.

Given a set of equational axioms B used for deduction modulo B, a preregular OS signature Σ is called *B-preregular*[1] iff for each $u = v \in B$ and substitutions ρ, $ls(u\rho) = ls(v\rho)$. The axioms B are called *collapse-free*) iff for each $(u = v) \in B$ neither u not v are variables.

At first sight, the above definition of order-sorted first-order logic seems too restrictive, since we might like to consider more general order-sorted first-order theories (OS-FO theories) having signatures of the form (Σ, Π), where Σ is an OS-signature of function symbols as before, and Π is a signature of typed predicate symbols of the form $p : s_1 \ldots s_n$, whose arguments have sorts $s_1 \ldots s_n$. However, as explained in [19], there is no real loss of generality in assuming that all atomic formulas are equations: atomic predicates with symbols in Π can be specified as equations by turning predicates into new function symbols of an added sort *Pred* having a constant *tt*, so that each predicate $p : s_1 \ldots s_n$ is now viewed as a function symbol $p : s_1 \ldots s_n \to Pred$. Then, any formula φ in the FO signature (Σ, Π) can be transformed into an equational formula $\widetilde{\varphi}$ in the order-sorted signature $\Sigma \cup \Pi$, where *Pred* and *tt* have been added, but where each $p : s_1 \ldots s_n$ in the original Π is now represented as a function symbol $p : s_1 \ldots s_n \to Pred$. The $\varphi \mapsto \widetilde{\varphi}$ transformation is very simple: each atom $p(t_1, \ldots, t_n)$ is replaced by the equational atom $p(t_1, \ldots, t_n) = tt$. In this way, if Γ is a set of first-order formulas in the OS-FO signature (Σ, Π), then $\widetilde{\Gamma}$ is a set of equational first-order formulas in the functional signature $\Sigma \cup \Pi$. Since an OS-FO *theory* is just a pair $((\Sigma, \Pi), \Gamma)$ with Γ a set of first-order (Σ, Π)-formulas, we then get a *semantically equivalent* [19] theory $(\Sigma \cup \Pi, \widetilde{\Gamma})$. By abuse of language we call $((\Sigma, \Pi), \Gamma)$ *equational* iff $(\Sigma \cup \Pi, \widetilde{\Gamma})$ is an equational theory. The semantic equivalence between these two formulations involves also the fact that equational theories in this sense both have initial models, which can be recovered from each other. In particular, we can recover from the initial algebra $T_{\Sigma\cup\Pi/\widetilde{\Gamma}}$ the initial model of $((\Sigma, \Pi), \Gamma)$ [19].

2.2 Convergent Theories, Constructors and Narrowing

Given an order-sorted equational theory $\mathcal{E} = (\Sigma, E \cup B)$, where B is a collection of associativity and/or commutativity and/or identity axioms and Σ is B-preregular, we can associate to it a corresponding *rewrite theory* [17] $\vec{\mathcal{E}} = (\Sigma, B, \vec{E})$ by orienting the equations E as left-to right rewrite rules. That is, each $(u = v) \in E$ is transformed into a rewrite rule $u \to v$. The main purpose of the rewrite theory $\vec{\mathcal{E}}$ is to reduce the complex bidirectional reasoning with equations to the much simpler unidirectional reasoning with rules under suitable assumptions. We assume familiarity with the notion of subterm $t|_p$ of t at a term position p and of term replacement $t[w]_p$ of $t|_p$ by w at position p (see, e.g., [5]). The rewrite relation $t \to_{\vec{E},B} t'$ (which can be abbreviated to $t \to_{\vec{\mathcal{E}}} t'$)

[1] If $B = B_0 \uplus U$, with B_0 associativity and/or commutativity axioms, and U identity axioms, the B-preregularity notion can be *broadened* by requiring only that: (i) Σ is B_0-preregular in the standard sense that $ls(u\rho) = ls(v\rho)$ for all $u = v \in B_0$ and substitutions ρ; and (ii) the axioms U oriented as rules $\vec{U}$ are *sort-decreasing* in the sense explained in Sect. 2.2.

holds iff there is a subterm $t|_p$ of t, a rule $(u \to v) \in \vec{E}$ and a substitution θ such that $u\theta =_B t|_p$, and $t' = t[v\theta]_p$. We denote by $\to^*_{\vec{E},B}$ the reflexive-transitive closure of $\to_{\vec{E},B}$. The requirements on $\vec{\mathcal{E}}$ allowing us to reduce equational reasoning to rewriting are the following: (i) $vars(v) \subseteq vars(u)$; (ii) *sort-decreasingness*: for each substitution θ we must have $ls(u\theta) \geqslant ls(v\theta)$; (iii) *strict B-coherence*: if $t_1 \to_{\vec{E},B} t'_1$ and $t_1 =_B t_2$ then there exists $t_2 \to_{\vec{E},B} t'_2$ with $t'_1 =_B t'_2$; (iv) *confluence*: for each term t if $t \to^*_{\vec{E},B} v_1$ and $t \to^*_{\vec{E},B} v_2$, then there exist rewrite sequences $v_1 \to^*_{\vec{E},B} w_1$ and $v_2 \to^*_{\vec{E},B} w_2$ such that $w_1 =_B w_2$; (v) *termination*: the relation $\to_{\vec{E},B}$ is well-founded. If $\vec{\mathcal{E}}$ satisfies conditions (i)–(v) then it is called *convergent*. The key point is that then, given a term t, all terminating rewrite sequences $t \to^*_{\vec{E},B} w$ end in a term w, denoted $t!_{\vec{\mathcal{E}}}$, that is unique up to B-equality, and its called t's *canonical form*. Three major results then follow for the ground convergent case: (1) (Church-Rosser Theorem) for any terms t, t' we have $t =_{E \cup B} t'$ iff $t!_{\vec{\mathcal{E}}} =_B t'!_{\vec{\mathcal{E}}}$, (2) the canonical forms of ground terms are the elements of the *canonical term algebra* $C_{\Sigma/E,B}$, where for each $f : s_1 \ldots s_n \to s$ in Σ and canonical terms $t_1 \ldots t_n$ with $ls(t_i) \leqslant s_i$ the operation $f_{C_{\Sigma/E,B}}$ is defined by the identity: $f_{C_{\Sigma/E,B}}(t_1 \ldots t_n) = f(t_1 \ldots t_n)!_{\vec{\mathcal{E}}}$, and (3) we have a Σ-isomorphism $T_{\mathcal{E}} \cong C_{\Sigma/E,B}$.

Given a convergent rewrite theory $\vec{\mathcal{E}} = (\Sigma, B, \vec{E})$ and a subsignature Ω on the same poset of sorts, a *constructor subspecification* is a convergent rewrite subtheory $\vec{\mathcal{E}}_\Omega = (\Omega, B_\Omega, \vec{E}_\Omega)$ of $\vec{\mathcal{E}}$ (i.e., we have an inclusion of convergent theories $(\Omega, B_\Omega, \vec{E}_\Omega) \subseteq (\Sigma, B, \vec{E})$) such that: (i) for each ground term t, $t!_{\vec{\mathcal{E}}} \in T_\Omega$, and (ii) $T_{\mathcal{E}}|_\Omega \cong T_{\mathcal{E}_\Omega}$. Furthermore, if $E_\Omega = \emptyset$, Ω is then called a signature of *free constructors modulo axioms* B_Ω. Furthermore, if $\vec{\mathcal{E}}_\Omega \subseteq \vec{\mathcal{E}}$ is a constructor subspecification we say that $\vec{\mathcal{E}}$ *sufficiently complete* w.r.t. Ω.

Whenever we have an inclusion of convergent theories $\vec{\mathcal{E}} \subseteq \vec{\mathcal{E}}'$, with respective signatures Σ and Σ', such that $T_{\mathcal{E}'}|_\Sigma \cong T_{\mathcal{E}}$, we say that $\vec{\mathcal{E}}'$ *protects* $\vec{\mathcal{E}}$. Therefore, condition (ii) above just states that $\vec{\mathcal{E}}$ protects $\vec{\mathcal{E}}_\Omega$.

Narrowing. Given a convergent $\vec{\mathcal{E}} = (\Sigma, B, \vec{E})$ such that B has a (not necessarily finitary) unification algorithm, by replacing B-matching by B-unification, we can generalize the rewrite relation $t \to_{\vec{\mathcal{E}}} t'$ to the *narrowing relation* $t \rightsquigarrow_{\vec{\mathcal{E}}} t'$, often decorated as $t \overset{\theta}{\rightsquigarrow}_{\vec{\mathcal{E}}} t'$, which holds between Σ-terms t and t' iff there is a *non-variable* position p in t, a rewrite rule $(l \to r) \in \vec{E}$ (renamed if necessary so as not to share variables with t), and a B-unifier $\theta \in Unif_B(l = t|_p)$, with $ran(\theta)$ all fresh new variables "standardized apart," i.e., never generated before in the same narrowing process, such that $t' = (t[r]_p)\theta$. Likewise, in $t \overset{\theta}{\rightsquigarrow}{}^*_{\vec{\mathcal{E}}} t'$, the relation $\rightsquigarrow^*_{\vec{\mathcal{E}}}$ denotes the reflexive-transitive closure of $\rightsquigarrow_{\vec{\mathcal{E}}}$, and θ denotes the composition $\theta = \theta_1 \ldots \theta_n$ of the substitutions appearing in the n steps of the narrowing sequence, or the identity substitution when the sequence has length 0. What narrowing a term t with $\rightsquigarrow_{\vec{\mathcal{E}}}$, means is to *symbolically execute* t in the theory $\vec{\mathcal{E}}$. That is, even though t may be in $\vec{\mathcal{E}}$-canonical form and may not be executable by rewriting with $\to_{\vec{\mathcal{E}}}$, by instantiating it with $\rightsquigarrow_{\vec{\mathcal{E}}}$ in all possible "most general" ways, it *becomes* executable. Specifically, if $t \overset{\theta}{\rightsquigarrow}{}^*_{\vec{\mathcal{E}}} t'$ holds, then $t\theta \to^*_{\vec{\mathcal{E}}} t'$ also holds and, conversely, (the so-called "Lifting Lemma" [13]), if γ is an $\vec{\mathcal{E}}$-canonical substitution and $t\gamma \to^*_{\vec{\mathcal{E}}} u$ holds, then there is a narrowing sequence $t \overset{\theta}{\rightsquigarrow}{}^*_{\vec{\mathcal{E}}} t'$ of same length as

$t\gamma \rightarrow^{*}_{\vec{\mathcal{E}}} u$, and with same term positions and rules at each step, and a substitution δ such that $t'\delta =_B u$.

2.3 Parameterized Theories

The general semantics and formal reasoning methods for order-sorted parameterized theories have been developed in [16]. In general, and as supported by Maude [3], the parameter theory $\mathcal{P}$ of a parameterized module $\mathcal{E}[\mathcal{P}]$ can be an order-sorted theory and can have *initiality constraints* [9]. However, for our present purposes in this paper a much simpler, yet commonly occurring, special case, namely, parameterized theories of the form $\mathcal{E}[X]$, where X is just a *parameter sort* (specified in Maude by the "trivial theory" TRIV [3]) will suffice and will allow a quite simple and self-contained explanation. For example, parameterized data types of lists, **List**$[X]$, sets, **Set**$[X]$, or multisets, **MSet**$[X]$, are all parametric on a parameter sort X. Any parameterized module $\mathcal{E}[X]$ like this, with a parameter sort X can then be *instantiated* to any chosen sort s in any order-sorted equational theory $\mathcal{M}$. We denote such an instantiation as $\mathcal{E}[\mathcal{M}, X \mapsto s]$ For example, $\mathcal{M}$ can be the theory **Nat** of natural numbers with addition and multiplication, and the sort s the subsort *NzNat* of non-zero natural numbers. Then **MSet**[**Nat**, $X \mapsto$ *NzNat*] denotes the instantiation of **MSet**$[X]$ to multisets whose elements are non-zero natural numbers.

In the simple setting of a parameterized theory $\mathcal{E}[X]$ with parameter sort X, its formal parameter X is just a *chosen sort* X in the order-sorted signature $\Sigma_{\mathcal{E}}$ of the order-sorted theory $\mathcal{E}$, i.e., $\mathcal{E}[X]$ just denotes the choice of sort X in $\mathcal{E}$. What is the *semantics* of such instantiations $\mathcal{E}[\mathcal{M}, X \mapsto s]$? This question can be split in two: (i) what *theory* is denoted by $\mathcal{E}[\mathcal{M}, X \mapsto s]$? and (ii) what *algebra* is specified by $\mathcal{E}[\mathcal{M}, X \mapsto s]$? Let us answer question (i). We will *always assume* that X is a *minimal element* in the poset of sorts $(S_{\mathcal{E}}, <)$ of $\mathcal{E}$. The theory $\mathcal{E}[\mathcal{M}, X \mapsto s]$ is defined as the result of a *theory transformation*

$$(\mathcal{M}, s) \mapsto \mathcal{E}[\mathcal{M}, X \mapsto s]$$

where $(\mathcal{M}, s)$ is a pair consisting of an order-sorted equational theory $\mathcal{M}$ and a sort s in the poset of sorts $(S_{\mathcal{M}}, <')$ of its signature $\Sigma_{\mathcal{M}}$. Then, the resulting order-sorted theory $\mathcal{E}[\mathcal{M}, X \mapsto s]$ is defined as follows: (i) its signature is the signature $(\Sigma_{\mathcal{E}} \uplus \Sigma_{\mathcal{M}})/\overline{\{X = s\}}$ obtained by (a) forming the disjoint union of signatures (to ensure disjoint sorts and operations) $\Sigma_{\mathcal{E}} \uplus \Sigma_{\mathcal{M}}$, and (b) identifying the sorts X and s in the disjoint union of posets $(S_{\mathcal{E}}, <) \uplus (S_{\mathcal{M}}, <')$ to get the quotient poset $((S_{\mathcal{E}}, <) \uplus (S_{\mathcal{M}}, <'))/\overline{\{X = s\}}$. Thanks to the assumption that X is a minimal element in $(S_{\mathcal{E}}, <)$, this quotient poset has a very easy description. Its set of sorts is the quotient set $(S_{\mathcal{E}} \uplus S_{\mathcal{M}})/\overline{\{X = s\}}$ under the equivalence relation $\overline{\{X = s\}}$ generated by the pair (X, s), i.e., $\overline{\{X = s\}} = \{(X, s), (s, X), (X, X), (s, s)\}$, so that we just "identify" X and s an leave the other sorts untouched, and its order relation is just $(< \cup <') \cup (<'; <)$, which can be easily shown to be irreflexive and transitive, where we assume $<$ and $<'$ already disjoint. The answer to question (ii) is now straight forward: the *algebra* denoted by the theory instantiation $\mathcal{E}[\mathcal{M}, X \mapsto s]$ is just the *initial algebra*, let us denote is $T_{\mathcal{E}[\mathcal{M}, X \mapsto s]}$, of the theory $\mathcal{E}[\mathcal{M}, X \mapsto s]$. For example, the initial algebra of **MSet**[**Nat**, $X \mapsto$ *NzNat*] has indeed (finite) multisets of non-zero natural numbers as its elements.

Note that, as further discussed in [16] all the notions about convergent theories and sufficient completeness extend to the parameterized case. Therefore, the instantiation $\mathcal{E}[\mathcal{M}, X \mapsto s]$ yields also an instantiation of rewrite theories $\vec{\mathcal{E}}[\vec{\mathcal{M}}, X \mapsto s]$, which under suitable modularity conditions is convergent if both $\vec{\mathcal{E}}$ and $\vec{\mathcal{M}}$ are so, and is sufficiently complete relative to a constructor signature $(\Omega_{\mathcal{E}} \uplus \Omega_{\mathcal{M}})/\overline{\{X = s\}}$ in a way that can be checked by the methods developed in [16] assuming constructor signatures $\Omega_{\mathcal{E}}$, resp. $\Omega_{\mathcal{M}}$ for $\mathcal{E}$, resp. $\mathcal{M}$.

2.4 Variant Satisfiability in a Nutshell

Given a convergent rewrite theory $\vec{\mathcal{E}} = (\Sigma, B, \vec{E})$ associated to an equational theory $\mathcal{E}$ a *variant* of a term t is a pair (u, θ) such that θ is a substitution in canonical form, i.e., $\theta(x) = \theta(x)!_{\vec{\mathcal{E}}}$ for each x, and $u =_B (t\theta)!_{\vec{\mathcal{E}}}$. $\vec{\mathcal{E}}$ has the *finite variant property* (FVP) iff for any term t there is a finite set $[\![t]\!]_{\vec{\mathcal{E}}} = \{(u_1, \theta_1), \ldots, (u_n, \theta_n)\}$ of variants of t that are *most general possible* among all such variants, where the "most general" relation $\sqsupseteq$ between variants is defined by the equivalence: $(v, \alpha) \sqsupseteq (w, \beta) \;\Leftrightarrow\; \exists\gamma(\beta =_B \alpha\gamma \wedge v\gamma =_B w)$. Furthermore, if B has a finitary unification algorithm, a finite set of most general variants in $[\![t]\!]_{\vec{\mathcal{E}}}$ can be effectively computed for any t by *folding variant narrowing* [11].

There are two ways to understand variants and FVP. One is in terms of the notion of a *pattern*, i.e., a term u with variables describing *something*. The variants $\{(u_1, \theta_1), \ldots, (u_n, \theta_n)\}$ of a term t in an FVP theory $\vec{\mathcal{E}}$ are clearly patterns $u_1, \ldots, u_n$ (plus the added technical monkeys $\theta_1, \ldots, \theta_n$). But what do they describe? Obviously, up to B-equality, the infinite set of *all* patterns of the form $(t\theta)!_{\vec{\mathcal{E}}}$ for a given term t. But there is a second, equivalent way of understanding the FVP notion. Implicit in the idea that for *any* variant (w, β) of t there is a most general one $(u_1, \theta_1) \in [\![t]\!]_{\vec{\mathcal{E}}}$ lies the property, called the *boundedness property* [4]: that *all variants* of a term t can be computed in a finite number of rewriting steps smaller or equal to a *fixed bound* $bd(t)$ depending on t. Why so? Because: (1) we can choose $bd(t)$ to be the maximum of the smallest rewriting depths needed to compute $(t\theta_i)!_{\vec{\mathcal{E}}} = u_i$ for $1 \leqslant i \leqslant n$, and (2) since for each variant (w, β) of t there is a $(u_i, \theta_i) \in [\![t]\!]_{\vec{\mathcal{E}}}$ such that $(u_i, \theta_i) \sqsupseteq (w, \beta) \;\Leftrightarrow\; \exists\gamma(\beta =_B \theta_i\gamma \wedge u_i\gamma =_B w)$, by the fact that the rewrite relation is B-coherent, we can obtain a rewrite sequence from $t\beta$ to $(t\beta)!_{\vec{\mathcal{E}}} =_B w$ of length l with $l \leqslant bd(t)$ just by instantiating by γ the sequence of length l from $t\theta_i$ to $(t\theta_i)!_{\vec{\mathcal{E}}} =_B u_i$.

In fact we have the following equivalence (see [4], and for a more precise statement, [2]).

Theorem 1. *(FVP iff Boundedness). Given a convergent $\vec{\mathcal{E}} = (\Sigma, B, \vec{E})$ associated to an equational theory $\mathcal{E}$ such that B has a finitary unification algorithm, $\vec{\mathcal{E}}$ is FVP iff $\vec{\mathcal{E}}$ has the boundedness property.*

Furthermore, since for *any* convergent $\vec{\mathcal{E}} = (\Sigma, B, \vec{E})$ such that B has a finitary unification a complete (but not necessarily finite) set of $\vec{\mathcal{E}}$-variants of a term t can be effectively generated by folding variant narrowing [11], and in fact this has been mechanized in Maude, as proved in [2], there is a simple semi-decision procedure to check whether such an $\vec{\mathcal{E}}$ is FVP: it is so if and only if for each $f \in \Sigma$ the term $f(x_1, \ldots, x_n)$, with variables $x_1, \ldots, x_n$ of most general possible sorts, has a finite number of most general $\vec{\mathcal{E}}$-variants. Call this property the *Σ-boundedness* property.

Another key point about $\vec{\mathcal{E}}$ being FVP is that, as proved in [11], if B has a finitary unification algorithm, then $E \cup B$ has also a finitary unification algorithm called *variant unification*. If $\vec{\mathcal{E}}$ is FVP and it has a constructor subspecification $\vec{\mathcal{E}}_\Omega \subseteq \vec{\mathcal{E}}$, say with $\vec{\mathcal{E}}_\Omega = (\Omega, B_\Omega, \vec{E}_\Omega)$, then several more notions appear: (1) A *constructor variant* of t is a variant (u, θ) of t such that u is an Ω-term. The set of constructor variants of t is denoted $[\![t]\!]^\Omega_{\vec{\mathcal{E}}}$. (2) A *constructor unifier* of a system of Σ-equations $u_1 = v_1 \wedge \ldots \wedge u_n = v_n$ is a $E \cup B$-unifier α such that for $1 \leqslant i \leqslant n$, $u_i\alpha!_{\vec{\mathcal{E}}}$ is an Ω-term. As explained in [19,20], under very mild conditions on the constructor subspecification $\vec{\mathcal{E}}_\Omega \subseteq \vec{\mathcal{E}}$, if $\vec{\mathcal{E}}$ is FVP and B and B_Ω have finitary unification algorithms, there is an effectively computable finite subset $\{(u_1, \theta_1), \ldots, (u_n, \theta_n)\}$ of most general constructor variants in $[\![t]\!]^\Omega_{\vec{\mathcal{E}}}$. Also, under the same assumptions, for any system of Σ-equations $\phi \equiv u_1 = v_1 \wedge \ldots \wedge u_n = v_n$ there is an algorithm computing a finite set $Unif^\Omega_{E \cup B}(\phi)$ of most general constructor unifiers. In particular, since any ground substitution $\rho : Y \to T_\Sigma$ is $E \cup B$-equivalent to the ground constructor substitution $\rho!_{\vec{\mathcal{E}}}$, any ground unifier of ϕ is $E \cup B$-equivalent to a ground constructor unifier that is an instance up to $E \cup B$-equality of a constructor unifier in $Unif^\Omega_{E \cup B}(\phi)$.

But there is more. If $\vec{\mathcal{E}}$ is FVP, has a constructor subspecification $\vec{\mathcal{E}}_\Omega \subseteq \vec{\mathcal{E}}$, with both B and B_Ω having finitary unification algorithms, *and* satisfiability of QF Ω-formulas in $T_{\mathcal{E}_\Omega}$ is decidable, then satisfiability of QF Σ-formulas in $T_{\mathcal{E}}$ is also decidable by a *variant satisfiability* algorithm [19,20].

The plot then thickens, since to prove decidable satisfiability in $T_{\mathcal{E}}$, we just need criteria ensuring decidable satisfiability in the initial algebra of constructors $T_{\mathcal{E}_\Omega}$. The simplest, yet commonly occurring, case is when $\vec{\mathcal{E}}_\Omega$ has the form: $\vec{\mathcal{E}}_\Omega = (\Omega, B_\Omega, \emptyset)$, i.e., the constructors are free modulo B_Ω, and B_Ω is any combination of associativity and/or commutativity and/or identity axioms, except associativity without commutativity [19]. This result is a special instance of a more general criterion, called *OS-compactness*. Here is the definition, slightly extended to include the notion of *weakly OS-compact* theory that we shall need to deal with associative but not commutative axioms as those of strings:

Definition 1. *(OS-Compactness and weak OS-Compactness). An equational OS-FO theory $((\Sigma, \Pi), \Gamma)$ is called* OS-compact *(resp.* weakly OS-compact*) iff: (i) for each sort s in Σ we can effectively determine whether s is finite or infinite in $T_{\Sigma \cup \Pi/\widetilde{\Gamma}}$, and, if finite, we can effectively compute a representative ground term $rep([u]) \in [u]$ for each $[u] \in T_{\Sigma \cup \Pi/\widetilde{\Gamma},s}$; (ii) $=_{\widetilde{\Gamma}}$ is decidable; (iii) $\widetilde{\Gamma}$ has a finitary unification algorithm (resp. a unification algorithm); and (iv) if $\bigwedge D$ is a finite conjunction of negated (Σ, Π)-atoms whose variables have all infinite sorts and for each $u \neq v$ in $\bigwedge \widetilde{D}$ we have $u \neq_{\widetilde{\Gamma}} v$, then $\bigwedge D$ is satisfiable in $T_{\Sigma \cup \Pi/\widetilde{\Gamma}}$.*

*We call an OS equational theory (Σ, E) OS-*compact *(resp.* weakly OS-compact*) iff the OS-FO theory $((\Sigma, \emptyset), E)$ is OS-*compact *(resp.* weakly OS-compact*).*

The proof that $\vec{\mathcal{E}}_\Omega = (\Omega, B_\Omega, \emptyset)$ is OS-compact when B_Ω is any combination of associativity and/or commutativity and/or identity axioms, except associativity without commutativity, relies on the crucial fact that then any equation $u = v$ involving a single variable x has a *finite* set of solutions modulo B_Ω. That is why, up to now, no variant satisfiability results have been proved when some of the constructor axioms in B_Ω are associative but not commutative: the OS-compactness proof does not extend to that case. For example, if $\_\ \_$ is an associative operator and a a constant to which it can be applied, the equation $a\ x = x\ a$ does *not* have a finite set of solutions modulo associativity, but the infinite set of solutions $\{x = a,\ x = a\,a,\ x = a\,a\,a,\ \ldots,\ x = a \overset{n}{\ldots} a,\ \ldots\}$. In fact, to deal with the variant-related properties of convergent theories having axioms B for which B-unification is infinitary new concepts and results are needed. Fortunately, those needed in this paper have recently been developed in the companion paper [15], which I summarize in what follows.

2.5 Variants and FVP When *B*-unification Is Infinitary

The first main difference between the finitary and infinitary B-unification cases is that in the infinitary case Theorem 1 no longer holds: all we have then is that FVP implies the boundedness property [15]. The reason for this discrepancy is that a convergent theory may enjoy the boundedness property but may fail to be FVP because the narrowing tree of a term may be infinitely branching for some nodes due to the infinitary nature of B-unification, so in general there isn't anymore a finite set of nodes in the narrowing tree of t up to bound $bd(t)$ from which we can gather a *finite* set of most general variants. To recover the equivalence between the boundedness property and FVP in the infinitary case, either for a convergent theory $\vec{\mathcal{E}}$, or for a class of instances of a parameterized theory $\vec{\mathcal{E}}[X]$ with parameter sort X in the sense explained in Sect. 2.3. we need the new notion of an FB theory (resp. parametric FB theory):

Definition 2. *(FB, FB Instance, and Parametric FB). A convergent theory* $\vec{\mathcal{E}} = (\Sigma, B, \vec{E})$ *having a B-unification algorithm is called* finitely branching *(FB) iff for each* $(l \to r) \in \vec{E}$ *and any equality* $l = w$ *such that* w *is not a variable and* $vars(l) \cap vars(w) = \emptyset$*, the set* $Unif_B(l = w)$ *is finite.*

Given a convergent parameterized theory $\vec{\mathcal{E}}[X]$*, an, also convergent, instantiation* $\vec{\mathcal{E}}[\vec{\mathcal{M}}, X \mapsto s]$ *is called a* finitely branching *(FB)* instance *of* $\vec{\mathcal{E}}[X]$ *iff* $\vec{\mathcal{E}}[\vec{\mathcal{M}}, X \mapsto s]$ *is FB.*

Given a convergent parameterized theory $\vec{\mathcal{E}}[X]$ *and a class C of convergent theories such that for all pairs* $(\vec{\mathcal{M}}, s)$ *with* $\vec{\mathcal{M}} \in C$ *and* s *a sort in* $\mathcal{M}$, $\vec{\mathcal{E}}[\vec{\mathcal{M}}, X \mapsto s]$ *is also convergent, we call* $\vec{\mathcal{E}}[X]$ parametrically FB *with respect to C iff each* $\vec{\mathcal{E}}[\vec{\mathcal{M}}, X \mapsto s]$*, with* $\vec{\mathcal{M}} \in C$ *and* s *a sort in* $\mathcal{M}$*, is an FB instance of* $\vec{\mathcal{E}}[X]$.

The nice result about the FB property is that if: (i) $\vec{\mathcal{E}}$ is FB and (i) enjoys the easy to check Σ-boundedness property, then $\vec{\mathcal{E}}$ is FVP (Theorem 5 in [15]). Furthermore, then the finite set of variants for any term t can be computed by folding variant narrowing *in exactly the same way* as in the finitary case. One important difference, however, is that, in general, the variant $E \cup B$-unification algorithm for an FVP theory is no longer finitary. This is to be expected, since variant $E \cup B$-unification relies on B-unification, which is itself infinitary.

This infinitary nature of $E \cup B$-unification poses some substantial challenges, but they are not unsurmountable. Specifically, assuming that B is a combination of associativity and/or commutativity and/or identity axioms which include some associative axioms for non-commutative operators, these substantial challenges have already been addressed by the *incomplete*, but complete in a large number of practical cases, B-unification algorithm designed by Steven Eker in [10] and summarized in [7], which is supported by Maude 3 [6]. Let me summarize this incomplete algorithm. Let us call it $IUnif_B$. Given a system of equations ϕ, $IUnif_B$ provides a generally *incomplete* but *finitary* algorithm computing $E \cup B$-unifiers $IUnif_B(\phi)$ instead of the *complete* but generally *infinitary* algorithm $Unif_B(\phi)$. $IUnif_B(\phi)$ works as follows: for each B-unification system of equations ϕ *always responds* with a *pair* (Θ, f), where Θ is a finite set of B-unifiers of ϕ, and where f is a Boolean flag indicating completeness, so that if $f = true$, then we *know* that $\Theta = Unif_B(\phi)$. Instead, if $f = false$, we only know that $\Theta \subseteq Unif_B(\phi)$. Since, at least in Maude, all we actually have available is the pragmatically useful $IUnif_B(\phi)$, we are *always* potentially incomplete anyway, except for computing the variants of a term t when $\vec{\mathcal{E}}$ is FB and enjoys the Σ-boundedness property. This can have a liberating effect. After all, we may as well just relax the FVP requirement and keep only the easy to check requirement that our convergent $\vec{\mathcal{E}}$ has the Σ-boundedness property. *If* for the computations of the $\vec{\mathcal{E}}$-variants of a term t, or the variant $E \cup B$ unifiers of a system of equations ϕ, Maude does not give any warnings about the underlying $IUnif_B$ algorithm having returned an incomplete solution set, *then* our results are *complete*, and all our variant-related algorithms, and all our theoretical claims are *exactly the same* as in the finitary B-unifications case. In practice, this ideal scenario can happen considerably more often than one might expect.

3 Variant Satisfiability for Two Parameterized String Data Types

I begin with a parameterized data type **St**$[X]$ of strings with an associative string concatenation operator $\_\ \_$ that enjoys the Σ-boundedness property and ensures the FB property (and therefore the FVP) for any instance **St**$[s]$ under reasonable assumptions. I then extend **St**$[X]$ to a parameterized data type $\mathbf{St}^{\in}[X]$ by adding a string membership predicate. $\mathbf{St}^{\in}[X]$ enjoys the Σ-boundedness property but *not* the FB property. $\mathbf{St}^{\in}[X]$ is not FVP but, as just mentioned in Sect. 2.5, this is no real obstacle in practice when we rely on the underlying $IUnif_B$ algorithm: if some incompleteness problem is found, we will know about it and, as explained below, even this may not hinder us from achieving our desired verification goals. I then show how, for any instances of **St**$[X]$, resp. $\mathbf{St}^{\in}[X]$, satisfiability problems in the initial algebra of such an instance can be either decided, or may instead receive the "unknown" answer, depending on the possible warnings of the underlying $IUnif_B$ algorithm. Let me describe **St**$[X]$.

Example 1. (Strings Parameterized Data Type **St**$[X]$). Consider the following algebraic data type of strings, where X is its *parameter sort*. Its rewrite theory $\vec{\mathbf{St}}[X] = (\Sigma, A, \vec{E})$ has signature Σ with sorts X,[2] *NeSt* and *St*, subsort inclusions $X < NeSt < St$, a constant ε of sort *St*, a subsort-overloaded string concatenation operator $\_\ \_ : St\ St \to St$, $\_\ \_ : NeSt\ NeSt \to NeSt$, two functions $first, last : NeSt \to X$, and two other functions $rest, prior : NeSt \to St$. The only axiom in A is the associativity axiom $(u\ v)\ w = u\ (v\ w)$, were u, v, w are variables of sort *St*, p, q, r variables of sort *NeSt*, and x is a variable of sort X. The rules $\vec{E}$ are: (i) the identity rules $u\ \ \varepsilon \to u$ and $\varepsilon\ \ u \to u$, (ii) the

[2] In Maude, X would be the sort `Elt` of the `TRIV` parameter theory.

first and *rest* rules $first(x) \to x$, $first(x\ q) \to x$, $rest(x) \to \varepsilon$, $rest(x\ q) \to q$, and (iii) the *last* and *prior* rules $last(x) \to x$, $last(q\ x) \to x$, $prior(x) \to \varepsilon$, $prior(q\ x) \to q$. $\vec{\mathbf{St}}$ has a constructor subtheory[3] $\vec{\mathbf{St}}_\Omega = (\Omega, A_\Omega, \emptyset)$ with same sorts and subsorts and where Ω has the constant ε and the concatenation operator for non-empty strings $\_\ \_ : NeSt\ NeSt \to NeSt$, and A_Ω has just the associativity *axiom* $(p\ q)\ r = p\ (q\ r)$. The theory $\vec{\mathbf{St}}$ is clearly terminating, since the associativity axiom is term-size-preserving, and all the rules are term-size-decreasing. It is also sort-decreasing and strictly A-coherent. The only critical pairs modulo A are those between the rules $u\ \varepsilon \to u$ and $\varepsilon\ u \to u$, which are clearly joinable, so $\vec{\mathbf{St}}$ is also confluent and therefore convergent. It satisfies also the Σ-boundedness property: for each non-constant symbol $f \in \Sigma$, the term $f(x_1, \ldots, x_n)$ has exactly 3 most general variants.

A natural question to ask is: when are the instances of $\mathbf{St}[X]$ FVP? This question has been answered and proved in [15] as follows:

Theorem 2. *[15] ($\vec{\mathbf{St}}[X]$ is parametrically FB relative to C). Let C be the class of convergent order-sorted theories $\mathbf{M} \in C$ such that: (i) axioms $B_\mathbf{M}$ of $\mathbf{M}$ are any combination of associativity and/or commutativity axioms,[4] (ii) have the boundedness property, (iii) are FB, and (iv) for any sort s in $\mathbf{M}$, $\vec{\mathbf{St}}[\vec{\mathbf{M}}, X \mapsto s]$ is convergent. Then, $\vec{\mathbf{St}}[X]$ is parametrically FB relative to C. Therefore, by Theorem 5 in [15], $\vec{\mathbf{St}}[\vec{\mathbf{M}}, X \mapsto s]$ is FVP for any $\mathbf{M} \in C$ and sort s in $\mathbf{M}$.*

Let me now describe the $\vec{\mathbf{St}}^{\in}[X]$ extension:

Example 2. (Strings Parameterized Data Type $\vec{\mathbf{St}}^{\in}[X]$). The extension $\vec{\mathbf{St}}^{\in}[X]$ has the form: $\vec{\mathbf{St}}^{\in}[X] = (\Sigma \cup \Pi, A, \vec{E} \cup \vec{\Gamma})$ and is obtained from an OS-FO theory $\mathbf{St}^{\in}[X] = ((\Sigma, \Pi), A, E \cup \Gamma)$ where Π has just a string membership predicate $\_ \in \_ : X\ St$, which is expressed functionally in $\Sigma \cup \Pi$ as $\_ \in \_ : X\ St \to Pred$, where the new sort *Pred* with constant *tt* has been added to Π. The string membership axioms Γ are: $x \in x$, $x \in x\ u$, $x \in u\ x$, $x \in u\ x\ v$, and are expressed in $\vec{\mathbf{St}}^{\in}[X]$ as the following string membership rules $\vec{\vec{\Gamma}}$: $x \in x \to tt$, $x \in x\ u \to tt$, $x \in u\ x \to tt$, and $x \in u\ x\ v \to tt$. That is, $\vec{\mathbf{St}}^{\in}[X]$ just adds to $\vec{\mathbf{St}}[X]$ the rules $\vec{\vec{\Gamma}}$ and Π with its new sort *Pred*. $\vec{\mathbf{St}}^{\in}[X]$ is convergent and has a constructor subtheory $\vec{\mathbf{St}}^{\in}_{\Omega \cup \Pi}[X] = (\Omega \cup \Pi, A_\Omega, \vec{\vec{\Gamma}})$. Furthermore, $\vec{\mathbf{St}}^{\in}$ satisfies the Σ-boundedness property: for the new operator $\_ \in \_$, the most general term $x \in u$ has 5 variants. However, as explained in [15], the new rules in $\vec{\vec{\Gamma}}$ are *not* FB, so we cannot expect $\vec{\mathbf{St}}^{\in}$ to produce FVP instances; but it can produce instances satisfying the Σ-boundedness property, which, as we shall see, for variant satisfiability purposes may be just enough.

[3] For more details about sufficient completeness of parameterized OS theories and methods for checking it see [16].

[4] I am purposefully avoiding identity axioms because, thanks to the theory transformation $\vec{\mathcal{E}} \mapsto \vec{\mathcal{E}}_U$ in [8] mapping a convergent $\vec{\mathcal{E}}$ with identity axioms U into a semantically equivalent convergent $\vec{\mathcal{E}}_U$ where such axioms have been transformed into rewrite rules, this involves no real loss of generality.

Let now $\vec{\mathbf{M}} = (\Sigma_{\mathbf{M}}, B_{\mathbf{M}}, \vec{E}_{\mathbf{M}})$ have only associative and/or commutative axioms $B_{\mathbf{M}}$, be convergent, enjoy the Σ-boundedness property, and have a constructor subtheory $\vec{\mathbf{M}}_{\Omega} = (\Sigma_{\mathbf{M}_{\Omega}}, B_{\mathbf{M}_{\Omega}}, \vec{E}_{\mathbf{M}_{\Omega}})$ enjoying the same properties. Let now s be a sort in $\vec{\mathbf{M}}$ such that $\vec{\mathbf{St}}^{\in}[\mathbf{M}, X \mapsto s]$ is convergent and let us consider the relationship between $\vec{\mathbf{St}}^{\in}[\mathbf{M}, X \mapsto s]$ and $\mathbf{St}^{\in}_{\Omega\cup\Pi}[\mathbf{M}_{\Omega}, X \mapsto s]$. Since in $\mathbf{St}^{\in}_{\Omega\cup\Pi}[X]$ the only terms of sort X are variables $x, y, \ldots$ of sort X, and $\mathbf{St}^{\in}_{\Omega\cup\Pi}[X]$ is made up of constructors, we have the following protecting relationships between the corresponding initial algebras (again, see [16] for more details about sufficient completeness of parameterized OS theories): (1) (parameter protection) $T_{\mathbf{St}^{\in}[\mathbf{M},X\mapsto s]}|_{\Sigma_{\mathbf{M}}} \cong T_{\mathbf{M}}$, (2) (parameter constructor protection) $T_{\mathbf{St}^{\in}_{\Omega\cup\Pi}[\mathbf{M}_{\Omega},X\mapsto s]}|_{\Sigma_{\mathbf{M}_{\Omega}}} \cong T_{\mathbf{M}_{\Omega}}$, and (3) (instance protection): $T_{\mathbf{St}^{\in}[\mathbf{M},X\mapsto s]}|_{\Sigma_{\mathbf{M}}\cup\Omega\cup\Pi} \cong T_{\mathbf{St}^{\in}_{\Omega\cup\Pi}[\mathbf{M}_{\Omega},X\mapsto s]}$. In particular, by (3), $\mathbf{St}^{\in}_{\Omega\cup\Pi}[\mathbf{M}_{\Omega}, X \mapsto s]$ is the constructor subtheory of $\mathbf{St}^{\in}[\mathbf{M}, X \mapsto s]$. (4) $\vec{\mathbf{St}}^{\in}[\mathbf{M}, X \mapsto s]$ has the Σ-boundedness property because both $\vec{\mathbf{St}}^{\in}[X]$ and $\vec{\mathbf{M}}$ do and, due to the disjointness of the signatures and the axiom sets, the computations of variants for operators with maximal arguments in either of the disjoint signatures can be computed by folding variant narrowing exactly as before: no operator from the other signature can ever show up in such narrowing trees. In particular, Σ-boundedness is also enjoyed by $\mathbf{St}^{\in}_{\Omega\cup\Pi}[\mathbf{M}_{\Omega}, X \mapsto s]$.

3.1 Variant Satisfiability of St[X]

A fortiori, all the above properties (1)–(4) are also satisfied by $\vec{\mathbf{St}}[\mathbf{M}, X \mapsto s]$, $\vec{\mathbf{St}}_{\Omega}[\mathbf{M}_{\Omega}, X \mapsto s]$, and all the associated initial algebras and reducts. Suppose, further, that $\vec{\mathbf{M}}$ belongs to the class C of theories specified in Theorem 2. Then, by Theorem 2, $\vec{\mathbf{St}}[\mathbf{M}, X \mapsto s]$, $\vec{\mathbf{St}}_{\Omega}[\mathbf{M}_{\Omega}, X \mapsto s]$, $\vec{\mathbf{M}}$, and $\vec{\mathbf{M}}_{\Omega}$ are all FVP. Suppose that $\vec{\mathbf{M}}_{\Omega}$ is also weakly OS-compact and that $T_{\mathbf{M},s}$ is an infinite set, and therefore so is $T_{\mathbf{M}_{\Omega},s}$. Note that, then: (5) by weak OS-compactness of $\vec{\mathbf{M}}_{\Omega}$ and (2), we can effectively determine whether any sort in $\mathbf{St}_{\Omega}[\mathbf{M}_{\Omega}, X \mapsto s]$ is finite or infinite and can compute representative ground terms for finite sorts; (6) since $\mathbf{St}_{\Omega}[\mathbf{M}_{\Omega}, X \mapsto s]$ is FVP, it has a unification algorithm. Therefore, $\mathbf{St}_{\Omega}[\mathbf{M}_{\Omega}, X \mapsto s]$ satisfies conditions (i)–(iii) in Definition 1 of weak OS-compactness. The key pending question then is: does it also satisfy condition (iv) so that $\mathbf{St}_{\Omega}[\mathbf{M}_{\Omega}, X \mapsto s]$ is actually weakly OS-compact? The answer to this question is provided by the following theorem, whose proof is similar to that for parameterized lists in Theorem 9 of [19].

Theorem 3. *(Preservation of Weak OS-Compactness). Under the above assumptions on* $\vec{\mathbf{M}}$ *and* s*,* $\mathbf{St}_{\Omega}[\mathbf{M}_{\Omega}, X \mapsto s]$ *is weakly OS-compact.*

Let me now explain how, for each $\vec{\mathbf{M}}$ in the class C of theories specified in Theorem 2, Theorem 3 provides a "knowingly incomplete" satisfiability decision procedure for satisfiability of QF Σ-formulas in the initial algebra $T_{\mathbf{St}[\mathbf{M},X\mapsto s]}$ when $\mathbf{M}_{\Omega}$ is weakly OS-compact and s is an infinite sort. This "knowingly incomplete" decision procedure is the natural extension to the infinitary unification case of the variant satisfiability procedure in [19]. By putting QF formulas in disjunctive normal form it is enough to consider conjunctions of literals of the form $\bigwedge G \wedge \bigwedge D$, with the G equalities and the D disequalities. Since $\vec{\mathbf{St}}[\mathbf{M}, X \mapsto s]$ is FVP, we can compute the variant unifiers of $\bigwedge G$ modulo $\mathbf{St}[\mathbf{M}, X \mapsto s]$ by folding variant narrowing modulo axioms $A \cup B_{\mathbf{M}}$. The $A \cup B_{\mathbf{M}}$-unification calls made by the folding variant narrowing algorithm will be computed by $IUnif_{A \cup B_{\mathbf{M}}}$. Since for some calls the number of $Unif_{A \cup B_{\mathbf{M}}}$-unifiers may be infinite, two things can happen for the input $\bigwedge G$. **Case** (a): the variant-unification algorithm returns with a finite number Θ of $\vec{\mathbf{St}}[\mathbf{M}, X \mapsto s]$-unifiers and no warning from $IUnif_{A \cup B_{\mathbf{M}}}$. Then, we know that such a finite set is complete and can reduce the satisfiability of $\bigwedge G \wedge \bigwedge D$, to that of $\bigvee_{\theta \in \Theta} (\bigwedge D)\theta$. As an optimization, we may first compute the constructor variant unifiers of $\bigwedge G$ from Θ as explained in [20], but this is not essential. Then for each disjunct $(\bigwedge D)\theta$ we can effectively compute its constructor variants, which are conjunctions in $\mathbf{St}_{\Omega}[\mathbf{M}_{\Omega}, X \mapsto s]$, and for each such constructor variant and all variables of finite sort in it (which sorts must be in $\mathbf{M}_{\Omega}$) the canonical forms of all the substitutions of those variables by all the choices of effectively computable ground representatives of those sorts, which we can do thanks to the weak OS-compactness of $\mathbf{M}_{\Omega}$. Then, our original conjunction is satisfiable thanks to Theorem 3 if and only if at least one of those normalized conjunctions of constructor disequalities, whose variables are all infinite, is axiom-consistent.

The "knowingly incomplete" case of this satisfiability decision procedure appears in **Case** (b): we obtain an incompleteness warning from the underlying $IUnif_{A \cup B_{\mathbf{M}}}$ and therefore an incomplete set Θ of variant unifiers of $\bigwedge G$. We then proceed as in the complete case, and can also prove satisfiability of $\bigwedge G \wedge \bigwedge D$ if we can find in the end some axiom-consistent normalized conjunction of constructor disequalities (whose variables are all infinite). However, if we cannot find any such conjunction of constructor disequalities our "knowingly incomplete" procedure must reply: "don't know." Let us see some examples.

First of all, by the syntactic disjointness assumption between $\mathbf{M}$ and $\mathbf{St}[X]$, it is possible to prove *generic theorems* in $\mathbf{St}[X]$, i.e., theorems only involving the syntax of $\mathbf{St}[X]$ which will apply to all instances $\mathbf{St}[\mathbf{M}, X \mapsto s]$ under the above assumptions on $\mathbf{M}$ and s. This is because, by the disjointness assumption, up to sort renaming for X, constructor variants and constructor variant unifiers for pure $\mathbf{St}[X]$ formulas coincide in $\mathbf{St}[X]$ and in $\mathbf{St}[\mathbf{M}, X \mapsto s]$. Here are two simple such generic theorems, where q has sort *NeSt*:

1. $q = \mathit{first}(q)\ \mathit{rest}(q)$
2. $q = \mathit{prior}(q)\ \mathit{last}(q)$

Let us see how (1) is proved; the proof of (2) is entirely similar. We just need to show that $q \neq \mathit{first}(q)\ \mathit{rest}(q)$ is unsatisfiable. We can do so by computing its constructor variants, which are:

1. $x \neq x$,and
2. $x\ q' \neq x\ q'$

which are both obviously unsatisfiable.

A somewhat more interesting generic theorem is the following equivalence, relating the four functions *first*, *rest*, *prior* and *last*, where x, y have sort X and q, q' sort *NeSt*:

$$\mathit{first}(q) = x \wedge \mathit{last}(q) = y \wedge \mathit{prior}(q) = q' \Leftrightarrow q = x\ \mathit{rest}(q')\ y \wedge \mathit{prior}(q) = q'$$

where the condition $prior(q) = q'$ just states that the string q has length $\geqslant 2$. Note that the simpler equivalence $first(q) = x \wedge last(q) = y \Leftrightarrow q = x\ rest(q')\ y$ is *invalid* for strings, because it fails for strings of length 1. For example, for $q = x$ it yields the contradiction $x = x\ x$.

Proving the above equivalence requires proving for the ($\Rightarrow$) part that:

1. $first(q) = x \wedge last(q) = y \wedge prior(q) = q' \wedge q \neq x\ rest(q')\ y$, and
2. $first(q) = x \wedge last(q) = y \wedge prior(q) = q' \wedge prior(q) \neq q'$

are both unsatisfiable. But (2) is always false, so unsatisfiable, and we only need to deal with (1).

Likewise, for proving the ($\Leftarrow$) side we need to show that

1. $q = x\ rest(q')\ y \wedge prior(q) = q' \wedge first(q) \neq x$
2. $q = x\ rest(q')\ y \wedge prior(q) = q' \wedge last(q) \neq y$
3. $q = x\ rest(q')\ y \wedge prior(q) = q' \wedge piror(q) \neq q'$

are all unsatisfiable. But (3) is always false, thus unsatisfiable, so we only need to deal with (1) and (2).

For proving the ($\Rightarrow$) implication we only need to deal with (1). But selecting the constructor variants unifiers of $first(q) = x \wedge last(q) = y \wedge prior(q) = q'$ among all other we get:

```
Unifier #2
q --> %2:X %3:NeSt %1:X
x --> %2:X
y --> %1:X
q' --> %2:X %3:NeSt

Unifier #3
q --> %2:X %1:X
x --> %2:X
y --> %1:X
q' --> %2:X
```

We can then instantiate $rest(q')$ by these two unifiers to get:

```
Maude> reduce rest(%2:X %3:NeList) .
result NeSt: %3:NeList

Maude> reduce rest(%2:X) .
result St: nil
```

So that the constructor variants of the instances of $q \neq x\ rest(q')\ y$ by unifiers #2 and #3 are, respectively:

```
%2:X %3:NeList %1:X =/=  %2:X %3:NeList %1:X

%2:X %1:X =/= %2:X %1:X
```

which are both unsatisfiable.

For proving the ($\Leftarrow$) part, the constructor unifiers of $q = x\ rest(q')\ y \wedge prior(q) = q'$ are:

```
Unifier #1
rewrites: 15 in 5ms cpu (6ms real) (2676 rewrites/second)
q --> %1:X %2:X
x --> %1:X
q' --> %1:X
y --> %2:X

Unifier #2
rewrites: 15 in 5ms cpu (6ms real) (2632 rewrites/second)
q --> %1:X %2:NeList %3:X
x --> %1:X
q' --> %1:X %2:NeList
y --> %3:X
```

It is enough to show that the normalized substitution instances by unifiers #1 and #2 of the disequalities are unsatisfiable constructor variants of: (i) $\mathit{first}(q) \neq x$ and (ii) $\mathit{last}(q) \neq y$. For (i) this follows from

```
Maude> red first(#1:X #2:X) .
result X: #1:X
```

yielding an unsatisfiable constructor disequality summarized as: $x_1 \neq x_1$, and

```
Maude> red first(#1:X #2:NeList #3:X) .
result X: #1:X
```

yielding an unsatisfiable constructor disequality summarized as: $x_1 \neq x_1$.
For (ii) this follows from:

```
Maude> red last(#1:X #2:X) .
result X: #2:X
```

yielding an unsatisfiable constructor disequality summarized as: $x_2 \neq x_2$, and

```
Maude> red last(#1:X #2:NeSt #3:X) .
result X: #3:X
```

yielding an unsatisfiable constructor disequality summarized as: $x_3 \neq x_3$.

3.2 Variant Satisfiability of $\mathbf{St}^{\in}[X]$

In the case of the parameterized module $\mathbf{St}^{\in}[X]$, we cannot rely anymore on the preservation of weak OS-Compactness provided by Theorem 3. But we still have properties (1)–(4). This means that it is sound to still follow the same approach as for $\mathbf{St}[X]$, but we may have somewhat weaker chances of success because, besides having to cope a fortiori with the fact that variant unification using $\mathit{IUnif}_{A \cup B_M}$ as our underlying mechanism will in general be incomplete, we need to face the additional potential source of incompleteness associated with not being able in general to compute complete finite sets of variants/constructor variants. However, if we do not get any warnings from $\mathit{IUnif}_{A \cup B_M}$ when performing either task, we can still be able to decide the initial satisfiability of the given QF formula (and even, after getting warnings, we may still find a witness θ proving satisfiability of the given formula). This is the case for two reasons: (A). Since $\mathbf{St}^{\in}[X]$ only adds the new sort *Pred* to $\mathbf{St}[X]$ and the predicates do not affect at all the terms in the original sort, it is easy to show that $\mathbf{St}^{\in}[X]$ *protects* $\mathbf{St}[X]$. Therefore, if we instantiate $\mathbf{St}^{\in}[X]$ to $\mathbf{St}^{\in}[\mathbf{M}, X \mapsto s]$ with $\vec{\mathbf{M}}$ and s satisfying the assumptions in Theorem 3, $\mathbf{St}[\mathbf{M}, X \mapsto s]$ will still be FVP, and Theorem 3 will still apply to the reduct $\mathbf{St}_{\Omega}[\mathbf{M}_{\Omega}, X \mapsto s]$ of $\mathbf{St}^{\in}_{\Omega \cup Pi}[\mathbf{M}_{\Omega}, X \mapsto s]$. (B). But (A) means that, since the "data" as opposed to the "predicate" part has not been affected, given a conjunction $\bigwedge G \wedge \bigwedge D$ for which we have been able to compute some variant unifiers of $\bigwedge G$ we can still compute a complete set of constructor variants for the "data disequalies" in $\bigwedge D$. However, we may or may not be able to compute a complete set of constructor variants for the "predicate disequalities". But for any canonical and axiom-consistent constructor variant, say, $\bigwedge D'$, of $(\bigwedge D)\theta$ with variables only of infinite sorts associated to any unifier θ of $\bigwedge G$ that we may have obtained, we can soundly *conclude* that the original conjunction $\bigwedge G \wedge \bigwedge D$ is satisfiable in the initial algebra. The reason why this is so is because, reasoning as in the proof of Theorem 3: (i) we can first *reduce* the initial satisfiability of $\bigwedge D'$ to that of the substitution $\bigwedge D'\{\overline{Y} \mapsto \overline{y}\}$ explained in the proof of Theorem 3, which will also be in canonical form and axiom-consistent; (ii) we can then transform the "data disequalities" in $\bigwedge D'\{\overline{Y} \mapsto \overline{y}\}$ into corresponding canonical and axiom-consistent $\mathbf{M}_{\Omega}$-disequalities as in the proof of Theorem 3; and (iii) we can do so also for the "predicate disequalities", which must be of one of the following two forms: (a) $t \in \varepsilon \neq tt$, which is always valid and can be disregarded; or (b) $t \in t_1 \ \ldots \ t_n \neq tt$, with $n \geqslant 1$, which is semantically equivalent to the conjunction of $\mathbf{M}_{\Omega}$-disequalities $t \neq t_1 \wedge \ldots \wedge t \neq t_n$. In this way, we can reduce $\bigwedge D'\{\overline{Y} \mapsto \overline{y}\}$ to an equivalent conjunction of canonical and axiom-consistent disequalities, showing that our original $\bigwedge D'$ was satisfiable in the initial algebra and therefore the decision method is sound. Of course, as in the $\mathbf{St}[X]$ case, if at any point in the entire process of computing unifiers θ for $\bigwedge G$, and then constructor variants with only infinite sort variables for $(\bigwedge D)\theta$, we get an incompleteness warning from the underlying $IUnif_{A \cup B_{\mathbf{M}}}$ algorithm and we have not been able to find a canonical and axiom-consistent constructor disequality variant, we must answer "don't know."

Let us see an example illustrating two facts: (i) that by performing instantiations $\mathbf{St}^{\in}[\mathbf{M}, X \mapsto s]$ with $\vec{\mathbf{M}}$ and s satisfying the assumptions in Theorem 3, we obtain for free a kind of implicit "Nelson-Oppen" combination of the variant satisfiability algorithm available for $\mathbf{M}$ and that for $\mathbf{St}^{\in}[X]$, and (ii) that the instantiation process can be nested, either with some other variant-satisfiable parameterized module or with $\mathbf{St}^{\in}[X]$ itself. We can consider, for example, a nested instantiation of the form $\mathbf{St}^{\in}[\mathbf{St}^{\in}[\mathbf{N}, X \mapsto Nat]X \mapsto NeSt']$ describing lists of lists of natural numbers. To ensure syntax disjointness, in the inner instantiation all sorts and operators must be renamed to, say, a primed form, except that we can rename _ _ to _;_. Also, to ensure that no identity axioms are used, $\mathbf{N}$ is assumed to be a specification of Presburger arithmetic where + is AC, which can be specified in a way similar to the one used in [19], except that we use a subsort relation $NzNat < Nat$, specify + in both sorts, but declare it as a constructor in *NzNat*, and declare 0 of sort *Nat*, 1 of sort *NzNat*, declare the rewrite rule $n + 0 \rightarrow n$ as well as those defining, say > as a Boolean predicate.

Here is a somewhat amusing, domain-specific theorem that is valid in the initial algebra of $\mathbf{St}^{\in}[\mathbf{St}^{\in}[\mathbf{N}, X \mapsto Nat]X \mapsto NeSt']$:

$$(first'(first(q)) > 0 = true \wedge first'(first(q)) = first(q)) \Rightarrow (0 \in' first(q) \neq tt)$$

This property can be shown valid for the data type of strings of strings of natural numbers because Maude cannot find any variant unifiers satisfying its negation, that is, the conjunction:

$$\mathit{first}'(\mathit{first}(q)) > 0 = \mathit{true} \wedge \mathit{first}'(\mathit{first}(q)) = \mathit{first}(q) \wedge 0 \in' \mathit{first}(q) \neq tt$$

Intuitively, the theorem says that, for q a non-empty string of non-empty strings of natural numbers, if the first element of its first element is greater than 0 and $\mathit{first}'(\mathit{first}(q)) = \mathit{first}(q)$, then 0 cannot appear in the string of natural numbers $\mathit{first}(q)$.

4 Related Work and Conclusions

Three types of most closely related work are: (1) Decision procedures for strings in current SMT solvers, e.g., [1, 14, 21, 22]. As pointed out in the Introduction, they are parametric on a finite alphabet, whereas $\mathbf{St}[X]$ and $\mathbf{St}^{\in}[X]$ are parametric on an infinite user-definable algebraic data type of string elements. They cannot be compared directly with each other: they cover complementary cases and different applications. An advantage of $\mathbf{St}[X]$ and $\mathbf{St}^{\in}[X]$ is that they are directly suited to reason about the initial models of order-sorted user-defined data types *and* their composition by both importations an instantiations of parametric data types. This can be quite useful when reasoning about the correctness of declarative rule-based programs and in many other applications. (2) Previous work on variant satisfiability, e.g., [19, 20]. In comparison with that work, what this work adds is to bring data types with associative but not commutative axioms, including parameterized ones, within the fold of variant satisfiability. (3) The recent work by Steven Eker in defining and building his very efficient and practical and order-sorted A- and B-unification algorithm $A \subseteq B$ [6, 10], here denoted IUnif_B, has been crucial for this work.

Much work remains ahead. Just the definition of $\mathbf{St}[X]$ and $\mathbf{St}^{\in}[X]$, their properties, theoretical framework needed, and some simple experiments is what has been possible to do for the moment. Two items for near-term work include the optimization and integration of $\mathbf{St}[X]$ and $\mathbf{St}^{\in}[X]$ within the current variant satisfiablity prototype tool [20], and substantial experimentation and exploration of synergies with the traditional SMT-based string procedures.

Acknowledgements. I cordially thank the referees for their very helpful suggestions to improve the paper. This work has been partially supported by NRL under contract N00173-17-1-G002.

References

1. Abdulla, P.A., et al.: Norn: an SMT solver for string constraints. In: Kroening, D., Păsăreanu, C.S. (eds.) CAV 2015, Part I. LNCS, vol. 9206, pp. 462–469. Springer, Cham (2015). https://doi.org/10.1007/978-3-319-21690-4_29
2. Cholewa, A., Meseguer, J., Escobar, S.: Variants of variants and the finite variant property. Technical report, CS Department, University of Illinois at Urbana-Champaign, February 2014. http://hdl.handle.net/2142/47117

3. Clavel, M., et al.: All About Maude - A High-Performance Logical Framework. LNCS, vol. 4350. Springer, Heidelberg (2007). https://doi.org/10.1007/978-3-540-71999-1
4. Comon-Lundh, H., Delaune, S.: The finite variant property: how to get rid of some algebraic properties. In: Giesl, J. (ed.) RTA 2005. LNCS, vol. 3467, pp. 294–307. Springer, Heidelberg (2005). https://doi.org/10.1007/978-3-540-32033-3_22
5. Dershowitz, N., Jouannaud, J.P.: Rewrite systems. In: van Leeuwen, J. (ed.) Handbook of Theoretical Computer Science, vol. B, pp. 243–320, North-Holland (1990)
6. Durán, F., et al.: Programming and symbolic computation in Maude. J. Log. Algebr. Methods Program. **110**, 1–57, 100497 (2020). https://doi.org/10.1016/j.jlamp.2019.100497
7. Durán, F., Eker, S., Escobar, S., Martí-Oliet, N., Meseguer, J., Talcott, C.: Associative unification and symbolic reasoning modulo associativity in Maude. In: Rusu, V. (ed.) WRLA 2018. LNCS, vol. 11152, pp. 98–114. Springer, Cham (2018). https://doi.org/10.1007/978-3-319-99840-4_6
8. Durán, F., Lucas, S., Meseguer, J.: Termination modulo combinations of equational theories. In: Ghilardi, S., Sebastiani, R. (eds.) FroCoS 2009. LNCS (LNAI), vol. 5749, pp. 246–262. Springer, Heidelberg (2009). https://doi.org/10.1007/978-3-642-04222-5_15
9. Durán, F., Meseguer, J.: Structured theories and institutions. Theor. Comput. Sci. **309**(1–3), 357–380 (2003)
10. Eker, S.: A pragmatic approach to implementing associative unification, unpublished manuscript, SRI International, circa (2015)
11. Escobar, S., Sasse, R., Meseguer, J.: Folding variant narrowing and optimal variant termination. J. Algebr. Logic Program. **81**, 898–928 (2012)
12. Goguen, J., Meseguer, J.: Order-sorted algebra I: equational deduction for multiple inheritance, overloading, exceptions and partial operations. Theor. Comput. Sci. **105**, 217–273 (1992)
13. Jouannaud, J.-P., Kirchner, C., Kirchner, H.: Incremental construction of unification algorithms in equational theories. In: Diaz, J. (ed.) ICALP 1983. LNCS, vol. 154, pp. 361–373. Springer, Heidelberg (1983). https://doi.org/10.1007/BFb0036921
14. Liang, T., Tsiskaridze, N., Reynolds, A., Tinelli, C., Barrett, C.: A decision procedure for regular membership and length constraints over unbounded strings. In: Lutz, C., Ranise, S. (eds.) FroCoS 2015. LNCS (LNAI), vol. 9322, pp. 135–150. Springer, Cham (2015). https://doi.org/10.1007/978-3-319-24246-0_9
15. Meseguer, J.: Variants in the infinitary unification wonderland, submitted to WRLA 2020
16. Meseguer, J.: Order-sorted parameterization and induction. In: Palsberg, J. (ed.) Semantics and Algebraic Specification. LNCS, vol. 5700, pp. 43–80. Springer, Heidelberg (2009). https://doi.org/10.1007/978-3-642-04164-8_4
17. Meseguer, J.: Conditional rewriting logic as a unified model of concurrency. Theor. Comput. Sci. **96**(1), 73–155 (1992)
18. Meseguer, J.: Membership algebra as a logical framework for equational specification. In: Presicce, F.P. (ed.) WADT 1997. LNCS, vol. 1376, pp. 18–61. Springer, Heidelberg (1998). https://doi.org/10.1007/3-540-64299-4_26
19. Meseguer, J.: Variant-based satisfiability in initial algebras. Sci. Comput. Program. **154**, 3–41 (2018)
20. Skeirik, S., Meseguer, J.: Metalevel algorithms for variant satisfiability. J. Log. Algebr. Methods Program. **96**, 81–110 (2018)
21. Trinh, M., Chu, D., Jaffar, J.: S3: a symbolic string solver for vulnerability detection in web applications. In: Proceedings of the 2014 ACM SIGSAC Conference on Computer and Communications Security, pp. 1232–1243 (2014)
22. Zheng, Y., et al.: Z3str2: an efficient solver for strings, regular expressions, and length constraints. Formal Methods Syst. Des. **50**(2), 249–288 (2016). https://doi.org/10.1007/s10703-016-0263-6

Inductive Reasoning with Equality Predicates, Contextual Rewriting and Variant-Based Simplification

José Meseguer(✉) and Stephen Skeirik

Department of Computer Science, University of Illinois at Urbana-Champaign, Urbana, USA
{meseguer,skeirik2}@illinois.edu

Abstract. We present an inductive inference system for proving validity of formulas in the initial algebra $T_{\mathcal{E}}$ of an order-sorted equational theory $\mathcal{E}$ with 17 inference rules, where only 6 of them require user interaction, while the remaining 11 can be automated as *simplification rules* and can be combined together as a limited, yet practical, automated inductive theorem prover. The 11 simplification rules are based on powerful equational reasoning techniques, including: equationally defined equality predicates, constructor variant unification, variant satisfiability, order-sorted congruence closure, contextual rewriting and recursive path orderings. For $\mathcal{E} = (\Sigma, E \uplus B)$, these techniques work modulo B, with B a combination of associativity and/or commutativity and/or identity axioms.

1 Introduction

In inductive theorem proving for equational specifications there is a tension between automated approaches and explicit induction ones. For two examples of automated equational inductive provers we can mention, among various others, Spike [1] and the superposition-based "inductionless induction" prover in [5]; and for explicit induction equational provers we can mention, again among various others, RRL [15], the OTS/CafeOBJ Method [10], and the Maude ITP [4,14]. The well-known ACL2 prover [16] does not support inductive reasoning about general algebraic specifications. It does instead support powerful inductive reasoning about LISP-style data structures. One way to relate ACL2 to the above-mentioned equational inductive provers is to view it as a domain-specific explicit induction equational theorem prover for recursive functions defined over LISP-style data structures. The advantage of automated provers is that they do not need interaction, although they often require proving auxiliary lemmas. Explicit induction is less automated, but provides substantial flexibility. This work presents an approach that combines automated and explicit-induction theorem proving in the context of proving validity in the initial algebra $T_{\mathcal{E}}$ of an order-sorted equational theory $\mathcal{E}$ for both arbitrary quantifier-free (QF) formulas (expressed as conjunctions of clauses, some of which can be combined together as "superclauses" in the sense of Sect. 3.1) and existential closures of such clauses/superclauses.

The combination is achieved by an inference system having 17 inference rules, where 11 of them are *goal simplification rules* that can be fully automated, whereas

S. Escobar and N. Martí-Oliet (Eds.): WRLA 2020, LNCS 12328, pp. 114–135, 2020.
https://doi.org/10.1007/978-3-030-63595-4_7

the remaining 6 require explicit user commands. In fact, we have combined 9 of those simplification rules into an automated inductive simplification strategy that we call *ISS*. An even more powerful ISS^+ combining all the 11 simplification rules could likewise be developed. Because the simplification rules are very powerful, *ISS* can be used on its own as an automatic *oracle* to answer inductive validity questions, that is, as a limited, yet quite practical, automated inductive theorem prover. How practical? As we explain in Sect. 4.3, practical enough to prove *all* the thousands of inductive validity verification conditions (VCs) that were generated in the deductive verification proof in constructor-based reachability logic of the security properties of the IBOS Browser described in [30,31]. It was the remarkable effectiveness of (a simplified version of) *ISS* as a backend oracle in the IBOS proof that gave us the stimulus for this work.

So, what is the secret of such effectiveness? There isn't a secret as such, but a novel *combination* of powerful *automatable* equational reasoning techniques that, to the best of our knowledge, have never before been combined together for inductive theorem proving purposes. They include: (1) equationally defined equality predicates [13]; (2) constructor variant unification [22,32]; (3) variant satisfiability [22,32]; (4) order-sorted congruence closure [21]; (5) contextual rewriting [36]; and (6) recursive path orderings [12,26]. All these techniques work modulo axioms B.

2 Preliminaries

2.1 Background on Order-Sorted First-Order Logic

We assume familiarity with the notions of an order-sorted signature Σ on a poset of sorts $(S, \leqslant)$, an order-sorted Σ-algebra A, and the term Σ-algebras T_Σ and $T_\Sigma(X)$ for X an S-sorted set of variables. We also assume familiarity with the notions of: (i) Σ-homomorphism $h : A \to B$ between Σ-algebras A and B, so that Σ-algebras and Σ-homomorphisms form a category $\mathbf{OSAlg}_\Sigma$; (ii) order-sorted (i.e., sort-preserving) substitution θ, its domain $dom(\theta)$ and range $ran(\theta)$, and its application $t\theta$ to a term t; (iii) *preregular* order-sorted signature Σ, i.e., a signature such that each term t has a least sort, denoted $ls(t)$; (iv) the set $\widehat{S} = S/(\geqslant \cup \leqslant)^+$ of *connected components* of $(S, \leqslant)$; and (v) for A a Σ-algebra, the set A_s of it elements of sort $s \in S$, and the set $A_{[s]} = \bigcup_{s' \in [s]} A_{s'}$ for $[s] \in \widehat{S}$. We furthermore assume that all signatures Σ have *non-empty sorts*, i.e., $T_{\Sigma,s} \neq \emptyset$ for each $s \in S$. All these notions are explained in detail in [11,20]. The material below is adapted from [22].

The first-order language of *equational Σ-formulas* is defined in the usual way: its atoms[1] are *Σ-equations* $t = t'$, where $t, t' \in T_\Sigma(X)_{[s]}$ for some $[s] \in \widehat{S}$ and each X_s is assumed countably infinite. The set $Form(\Sigma)$ of *equational Σ-formulas* is then inductively built from atoms by: conjunction ($\wedge$), disjunction ($\vee$), negation ($\neg$), and universal ($\forall x_1 : s_1, \ldots, x_n : s_n$) and existential ($\exists x_1 : s_1, \ldots, x_n : s_n$) quantification with distinct sorted variables $x_1 : s_1, \ldots, x_n : s_n$, with $s_1, \ldots, s_n \in S$ (by convention, for $\emptyset$

[1] As explained in [22], there is no real loss of generality in assuming that all atomic formulas are equations: predicates can be specified by equational formulas using additional function symbols of a fresh new sort *Pred* with a constant *tt*, so that a predicate $p(t_1, \ldots, t_n)$ becomes $p(t_1, \ldots, t_n) = tt$.

the empty set of variables and φ a formula, we define $(\forall\emptyset)\ \varphi \equiv (\exists\emptyset)\ \varphi \equiv \varphi$). A literal $\neg(t = t')$ is denoted $t \neq t'$. Given a Σ-algebra A, a formula $\varphi \in Form(\Sigma)$, and an assignment $\alpha \in [Y{\rightarrow}A]$, where $Y \supseteq fvars(\varphi)$, with $fvars(\varphi)$ the free variables of φ, the *satisfaction relation* $A, \alpha \models \varphi$ is defined inductively as usual: for atoms, $A, \alpha \models t = t'$ iff $t\alpha = t'\alpha$; for Boolean connectives it is the corresponding Boolean combination of the satisfaction relations for subformulas; and for quantifiers: $A, \alpha \models (\forall x_1 : s_1, \ldots, x_n : s_n)\ \varphi$ (resp. $A, \alpha \models (\exists x_1 : s_1, \ldots, x_n : s_n)\ \varphi$) holds iff for all $(a_1, \ldots, a_n) \in A_{s_1} \times \ldots \times A_{s_n}$ (resp. for some $(a_1, \ldots, a_n) \in A_{s_1} \times \ldots \times A_{s_n}$) we have $A, \alpha[x_1 : s_1 := a_1, \ldots, x_n : s_n := a_n] \models \varphi$, where if $\alpha \in [Y{\rightarrow}A]$, then $\alpha[x_1 : s_1 := a_1, \ldots, x_n : s_n := a_n] \in [(Y \cup \{x_1 : s_1, \ldots, x_n : s_n\}){\rightarrow}A]$ and is such that for $y : s \in (Y \setminus \{x_1 : s_1, \ldots, x_n : s_n\})$, $\alpha[x_1 : s_1 := a_1, \ldots, x_n : s_n := a_n](y : s) = \alpha(y : s)$, and $\alpha[x_1 : s_1 := a_1, \ldots, x_n : s_n := a_n](x_i : s_i) = a_i$, $1 \leqslant i \leqslant n$. We say that φ is *valid* in A (resp. is *satisfiable* in A) iff $A, \underline{\emptyset} \models (\forall Y)\ \varphi$ (resp. $A, \underline{\emptyset} \models (\exists Y)\ \varphi$), where $Y = fvars(\varphi)$ and $\underline{\emptyset} \in [\underline{\emptyset}{\rightarrow}A]$ denotes the empty S-sorted assignment of values in A to the empty S-sorted family $\underline{\emptyset}$ of variables. The notation $A \models \varphi$ abbreviates validity of φ in A. More generally, a set of formulas $\Gamma \subseteq Form(\Sigma)$ is called *valid* in A, denoted $A \models \Gamma$, iff $A \models \varphi$ for each $\varphi \in \Gamma$. For a subsignature $\Omega \subseteq \Sigma$ and $A \in \mathbf{OSAlg}_{\Sigma}$, the *reduct* $A|_{\Omega} \in \mathbf{OSAlg}_{\Omega}$ agrees with A in the interpretation of all sorts and operations in Ω and discards everything in $\Sigma \setminus \Omega$. If $\varphi \in Form(\Omega)$ we have the equivalence $A \models \varphi \Leftrightarrow A|_{\Omega} \models \varphi$.

An OS *equational theory* is a pair $T = (\Sigma, E)$, with E a set of (possibly conditional) Σ-equations. $\mathbf{OSAlg}_{(\Sigma,E)}$ denotes the full subcategory of $\mathbf{OSAlg}_{\Sigma}$ with objects those $A \in \mathbf{OSAlg}_{\Sigma}$ such that $A \models E$, called the *(Σ, E)-algebras*. $\mathbf{OSAlg}_{(\Sigma,E)}$ has an *initial algebra* $T_{\Sigma/E}$ [20]. Given $T = (\Sigma, E)$ and $\varphi \in Form(\Sigma)$, we call φ *T-valid*, written $E \models \varphi$, iff $A \models \varphi$ for all $A \in \mathbf{OSAlg}_{(\Sigma,E)}$. We call φ *T-satisfiable* iff there exists $A \in \mathbf{OSAlg}_{(\Sigma,E)}$ with φ satisfiable in A. Note that φ is *T-valid* iff $\neg\varphi$ is *T-unsatisfiable*. The inference system in [20] is *sound and complete* for OS equational deduction, i.e., for any OS equational theory (Σ, E), and Σ-equation $u = v$ we have an equivalence $E \vdash u = v \Leftrightarrow E \models u = v$. Deducibility $E \vdash u = v$ is abbreviated as $u =_E v$, called *E-equality*. An *E-unifier* of a system of Σ-equations, i.e., of a conjunction $\phi = u_1 = v_1 \wedge \ldots \wedge u_n = v_n$ of Σ-equations, is a substitution σ such that $u_i\sigma =_E v_i\sigma$, $1 \leqslant i \leqslant n$. An *$E$-unification algorithm* for (Σ, E) is an algorithm generating a *complete set* of E-unifiers $Unif_E(\phi)$ for any system of Σ equations ϕ, where "complete" means that for any E-unifier σ of ϕ there is a $\tau \in Unif_E(\phi)$ and a substitution ρ such that $\sigma =_E (\tau\rho)|_{dom(\sigma)\cup dom(\tau)}$, where $=_E$ here means that for any variable x we have $x\sigma =_E x(\tau\rho)|_{dom(\sigma)\cup dom(\tau)}$. The algorithm is *finitary* if it always terminates with a *finite set* $Unif_E(\phi)$ for any ϕ.

Given a set of equations B used for deduction modulo B, a preregular OS signature Σ is called *B-preregular*[2] iff for each $u = v \in B$ and substitutions ρ, $ls(u\rho) = ls(v\rho)$.

---

[2] If $B = B_0 \uplus U$, with B_0 associativity and/or commutativity axioms, and U identity axioms, the B-preregularity notion can be *broadened* by requiring only that: (i) Σ is B_0-preregular in the standard sense that $ls(u\rho) = ls(v\rho)$ for all $u = v \in B_0$ and substitutions ρ; and (ii) the axioms U oriented as rules $\vec{U}$ are *sort-decreasing* in the sense explained in Sect. 2.2.

2.2 Background on Convergent Theories and Constructors

Given an order-sorted equational theory $\mathcal{E} = (\Sigma, E \cup B)$, where B is a collection of associativity and/or commutativity and/or identity axioms and Σ is B-preregular, we can associate to it a corresponding *rewrite theory* [19] $\vec{\mathcal{E}} = (\Sigma, B, \vec{E})$ by orienting the equations E as left-to right rewrite rules. That is, each $(u = v) \in E$ is transformed into a rewrite rule $u \to v$. For simplicity we recall here the case of unconditional equations; for how conditional equations (whose conditions are conjunctions of equalities) are likewise transformed into conditional rewrite rules see, e.g., [17]. The main purpose of the rewrite theory $\vec{\mathcal{E}}$ is to reduce the complex bidirectional reasoning with equations to the much simpler unidirectional reasoning with rules under suitable assumptions. We assume familiarity with the notion of subterm $t|_p$ of t at a term position p and of term replacement $t[w]_p$ of $t|_p$ by w at position p (see, e.g., [6]). The rewrite relation $t \to_{\vec{E},B} t'$ holds iff there is a subterm $t|_p$ of t, a rule $(u \to v) \in \vec{E}$ and a substitution θ such that $u\theta =_B t|_p$, and $t' = t[v\theta]_p$. We denote by $\to^*_{\vec{E},B}$ the reflexive-transitive closure of $\to_{\vec{E},B}$. The requirements on $\vec{\mathcal{E}}$ allowing us to reduce equational reasoning to rewriting are the following: (i) $vars(v) \subseteq vars(u)$; (ii) *sort-decreasingness*: for each substitution θ we must have $ls(u\theta) \geqslant ls(v\theta)$; (iii) *strict B-coherence*: if $t_1 \to_{\vec{E},B} t_1'$ and $t_1 =_B t_2$ then there exists $t_2 \to_{\vec{E},B} t_2'$ with $t_1' =_B t_2'$; (iv) *confluence* (resp. *ground confluence*) modulo B: for each term t (resp. ground term t) if $t \to^*_{\vec{E},B} v_1$ and $t \to^*_{\vec{E},B} v_2$, then there exist rewrite sequences $v_1 \to^*_{\vec{E},B} w_1$ and $v_2 \to^*_{\vec{E},B} w_2$ such that $w_1 =_B w_2$; (v) *termination*: the relation $\to_{\vec{E},B}$ is well-founded (for $\vec{E}$ conditional, we require *operational termination* [17]). If $\vec{\mathcal{E}}$ satisfies conditions (i)–(v) (resp. the same, but (iv) weakened to ground confluence modulo B), then it is called *convergent* (resp. *ground convergent*). The key point is that then, given a term (resp. ground term) t, all terminating rewrite sequences $t \to^*_{\vec{E},B} w$ end in a term w, denoted $t!_{\vec{\mathcal{E}}}$, that is unique up to B-equality, and its called t's *canonical form*. Three major results then follow for the ground convergent case: (1) for any ground terms t, t' we have $t =_{E \cup B} t'$ iff $t!_{\vec{\mathcal{E}}} =_B t'!_{\vec{\mathcal{E}}}$, (2) the B-equivalence classes of canonical forms are the elements of the *canonical term algebra* $C_{\Sigma/E,B}$, where for each $f : s_1 \ldots s_n \to s$ in Σ and B-equivalence classes of canonical terms $[t_1], \ldots, [t_n]$ with $ls(t_i) \leqslant s_i$ the operation $f_{C_{\Sigma/E,B}}$ is defined by the identity: $f_{C_{\Sigma/E,B}}([t_1] \ldots [t_n]) = [f(t_1 \ldots t_n)!_{\vec{\mathcal{E}}}]$, and (3) we have an isomorphism $T_{\mathcal{E}} \cong C_{\Sigma/E,B}$.

A ground convergent rewrite theory $\vec{\mathcal{E}} = (\Sigma, B, \vec{E})$ is called *sufficiently complete* with respect to a subsignature Ω, whose operators are then called *constructors*, iff for each ground Σ-term t, $t!_{\vec{\mathcal{E}}} \in T_\Omega$. Furthermore, for $\vec{\mathcal{E}} = (\Sigma, B, \vec{E})$ sufficiently complete w.r.t. Ω, a ground convergent rewrite subtheory $(\Omega, B_\Omega, \vec{E}_\Omega) \subseteq (\Sigma, B, \vec{E})$ is called a *constructor subspecification* iff $T_{\mathcal{E}}|_\Omega \cong T_{\Omega/E_\Omega \cup B_\Omega}$. If $E_\Omega = \varnothing$, then Ω is called a signature of *free constructors modulo axioms* B_Ω.

2.3 Equationally Defined Equality Predicates in a Nutshell

Equationally-defined equality predicates [13] achieve a remarkable feat for QF formulas in initial algebras under reasonable executability conditions: they *reduce* first-order logic satisfaction of QF formulas in an initial algebra $T_{\mathcal{E}}$ to *purely equational reasoning*. This is achieved by a theory transformation[3] $\mathcal{E} \mapsto \mathcal{E}^{=}$ such that, provided: $\mathcal{E} = (\Sigma, E \cup B)$, with B any combination of associativity and/or commutativity axioms, is ground convergent and operationally terminating modulo B, and is sufficiently complete with respect to a subsignature Ω of constructors such that $T_{\mathcal{E}}|_{\Omega} \cong T_{\Omega/B_{\Omega}}$, with $B_{\Omega} \subseteq B$, then: (i) $\mathcal{E}^{=}$ is ground convergent operationally terminating and sufficiently complete and protects[4] a new copy of the Booleans, of sort *NewBool*, where true and false are respectively denoted $\top$, $\bot$, conjunction and disjunction are respectively denoted $\wedge$, $\vee$, negation is denoted $\neg$, and a QF Σ-formula φ is a term of sort *NewBool*. Furthermore, for any ground QF Σ-formula φ we have:

$$T_{\mathcal{E}} \models \varphi \;\Leftrightarrow\; \varphi!_{\vec{\mathcal{E}}^{=}} = \top \qquad \textit{and} \qquad T_{\mathcal{E}} \not\models \varphi \;\Leftrightarrow\; \varphi!_{\vec{\mathcal{E}}^{=}} = \bot.$$

That is, we can decide the validity of ground QF Σ-formulas in $T_{\mathcal{E}}$ by reducing them to canonical form with the ground convergent rules in $\vec{\mathcal{E}}^{=}$. In particular, and this is the property that we will systematically exploit in Sect. 3.2, for any QF Σ-formula φ, possibly with variables, we have $T_{\mathcal{E}} \models (\varphi \Leftrightarrow \varphi!_{\vec{\mathcal{E}}^{=}})$, where $\varphi!_{\vec{\mathcal{E}}^{=}}$ may be a much simpler formula, sometimes just $\top$ or $\bot$. Since the $\mathcal{E} \mapsto \mathcal{E}^{=}$ transformation excludes identity axioms from $\mathcal{E}$, one lingering doubt is what to do when $\mathcal{E}$ has also identity axioms U. The answer is that we can use the semantics-preserving theory transformation $\mathcal{E} \mapsto \mathcal{E}_U$ defined in [7], which turns U into rules $\vec{U}$ and preserves ground convergence, to reduce to the case $U = \emptyset$, provided we have $T_{\mathcal{E}_U}|_{\Omega} \cong T_{\Omega/B_{\Omega}}$.

2.4 Order-Sorted Congruence Closure in a Nutshell

Let (Σ, B) be an order-sorted theory where the axioms B are only associativity-commutativity (AC) axioms and Σ is B-preregular. Now let Γ be a set of ground Σ-equations. The question is: is $B \cup \Gamma$-equality *decidable*? (when Σ has just a binary AC operator, this is called the "word problem for commutative semigroups"). The answer, provided in [21], is yes! We can perform a ground Knuth-Bendix completion of Γ into an equivalent (modulo B) set of ground rewrite rules $cc^{\succ}_{B}(\Gamma)$ that is convergent modulo B, so that $t =_{B \cup \Gamma} t'$ iff $t!_{\vec{\mathcal{E}}_{cc^{\succ}_{B}(\Gamma)}} =_{B^{\square}} t'!_{\vec{\mathcal{E}}_{cc^{\succ}_{B}(\Gamma)}}$, where $\vec{\mathcal{E}}_{cc^{\succ}_{B}(\Gamma)}$ is the rewrite theory $\vec{\mathcal{E}}_{cc^{\succ}_{B}(\Gamma)} = (\Sigma^{\square}, B^{\square}, cc^{\succ}_{B}(\Gamma))$, with $\Sigma^{\square}$ the "kind completion" of Σ, which is automatically computed by Maude by adding a so-called "kind" sort $\top_{[s]}$ above each connected component $[s] \in S$ of $(S, \leqslant)$ and lifting each operation $f : s_1 \cdots s_n \to s$ to its kinded version $f : \top_{[s_1]} \cdots \top_{[s_n]} \to \top_{[s]}$, and where $B^{\square}$ is obtained from B by replacing each variable of sort s in B by a corresponding variable of sort $\top_{[s]}$. The symbol $\succ$ in $cc^{\succ}_{B}(\Gamma)$ is a total well-founded order on ground terms modulo B that is used to orient the equations into rules. In all our uses we will take $\succ$ to be an AC RPO based on a total order on function

[3] In [13] the equality predicate is denoted $\_ \sim \_$, instead of the standard notation $\_ = \_$. Here we use $\_ = \_$ throughout. This has the pleasant effect that a QF formula φ is both a formula and a Boolean expression, which of course amounts to mechanizing by equational rewriting the Tarskian semantics of QF formulas in first-order-logic for initial algebras.

[4] That is, there is a subtheory inclusion $\mathcal{B} \subseteq \mathcal{E}$, with $\mathcal{B}$ having signature $\Sigma_{\mathcal{B}}$ and only sort *NewBool* such that: (i) $T_{\mathcal{B}}$ the initial algebra of the Booleans, and (ii) $T_{\mathcal{E}^{=}}|_{\Sigma_{\mathcal{B}}} \cong T_{\mathcal{B}}$.

symbols [27]. The need to extend Σ to $\Sigma^{\square}$ is due to the fact that some terms in $cc_B^{>}(\Gamma)$ may be $\Sigma^{\square}$-terms that fail to be Σ-terms.

Extending the above congruence closure framework from AC axioms B to axioms B that contain any combination of associativity and/or commutativity axioms is quite smooth, but requires a crucial caveat: if some operator $f \in \Sigma$ is only associative, then $cc_B^{>}(\Gamma)$ may be an infinite set that cannot be computed in practice. This is due to the undecidability of the "word problem for semigroups." The Maude implementation of $cc_B^{>}(\Gamma)$ used in Sect. 4 supports this more general combination of axioms B, but when some $f \in \Sigma$ is only associative, it has a bound on the number of iterations of the ground completion cycle. This of course means that, if the completion process has not terminated before the bound is reached, the above decidability result does not hold. However, for our inductive simplification purposes it is enough to obtain a set of ground rules $cc_B^{>}(\Gamma)$ that is guaranteed to be *terminating* modulo B, and that, thanks to the, perhaps partial, completion, "approximates convergence" much better than the original Γ.

2.5 Contextual Rewriting in a Nutshell

Let (Σ, B) be an order-sorted theory where the axioms B contain any combination of associativity and/or commutativity axioms. What can we do to prove that in (Σ, B) an implication of the form $\Gamma \rightarrow u = v$, with variables $vars(\Gamma \rightarrow u = v) = X$ and Γ a conjunction of equations, is valid? We can: (i) add to Σ a set of fresh new constants $\overline{X}$ obtained from X by changing each $x \in X$ into a constant $\overline{x} \in \overline{X}$ of same sort as x, (ii) replace the conjunction Γ by the ground conjunction $\overline{\Gamma}$ obtained by replacing each $x \in X$ in Γ by its corresponding $\overline{x} \in \overline{X}$, and obtaining likewise the ground equation $\overline{u} = \overline{v}$. By the Lemma of Constants and the Deduction Theorem we have [20]:

$$(\Sigma, B) \vdash \Gamma \rightarrow u = v \quad \Leftrightarrow \quad (\Sigma(\overline{X}), \cup B \cup \{\overline{\Gamma}\}) \vdash \overline{u} = \overline{v}$$

where $\Sigma(\overline{X})$ is obtained from Σ by adding the fresh new constants $\overline{X}$, and $\{\overline{\Gamma}\}$ denotes the set of ground equations associated to the conjunction $\overline{\Gamma}$. But, disregarding the difference between $\overline{\Gamma}$ and $\{\overline{\Gamma}\}$, and realizing that $cc_B^{>}(\overline{\Gamma})$ is equivalent modulo $B^{\square}$ to $\overline{\Gamma}$, if we can prove $\overline{u}!_{\vec{\mathcal{E}}_{cc_B^{>}(\overline{\Gamma})}} =_{B^{\square}} \overline{v}!_{\vec{\mathcal{E}}_{cc_B^{>}(\overline{\Gamma})}}$, then we have proved $(\Sigma(\overline{X}), \cup B \cup \{\overline{\Gamma}\}) \vdash \overline{u} = \overline{v}$ and therefore $(\Sigma, B) \vdash \Gamma \rightarrow u = v$, where $\vec{\mathcal{E}}_{cc_B^{>}(\overline{\Gamma})} = (\Sigma(\overline{X})^{\square}, B^{\square}, cc_B^{>}(\overline{\Gamma}))$. Furthermore, if $\vec{\mathcal{E}}_{cc_B^{>}(\overline{\Gamma})}$ is *convergent* (this may only fail to be the case if some $f \in \Sigma$ is associative but not commutative) this is an *equivalence*: $(\Sigma, B) \vdash \Gamma \rightarrow u = v$ iff $\overline{u}!_{\vec{\mathcal{E}}_{cc_B^{>}(\overline{\Gamma})}} =_{B^{\square}} \overline{v}!_{\vec{\mathcal{E}}_{cc_B^{>}(\overline{\Gamma})}}$, and therefore a decision procedure. Rewriting with $\vec{\mathcal{E}}_{cc_B^{>}(\overline{\Gamma})}$ is called *contextual rewriting* [36], since we are using the "context" $\overline{\Gamma}$ suitably transformed into $cc_B^{>}(\overline{\Gamma})$. Many increasingly more powerful variations on this method are possible. For example, we may replace (Σ, B) by $\mathcal{E} = (\Sigma, E \cup B)$, with $\vec{\mathcal{E}}$ ground convergent and then rewrite $\overline{u} = \overline{v}$ not only with $cc_B^{>}(\overline{\Gamma})$ but also with $\vec{\mathcal{E}}$. Likewise, we may consider not just a ground equation $\overline{u} = \overline{v}$, but a ground QF formula $\overline{\varphi}$ and rewrite $\overline{\varphi}$ not only with $cc_B^{>}(\overline{\Gamma})$ but also with $\vec{\mathcal{E}}_U^{=}$.

2.6 Variant Unification and Satisfiability in a Nutshell

Consider an order-sorted equational theory $\mathcal{E} = (\Sigma, E \cup B)$ such that $\vec{\mathcal{E}}$ is ground convergent and suppose we have a constructor subspecification $(\Omega, B_\Omega, \varnothing) \subseteq (\Sigma, B, \vec{E})$, so that $T_{\mathcal{E}}|_\Omega \cong T_{\Omega/B_\Omega}$. Suppose, further, that we have a subtheory $\mathcal{E}_1 \subseteq \mathcal{E}$ such that: (i) $\vec{\mathcal{E}_1}$ is convergent and has the finite variant property[5] (FVP) [9], (ii) $\vec{\mathcal{E}_1}$ can be "sandwiched" between $\vec{\mathcal{E}}$ and the constructors as $(\Omega, B_\Omega, \varnothing) \subseteq (\Sigma_1, B_1, \vec{E_1}) \subseteq (\Sigma, B, \vec{E})$, (iii) B_1 can involve any combination of associativity and/or commutativity and/or identity axioms, except associativity without commutativity; and (iv) $T_{\mathcal{E}}|_{\Sigma_1} \cong T_{\mathcal{E}_1}$, which forces $T_{\mathcal{E}_1}|_\Omega \cong T_{\Omega/B_\Omega}$.

Then, if Γ is a conjunction of Σ_1-equations, since $T_{\mathcal{E}}|_\Omega \cong T_{\Omega/B_\Omega}$, a ground $\mathcal{E}$-unifier ρ of Γ is always $\mathcal{E}$-equivalent to its normal form to $\rho!_{\vec{\mathcal{E}}}$, with $\rho!_{\vec{\mathcal{E}}}(x) = \rho(x)!_{\vec{\mathcal{E}}}$, which is a ground Ω-substitution, that is, a *constructor* ground $\mathcal{E}$-unifier of Γ. But since $\Omega \subseteq \Sigma_1$ and $T_{\mathcal{E}}|_{\Sigma_1} \cong T_{\mathcal{E}_1}$, which implies $C_{\Sigma/E,B}|_{\Sigma_1} \cong C_{\Sigma_1/E_1,B_1}$, this makes $\rho!_{\vec{\mathcal{E}}}$ a *constructor* ground $\mathcal{E}_1$-unifier of Γ. But, under the assumptions for B_Ω, by the results in [22,32] we can compute a complete, finite set $Unif^{\Omega}_{\mathcal{E}_1}(\Gamma)$ of constructor $\mathcal{E}_1$-unifiers of Γ, so that any constructor ground $\mathcal{E}_1$-unifier of Γ, and therefore up to $\mathcal{E}$-equivalence any ground $\mathcal{E}$-unifier of Γ, is an instance of a unifier in $Unif^{\Omega}_{\mathcal{E}_1}(\Gamma)$.

Note, furthermore, that under the assumptions on B_1, (Ω, B_Ω) is an OS-compact theory [22]. Therefore, again by [22], satisfiability (and therefore validity) of any QF Σ_1-formula in $T_{\mathcal{E}_1}$, and by $T_{\mathcal{E}}|_{\Sigma_1} \cong T_{\mathcal{E}_1}$ also in $T_{\mathcal{E}}$, is *decidable*.

3 Superclause-Based Inductive Reasoning

3.1 Superclauses and Inductive Theories

Since predicate symbols can always be transformed into function symbols by adding a fresh new sort *Pred*, we can reduce all of order-sorted first-order logic to just reasoning about equational formulas whose only atoms are equations. Any quantifier-free formula ϕ can therefore be put in conjunctive normal form (CNF) as a conjunction of equational clauses $\phi \equiv \bigwedge_{i \in I} \Gamma_i \to \Delta_i$, where Γ_i, denoted $u_1 = v_1, \cdots, u_n = v_n$, is a *conjunction* of equations $\bigwedge_{1 \leqslant i \leqslant n} u_i = v_i$ and Δ_i, denoted $w_1 = w'_1, \cdots, w_m = w'_m$, is a *disjunction* of equations $\bigvee_{1 \leqslant k \leqslant m} w_k = w'_k$. In our inductive inference system, higher efficiency can be gained by applying the inference rules not to a single clause, but to a conjunction of related clauses sharing the same condition Γ. Thus, we will assume that all clauses $\{\Gamma \to \Delta_l\}_{l \in L}$ with the same condition Γ in the CNF of ϕ have been gathered together into a semantically equivalent formula of the form $\Gamma \to \bigwedge_{l \in L} \Delta_l$, which we call a *superclause*. We will use the notation Λ to abbreviate $\bigwedge_{l \in L} \Delta_l$. Therefore, Λ denotes a conjunction of disjunctions of equations. Superclauses, of course, generalize clauses, which generalize conditional equations, which, in turn, generalize

[5] An $\vec{\mathcal{E}_1}$-*variant* (or $\vec{E}_1, B_1$-*variant*) of a Σ_1-term t is a pair (v, θ), where θ is a substitution in canonical form, i.e., $\theta = \theta!_{\vec{\mathcal{E}_1}}$, and $v =_{B_1} (t\theta)!_{\vec{\mathcal{E}_1}}$. $\vec{\mathcal{E}_1}$ is FVP iff any such t has a finite set of variants $\{(u_1, \alpha_1), \ldots, (u_n, \alpha_n)\}$ which are "most general possible" in the precise sense that for any variant (v, θ) of t there exist i, $1 \leqslant i \leqslant n$, and substitution γ such that: (i) $v =_{B_1} u_i\gamma$, and (ii) $\theta =_{B_1} \alpha_i\gamma$.

equations. Thus, superclauses give us a more general setting for inductive reasoning, because superclauses are more general formulas.

What is an *inductive theory*? In an order-sorted equational logic framework, the simplest possible inductive theories we can consider are order-sorted conditional equational theories $\mathcal{E} = (\Sigma, E \cup B)$, where E is a set of conditional equations (i.e., Horn clauses) of the form $u_1 = v_1 \wedge \cdots \wedge u_n = v_n \rightarrow w = w'$, and B is a set of equational axioms such as associativity and/or commutativity and/or identity. Inductive properties are then properties satisfied in the *initial algebra* $T_{\mathcal{E}}$ associated to $\mathcal{E}$. Note that this is exactly the initial semantics of functional modules in the Maude language. So, as a first approximation, a Maude user can think of an inductive theory as an order-sorted functional module. The problem, however, is that as we perform inductive reasoning, the inductive theory of $\mathcal{E}$, which we denote by $[\mathcal{E}]$ to emphasize its initial semantics, needs to be extended by: (i) extra constants, and; (ii) extra formulas such as: (a) induction hypotheses, (b) lemmas, and (c) hypotheses associated to modus ponens reasoning. Thus, we will consider general inductive theories of the form $[\overline{X}, \mathcal{E}, H]$, where $\overline{X}$ is a fresh set of constants having sorts in Σ and H is a set of $\Sigma(\overline{X})$ clauses[6], corresponding to formulas of types (a)-(c) above. The *models* of an inductive theory $[\overline{X}, \mathcal{E}, H]$ are exactly the $\Sigma^{\square}(\overline{X})$-algebras A such that $A|_{\Sigma^{\square}} \cong T_{\mathcal{E}^{\square}}$ and $A \models H$, where $\mathcal{E}^{\square} = (\Sigma^{\square}, E \cup B^{\square})$ and $\Sigma^{\square}$ is the kind completion of Σ defined in Sect. 2.4. Note that, since $T_{\mathcal{E}^{\square}}|_{\Sigma} = T_{\mathcal{E}}$ [21], the key relation for reasoning is $A|_{\Sigma} \cong T_{\mathcal{E}}$. Such algebras A have a very simple description: they are pairs $(T_{\mathcal{E}^{\square}}, a)$ where $a : \overline{X} \rightarrow T_{\mathcal{E}}$ is the assignment interpreting constants $\overline{X}$. In Maude, such inductive theories $[\overline{X}, \mathcal{E}, H]$ can be defined as *functional theories* which *protect* the functional module $[\mathcal{E}]$, which in our expanded notation is identified with the inductive theory $[\emptyset, \mathcal{E}, \emptyset]$ with neither extra constants nor extra hypotheses, lemmas, or assumptions.

We will furthermore assume that $\vec{\mathcal{E}} = (\Sigma, B, \vec{E})$, with $B = B_0 \uplus U$, is ground convergent, with a total RPO order modulo B_0 $\succ$ making $\vec{\mathcal{E}}_U$ operationally terminating, and that there is a "sandwich" $(\Omega, B_{\Omega}, \emptyset) \subseteq (\Sigma_1, B_1, \vec{E}_1) \subseteq (\Sigma, B, \vec{E})$ with $B_{\Omega} \subseteq B_0$ satisfying all the requirements in Sect. 2.6, including the sufficient completeness of $\vec{\mathcal{E}}$ w.r.t. Ω, the finite variant property of $\mathcal{E}_1$, and the OS-compactness of (Ω, B_{Ω}).

We finally assume that the clauses H in an inductive theory $[\overline{X}, \mathcal{E}, H]$ have been decomposed into the disjoint union $H = H_e \cup H_{ne}$ where H_{e_U} are the *executable* hypotheses, which are conditional equations, that are *orientable* using the same RPO order $\succ$ modulo B_0 that makes $\vec{\mathcal{E}} = (\Sigma, B, \vec{E})$ ground convergent, so $\vec{E}_U \cup \vec{H}_{e_U}$ is ground operationally terminating modulo B_0.

Under the above assumptions, up to isomorphism, and identifying $T_{\mathcal{E}^{\square}}$ with $C_{\Sigma^{\square}/E,B}$, a model (A, a) of an inductive theory $[\overline{X}, \mathcal{E}, H]$ has a very simple description as a pair $(T_{\mathcal{E}^{\square}}, [\overline{\alpha}])$, where $\alpha : X \rightarrow T_{\Omega}$ is a ground constructor substitution, $[\alpha]$ denotes the composition $X \overset{\alpha}{\rightarrow} T_{\Omega} \overset{[\_]}{\rightarrow} T_{\Omega/B_{\Omega}}$, with $[\_]$ the unique Ω-homomorphism mapping each term t to its B_{Ω}-equivalence class $[t]$, and where $[\overline{\alpha}] : \overline{X} \rightarrow T_{\mathcal{E}^{\square}}$ maps each $\overline{x} \in \overline{X}$ to $[\alpha](x)$, where $x \in X$ is the variable with same sort associated to $\overline{x} \in \overline{X}$. The fact that for

[6] Even when, say, an induction hypothesis in H might originally be a superclause $\Gamma \rightarrow \bigwedge_{l \in L} \Delta_l$, for executability reasons we will always decompose it into its corresponding set of clauses $\{\Gamma \rightarrow \Delta_l\}_{l \in L}$.

each clause $\Gamma \to \Delta$ in H we must have $(T_{\mathcal{E}^{\square}}, [\overline{\alpha}]) \models \Gamma \to \Delta$ has also a very simple expression. Let $Y = vars(\Gamma \to \Delta)$. Then, $(T_{\mathcal{E}^{\square}}, [\overline{\alpha}]) \models \Gamma \to \Delta$ exactly means that for each ground constructor substitution $\beta : Y \to T_{\Omega}$ we have $T_{\mathcal{E}^{\square}}, [\alpha] \uplus [\beta] \models (\Gamma \to \Delta)^{\circ}$, where $(\Gamma \to \Delta)^{\circ}$ is obtained from $\Gamma \to \Delta$ by replacing each constant $\overline{x} \in \overline{X}$ appearing in it by its corresponding variable $x \in X$.

3.2 Inductive Inference System

The inductive inference system that we present below transforms *inductive goals* of the form: $[\overline{X}, \mathcal{E}, H] \Vdash \Gamma \to \Lambda$—where $[\overline{X}, \mathcal{E}, H]$ is an inductive theory and $\Gamma \to \Lambda$ is a $\Sigma^{\square}(\overline{X})$-superclause—into sets of goals, with the empty set of goals denoted $\top$, suggesting that the goal from which it was generated has been proved (is a *closed* goal). However, in the special case of goals of the form $[\varnothing, \mathcal{E}, \varnothing] \Vdash \Gamma \to \Lambda$, called *initial goals*, we furthermore require that $\Gamma \to \Lambda$ is a Σ-superclause; and we also allow *existential initial goals* of the form $[\varnothing, \mathcal{E}, \varnothing] \Vdash \exists(\Gamma \to \Lambda)$, with $\exists(\Gamma \to \Lambda)$ the existential closure of a Σ-superclause. A *proof tree* is a tree of goals where at the root we have the original goal that we want to prove and the children of each node in the tree have been obtained by applying an inference rule in the usual bottom-up proof search fashion. Goals in the leaves are called the *pending goals*. A proof tree is *closed* if it has no pending goals, i.e., all the leaves are marked $\top$. Soundness of the inference system means that if the goal $[\overline{X}, \mathcal{E}, H] \Vdash \phi$ is the root of a closed proof tree, then ϕ is valid in the inductive theory $[\overline{X}, \mathcal{E}, H]$, i.e., it is satisfied by all the models $(T_{\mathcal{E}^{\square}}, [\overline{\alpha}])$ of $[\overline{X}, \mathcal{E}, H]$ in the sense explained above.

The inductive inference system presented below consists of two sets of inference rules: (1) *simplification rules*, which are easily amenable to automation, and (2) *standard rules*, which are typically applied under user guidance, although they could also be automated by tactics.

Inductive Simplification Rules
Equality Predicate Simplification (EPS)

$$\frac{[\overline{X}, \mathcal{E}, H] \Vdash (\Gamma \to \Lambda)!_{\vec{\mathcal{E}}^{=}_{\overline{X}_U} \cup \vec{H}_{e_U}}}{[\overline{X}, \mathcal{E}, H] \Vdash \Gamma \to \Lambda}$$

where $B = B_0 \cup U$ is the decomposition of B into unit axioms U and the remaining associative and/or commutative axioms B_0, and $\vec{\mathcal{E}}_{\overline{X}_U} = (\Sigma(\overline{X}), B_0, \vec{E}_U \cup \vec{U})$ is the semantically equivalent rewrite theory obtained from $\vec{\mathcal{E}}_{\overline{X}} = (\Sigma(\overline{X}), B, \vec{E})$ using the $\vec{\mathcal{E}} \mapsto \vec{\mathcal{E}}_U$ transformation specified in [7]. That is, we add the axioms U as rules $\vec{U}$ and transform the equations $\vec{E}$ into $\vec{E}_U$ by mapping each $(l \to r) \in \vec{E}$ to the set of rules $\{l_i \to r\alpha_i \mid 1 \leqslant i \leqslant n\}$, where $\{(l_i, \alpha_i)\}_{1 \leqslant i \leqslant n}$ is the finite set of $\vec{U}, B_0$-variants of l. For example, if $\_,\_$ is an ACU multiset union operator of sort $MSet$ with identity $\varnothing$ and with subsort Elt of elements, a membership rewrite rule $x \in x, S \to true$ modulo ACU with x of sort Elt and S of sort $MSet$ is mapped to the set of rules $\{x \in x \to true, x \in x, S \to true\}$ modulo AC. Since these theories are semantically equivalent, we have $T_{\mathcal{E}_{\overline{X}}} \cong T_{\mathcal{E}_{\overline{X}_U}}$. $\vec{\mathcal{E}}^{=}_{\overline{X}_U}$ is the theory obtained from $\vec{\mathcal{E}}_{\overline{X}_U}$ by adding to it the equationally defined equality predicates defined in [13].

We also assume that in $\mathcal{E}_\Omega = (\Omega, B_\Omega)$, the axioms B_Ω decompose as $B_\Omega = Q_\Omega \uplus U_\Omega$ with U_Ω the unit axioms and Q_Ω the associative and/or commutative axioms such that $T_{\mathcal{E}_\Omega} \cong T_{\Omega/Q_\Omega}$. This can be arranged with relative ease in many cases by subsort overloading, so that the rules in $\vec{U}_\Omega$ only apply to subsort-overloaded operators that are *not* constructors.

For example, consider sorts *Elt* < *NeList* < *List* and Ω with operators *nil* of sort *List* and _;_ : *NeList NeList* → *NeList* and B_Ω associativity of _;_ with identity *nil*, but where _;_ : *List List* → *List*, declared with the same axioms, is in $\Sigma\backslash\Omega$. Then Q_Ω is just the associativity axiom for (_;_). Finally, note that the executable hypotheses H_e in the theory $[\overline{X}, \mathcal{E}, H]$, transformed as rules $\vec{H}_{e_U}$ exactly as for $\vec{E}_U$, are also added to the theory $\vec{\mathcal{E}}^{=}_{\overline{X}_U}$ as extra rewrite rules.

In summary, this inference rule simplifies a superclause $\Gamma \to \Lambda$ with: (i) the rules in $\vec{E}_U$, (ii) the equality predicate rewrite rules, and (iii) the executable hypotheses rewrite rules $\vec{H}_{e_U}$.[7]

Constructor Variant Unification Left (CVUL)

$$\frac{\left\{[\overline{X}, \mathcal{E}, H] \Vdash (\Gamma' \to \Lambda)\gamma\right\}_{\gamma \in Unif^{\Omega}_{\mathcal{E}_1}(\Gamma)}}{[\overline{X}, \mathcal{E}, H] \Vdash \Gamma, \Gamma' \to \Lambda}$$

where Γ is a conjunction of $\mathcal{E}_1$-equalities (therefore not containing any constants in $\overline{X}$), Γ' contains no extra such $\mathcal{E}_1$-equalities, and $Unif^{\Omega}_{\mathcal{E}_1}(\Gamma)$ denotes the set of constructor $\mathcal{E}_1$-unifiers of Γ [22,32].

Constructor Variant Unification Failure Left (CVUFL)

$$\frac{\top}{[\overline{X}, \mathcal{E}, H] \Vdash \Gamma, \Gamma' \to \Lambda}$$

where Γ is a conjunction of $\mathcal{E}_{1\overline{X}}$-equalities, Γ' contains no extra such $\mathcal{E}_{1\overline{X}}$-equalities, Γ° is the conjunction of $\mathcal{E}_1$-equalities obtained by replacing the constants $\overline{x} \in \overline{X}$ by corresponding variables $x \in X$, and $Unif^{\Omega}_{\mathcal{E}_1}(\Gamma^\circ) = \emptyset$.

Constructor Variant Unification Failure Right (CVUFR)

$$\frac{[\overline{X}, \mathcal{E}, H] \Vdash \Gamma \to \Lambda \wedge \Delta}{[\overline{X}, \mathcal{E}, H] \Vdash \Gamma \to \Lambda \wedge (u = v, \Delta)}$$

where $u = v$ is a $\mathcal{E}_{1\overline{X}}$-equality and $Unif^{\Omega}_{\mathcal{E}_1}((u = v)^\circ) = \emptyset$.

[7] Recall that Γ is a conjunction and Λ a conjunction of disjunctions. Therefore, the equality predicate rewrite rules together with $\vec{H}_{e_U}$ may have powerful "cascade effects." For example, if either $\Gamma!_{\vec{\mathcal{E}}^{=}_{\overline{X}_U} \cup \vec{H}_{e_U}} = \bot$ or $\Lambda!_{\vec{\mathcal{E}}^{=}_{\overline{X}_U} \cup \vec{H}_{e_U}} = \top$, then $(\Gamma \to \Lambda)!_{\vec{\mathcal{E}}^{=}_{\overline{X}_U} \cup \vec{H}_{e_U}}$ is a tautology and the goal is proved.

Substitution Left (SUBL)

$$\frac{[\overline{X},\mathcal{E},H] \Vdash (\Gamma \to \Lambda)\{x \mapsto u\}}{[\overline{X},\mathcal{E},H] \Vdash x = u,\ \Gamma \to \Lambda}$$

where: (i) x is a variable of sort s, $ls(u) \leqslant s$, and $x \notin vars(u)$; and (ii) u is not a Σ_1-term, or if so, then Γ contains no other Σ_1-equations. Note that $\_ = \_$ is assumed commutative, so cases $x = u$ and $u = x$ are both covered.

Substitution Right (SUBR)

$$\frac{[\overline{X},\mathcal{E},H] \Vdash \Gamma \to x = u \qquad [\overline{X},\mathcal{E},H] \Vdash (\Gamma \to \Lambda)\{x \mapsto u\}}{[\overline{X},\mathcal{E},H] \Vdash \Gamma \to \Lambda \wedge x = u}$$

with x a variable of sort s, $ls(u) \leqslant s$, and $x \notin vars(u)$. Cases $x = u$ and $u = x$ are both covered.

Clause Subsumption (CS)

$$\frac{[\overline{X},\mathcal{E},H \cup \{\Gamma \to \Delta\}] \Vdash \Gamma\theta, \Gamma' \to \Lambda}{[\overline{X},\mathcal{E},H \cup \{\Gamma \to \Delta\}] \Vdash \Gamma\theta, \Gamma' \to \Lambda \wedge (\Delta\theta, \Delta')}$$

Note that in the application of the **CS** inference rule to a *concrete* superclause we implicitly use ACU-matching in the following two ways: (i) on the *left* we identify the meta-notation $\_,\_$ with $\wedge$ as a single ACU symbol with identity $\top$; and (ii) on the *right* we identify the meta-notation $\_,\_$ with $\vee$ as a single ACU symbol with identity $\bot$. Therefore, desugaring $\_,\_$ on the left as $\wedge$ and on the right as $\vee$, what this inference rule is really doing is matching the given concrete superclause goal against the *pattern* $\Gamma \wedge \Gamma' \to (\Delta \vee \Delta') \wedge \Lambda$, where $\Gamma \to \Delta$ is a *concrete clause* in the given theory's hypotheses, whereas Γ', Δ', and Λ are *meta-variables*. But if this ACU match succeeds, the *concrete superclause* must have the form: $\Gamma\theta \wedge \Gamma'_0 \to \Lambda_0 \wedge (\Delta\theta \vee \Delta'_0)$, where now Γ'_0, Δ'_0, and Λ_0 are all *concrete*. In particular, since $\_ \wedge \_$ is ACU with identity $\top$, we could have $\Lambda_0 \equiv \top$, so that our concrete superclause was actually a *clause*. But then, the bottom-up application of the **CS** rule to this concrete clause will result in the tautology goal $\Gamma\theta \wedge \Gamma'_0 \to \top$, so that in this case the **CS** rule *proves* the given clause goal.

Equation Rewriting (Left and Right) (ERL and ERR)

$$\textbf{(ERL)}\ \frac{[\overline{X},\mathcal{E},H] \Vdash (u' = v')\theta, \Gamma \to \Lambda \qquad [\varnothing,\mathcal{E},\varnothing] \Vdash u = v \Leftrightarrow u' = v'}{[\overline{X},\mathcal{E},H] \Vdash (u = v)\theta, \Gamma \to \Lambda}$$

$$\textbf{(ERR)}\ \frac{[\overline{X},\mathcal{E},H] \Vdash \Gamma \to \Lambda \wedge ((u' = v')\theta, \Delta) \qquad [\varnothing,\mathcal{E},\varnothing] \Vdash u = v \Leftrightarrow u' = v'}{[\overline{X},\mathcal{E},H] \Vdash \Gamma \to \Lambda \wedge ((u = v)\theta, \Delta)}$$

where $vars(u' = v') \subseteq vars(u = v)$. When using the equational equivalence as a rewrite rule $(u = v) \to (u' = v')$ two additional requirements are imposed:

1. The equivalence $(u = v) \Leftrightarrow (u' = v')$ should be verified ahead of time as a separate proof obligation, so that it can be used automatically to simplify many goals without requiring reproving $(u = v) \Leftrightarrow (u' = v')$ each time.
2. The rewrite theory $\vec{\mathcal{E}}_U^{=}$ axiomatizing the equality predicates should remain terminating when the rule $(u = v) \rightarrow (u' = v')$ is added to it.

In fact, what requirements (1)–(2) provide is a general method to fully *automate* rules **(ERL)** and **(ERR)** so that they are *subsumed*[8] by a more powerful version of the **(EPS)** simplification rule in which the equality predicate theory $\vec{\mathcal{E}}_U^{=}$ has been extended with rules of the form $(u = v) \rightarrow (u' = v')$ proved as lemmas.[9] For an example of a useful rewrite rule of this kind, namely, the clearly terminating rewrite rule $x * z' = y * z' \rightarrow x = y$ for the equality predicate of natural numbers, where x, y range over naturals and z' over non-zero naturals, as well as its proof allowing it to be added to the equality predicate theory $\vec{\mathcal{N}}_U^{=}$ of the natural numbers, see Sects. 3.3 and 4.3.

Inductive Congruence Closure (ICC)

$$\frac{[\overline{X}, \mathcal{E}, H] \Vdash \top}{[\overline{X}, \mathcal{E}, H] \Vdash \Gamma \rightarrow \Lambda} \quad \text{if} \quad \begin{array}{c} \overline{\Gamma'} = \bot \\ \text{or } \top \in \overline{\Lambda}!_{\vec{\mathcal{E}}_{\overline{X}_U}^{=} \cup \vec{H}_{e_U} \cup \vec{\overline{\Gamma'}}} \end{array}$$

$$\frac{[\overline{X}, \mathcal{E}, H] \Vdash \Gamma' \rightarrow \Lambda'}{[\overline{X}, \mathcal{E}, H] \Vdash \Gamma \rightarrow \Lambda} \quad \text{if} \quad \begin{array}{c} \overline{\Gamma'} \neq \bot \\ \text{and } \top \notin \overline{\Lambda}!_{\vec{\mathcal{E}}_{\overline{X}_U}^{=} \cup \vec{H}_{e_U} \cup \vec{\overline{\Gamma'}}} \text{ and } \overline{\Lambda}' \in \overline{\Lambda}!_{\vec{\mathcal{E}}_{\overline{X}_U}^{=} \cup \vec{H}_{e_U} \cup \vec{\overline{\Gamma'}}} \end{array}$$

where the notation in the side conditions of the two versions of the **ICC** rule is explained below, and, as explained in Sect. 2.5, the goal $[\overline{X}, \mathcal{E}, H] \Vdash \Gamma \rightarrow \Lambda$ is semantically equivalent to the goal $[\overline{X} \uplus \overline{Y}, \mathcal{E}, H \cup \{\overline{\Gamma}\}] \Vdash \overline{\Lambda}$, where $Y = vars(\Gamma \rightarrow \Lambda)$. Assuming that $\mathcal{E}$ has axioms $B = B_0 \uplus U$ and recalling the definition of the congruence closure $cc^{\succ}_{B_0}(\overline{\Gamma})$ in Sect. 2.4, let us then define

$$\overline{\Gamma'} = \Big(\bigwedge_{(l \rightarrow r) \in cc^{\succ}_{B_0}(\overline{\Gamma})} l = r \Big)!_{\vec{\mathcal{E}}_{\overline{X}_U} \cup \vec{H}_{e_U}}.$$

Assuming $\overline{\Gamma'} \neq \bot$, and disregarding the difference between sets and conjunctions of equations, let us also define

$$\vec{\overline{\Gamma'}} = \text{orient}^{\succ}(\overline{\Gamma'})$$

[8] The net effect is not only that **(EPS)** both subsumes **(ERL)** and **(ERR)** and becomes more powerful: by adding such extra rules to $\vec{\mathcal{E}}_U^{=}$, the **ICC** simplification rule discussed next, which also performs simplification with equality predicates, also becomes more powerful.

[9] More generally, the equality predicate theory $\vec{\mathcal{E}}_U^{=}$ can be extended by adding to it *conditional rewrite rules* that orient inductive theorems of $\mathcal{E}$ or $\mathcal{E}_U^{=}$, are executable, and keep $\vec{\mathcal{E}}_U^{=}$ operationally terminating. For example, if c and c' are *different* constructors whose sorts belong to the same connected component having a top sort, say, s, then the conditional rewrite rule $x = c(x_1, \ldots, x_n) \wedge x = c'(y_1, \ldots, y_m) \rightarrow \bot$, where x has sort s orients an inductively valid lemma, clearly terminates, and can thus be added to $\vec{\mathcal{E}}_U^{=}$. In particular, if p is a Boolean-valued predicate and $u_i =_{B_0} v_i$, $p(u_1, \ldots, u_n) = true \wedge p(v_1, \ldots, v_n) = false$ rewrites to $\bot$.

where for any ground equation $u = v$, we define $\text{orient}^{\succ}(u = v) = \underline{\text{if}}\ u \succ v\ \underline{\text{then}}\ u \to v\ \underline{\text{else}}\ v \to u\ \underline{\text{fi}}$, with $\succ$ an RPO order modulo B_0 total on B_0-equivalence classes of ground terms. Intuitively, what we want is to reduce if possible $\overline{\Lambda}$ to $\top$ using the combined power of $\vec{\mathcal{E}}^{=}_{\overline{X}_U} \cup \vec{H}_{e_U} \cup \vec{\overline{\Gamma}}'$. However, since these combined rules, although operationally terminating by construction, need not be confluent, we will increase our chances of reaching the desired $\top$ result if we explore the entire *set* of *all canonical forms* of $\overline{\Lambda}$ under those rules. By abuse of notation, we denote this set—which can be computed in Maude by means of the `search =>!` command— as $\overline{\Lambda}!_{\vec{\mathcal{E}}^{=}_{\overline{X}_U} \cup \vec{H}_{e_U} \cup \vec{\overline{\Gamma}}'}$. The purpose of the rule transformation $cc^{\succ}_{B_0}(\overline{\Gamma}) \mapsto \vec{\overline{\Gamma}}'$ is to further increase the chances of success in simplifying $\overline{\Lambda}$, as compared to just using $cc^{\succ}_{B_0}(\overline{\Gamma})$. In the context of the other rules, $\vec{\mathcal{E}}^{=}_{\overline{X}_U} \cup \vec{H}_{e_U}$, these chances can be further increased in two ways: (i) the lefthand side l of a rule $(l \to r) \in cc^{\succ}_{B_0}(\overline{\Gamma})$ may be reducible by $\vec{\mathcal{E}}^{=}_{\overline{X}_U} \cup \vec{H}_{e_U}$, thus preventing its application, whereas this can never happen for rules in $\vec{\overline{\Gamma}}'$; (ii) suppose, as an example, a rule in $cc^{\succ}_{B_0}(\overline{\Gamma})$ of the form $s(u) \to s(v)$, where s is the successor constructor for natural numbers, and assume for simplicity that u, v are irreducible by $\vec{\mathcal{E}}^{=}_{\overline{X}_U} \cup \vec{H}_{e_U}$; then, thanks to its reduction by $\vec{\mathcal{E}}^{=}_{\overline{X}_U}$, in $\vec{\overline{\Gamma}}'$ this rule will become the rule $u \to v$, which is much more widely applicable than the original rule $s(u) \to s(v)$.

In summary, the first version of the **ICC** rule can fully prove a goal $\Gamma \to \Lambda$ if either: (i) $\overline{\Gamma}$ can be proved unsatisfiable by simplifying to $\bot$ the conjunction associated to its congruence closure using $\vec{\mathcal{E}}_{\overline{X}_U} \cup \vec{H}_{e_U}$, or (ii) we can simplify $\overline{\Lambda}$ to $\top$ using the combined power of $\vec{\mathcal{E}}^{=}_{\overline{X}_U} \cup \vec{H}_{e_U} \cup \vec{\overline{\Gamma}}'$. However, if a full proof by either (i) or (ii) cannot be obtained, we can still use the second version of the **ICC** rule to derive a hopefully simpler goal $\Gamma' \to \Lambda'$ (where the choice of $\overline{\Lambda}' \in \overline{\Lambda}!_{\vec{\mathcal{E}}^{=}_{\overline{X}_U} \cup \vec{H}_{e_U} \cup \vec{\overline{\Gamma}}'}$ is arbitrary but could be optimized according to some criteria) as partial progress in the proof effort short of actually proving the goal.

Variant Satisfiability (VARSAT)

$$\frac{\top}{[\overline{X}, \mathcal{E}, H] \Vdash \Gamma \to \Lambda}$$

if $\Gamma \to \Lambda$ is an $\mathcal{E}_1$-formula and $\neg(\Gamma^\circ \to \Lambda^\circ)$ is unsatisfiable in $T_{\mathcal{E}_1}$, where $\Gamma^\circ \to \Lambda^\circ$ is obtained from $\Gamma \to \Lambda$ by replacing constants in $\overline{X}$ by corresponding variables in X.

Standard Inductive Rules
Cover Set Induction (CSI)

$$\frac{\{[\overline{X} \uplus \overline{Y}_i, \mathcal{E}, H \uplus \{(\Gamma \to \Delta_j)\{z \to \overline{y}\}\}^{j \in J}_{\overline{y} \in \overline{Y}_{i \preccurlyeq s}}] \Vdash (\Gamma \to \bigwedge_{j \in J} \Delta_j)\{z \mapsto \overline{u}_i\}\}_{1 \leqslant i \leqslant n}}{[\overline{X}, \mathcal{E}, H] \Vdash \Gamma \to \bigwedge_{j \in J} \Delta_j}$$

where $z \in vars(\Gamma \to \bigwedge_{j\in J}\Delta_j)$ has sort s, $\{u_1 \cdots u_n\}$ is a *cover set*[10] for s with fresh variables $Y_i = vars(u_i)$ for $1 \leqslant i \leqslant n$, $Y_{i\leqslant s} = \{y \in Y_i \mid sort(y) \leqslant s\}$, $\overline{Y_i}$ are fresh constants of the same sorts for each Y_i, and $\overline{u}_i$ is the instantiation of u_i by such fresh constants.

Existential ($\exists$)

$$\frac{[\varnothing, \mathcal{E}, \varnothing] \Vdash (\Gamma \to \Lambda)\theta}{[\varnothing, \mathcal{E}, \varnothing] \Vdash (\exists X)(\Gamma \to \Lambda)}$$

where $vars(\Gamma \to \Lambda) = X$ and θ is a substitution. Note that the ($\exists$) rule only applies when the inductive theory is $[\varnothing, \mathcal{E}, \varnothing]$, that is, at the beginning of the inductive reasoning process, and that θ must be provided by the user as a witness.

Lemma Enrichment (LE)

$$\frac{[\varnothing, \mathcal{E}, \varnothing] \Vdash \Gamma' \to \bigwedge_{j\in J}\Delta'_j \qquad [\overline{X}, \mathcal{E}, H \uplus \{\Gamma' \to \Delta'_j\}_{j\in J}] \Vdash \Gamma \to \Lambda}{[\overline{X}, \mathcal{E}, H] \Vdash \Gamma \to \Lambda}$$

Split (SP)

$$\frac{\{[\overline{X}, \mathcal{E}, H] \Vdash (u_i = v_i)\theta, \Gamma \to \Lambda\}_{1\leqslant i\leqslant n} \qquad [\varnothing, \mathcal{E}, \varnothing] \Vdash u_1 = v_1 \vee \cdots \vee u_n = v_n}{[\overline{X}, \mathcal{E}, H] \Vdash \Gamma \to \Lambda}$$

where $vars((u_1 = v_1 \vee \cdots \vee u_n = v_n)\theta) \subseteq vars(\Gamma \to \Lambda)$.

Case (CAS)

$$\frac{\left\{[\overline{X}, \mathcal{E}, H] \Vdash (\Gamma \to \Lambda)\{z \mapsto u_i\}\right\}_{1\leqslant i\leqslant n}}{[\overline{X}, \mathcal{E}, H] \Vdash \Gamma \to \Lambda}$$

where $z \in vars(\Gamma \to \Lambda)$ has sort s and $\{u_1, \cdots, u_n\}$ is a cover set for sort s with the u_i for $1 \leqslant i \leqslant n$ having fresh variables.

Variable Abstraction (VA)

$$\frac{[\overline{X}, \mathcal{E}, H] \Vdash u = w,\ x_1 = v_1, \cdots,\ x_n = v_n,\ \Gamma \to \Lambda}{[\overline{X}, \mathcal{E}, H] \Vdash u = v,\ \Gamma \to \Lambda}$$

where u and w are Σ_1-terms but v is not and $x_1, \ldots, x_n$ are fresh variables whose sorts are respectively the least sorts of the $v_1, \ldots, v_n$, which are subterms of v such that their top symbols are not in Σ_1, and $v =_B w\{x_1 \mapsto v_1, \ldots, x_n \mapsto v_n\}$.

The main property about the above inference system is the following Soudness Theorem, whose proof can be found in the technical report [23]:

Theorem 1 (Soundness Theorem). *If a closed proof tree can be built from a goal of the form* $[\overline{X}, \mathcal{E}, H] \Vdash \Gamma \to \Lambda$, *then* $[\overline{X}, \mathcal{E}, H] \models \Gamma \to \Lambda$.

Although the Soundness Theorem is stated in full generality, in practice, of course, its main application will be to initial goals of the form $[\varnothing, \mathcal{E}, \varnothing] \Vdash \Gamma \to \Lambda$.

---

[10] A *cover set* for s is a finte set of Ω-terms such that $ls(u_i) \leqslant s$, $1 \leqslant i \leqslant n$, and generating all constructor ground terms of sort s modulo B_Ω, i.e., $T_{\Omega/B_\Omega,s} = \bigcup_{1\leqslant i\leqslant n}\{[u_i\rho] \mid \rho \in [Y_i \to T_\Omega]\}$.

3.3 Inductive Inference System Example

Suppose we wish to prove the cancellation law for natural number multiplication

$$x * z' = y * z' \Rightarrow x = y$$

where z' is a non-zero natural number while x and y are natural numbers. We specify natural number addition and multiplication as associative-commutative operators in theory $\mathcal{N}$ having a subsort relation $NzNat < Nat$ of non-zero numbers as subset of all naturals (see Appendix A for a detailed specification of $\mathcal{N}$). Of course, since the proof of the reverse implication $x = y \Rightarrow x * z' = y * z'$ follows trivially by simplification with the **(ICC)** rule, what we are really proving is the equivalence $x*z' = y*z' \Leftrightarrow x = y$. Therefore, as discussed when introducing the **(ERL)** and **(ERR)** rules, once the above cancellation rule has been proved, the rewrite rule $x * z' = y * z' \rightarrow x = y$ can be added to the equality predicate theory $\vec{\mathcal{N}}^{=}$ ($\mathcal{N}$ has no U axioms, i.e., $\vec{\mathcal{N}}^{=}_{U} = \vec{\mathcal{N}}^{=}$) to obtain a more powerful version of the **(EPS)** simplification rule.
We begin with the goal:

$$G : [\emptyset, \mathcal{N}, \emptyset] \Vdash x * z' = y * z' \rightarrow x = y$$

After applying the rule **CSI** to the variable x with the cover set $\{0, 1+x_1\}$ and simplifying by **EPS** we obtain:

$$G_1 : [\emptyset, \mathcal{N}, \emptyset] \Vdash 0 = y * z' \rightarrow 0 = y$$
$$G_2 : [\{\overline{x}_1\}, \mathcal{N}, \overline{x}_1 * z' = y * z' \rightarrow \overline{x}_1 = y] \Vdash z' + (\overline{x}_1 * z') = y * z' \rightarrow \overline{x}_1 + 1 = y$$

We first prove G_1 by: (a) applying the **CAS** rule to variable y with the cover set $\{0, y'\}$, where y' has the non-zero natural sort *NzNat*; and (b) applying the **EPS** rule to obtain:

$$G_{1.1} : [\emptyset, \mathcal{N}, \emptyset] \Vdash 0 = 0 \rightarrow 0 = 0$$
$$G_{1.2} : [\emptyset, \mathcal{N}, \emptyset] \Vdash 0 = y' * z' \rightarrow 0 = y'$$

To solve $G_{1.1}$, apply **EPS** to obtain $\top$. To solve $G_{1.2}$, apply **VA** to the term $y' * z'$ which has least sort *NzNat* to obtain:

$$G_{1.2.1} : [\emptyset, \mathcal{N}, \emptyset] \Vdash 0 = z'', z'' = y' * z' \rightarrow 0 = y'$$

where z'' also has sort *NzNat*. Finally apply **CVUL** to obtain $\top$, since the equation $0 = z''$ has no unifiers. This finishes the proof of G_1. We now prove G_2 by: (a) applying the **CAS** rule to variable y with cover set $\{0, y_1 + 1\}$; and (b) applying the **EPS** rule to obtain:

$$G_{2.1} : [\{\overline{x}_1\}, \mathcal{N}, \overline{x}_1 * z' = y * z' \rightarrow \overline{x}_1 = y] \Vdash z' + (\overline{x}_1 * z') = 0 \rightarrow \overline{x}_1 + 1 = 0$$

$$G_{2.2} : [\{\overline{x}_1\}, \mathcal{N}, \overline{x}_1 * z' = y * z' \rightarrow \overline{x}_1 = y] \Vdash \begin{array}{l} z' + (\overline{x}_1 * z') = (y_1 * z') + z' \\ \rightarrow \overline{x}_1 + 1 = y_1 + 1 \end{array}$$

To solve $G_{2.1}$, apply **VA** to the term $z' + (\overline{x}_1 * z')$ which has least sort *NzNat* to obtain:

$$G_{2.1.1} : [\{\overline{x}_1\}, \mathcal{N}, \overline{x}_1 * z' = y * z' \to \overline{x}_1 = y] \Vdash \begin{array}{r} z' + (\overline{x}_1 * z') = z'', z'' = 0 \\ \to \overline{x}_1 + 1 = 0 \end{array}$$

where z'' also has sort *NzNat*. As in $G_{1.2.1}$, apply **CVUL** to obtain $\top$. Finally, to solve $G_{2.2}$, we apply **ERL** and **ERR** with the equivalence $z_1 + z_2 = z_1 + z_3 \Leftrightarrow z_2 = z_3$ (which can be proved by variant satisfiability) to obtain:

$$G_{2.2.1} : [\{\overline{x}_1\}, \mathcal{N}, \overline{x}_1 * z' = y * z' \to \overline{x}_1 = y] \Vdash \overline{x}_1 * z' = y_1 * z' \to \overline{x}_1 = y_1$$

But note that a proof of $G_{2.2.1}$ immediately follows by **CS**. In summary, we completed the proof after 14 applications of our inference rules.

4 Inference System Mechanization and Examples

Given the extensive nature of the inductive inference system we introduced (with 17 rules), a natural question to ask is: do any effective strategies exist? In fact, a well-chosen answer to this question can be the key differentiator between a tedious proof assistant requiring the user to apply one rule at a time, and an efficient proof assistant automating large parts of a proof. Automating away the rote and tedious parts of mechanical proof allows the user to reason at a higher level of abstraction. As mentioned before, there is a core subset of proof rules, the 11 so-called simplification rules, that can be automated, leaving only the 6 standard rules to be applied by the user. In this section we present: (a) an inductive simplification strategy *ISS* that applies 9 of the 11 simplification rules in combination until a fixpoint is reached (**VARSAT** and **CVUFL** are not included; they will be added in an ISS^+ extension); (b) an overview of how our inductive simplification strategy has been implemented in Maude; (c) a simple example illustrating how the inductive simplification strategy operates in practice; and (d) our encouraging experience using a simplified version of this inductive simplification strategy to automatically prove all VCs generated by the proof of security of the IBOS browser.

4.1 Inductive Simplification Strategy

The strategy we present takes as input a set of goals Φ and outputs a set of goals Φ'. Let $\mathcal{G}$ denote the set of all goals over some ground convergent $\vec{\mathcal{E}}$. Then each individual inductive simplification inference rule R is a function $R \in [\mathcal{G} \to \mathcal{P}(\mathcal{G}) \uplus \{\bot\}]$. That is, each R is a function that takes a single goal as input and either fails to evaluate because the side-condition does not provably hold or else outputs: (i) a non-empty set of goals; (ii) an empty set of goals (equivalently $\top$), that is, the rule closes a branch of the proof tree; or (iii) a counterexample (equivalently $\bot$), that is, the proof immediately terminates in failure. For simplicity, we treat rule side-condition failure (or the rule not matching) as identity (i.e., the original goal is returned unchanged).

Then, for each inference rule R, we can consider the set-lifting of that rule R_{set}, i.e., $R_{\text{set}} \in [\mathcal{P}(\mathcal{G} \uplus \{\bot\}) \to \mathcal{P}(\mathcal{G} \uplus \{\bot\})]$ which is defined by $R_{\text{set}}(\Phi) = \bigcup_{\phi \in \Phi} R(\phi)$. For simplicity of notation, let semicolon (;) denote in-order function composition. For an order-continuous function $f \in [A \to A]$, let $f!$ denote the recursive fixpoint construction of f, i.e.,

$$f!(a) = \begin{cases} a & \text{if } a = f(a) \\ f!(f(a)) & \text{otherwise} \end{cases}$$

Then we define our inductive simplification strategy (*ISS*) by means of a variant simplification strategy (*VSS*). We have:

$$VSS = (\textbf{EPS}_{\text{set}} \,;\, \textbf{ERL}_{\text{set}}! \,;\, \textbf{ERR}_{\text{set}}! \,;\, \textbf{SUBL}_{\text{set}}! \,;\, \textbf{SUBR}_{\text{set}}! \,;\, \textbf{CVUL}_{\text{set}} \,;\, \textbf{CVUR}_{\text{set}})!$$
$$ISS = (\textbf{CS}_{\text{set}} \,;\, VSS \,;\, \textbf{ICC}_{\text{set}} \,;\, \textbf{CS}_{\text{set}})!$$

The inner strategy simplifies a set of goals by equality predicate simplification, substitution elimination, and variant unification to the limit. The outer strategy takes a set of variant-simplified goals and applies the inductive congruence closure rule. The reason for this stratification is simple: the inductive congruence closure rule (**ICC**) is computationally expensive because the congruence closure algorithm may require many iterations before convergence. By simplifying the input goals as much as possible before applying congruence closure, we increase the speed of convergence.

4.2 Inductive Simplification Strategy Mechanization

The strategy presented above has been mechanized in Maude. Recall that our inference system assumes a ground convergent theory $\vec{\mathcal{E}}$ with $B = B_0 \uplus U$ and such that $\vec{\mathcal{E}}_U$ is operationally terminating via a recursive path ordering (RPO) ($\succ$) modulo B_0 that is total on ground terms and that has constructor and finite variant subtheories respectively $(\Omega, B_\Omega, \emptyset) \subseteq (\Sigma_1, B_1, \vec{E}_1) \subseteq (\Sigma, B, \vec{E})$. Since rewriting logic is reflective, for any rewriting logic derivation $\mathcal{R} \vdash t \to t'$, there is a universal rewrite theory that can internalize the theory $\mathcal{R}$ as well as terms t, t' and the derivation $\mathcal{U} \vdash \overline{\mathcal{R} \vdash t \to t'}$. In Maude, key functionality of this universal theory is defined by the prelude module META-LEVEL [3].

Thus, our inductive simplification strategy is defined by a Maude rewrite theory $ISS_{\mathcal{R}}$ that protects META-LEVEL and takes as input: (i) an inductive theory $[\overline{X}, \mathcal{E}, H]$, specified as a functional theory in Maude (or a functional module if $\overline{X} = \emptyset$ and $H = \emptyset$), where each symbol $f \in \Sigma$ is annotated with a natural number that denotes its order in the RPO (the numbers for the fresh constants in $\overline{X}$ are added automatically), and where the functional submodule $\mathcal{E}$ has specified subtheories $(\Omega, B_\Omega, \emptyset)$ and $(\Sigma_1, B_1, \vec{E}_1)$; (ii) a quantifier-free $\Sigma(\overline{X})$-superclause ϕ to be proved.

The equality predicate simplification [13], B-recursive path ordering [12,26], variant unification [22,32], and order-sorted congruence closure modulo B [21] algorithms have all been implemented in Maude. This work combines all of those existing algorithms together into a powerful inductive simplification strategy.

4.3 Inductive Simplification Strategy Example and IBOS VC Proofs

To conclude this section, we first recall the multiplication cancellation law proof from Sect. 3.3. To recap, we wanted to show:

$$x * z' = y * z' \Rightarrow x = y$$

in the theory $\mathcal{N}$ of naturals mentioned in Sect. 3.3, where z' is a non-zero natural number and x and y are natural numbers. For our semi-automated proof, we first prove the equivalence $z_1 + z_2 = z_1 + z_3 \Leftrightarrow z_2 = z_3$ by variant satisfiability and make this equivalence available to the tool as a simplification lemma. The proof proceeds as before *except* that we apply our strategy *ISS* at the beginning of the proof *and* after each inference step. Thus, begin with goal:

$$G : [\varnothing, \mathcal{N}, \varnothing] \Vdash x * z' = y * z' \rightarrow x = y$$

Then apply **CSI** on variable x with cover set $\{0, x_1 + 1\}$ to obtain:

$$G_1 : [\varnothing, \mathcal{N}, \varnothing] \Vdash 0 = y * z' \rightarrow 0 = y$$

$$G_2 : [\{\overline{x}_1\}, \mathcal{N}, \overline{x}_1 * z' = y * z' \rightarrow \overline{x}_1 = y] \Vdash z' + (\overline{x}_1 * z') = y * z' \rightarrow \overline{x}_1 + 1 = y$$

To prove G_1, we apply the **CAS** rule to variable y with the cover set $\{0, y'\}$ where y' has sort *NzNat*. Since the $\{y \mapsto 0\}$ case is blown away by *ISS* automatically, we obtain the following goal:

$$G_{1.1} : [\varnothing, \mathcal{N}, \varnothing] \Vdash 0 = y' * z' \rightarrow 0 = y'$$

To solve $G_{1.1}$, apply **VA** to the term $y' * z'$ which has least sort *NzNat*; the goal is then immediately closed by *ISS*. This finishes the proof of G_1. We now prove G_2 by applying the **CAS** rule to variable y with cover set $\{0, y_1 + 1\}$. Since the $y \mapsto y_1 + 1$ case is immediately closed by *ISS*, we obtain the following goal:

$$G_{2.1} : [\{\overline{x}_1\}, \mathcal{N}, \overline{x}_1 * z' = y * z' \rightarrow \overline{x}_1 = y] \Vdash z' + (\overline{x}_1 * z') = 0 \rightarrow \overline{x}_1 + 1 = 0$$

To solve $G_{2.1}$, apply **VA** to the term $z' + (\overline{x}_1 * z')$ which has least sort *NzNat*; the goal is then immediately closed by *ISS*. In summary, using the *ISS* strategy, we need only 5 inference rule applications versus 14 applications in the original proof. The above proof was carried out using our prototype *ISS* tool, with the not yet implemented standard inference rules applied by hand.

Inductive Simplification Strategy: Automatic Proof of IBOS VCs. The Illinois Browser Operating System (IBOS) [34,35] is an advanced web browser and operating system built on top of the L4Ka::Pistachio secure microkernel that was developed to push the limits of secure web browser design. In [28,29] a Maude specification of the IBOS system was developed for which the same-origin policy (SOP) and address bar correctness (ABC) properties were verified using a hand-written state abstraction proof plus bounded model checking. In [25], a first attempt at a fully automated deductive verification of SOP and ABC for IBOS was attempted, but had to be abandoned because thousands of inductive verification conditions (VCs) were generated. In [30,31], this deductive verification project was finally completed. Amazingly, using a simplified version of the above inductive simplification strategy as its automatic VC prover backend, the constructor-based reachability logic theorem prover [31,33] was able to verify all 7 claims corresponding to SOP and ABC for IBOS which in total required approximately 2K lines of Maude code for the system and property specifications and which generated thousands of goals to be solved by the backend VC prover.

5 Related Work and Conclusions

As already mentioned, this work combines automated, e.g., [1,5] and explicit induction, e.g., [4,10,14,15] equational inductive theorem proving in a novel way. Some of our automatable techniques have been used in some fashion in earlier work, but others have not. For example, congruence closure is used in many provers, but congruence closure modulo is considerably less used, and order-sorted congruence closure modulo is here used for the first time. Contextual rewriting goes back to the Boyer-More prover [2], later extended to ACL2 [16], and has also been used, for example, in RRL [5]; and clause subsumption is used in most automated theorem provers, including inductive ones. Equational simplification is used by everybody, but to the best of our knowledge simplification with equationally-defined equality predicates *modulo* axioms B_0 was only previously used in [24], although in the much easier free case equality predicates have been used to specify "consistency" properties of data types in, e.g., [5]. To the best of our knowledge, neither constructor variant unification nor variant satisfiability have been used in other general-purpose provers, although variant unification is used in various cryptographic protocol verification tools, e.g., [8,18]. Combining *all* these techniques appears to be new.

In summary, our combination of automated and explicit-induction theorem proving seems to be new and offers the possibility of an inference subsystem that can be automated as a practical oracle for inductive validity of VCs generated by other tools, and that allows a user to focus on applying just 6 inference rules. For the moment, only the *ISS* strategy has been implemented in Maude. Both the extension of *ISS* to ISS^+, and the implementation of an inductive theorem prover supporting the 17 inference rules are unproblematic. They are left for future work.

Acknowledgements. We cordially thank the referees for their very helpful suggestions to improve the paper. Work partially supported by NRL under contract N00173-17-1-G002.

A The Natural Numbers Theory $\mathcal{N}$

```
fmod NATURAL is
  sorts Zero NzNat Nat .
  subsorts Zero NzNat < Nat .

  op 0 : -> Zero   [ctor metadata "1"] .
  op 1 : -> NzNat [ctor metadata "2"] .
  op _+_ : NzNat NzNat -> NzNat [ctor assoc comm metadata "3"] .
  op _+_ : NzNat   Nat -> NzNat [      ditto      metadata "3"] .
  op _+_ : Nat   NzNat -> NzNat [      ditto      metadata "3"] .
  op _+_ : Nat   Nat   -> Nat   [      ditto      metadata "3"] .
  op _*_ : NzNat NzNat -> NzNat [      assoc comm metadata "4"] .
  op _*_ : Nat   Nat   -> Nat   [      ditto      metadata "4"] .

  vars X Y Z : Nat .

  eq X +  0      =  X .
  eq X *  0      =  0 .
  eq X *  1      =  X .
  eq X * (Y + Z) = (X * Y) + (X * Z) .
endfm
```

Fig. 1. Natural number theory specification.

Note that we have a "sandwich" of theories $\mathcal{N}_\Omega \subseteq \mathcal{N}_1 \subseteq \mathcal{N}$, where $\mathcal{N}_\Omega$ is given by the operators marked as `ctor` and the associativity-commutativity of $+$, and $\mathcal{N}_1$ is the FVP theory extending $\mathcal{N}_\Omega$ with the other symbols for $+$ and the equation for `0` as identity element for $+$ (Fig. 1).

References

1. Bouhoula, A., Rusinowitch, M.: SPIKE: a system for automatic inductive proofs. In: Alagar, V.S., Nivat, M. (eds.) AMAST 1995. LNCS, vol. 936, pp. 576–577. Springer, Heidelberg (1995). https://doi.org/10.1007/3-540-60043-4_79
2. Boyer, R., Moore, J.: A Computational Logic. Academic Press, San Diego (1980)
3. Clavel, M., et al.: All About Maude - A High-Performance Logical Framework. LNCS, vol. 4350. Springer, Heidelberg (2007). https://doi.org/10.1007/978-3-540-71999-1
4. Clavel, M., Palomino, M.: The ITP tool's manual, universidad Complutense, Madrid, April 2005. http://maude.sip.ucm.es/itp/
5. Comon, H., Nieuwenhuis, R.: Induction = i - axiomatization + first-order consistency. Inf. Comput. **159**(1–2), 151–186 (2000)
6. Dershowitz, N., Jouannaud, J.P.: Rewrite systems. In: van Leeuwen, J. (ed.) Handbook of Theoretical Computer Science, vol. B, pp. 243–320. North-Holland (1990)
7. Durán, F., Lucas, S., Meseguer, J.: Termination modulo combinations of equational theories. In: Ghilardi, S., Sebastiani, R. (eds.) FroCoS 2009. LNCS (LNAI), vol. 5749, pp. 246–262. Springer, Heidelberg (2009). https://doi.org/10.1007/978-3-642-04222-5_15

8. Escobar, S., Meadows, C., Meseguer, J.: Maude-NPA: cryptographic protocol analysis modulo equational properties. In: Aldini, A., Barthe, G., Gorrieri, R. (eds.) FOSAD 2007-2009. LNCS, vol. 5705, pp. 1–50. Springer, Heidelberg (2009). https://doi.org/10.1007/978-3-642-03829-7_1
9. Escobar, S., Sasse, R., Meseguer, J.: Folding variant narrowing and optimal variant termination. J. Algebraic Logic Programm. **81**, 898–928 (2012)
10. Găină, D., Lucanu, D., Ogata, K., Futatsugi, K.: On automation of OTS/CafeOBJ method. In: Iida, S., Meseguer, J., Ogata, K. (eds.) Specification, Algebra, and Software. LNCS, vol. 8373, pp. 578–602. Springer, Heidelberg (2014). https://doi.org/10.1007/978-3-642-54624-2_29
11. Goguen, J., Meseguer, J.: Order-sorted algebra I: equational deduction for multiple inheritance, overloading, exceptions and partial operations. Theoret. Comput. Sci. **105**, 217–273 (1992)
12. Gutiérrez, R., Meseguer, J., Skeirik, S.: The Maude termination assistant. In: Pre-Proceedings of WRLA 2018
13. Gutiérrez, R., Meseguer, J., Rocha, C.: Order-sorted equality enrichments modulo axioms. Sci. Comput. Program. **99**, 235–261 (2015)
14. Hendrix, J.D.: Decision procedures for equationally based reasoning. Ph.D. thesis, University of Illinois at Urbana-Champaign (2008). `http://hdl.handle.net/2142/10967`
15. Kapur, D., Zhang, H.: An overview of rewrite rule laboratory (RRL). In: Dershowitz, N. (ed.) RTA 1989. LNCS, vol. 355, pp. 559–563. Springer, Heidelberg (1989). https://doi.org/10.1007/3-540-51081-8_138
16. Kaufmann, M., Manolios, P., Moore, J.: Computer-Aided Reasoning: An Approach. Kluwer, Dordrecht (2000)
17. Lucas, S., Meseguer, J.: Normal forms and normal theories in conditional rewriting. J. Log. Algebr. Meth. Program. **85**(1), 67–97 (2016)
18. Meier, S., Schmidt, B., Cremers, C., Basin, D.: The TAMARIN prover for the symbolic analysis of security protocols. In: Sharygina, N., Veith, H. (eds.) CAV 2013. LNCS, vol. 8044, pp. 696–701. Springer, Heidelberg (2013). https://doi.org/10.1007/978-3-642-39799-8_48
19. Meseguer, J.: Conditional rewriting logic as a unified model of concurrency. Theoret. Comput. Sci. **96**(1), 73–155 (1992)
20. Meseguer, J.: Membership algebra as a logical framework for equational specification. In: Presicce, F.P. (ed.) WADT 1997. LNCS, vol. 1376, pp. 18–61. Springer, Heidelberg (1998). https://doi.org/10.1007/3-540-64299-4_26
21. Meseguer, J.: Order-sorted rewriting and congruence closure. In: Jacobs, B., Löding, C. (eds.) FoSSaCS 2016. LNCS, vol. 9634, pp. 493–509. Springer, Heidelberg (2016). https://doi.org/10.1007/978-3-662-49630-5_29
22. Meseguer, J.: Variant-based satisfiability in initial algebras. Sci. Comput. Program. **154**, 3–41 (2018)
23. Meseguer, J., Skeirik, S.: Inductive reasoning with equality predicates, contextual rewriting and variant-based simplification. Technical report, University of Illinois at Urbana-Champaign, Computer Science Department, July 2020. http://hdl.handle.net/2142/107774
24. Rocha, C., Meseguer, J.: Proving safety properties of rewrite theories. In: Corradini, A., Klin, B., Cîrstea, C. (eds.) CALCO 2011. LNCS, vol. 6859, pp. 314–328. Springer, Heidelberg (2011). https://doi.org/10.1007/978-3-642-22944-2_22
25. Rocha, C.: Symbolic reachability analysis for rewrite theories. Ph.D. thesis, University of Illinois at Urbana-Champaign (2012)
26. Rubio, A.: Automated deduction with constrained clauses. Ph.D. thesis, Universitat Politècnica de Catalunya (1994)

27. Rubio, A.: A fully syntactic AC-RPO. Inf. Comput. **178**(2), 515–533 (2002)
28. Sasse, R.: Security models in rewriting logic for cryptographic protocols and browsers. Ph.D. thesis, University of Illinois at Urbana-Champaign (2012). http://hdl.handle.net/2142/34373
29. Sasse, R., King, S.T., Meseguer, J., Tang, S.: IBOS: a correct-by-construction modular browser. In: Păsăreanu, C.S., Salaün, G. (eds.) FACS 2012. LNCS, vol. 7684, pp. 224–241. Springer, Heidelberg (2013). https://doi.org/10.1007/978-3-642-35861-6_14
30. Skeirik, S., Meseguer, J., Rocha, C.: Verification of the IBOS browser security properties in reachability logic. In: Escobar, S., Martí-Oliet, N. (eds.) WRLA 2020, LNCS 12328, pp. 176–196 (2020)
31. Skeirik, S.: Rewriting-based symbolic methods for distributed system verification. Ph.D. thesis, University of Illinois at Urbana-Champaign (2019)
32. Skeirik, S., Meseguer, J.: Metalevel algorithms for variant satisfiability. J. Log. Algebr. Meth. Program. **96**, 81–110 (2018)
33. Skeirik, S., Stefanescu, A., Meseguer, J.: A constructor-based reachability logic for rewrite theories. Fundam. Inform. **173**(4), 315–382 (2020)
34. Tang, S.: Towards secure web browsing. Ph.D. thesis, University of Illinois at Urbana-Champaign (2011), 25 May 2011. http://hdl.handle.net/2142/24307
35. Tang, S., Mai, H., King, S.T.: Trust and protection in the Illinois browser operating system. In: Proceedings of the 9th USENIX Symposium on Operating Systems Design and Implementation, OSDI 2010, Vancouver, BC, Canada, pp. 17–32, 4–6 October 2010. USENIX Association (2010)
36. Zhang, H.: Contextual rewriting in automated reasoning. Fundam. Inform. **24**(1/2), 107–123 (1995)

A Simplified Application of Howard's Vector Notation System to Termination Proofs for Typed Lambda-Calculus Systems

Mitsuhiro Okada[1(✉)] and Yuta Takahashi[2(✉)]

[1] Keio University, 2-15-45 Mita, Minato-ku, Tokyo 108-8345, Japan
mitsu@abelard.flet.keio.ac.jp
[2] IHPST (UMR 8590), Université Paris 1 Panthéon-Sorbonne, CNRS, 13, rue du Four, 75006 Paris, France
yuta.takahashi@univ-paris1.fr

Abstract. There have been some important methods of combining a recursive path ordering and Tait-Girard's computability argument to provide an ordering for termination proofs of higher-order rewrite systems. The higher-order recursive path ordering HORPO by Jouannaud and Rubio and the computability path ordering CPO by Blanqui, Jouannaud and Rubio are examples of such an ordering. In this paper, we give a case study of yet another direction of such extension of recursive path ordering, avoiding Tait-Girard's computability method plugged in the above mentioned works. This motivation comes from Lévy's question in the RTA open problem 19, which asks for a reasonably straightforward interpretation of simply typed λ-calculus $\lambda_{\rightarrow}$ in a certain well founded ordering. As in the cases of HORPO and CPO, the addition of λ-abstraction and application into path orderings might be considered as one solution, but the following question still remains; can the termination of $\lambda_{\rightarrow}$ be proved by an interpretation in a first-order well founded ordering in the sense that λ-abstraction/application are not directly built in the ordering? Reconsidering one of Howard's works on proof-theoretic studies, we introduce the path ordering with Howard algebra as a case study towards further studies on Lévy's question.

Keywords: Path orderings · Termination proofs · Term rewrite theory · Simply typed λ-calculus · Primitive recursive functionals of finite type

---

We thank the readers of the earlier version of this paper and the anonymous reviewers for their valuable comments. The first author is supported by JSPS (Japan Society for the Promotion of Science) KAKENHI Grand Numbers 17H02263, 17H02265 and 19KK0006. The second author is supported by JSPS Overseas Research Fellowship.

S. Escobar and N. Martí-Oliet (Eds.): WRLA 2020, LNCS 12328, pp. 136–155, 2020.
https://doi.org/10.1007/978-3-030-63595-4_8

1 Introduction

Since Jouannaud and Okada [10] showed a solution to a question of the termination problem, namely, the strong normalization problem on typed λ-calculus with higher-order rewrite rules by Tait-Girard's computability method, further improvements have been accumulated [1–4,11,12]. Among them, the higher-order recursive path ordering HORPO [12] by Jouannaud and Rubio and the computability path ordering CPO by Blanqui, Jouannaud and Rubio [4] give natural and good extension of recursive path ordering to treat higher-order rewrite systems. On the other hand, Lévy's question in the RTA open problem 19 asks for a termination proof for simply typed λ-calculus $\lambda_\rightarrow$ using a reasonably straightforward interpretation of $\lambda_\rightarrow$ in a well founded ordering.[1]

As in the cases of HORPO and CPO, the addition of λ-abstraction and application into path orderings with the use of computability method might be considered as one solution to Lévy's question, but the following question still remains; can the termination of $\lambda_\rightarrow$ be proved by an interpretation in a first-order well founded ordering in the sense that λ-abstraction and application are not directly built in the ordering? We are in particular interested in avoiding the computability method and questioning how to embed λ-abstraction/application into a first-order variant of some well-known path ordering (cf. [6–8]).[2]

The purpose of this paper is to revisit Howard's weak normalization proof for λ-formulation T of primitive recursive functionals of finite type in [9], and introduce a first-order variant of recursive path orderings which enables us to approach Lévy's question in the manner above. First of all, we restrict Howard's proof to $\lambda_\rightarrow$ since his proof did not show the termination of recursor reduction of T in the sense of strong normalization. Then, Howard's proof turns to a termination proof of $\lambda_\rightarrow$ using certain two step interpretations. Though this termination proof does not use the computability method, it can be improved for the purpose of finding an interpretation which is simpler and embeds λ-abstraction and application into a variant of some path ordering.

Below we simplify Howard's two step interpretations by introducing a path ordering with an algebra in which $\lambda_\rightarrow$ is embedded with one step. The well foundedness of this path ordering follows from Kruskal's tree theorem and so we do not need the computability method. Next, some extensions and comparisons of our path ordering are discussed. We adapt it to termination proofs for two combined systems of $\lambda_\rightarrow$ with additional higher-order rewrite rules, that is, the one with the rule for the map function and the one with the rule for the

[1] https://www.win.tue.nl/rtaloop/problems/19.html. See also the TLCA open problem 26 (http://tlca.di.unito.it/opltlca/opltlcasu33.html#x38-62000).

[2] If one takes the sequent-style formulation of logic, a reasonably straightforward mapping from proofs to a recursive path ordering (for example, a recursive path ordering of size of the ordinal $\varphi\omega 0$ in Veblen hierarchy) is enough for termination proofs. Lévy's question is open only when one considers the normalization by means of natural deduction, equivalently of typed λ-calculus, instead of sequent calculus. This fact also suggests that the key issue here, with respect to Lévy's question, is how to interpret the λ-abstraction/application in a natural way.

Ackermann function. Furthermore, we introduce another path ordering with an algebra in simplifying Wilken and Weiermann's two step mappings for their termination proof of the system T. To formulate it smoothly, we use membership equational logic [13]. Finally, we briefly compare our approach with some of the other approaches such as Blanqui, Jouannaud and Rubio's CPO and van de Pol's semantic termination method [14].

This paper is organized as follows. In Sect. 2, we first explain what our contribution is, and then give a termination proof of $\lambda_{\rightarrow}$ by means of our one step mapping obtained from a simplification of Howard's two step mappings. In Sect. 3, we discuss several extensions and comparisons of our path ordering, which were mentioned above.

2 A Termination Proof of Simply Typed λ-Calculus by a Path Ordering with an Algebra

In this section, we first introduce the *path ordering with Howard algebra* (Sect. 2.1). Next, we give a mapping from simply typed λ-calculus $\lambda_{\rightarrow}$ to our path ordering as Howard-style non-unique assignments of this ordering to λ-terms, and then verify that the β-rewrite relation decreases the order (Sect. 2.2).

2.1 Formulation of the Path Ordering with Howard Algebra

First of all, we outline Howard's termination proof of $\lambda_{\rightarrow}$ which can be found in [9], and then explain what our contribution is.[3] We follow [6,7] with respect to the terminology of term rewriting theory such as recursive path orderings RPO, and in particular we use the recursive path ordering with the status multiset only. Let $\mathcal{T}$ be the set of typed λ-terms of $\lambda_{\rightarrow}$ (the definition of $\mathcal{T}$ will be given in Sect. 2.2). Below "λ-terms" always means typed λ-terms. The set of all finite sequences from a given set $\mathcal{A}$ is denoted by $\mathcal{A}^{<\omega}$. We call a finite sequence of some elements of $\mathcal{A}$ a *vector* of elements of $\mathcal{A}$ as Howard did.

Howard's termination proof of $\lambda_{\rightarrow}$ in [9] proceeds as follows. First, he introduced the set of expressions, which we write as $\mathcal{N}$ in this paper (cf. [9, p. 448]). The set $\mathcal{N}^{<\omega}$ of all vectors of $\mathcal{N}$-elements forms the base-set of Howard's vector system, and λ-terms of $\mathcal{T}$ were mapped to this vector system. He mapped λ-terms of $\mathcal{T}$ to $\mathcal{N}^{<\omega}$ non-uniquely: Multiple vectors were assigned to each λ-term which includes some λ-abstraction term $\lambda X.A$ as its subterm. Howard used non-unique assignments to cope with the non-monotonicity of the delta operator, which was introduced to interpret λ-abstraction (cf. [9, pp. 456–457] and [16, p. 24]).

The ordering $\succeq$ on $\mathcal{N}^{<\omega}$ in Howard's vector system $(\mathcal{N}^{<\omega}, \succeq)$ was defined via the axiomatic theory $\mathcal{E}$ on $\mathcal{N}$, which consists of several equations and inequalities

[3] As stated in Sect. 1, it is not $\lambda_{\rightarrow}$ but the system T of primitive recursive functionals of finite type that Howard actually discussed in [9]. We restrict Howard's proof to $\lambda_{\rightarrow}$ because it did not prove the termination of primitive recursive functionals in the sense of strong normalization.

(cf. [9, p. 448, p. 457]). The theory $\mathcal{E}$ gave a quasi ordering on $\mathcal{N}$ which is not in path ordering-style but in axiomatic formulation, and $\succeq$ was obtained by extending this ordering to $\mathcal{N}^{<\omega}$ in a natural way. On the other hand, the well foundedness of $\succ$ does not follow from the definition of $\mathcal{E}$. To show the well foundedness of $\succ$, Howard used an interpretation of expressions of $\mathcal{N}$ in the set $\mathbb{N}$ of natural numbers.[4] Then, by showing that any reduction in $\lambda_{\rightarrow}$ decreases the order in $(\mathcal{N}^{<\omega}, \succeq)$, Howard finished his termination proof of $\lambda_{\rightarrow}$. In sum, Howard's termination proof used the following two step mappings, where non-unique assignments above are expressed as the double arrow.

$$\mathcal{T} \Longrightarrow (\mathcal{N}^{<\omega}, \succeq) \longrightarrow \mathbb{N}^{<\omega}$$

The first mapping and the set $\mathcal{N}^{<\omega}$ of vectors were used to show that the β-reduction decreases the order $\succeq$, and the second mapping was used to show that the order $\succeq$ is well founded.

Below we eliminate the right-hand mapping from the picture above: The resulting termination proof for $\lambda_{\rightarrow}$ has the structure below.

$$\mathcal{T} \Longrightarrow (\mathcal{N}^{<\omega}, \succeq_{\mathrm{po}})$$

We define an RPO-style ordering $\succeq_{\mathrm{po}}$ on $\mathcal{N}^{<\omega}$ directly, by using a normalizing function which results from some oriented equations of Howard's $\mathcal{E}$ above. A difficulty in defining an RPO-style ordering on $\mathcal{N}$ and $\mathcal{N}^{<\omega}$ directly will be revealed in Proposition 1 later. We first introduce the set H of rewrite rules on $\mathcal{N}$, which is obtained by orienting the two crucial equations of $\mathcal{E}$. This set gives the convergent rewrite system, and we consider a normalizing function $\mathrm{nf}(t)$ with respect to the H-rewrite relation. The ordering $\succeq_{\mathrm{nf}}$ on $\mathcal{N}$, which we call the *path ordering with Howard algebra* below, is defined by means of this normalizing function. The well foundedness of $\succeq_{\mathrm{nf}}$ follows from Kruskal's tree theorem, and the ordering $\succeq_{\mathrm{po}}$ on $\mathcal{N}^{<\omega}$ is obtained from a straightforward extension of $\succeq_{\mathrm{nf}}$ to $\mathcal{N}^{<\omega}$. In sum, we simplify Howard's two step mappings into a single mapping by introducing the well founded RPO-style ordering $(\mathcal{N}^{<\omega}, \succeq_{\mathrm{po}})$, in which λ-abstraction/application can be embedded (cf. Lévy's open question mentioned Sect. 1). Once our ordering is defined, the remaining parts of our proof are essentially the same as Howard's. We, in Sect.3, will simplify Wilken and Weiermann's two step mappings [16] for their termination proof of the system T in a similar manner.

Let Σ be a signature with a quasi ordering $\geq_{\Sigma}$ as its precedence relation, and $\mathcal{X}$ be a set of variables. We denote the set of terms over Σ and $\mathcal{X}$ by $\mathcal{T}(\Sigma, \mathcal{X})$. Below the following notations for an arbitrary quasi ordering $\geq$ are used: $t \approx s$ denotes $t \geq s \& s \geq t$, and $t > s$ denotes $t \geq s \& s \not\geq t$. The recursive path ordering on $\mathcal{T}(\Sigma, \mathcal{X})$ is denoted by $\succeq_{\mathrm{rpo}}$. For any term t of $\mathcal{T}(\Sigma, \mathcal{X})$, the equivalence class of t with respect to an equivalence relation R is denoted by $[t]_R$. Below we fix an arbitrary term-set $\mathcal{T}(\Sigma, \mathcal{X})$.

[4] Note that $\mathcal{N}$ is mapped to an ordinal notation system up to ε_0 if we do not restrict Howard's proof to $\lambda_{\rightarrow}$.

Definition 1 (A Path Ordering with an Algebra). *Let E be a set of equations on $\mathcal{T}(\Sigma, \mathcal{X})$, and R^E be the equivalence relation on $\mathcal{T}(\Sigma, \mathcal{X})$ induced by E. Moreover, let f be a choice function such that for any term t of $\mathcal{T}(\Sigma, \mathcal{X})$, $f([t]_{R^E}) \in [t]_{R^E}$ holds.*

Then, the path ordering with the algebra E with respect to f is the ordering $(\mathcal{T}(\Sigma, \mathcal{X}), \succeq_E)$, where $\succeq_E$ is defined as follows: For any two terms t and s of $\mathcal{T}(\Sigma, \mathcal{X})$, $t \succeq_E s$ holds if and only if $f([t]_{R^E}) \succeq_{\mathrm{rpo}} f([s]_{R^E})$ holds.

We write $E \vdash t = s$ if $t = s$ is derivable from E by means of reflexivity, symmetry, transitivity and the substitution rule. A quasi ordering $\succeq$ on $\mathcal{T}(\Sigma, \mathcal{X})$ and a set E of equations on $\mathcal{T}(\Sigma, \mathcal{X})$ are *compatible on* $\mathcal{T}(\Sigma, \mathcal{X})$ if $E \vdash t = s$ implies $t \approx s$ in the sense of $\succeq$, otherwise they are *incompatible on* $\mathcal{T}(\Sigma, \mathcal{X})$. Theorem 1 below is shown by Kruskal's tree theorem (cf. [5]), and Lemma 1 below is the key lemma to the construction of the path ordering with Howard algebra.

Theorem 1 ([5]). *If a quasi ordering $\geq$ on Σ is a well quasi ordering, then $\succeq_{\mathrm{rpo}}$ on $\mathcal{T}(\Sigma, \mathcal{X})$ is a well quasi ordering.*

Lemma 1. *Let $(\mathcal{T}(\Sigma, \mathcal{X}), \succeq_E)$ be the path ordering with an algebra E with respect to a choice function f, and assume that the precedence relation $\geq$ on Σ is a well quasi ordering. Then, $(\mathcal{T}(\Sigma, \mathcal{X}), \succeq_E)$ is a well quasi ordering on $\mathcal{T}(\Sigma, \mathcal{X})$ such that $\succeq_E$ and E are compatible on $\mathcal{T}(\Sigma, \mathcal{X})$.*

Proof. First, we show that $\succeq_E$ and E are compatible on $\mathcal{T}(\Sigma, \mathcal{X})$. If $E \vdash t = s$ holds, then we have $[t]_{R^E} = [s]_{R^E}$, where R^E is the equivalence relation induced by E. Therefore, $f([t]_{R^E}) = f([s]_{R^E})$ holds, and so $t \approx s$ holds in the sense of $\succeq_E$. Next, we show that $(\mathcal{T}(\Sigma, \mathcal{X}), \succeq_E)$ is a well quasi ordering. It is obvious that $(\mathcal{T}(\Sigma, \mathcal{X}), \succeq_E)$ is a quasi ordering. Let $t_0, t_1, \ldots$ be an infinite sequence of terms of $\mathcal{T}(\Sigma, \mathcal{X})$. We obtain the infinite sequence $f([t_0]_{R^E}), f([t_1]_{R^E}), \ldots$ and we have $f([t_i]_{R^E}) \succeq_{\mathrm{rpo}} f([t_j]_{R^E})$ for some i, j with $i > j$ by Theorem 1. Therefore, $t_i \succeq_E t_j$ holds by definition.

In the rest of this subsection, we modify Howard's set $\mathcal{N}$ of expressions to the path ordering with Howard algebra. Define $\mathcal{N}$ as the Σ-algebra $\mathcal{T}(\Sigma, \mathcal{X})$ where $\mathcal{X}$ is an infinite set of term variables and Σ consists of the constant 1, the binary function symbols $\#$ and h.[5] In Howard's notations, $\#$ and $\mathsf{h}(\cdot,\cdot)$ are written as $+$ and $(\cdot,\cdot)$, respectively. Howard intended $\#$ as the commutative sum on ordinals and (x, y) as the operation $2^x \otimes y$, where $\otimes$ is the commutative product on ordinals (cf. [9, p. 449]). The reason he added $(\cdot,\cdot)$ into the primitive symbols is that its nested structure is useful for interpreting λ-application/abstraction, as we will see in Sect. 2.2.

To define our path ordering on $\mathcal{N}$, we consider the flattened $\mathcal{N}$-terms. Let $\mathcal{N}^{\mathrm{fla}}$ be the set of all flattened $\mathcal{N}$-terms with respect to $\#$, that is, the set of terms obtained by stripping all nested occurrences of $\#$. When we consider $\mathcal{N}^{\mathrm{fla}}$,

---

5 Though Howard also used the constant 0, we omit it since it is not necessary and this makes the formulation of our path ordering simpler.

the function symbol # is treated as a variadic function symbol of arity ≥ 2. For example, the $\mathcal{N}$-term $\mathsf{h}(x, \mathsf{h}(\#(x,y), \#(\#(x,y),z)))$ is flattened as the $\mathcal{N}^{\text{fla}}$-term $\mathsf{h}(x, \mathsf{h}(\#(x,y), \#(x,y,z)))$. If no variable occurs in t then we say t is *closed.* We call a term of the form $\mathsf{h}(t,s)$ an h-*term*, and define the ordering $\geq_\Sigma$ on Σ as $\mathsf{h} >_\Sigma \# >_\Sigma 1$. The recursive path ordering on $\mathcal{N}^{\text{fla}}$ is a well quasi ordering by Theorem 1. Below we denote the recursive path ordering on $\mathcal{N}^{\text{fla}}$ by $\succeq_{\text{rpo}}$ as well. Put $(t,s) := \mathsf{h}(t,s)$, $t_1\#\cdots\#t_n := \#(t_1,\ldots,t_n)$ and for any $t = t_1\#\cdots\#t_n$ and $s = s_1\#\cdots\#s_m$ $(n, m \geq 1)$, $t\overline{\#}s := t_1\#\cdots\#t_n\#s_1\#\cdots\#s_m$.

The ordering $\succeq_{\text{rpo}}$ on $\mathcal{N}^{\text{fla}}$ is incompatible with the set E_H of the following two equations on $\mathcal{N}^{\text{fla}}$ (cf. [9, Axioms 2.8 and 2.13 in p. 448]): For any $n > 1$ and any $m, k \geq 1$,

1. $(x, y_1\#\cdots\#y_n) = (x, y_1)\#\cdots\#(x, y_n)$.
2. $(x_1\#\cdots\#x_m, (y_1\#\cdots\#y_k, z)) = (x_1\#\cdots\#x_m\#y_1\#\cdots\#y_k, z)$.

Proposition 1 (Incompatibility of $\succeq_{\text{rpo}}$ and E_H). *The ordering $\succeq_{\text{rpo}}$ and the algebra E_H are incompatible on $\mathcal{N}^{\text{fla}}$.*

Proof. First, we consider the Eq. 1 above. For any $t, s_1, \ldots, s_n \in \mathcal{N}^{\text{fla}}$, we have $(t, s_1\overline{\#}\cdots\overline{\#}s_n) \succ_{\text{rpo}} (t, s_1)\#\cdots\#(t, s_n)$, so this is incompatible with 1. Next, consider the Eq. 2. In this case, we have $(1, (1, 1)) \succ_{\text{rpo}} (1\#1, 1)$ while $E_H \vdash (1, (1, 1)) = (1\#1, 1)$ holds. We also have $((1, (1, 1))\#1, 1) \succ_{\text{rpo}} ((1, (1, 1)), (1, 1))$ and $E_H \vdash ((1, (1, 1))\#1, 1) = ((1, (1, 1)), (1, 1))$.

When a set E of equations on $\mathcal{T}(\Sigma, \mathcal{X})$ is given, we say a set of rewrite rule R is an *oriented set* of E if $R = \{F(t = s) \mid t = s \in E\}$ holds for some mapping F assigning a rewrite rule $t \to s$ or $s \to t$ to each equation $t = s$ in E. To define the path ordering with Howard algebra, we consider the oriented set H of E_H which is obtained by giving to the equations in E_H the direction from the left-hand side to the right-hand side. One can verify that the rewrite relation $\to_H$ is terminating by defining the polynomial interpretation $\tau(t)$ for any closed term t in $\mathcal{N}^{\text{fla}}$ as $\tau(1) := 2$, $\tau((t,s)) := \tau(t) \cdot \tau(s)$, $\tau(t_1\#\cdots\#t_n) := \tau(t_1) + \cdots + \tau(t_n) + 1$. The confluence of $\to_H$ can be shown by Knuth-Bendix's Critical Pair Lemma, so $\to_H$ is convergent. By the convergence of $\to_H$, any term has a unique H-normal form. We denote the H-normal form of t by $\text{nf}(t)$. Note that the H-normal form s of a term $t \in \mathcal{N}^{\text{fla}}$ is a term such that any h-subterm of s is of the form either (u, x) or $(u, 1)$. By defining $f_H([t]_{R^H}) := \text{nf}(t)$, where R^H is the equivalence relation induced by E_H, we have the choice function f_H for the set of equivalence classes with respect to R^H. We call the path ordering $(\mathcal{N}^{\text{fla}}, \succeq_{\text{nf}})$ with the algebra E_H with respect to f_H the *path ordering with Howard algebra.* By Lemma 1, we have the following proposition.

Proposition 2 (The Path Ordering $\succeq_{\text{nf}}$ with Howard Algebra). *The path ordering $(\mathcal{N}^{\text{fla}}, \succeq_{\text{nf}})$ with Howard algebra E_H is a well quasi ordering on $\mathcal{N}^{\text{fla}}$ such that $\succeq_{\text{nf}}$ and E_H are compatible on $\mathcal{N}^{\text{fla}}$.*

We extend $\succeq_{\text{nf}}$ to $\mathcal{N}$ by stipulating that $t \succeq_{\text{nf}} s$ holds for $t, s \in \mathcal{N}$ if and only if $\bar{t} \succeq_{\text{nf}} \bar{s}$ holds, where $\bar{t}$ and $\bar{s}$ are their flattened forms. We use # as an infix operator in $\mathcal{N}$ as well and treat it as left associative. The well quasi ordering $\succeq_{\mathrm{nf}}$ on $\mathcal{N}$ will be extended to the well founded ordering $\succeq_{\mathrm{po}}$ on $\mathcal{N}^{<\omega}$ further in the next subsection.

An advantage of the choice function f_H is as follows: The ordering $\succeq_{\mathrm{nf}}$ satisfies several properties which are satisfied by Howard's original ordering (cf. Lemma 2 below).[6] These properties guarantee that one can use $\succeq_{\mathrm{nf}}$ in a way similar to Howard's original ordering. For any term t, we define a substitution $t[x := s]$ of s for x in t in a usual way.

Lemma 2. *For any $t, t_1, s, u \in \mathcal{N}$, the following statements hold.*

1. *If $t \succ_{\mathrm{nf}} s$ and $t \succ_{\mathrm{nf}} u$ hold, then $(t, t_1) \succ_{\mathrm{nf}} (s, t_1)\#(u, t_1)$ holds.*
2. *If $t \succ_{\mathrm{nf}} s$ holds, then $(t, u) \succ_{\mathrm{nf}} (s, u)$ and $(u, t) \succ_{\mathrm{nf}} (u, s)$ hold.*
3. *If $t \succ_{\mathrm{nf}} s$ holds, then $t[x := u] \succ_{\mathrm{nf}} s[x := u]$ holds.*
4. *$(s, t) \succ_{\mathrm{nf}} t$ and $(t, s) \succ_{\mathrm{nf}} t$ hold.*

2.2 Non-Unique Assignments of the Vector System

In this subsection, we finish a termination proof of $\lambda_{\rightarrow}$ based on our ordering $(\mathcal{N}^{<\omega}, \succeq_{\mathrm{po}})$. Once this ordering is defined, the remaining parts of our proof are essentially the same as Howard's and so almost all proofs will be omitted below.

We define Howard's vector system $\mathcal{N}^{<\omega}$ by formulating a two-sorted Σ-algebra including both $\mathcal{N}^{<\omega}$ and $\mathcal{N}$. In the definition below, we follow the notations in [13]. Let Σ be the signature which consists of

- the set of sorts: $S = \{\mathtt{Ter}, \mathtt{Vec}\}$, and
- the $S^* \times S$-indexed family of sets: $\Sigma_{\lambda,\mathtt{Ter}} = \{1\}$, $\Sigma_{\mathtt{Ter\ Ter},\mathtt{Ter}} = \{\#, \mathsf{h}\}$, $\Sigma_{\lambda,\mathtt{Vec}} = \{\epsilon\}$ and $\Sigma_{\mathtt{Ter\ Vec},\mathtt{Vec}} = \{*\}$.

The constant ϵ denotes the empty sequence, and the function symbol $*$ denotes the cons operation for Vec. We take the S-indexed family $\mathcal{X}$ of sets of variables by stipulating that $\mathcal{X}_{\mathtt{Ter}}$ is the set of variables used to define $\mathcal{N}$ in the last subsection and $\mathcal{X}_{\mathtt{Vec}} = \emptyset$. Then, the set $\mathcal{T}(\Sigma, \mathcal{X})_{\mathtt{Ter}}$ is equal to $\mathcal{N}$, and Howard's vector system $\mathcal{N}^{<\omega}$ can be defined as the set $\mathcal{T}(\Sigma, \mathcal{X})_{\mathtt{Vec}}$. We denote $\mathcal{T}(\Sigma, \mathcal{X})_{\mathtt{Ter}}$ by $\mathcal{N}$ as in the last subsection.

While terms in $\mathcal{N}$ are called *terms* simply, terms in $\mathcal{N}^{<\omega}$ are called *vectors* and denoted by $\boldsymbol{t}, \boldsymbol{s}, \boldsymbol{u}, \boldsymbol{v}, \boldsymbol{a}, \boldsymbol{b}, \boldsymbol{c}, \boldsymbol{d}$ possibly with suffixes. Below a vector $t_0 * (t_1 * (\cdots (t_n * \epsilon) \cdots))$ is abbreviated as $\langle t_0, \ldots, t_n \rangle$. For any vector $\boldsymbol{t} = \langle t_0, \ldots, t_n \rangle$, if $0 \leq i \leq n$ holds then we put $(\boldsymbol{t})_i := t_i$, and if $i > n$ holds we put $(\boldsymbol{t})_i := e$, where e is an auxiliary symbol with $e\#s := s$ and $s\#e := s$ for any term s. The *level* $\mathrm{lv}(\boldsymbol{t})$ of $\boldsymbol{t}$ is defined as $\mathrm{lv}(\boldsymbol{t}) := n$. Here the auxiliary symbol e is used to define Howard's square operator $\square$ smoothly (cf. Definition 3 below). The path ordering $\succeq_{\mathrm{nf}}$ on $\mathcal{N}$ is obtained as in the last subsection. For the sake of brevity, we write the orderings $\succeq_{\mathrm{nf}}$ and $\succ_{\mathrm{nf}}$ on $\mathcal{N}$ as $\succeq$ and $\succ$, respectively. We define the well founded RPO-style ordering $\succeq_{\mathrm{po}}$ on $\mathcal{N}^{<\omega}$ as follows.

[6] The statement 1. of Lemma 2 below corresponds to Axiom 2.9 in [9, p. 448], the statement 2. corresponds to Axioms 2.10, 2.11 and the statement 3. corresponds to Axiom 4.1 of [9, p. 457]. The statement 4. has no counterpart in [9].

Definition 2 (The Ordering $(\mathcal{N}^{<\omega}, \succeq_{\mathrm{po}})$). *Let $\boldsymbol{t}, \boldsymbol{s}$ be two vectors with $\mathrm{lv}(\boldsymbol{t}) \geq \mathrm{lv}(\boldsymbol{s})$. The ordering $\boldsymbol{t} \succ_{\mathrm{po}} \boldsymbol{s}$ holds if and only if $(\boldsymbol{t})_0 \succ (\boldsymbol{s})_0$ holds and $(\boldsymbol{t})_i \succeq (\boldsymbol{s})_i$ holds for any i with $1 \leq i \leq \mathrm{lv}(\boldsymbol{s})$. The ordering $\boldsymbol{t} \succeq_{\mathrm{po}} \boldsymbol{s}$ holds if and only if either $\boldsymbol{t} \succ_{\mathrm{po}} \boldsymbol{s}$ or $\boldsymbol{t} = \boldsymbol{s}$ holds.*

Next, we define several operators on vectors to embed $\lambda_{\rightarrow}$ into Howard's vector system. The *sum operator* $+$ on vectors is defined by recursion: $\boldsymbol{t} + \epsilon = \boldsymbol{t}$, $\epsilon + \boldsymbol{t} = \boldsymbol{t}$ and $(t * \boldsymbol{t}) + (s * \boldsymbol{s}) = (t \# s) * (\boldsymbol{t} + \boldsymbol{s})$. In addition to the sum operator, Howard defined the *square operator* $\Box$ (cf. [9, p. 449]) to define the vectors assigned to λ-application terms, while he defined the *delta operator* δ (cf. [9, p. 452]) to define the vectors assigned to λ-abstraction terms. We define the square operator first, and the delta operator will be defined after Lemma 4.

Definition 3 (Square Operator). *Let $\boldsymbol{t}$ and $\boldsymbol{s}$ be arbitrary vectors. We define the vector $\boldsymbol{t}\Box\boldsymbol{s}$ of level $n = \max\{\mathrm{lv}(\boldsymbol{t}), \mathrm{lv}(\boldsymbol{s})\}$ by downward induction on n.*

$$(\boldsymbol{t}\Box\boldsymbol{s})_i := \begin{cases} (\boldsymbol{t})_i \# (\boldsymbol{s})_i, & \text{if } i = n, \\ ((\boldsymbol{t}\Box\boldsymbol{s})_{i+1}, (\boldsymbol{t})_i \# (\boldsymbol{s})_i), & \text{if } 0 \leq i < n. \end{cases}$$

The following lemma is provable by downward induction on i.

Lemma 3. *Let $\boldsymbol{t}$ and $\boldsymbol{s}$ be arbitrary two vectors such that $\mathrm{lv}(\boldsymbol{t}) = \mathrm{lv}(\boldsymbol{s}) = n$ holds and $t_i \succeq s_i$ holds for any i with $0 \leq i \leq n$. If there exists $j \leq n$ such that $t_i \succ s_i$ holds for any i with $0 \leq i \leq j$, then for any vector $\boldsymbol{u}$ and any i with $0 \leq i \leq j$, we have $(\boldsymbol{t}\Box\boldsymbol{u})_i \succ (\boldsymbol{s}\Box\boldsymbol{u})_i$ and $(\boldsymbol{u}\Box\boldsymbol{t})_i \succ (\boldsymbol{u}\Box\boldsymbol{s})_i$.*

From this lemma, one can see that if $\boldsymbol{t} \succ_{\mathrm{po}} \boldsymbol{s}$ holds then both $\boldsymbol{t}\Box\boldsymbol{u} \succ_{\mathrm{po}} \boldsymbol{s}\Box\boldsymbol{u}$ and $\boldsymbol{u}\Box\boldsymbol{t} \succ_{\mathrm{po}} \boldsymbol{u}\Box\boldsymbol{s}$ hold, hence the square operator is monotonic. Note that the square operator produces nested occurrences of $(\cdot,\cdot)$ in the position of the first argument. For example, we have

$$\langle t_0, t_1, t_2\rangle \Box \langle s_0, s_1\rangle = \langle ((t_2, t_1 \# s_1), t_0 \# s_0), (t_2, t_1 \# s_1), t_2\rangle.$$

Because of such nested occurrences of $(\cdot,\cdot)$, we have Lemma 4 below, which is used to verify that the β-reduction decreases the order $\succeq_{\mathrm{po}}$ (cf. Lemma 5 and Proposition 3 below). Lemma 4 is essentially the same as [9, Lemma 2.5, 2.6], so we omit its proof. It is crucial for the proof of Lemma 4.(2) that $\succeq$ and E_H are compatible on $\mathcal{N}^{\mathrm{fla}}$ (cf. Proposition 2 above). We denote $t\#t$ by $2t$ for any term t.

Lemma 4. *Let $\boldsymbol{a}, \boldsymbol{b}, \boldsymbol{t}, \boldsymbol{s}, \boldsymbol{u}$ be vectors with $\mathrm{lv}(\boldsymbol{a}) = \mathrm{lv}(\boldsymbol{b}) = \mathrm{lv}(\boldsymbol{t}) = \mathrm{lv}(\boldsymbol{s}) = n > \mathrm{lv}(\boldsymbol{u})$. Then, the following statements hold.*

1. *For any i with $0 \leq i \leq n$, $((\boldsymbol{a} + \boldsymbol{b})\Box\boldsymbol{u})_i \succeq ((\boldsymbol{a}\Box\boldsymbol{u}) + (\boldsymbol{b}\Box\boldsymbol{u}))_i$ holds.*
2. *For any vector $\boldsymbol{v}$ with $\mathrm{lv}(\boldsymbol{v}) \geq n$, if $(\boldsymbol{v})_n \succ 2(\boldsymbol{t})_n \# 2(\boldsymbol{s})_n$ holds and $(\boldsymbol{v})_i \succeq (\boldsymbol{t})_i \# (\boldsymbol{s})_i$ holds for any i with $0 \leq i < n$, then $(\boldsymbol{v}\Box\boldsymbol{u})_i \succ 2((\boldsymbol{t}\Box\boldsymbol{u})\Box(\boldsymbol{s}\Box\boldsymbol{u}))_i$ holds for any i with $0 \leq i \leq n$.*

Let $\mathcal{S}$ be a non-empty set of base types. *Types* are defined by induction: Any $P \in \mathcal{S}$ is a type and the *level* $\mathrm{lv}(P)$ of P is defined as $\mathrm{lv}(P) := 0$, and if σ and τ are types, then $\sigma \to \tau$ is a type and $\mathrm{lv}(\sigma \to \tau)$ is defined as $\max\{\mathrm{lv}(\sigma)+1, \mathrm{lv}(\tau)\}$. Below we use a set of $\lambda_{\to}$-variables such that each $\lambda_{\to}$-variable has a unique type and for any type σ, there are infinitely many $\lambda_{\to}$-variables of type σ enumerated as $X^{\sigma,0}, X^{\sigma,1}, \ldots$. We denote $\lambda_{\to}$-variables X, Y, Z possibly with suffixes and type annotations. *Typed $\lambda_{\to}$-terms* are defined by induction: (i) For any type σ, every variable of type σ is a $\lambda_{\to}$-term of type σ. (ii) If M is a $\lambda_{\to}$-term of type τ and X is a variable of type σ, then $\lambda X.M$ is a $\lambda_{\to}$-term of type $\sigma \to \tau$. (iii) If M is a $\lambda_{\to}$-term of type $\sigma \to \tau$ and N is a $\lambda_{\to}$-term of type σ, then MN is a term of type τ.

If no free $\lambda_{\to}$-variable occurs in a $\lambda_{\to}$-term M then we say M is *closed.* We often write a $\lambda_{\to}$-term M of type σ as M^{σ} to indicate the type of M. We treat $\to$ as right associative and application-terms MN as left associative. Substitution $M[X := N]$ of N for X in M and its simultaneous version are defined in a usual way, and we assume that when we write $M[X := N]$, no free $\lambda_{\to}$-variable in N is bound in $M[X := N]$. We denote by $\to_{\beta}$ the β-rewrite relation on λ-terms defined as follows: $M \to_{\beta} N$ holds if and only if for some $\lambda_{\to}$-term $(\lambda X.L_1)L_2$ and some position p in M, we have $M|_p = (\lambda X.L_1)L_2$ and $M[L_1[X := L_2]]_p = N$.

Below we assume a mapping which assigns a $\lambda_{\to}$-variable $X^{\sigma,k}$ to a vector $\boldsymbol{x}^{\sigma,k} := \langle x_0^{\sigma,k}, \ldots, x_n^{\sigma,k} \rangle$ of $\mathcal{N}$-variables ($n = \mathrm{lv}(\sigma)$) such that $\{x_0^{\sigma,k}, \ldots, x_n^{\sigma,k}\}$ and $\{x_0^{\tau,l}, \ldots, x_m^{\tau,l}\}$ are disjoint whenever $\sigma \neq \tau$ or $k \neq l$ holds. These vectors $\boldsymbol{x}^{\sigma,k}$ of $\mathcal{N}$-variables and their elements $x_0^{\sigma,k}, \ldots, x_n^{\sigma,k}$ are denoted by $\boldsymbol{x}^{\sigma}$ and $x_0^{\sigma}, \ldots, x_n^{\sigma}$ without the upper index k. To define Howard's delta operator δ on vectors, we first define the set $\mathcal{C}_i$ of terms for each $i \in \mathbb{N}$.

Definition 4 (The set $\mathcal{C}_i$). *For any $i \in \mathbb{N}$, we define the set $\mathcal{C}_i$ of terms by simultaneous induction:*

1. *If t is a closed term, then t belongs to $\mathcal{C}_i$.*
2. *For any type σ and any i with $0 \leq i \leq \mathrm{lv}(\sigma)$, $(\boldsymbol{x}^{\sigma})_i$ belongs to $\mathcal{C}_i$.*
3. *If t_1 and t_2 are terms in $\mathcal{C}_i$, then $t_1 \# t_2$ belongs to $\mathcal{C}_i$.*
4. *If t is a term in $\mathcal{C}_{i+1}$ and s is a term in $\mathcal{C}_i$, then (t, s) belongs to $\mathcal{C}_i$.*

Note that when $j > i$ holds, x_i^{σ} never occurs in any term of $\mathcal{C}_j$. We denote by $\boldsymbol{C}$ the set of all vectors $\boldsymbol{t}$ such that for any i with $0 \leq i \leq \mathrm{lv}(\boldsymbol{t})$, $(\boldsymbol{t})_i$ belongs to $\mathcal{C}_i$. It is obvious that $\boldsymbol{C}$ is closed under the square operator $\Box$. Howard's delta operator is first defined as the one from terms to vectors, then the delta operator from vectors to vectors is defined.

Definition 5 (Delta Operator for Terms). *For any vector $\boldsymbol{x}^{\sigma}$ of variables with $\boldsymbol{x}^{\sigma} = \langle x_0^{\sigma}, \ldots, x_{\mathrm{lv}(\sigma)}^{\sigma} \rangle$, any term t and any i with $t \in \mathcal{C}_i$, we define the vector $\delta^i \boldsymbol{x}^{\sigma}.t \in \boldsymbol{C}$ with $\mathrm{lv}(\delta^i \boldsymbol{x}^{\sigma}.t) = \mathrm{lv}(\sigma) + 1$ as follows.*

1. *If t does not contain any component of $\langle x_0^{\sigma}, \ldots, x_{\mathrm{lv}(\sigma)}^{\sigma} \rangle$, then for any j with $0 \leq j \leq \mathrm{lv}(\sigma) + 1$, we define $(\delta^i \boldsymbol{x}^{\sigma}.t)_j := t \# 1$ if $j = i$ holds, otherwise $(\delta^i \boldsymbol{x}^{\sigma}.t)_j := 1$.*

2. *Assume that t contains some component of $\langle x_0^\sigma, \ldots, x_{\mathrm{lv}(\sigma)}^\sigma \rangle$.*
   (a) *If t is the variable x_i^σ, then* $\delta^i \boldsymbol{x}^\sigma.t := \langle \underbrace{1, \ldots, 1}_{\mathrm{lv}(\sigma)+2 \ times} \rangle$.
   (b) *If t is of the form $t_1 \# t_2$ with $t_1, t_2 \in C_i$, then* $\delta^i \boldsymbol{x}^\sigma.t := \delta^i \boldsymbol{x}^\sigma.t_1 + \delta^i \boldsymbol{x}^\sigma.t_2$.
   (c) *If t is of the form (u, s) with $u \in C_{i+1}$ and $s \in C_i$, then for any j with $0 \leq j \leq \mathrm{lv}(\sigma) + 1$, we define*

$$(\delta^i \boldsymbol{x}^\sigma.t)_j := \begin{cases} (\delta^{i+1} \boldsymbol{x}^\sigma.u)_j \# (\delta^i \boldsymbol{x}^\sigma.s)_j, & \text{if } 0 \leq j \leq \mathrm{lv}(\sigma), \\ 2(\delta^{i+1} \boldsymbol{x}^\sigma.u)_j \# 2(\delta^i \boldsymbol{x}^\sigma.s)_j \# 1, & \text{if } j = \mathrm{lv}(\sigma) + 1. \end{cases}$$

Note that if $t \in C_i$ and $t \in C_j$ hold with $i \neq j$, then both of $\delta^i \boldsymbol{x}^\sigma.t$ and $\delta^j \boldsymbol{x}^\sigma.t$ are defined and they can be different from one another. The factor 2 in the clause 2.(c) above is crucial to use Lemma 4.(2) in a proof of Lemma 5.(1).

Definition 6 (Delta Operator for Vectors). *For any vector $\boldsymbol{x}^\sigma$ of variables and any vector $\boldsymbol{t}$ with $\boldsymbol{t} \in \boldsymbol{C}$ and* $\mathrm{lv}(\boldsymbol{t}) = n$, *we define the vector $\delta \boldsymbol{x}^\sigma.\boldsymbol{t} \in \boldsymbol{C}$ of level* $\max\{\mathrm{lv}(\sigma) + 1, n\}$ *as follows: For any j with* $0 \leq j \leq \max\{\mathrm{lv}(\sigma) + 1, n\}$,

$$(\delta \boldsymbol{x}^\sigma.\boldsymbol{t})_j := \begin{cases} (\delta^0 \boldsymbol{x}^\sigma.(\boldsymbol{t})_0)_j \# \cdots \# (\delta^n \boldsymbol{x}^\sigma.(\boldsymbol{t})_n)_j, & \text{if } 0 \leq j \leq \mathrm{lv}(\sigma) + 1, \\ (\boldsymbol{t})_j \# 1, & \text{if } \mathrm{lv}(\sigma) + 1 < j \leq n. \end{cases}$$

For any term t (resp. any vector $\boldsymbol{t}$), we define a simultaneous substitution $t[x_0 := s_0, \ldots, x_n := s_n]$ (resp. $\boldsymbol{t}[x_0 := s_0, \ldots, x_n := s_n]$) in a usual way. Let $\boldsymbol{s}$ be a vector with $\mathrm{lv}(\boldsymbol{s}) = n$. The substitution $t[\boldsymbol{x}^\sigma := \boldsymbol{s}]$ with $\boldsymbol{x}^\sigma = \langle x_0^\sigma, \ldots, x_n^\sigma \rangle$ is defined as $t[\boldsymbol{x}^\sigma := \boldsymbol{s}] := t[x_0^\sigma := (\boldsymbol{s})_0, \ldots, x_n^\sigma := (\boldsymbol{s})_n]$. The substitution $\boldsymbol{t}[\boldsymbol{x}^\sigma := \boldsymbol{s}]$ with $\boldsymbol{x}^\sigma = \langle x_0^\sigma, \ldots, x_n^\sigma \rangle$ is defined as $(\boldsymbol{t}[\boldsymbol{x}^\sigma := \boldsymbol{s}])_i := t_i[\boldsymbol{x}^\sigma := \boldsymbol{s}]$ for any i with $0 \leq i \leq \mathrm{lv}(\boldsymbol{t})$. One can prove the following lemma, which is a key lemma for the termination of $\lambda_\rightarrow$ (cf. Proposition 3 below), in the same way as [9].[7] Lemma 4 is used to verify Lemma 5.(1).

Lemma 5. *We have the following assertions.*

1. *For any $t \in C_i$ and any $\boldsymbol{x}^\sigma, \boldsymbol{s}$ with* $\mathrm{lv}(\boldsymbol{x}^\sigma) = \mathrm{lv}(\boldsymbol{s})$, $((\delta^i \boldsymbol{x}^\sigma.t) \Box \boldsymbol{s})_i \succ t[\boldsymbol{x}^\sigma := \boldsymbol{s}]$ *holds.*
2. *For any $\boldsymbol{t} \in \boldsymbol{C}$ and any $\boldsymbol{x}^\sigma, \boldsymbol{s}$ with* $\mathrm{lv}(\boldsymbol{x}^\sigma) = \mathrm{lv}(\boldsymbol{s})$, $((\delta \boldsymbol{x}^\sigma.\boldsymbol{t}) \Box \boldsymbol{s})_i \succ (\boldsymbol{t}[\boldsymbol{x}^\sigma := \boldsymbol{s}])_i$ *holds for any i with* $0 \leq i \leq \mathrm{lv}(\boldsymbol{t})$.

For any vector $\boldsymbol{t}$ of level n and any i with $0 \leq i \leq n$, the restriction $\boldsymbol{t} \restriction_i$ of $\boldsymbol{t}$ up to i is defined as $\boldsymbol{t} \restriction_i := \langle t_0, \ldots, t_i \rangle$. For any $\boldsymbol{x}^\sigma = \langle x_0^\sigma, \ldots, x_n^\sigma \rangle$, we denote $\boldsymbol{t}[x_0^\sigma := 1, \ldots, x_n^\sigma := 1]$ by $\boldsymbol{t}[\boldsymbol{x}^\sigma := \boldsymbol{1}]$. Below we define the non-unique assignments of vectors in $\boldsymbol{C}$ to $\lambda_\rightarrow$-terms by adapting Wilken and Weiermann's *assignment derivations* (cf. [16, Definition 3.1]) to the setting of $\lambda_\rightarrow$.[8] Roughly speaking, the structures of λ-abstraction terms and λ-application terms are reflected

[7] Lemma 5.(1) and (2) correspond to Lemma 2.11 and its corollary in [9], respectively.

[8] Assignment derivations were introduced to formulate Howard-style non-unique assignments of vectors perspicuously. Note that Wilken and Weiermann not only introduced assignment derivations, but also refined Howard's original non-unique assignments to cope with arbitrary recursor reduction rules of T. We restrict ourselves to $\lambda_\rightarrow$ here, so we need not use the refined part by Wilken and Weiermann.

on vectors in $\boldsymbol{C}$ by the delta operator and the square operator, respectively, so that the β-reduction decreases the order of vectors. The motivation for the non-unique assignments is explained after the definition.

Definition 7 (Assignment Derivations). *Assignment derivations, which assign vectors in* $\boldsymbol{C}$ *to* $\lambda_{\rightarrow}$*-terms non-uniquely, are derivations constructed by the following axioms and rules.*

Axioms. *The following axiom is an assignment derivation for* $X^{\sigma} \mapsto \boldsymbol{x}^{\sigma}$*.*

$$\frac{}{X^{\sigma} \mapsto \boldsymbol{x}^{\sigma}}$$

Application Rule. *If* d_0 *and* d_1 *are assignment derivations for* $M^{\sigma\to\tau} \mapsto \boldsymbol{a}$ *and* $N^{\sigma} \mapsto \boldsymbol{b}$*, respectively, then*

$$\frac{\begin{array}{cc} \vdots\, d_0 & \vdots\, d_1 \\ M \mapsto \boldsymbol{a} & N \mapsto \boldsymbol{b} \end{array}}{MN \mapsto (\boldsymbol{a}\Box\boldsymbol{b}) \restriction_{\mathrm{lv}(\tau)}}$$

is an assignment derivation for $MN \mapsto (\boldsymbol{a}\Box\boldsymbol{b}) \restriction_{\mathrm{lv}(\tau)}$*.*

Abstraction Rule. *If for some* $k \geq 0$, $d_0, \ldots, d_k$ *are assignment derivations for* $D_0 \mapsto \boldsymbol{d}^0, \ldots, D_k \mapsto \boldsymbol{d}^k$*, respectively, such that* $D_0 \rightarrow_{\beta} \cdots \rightarrow_{\beta} D_k = L$ *and* $\boldsymbol{d}^0 \succ_{\mathrm{po}} \cdots \succ_{\mathrm{po}} \boldsymbol{d}^k$ *hold, then*

$$\frac{\begin{array}{ccc} \vdots\, d_0 & & \vdots\, d_k \\ D_0 \mapsto \boldsymbol{d}^0 & \cdots & D_k \mapsto \boldsymbol{d}^k \end{array}}{\lambda X^{\sigma}.L \mapsto (\delta \boldsymbol{x}^{\sigma}.\boldsymbol{d}^0)\#\boldsymbol{d}^k[\boldsymbol{x}^{\sigma} := \mathbf{1}]}$$

is an assignment derivation for $\lambda X^{\sigma}.L \mapsto (\delta \boldsymbol{x}^{\sigma}.\boldsymbol{d}^0)\#\boldsymbol{d}^k[\boldsymbol{x}^{\sigma} := \mathbf{1}]$*.*

We say $\boldsymbol{a}$ *is a vector of a* $\lambda_{\rightarrow}$*-term* M *if and only if there is an assignment derivation for* $M \mapsto \boldsymbol{a}$*.*

Because of Abstraction Rule above, a $\lambda_{\rightarrow}$-term M with λ-abstraction subterms can have several assignment derivations which give different vectors to M, and this is the key ingredient of Howard-style non-unique assignments. Howard's this method enables one to overcome the following difficulty induced by the non-monotonicity of the delta operator. As shown in [16, p. 24], the delta operator is not even weakly monotonic, and thus it does not follow from $\boldsymbol{d} \succ_{\mathrm{po}} \boldsymbol{a}$ that $\delta \boldsymbol{x}^{\sigma}.\boldsymbol{d} \succ_{\mathrm{po}} \delta \boldsymbol{x}^{\sigma}.\boldsymbol{a}$ holds. Therefore, the interpretation of a λ-abstraction term $\lambda X^{\sigma}.M$ as the vector $\delta \boldsymbol{x}^{\sigma}.\boldsymbol{d}$, where $\boldsymbol{d}$ is the interpretation of M, cannot work in verifying that the ξ-rule $M \rightarrow_{\beta} N \Rightarrow \lambda X^{\sigma}.M \rightarrow_{\beta} \lambda X^{\sigma}.N$ decreases the order.

While the part $\boldsymbol{d}^k[\boldsymbol{x}^{\sigma} := \mathbf{1}]$ of $(\delta \boldsymbol{x}^{\sigma}.\boldsymbol{d}^0)\#\boldsymbol{d}^k[\boldsymbol{x}^{\sigma} := \mathbf{1}]$ in Abstraction Rule is not necessary to manage the case of β-reduction $(\lambda X^{\sigma}.L_1)L_2 \rightarrow_{\beta} L_1[X^{\sigma} := L_2]$, both of $\delta \boldsymbol{x}^{\sigma}.\boldsymbol{d}^0$ and $\boldsymbol{d}^k[\boldsymbol{x}^{\sigma} := \mathbf{1}]$ are necessary to manage the ξ-rule. Assume that a vector is assigned to $\lambda X^{\sigma}.M$. Abstraction Rule enables one to assign a vector $(\delta \boldsymbol{x}^{\sigma}.\boldsymbol{d}^0)\#\boldsymbol{a}[\boldsymbol{x}^{\sigma} := \mathbf{1}]$ to $\lambda X^{\sigma}.N$ relative to a reduction relation $M \rightarrow_{\beta} N$

so that $\delta \boldsymbol{x}^\sigma.\boldsymbol{d}^0$ is common to the vectors of $\lambda X^\sigma.M$ and $\lambda X^\sigma.N$ but $\boldsymbol{a}[\boldsymbol{x}^\sigma := \mathbf{1}]$ makes the vector of $\lambda X^\sigma.N$ smaller than the one of $\lambda X^\sigma.M$ (see the proof of Proposition 3 for details). In this way, one can overcome the difficulty above and verify that the ξ-rule decreases the order.

Lemma 6 below corresponds to [9, Lemma 3.1] (cf. also [16, Lemma 3.3]), and Proposition 3 below corresponds to [9, Theorem 4.1] (cf. also [16, Theorem 3.5]). Though one can prove these lemma and proposition in the same way as [16], we prove the assertion in the crucial cases of Proposition 3 for readers' convenience.

Lemma 6. *Let $\boldsymbol{t}$ and $\boldsymbol{s}$ be vectors of M and N, respectively. If M is of type σ, then $\boldsymbol{s}[\boldsymbol{x}^\sigma := \boldsymbol{t}]$ is a vector of $N[X^\sigma := M]$.*

Proposition 3. *Let M and N be arbitrary two $\lambda_\rightarrow$-terms of the same type σ with $M \rightarrow_\beta N$. For any vector $\boldsymbol{t}$ of M, there is a vector $\boldsymbol{s}$ of N such that $\boldsymbol{t} \succ_{\mathrm{po}} \boldsymbol{s}$ holds.*

Proof. By induction on the length of M. First, assume that $M = (\lambda X^\sigma.L_1)L_2$ and $L_1[X^\sigma := L_2] = N$ hold. Let a given vector of $\lambda X^\sigma.L_1$ be $(\delta \boldsymbol{x}^\sigma.\boldsymbol{d}^0)\#\boldsymbol{d}^k[\boldsymbol{x}^\sigma := \mathbf{1}]$ and a given vector of L_2 be $\boldsymbol{a}$. Then, we have

$$\begin{aligned}((\delta \boldsymbol{x}^\sigma.\boldsymbol{d}^0)\#\boldsymbol{d}^k[\boldsymbol{x}^\sigma := \mathbf{1}])\Box\boldsymbol{a} &\succ_{\mathrm{po}} (\delta \boldsymbol{x}^\sigma.\boldsymbol{d}^0)\Box\boldsymbol{a} && \text{By Lemma 3}\\ &\succ_{\mathrm{po}} \boldsymbol{d}^0[\boldsymbol{x}^\sigma := \boldsymbol{a}] && \text{By Lemma 5.(2)}\\ &\succ_{\mathrm{po}} \boldsymbol{d}^k[\boldsymbol{x}^\sigma := \boldsymbol{a}] && \text{By Lemma 2.(3),}\end{aligned}$$

hence we have the assertion since $\boldsymbol{d}^k[\boldsymbol{x}^\sigma := \boldsymbol{a}]$ is a vector of N by Lemma 6.

Next, assume that $M = \lambda X^\sigma.L_1 \rightarrow_\beta \lambda X^\sigma.L_2 = N$ holds and an assignment derivation d for $M \mapsto \boldsymbol{t}$ is given. Then, d consists of the immediate subderivations d_i of $D_i \mapsto \boldsymbol{d}^i$ for all i with $0 \leq i \leq k$ such that $D_k = L_1$ and $\boldsymbol{d}^0 \succ_{\mathrm{po}} \cdots \succ_{\mathrm{po}} \boldsymbol{d}^k$ hold. Since we have $L_1 \rightarrow_\beta L_2$, there is an assignment derivation d' of $L_2 \mapsto \boldsymbol{a}$ with $\boldsymbol{d}^k \succ_{\mathrm{po}} \boldsymbol{a}$ by IH. Therefore, by Lemma 2.(3), we can construct an assignment derivation of $\lambda X^\sigma.L_2 \mapsto \boldsymbol{s}$ from $d_0, \ldots, d_k$ and d' such that the assertion $\boldsymbol{t} = (\delta \boldsymbol{x}^\sigma.\boldsymbol{d}^0)\#\boldsymbol{d}^k[\boldsymbol{x}^\sigma := \mathbf{1}] \succ_{\mathrm{po}} (\delta \boldsymbol{x}^\sigma.\boldsymbol{d}^0)\#\boldsymbol{a}[\boldsymbol{x}^\sigma := \mathbf{1}] = \boldsymbol{s}$ holds.

Corollary 1. *Simply typed λ-calculus $\lambda_\rightarrow$ is terminating.*

Proof. Suppose that there is an infinite sequence $M_0 \rightarrow_\beta M_1 \rightarrow_\beta \cdots$ of β-rewrite relation. By putting $k = 0$ in all cases of Abstraction Rule (if any), we can assign a vector to M_0. Then, by Proposition 3, we have the infinite decreasing sequence $\boldsymbol{a}_0 \succ_{\mathrm{po}} \boldsymbol{a}_1 \succ_{\mathrm{po}} \cdots$ and this contradicts Proposition 2.

3 Extension and Comparison of the Path Ordering with Howard Algebra

In this section, we first discuss some extensions of the path ordering with Howard algebra: We sketch termination proofs of two combined systems of $\lambda_\rightarrow$ with higher-order rewrite rules, and introduce another path ordering with an algebra by simplifying Wilken and Weiermann's two step mappings, which was introduced to give their termination proof for the system T of primitive recursive functionals of finite type (Sect. 3.1). Next, we briefly compare our path ordering with Blanqui-Jouannaud-Rubio's computability path ordering CPO and van de Pol's semantic termination method (Sect. 3.2).

3.1 Extension to Some Combined Systems

We start from a sketch of termination proof for the combined system of $\lambda_{\rightarrow}$ and rewrite rules for the map function. In this case, the set $\mathcal{S}$ of base types consists of the type $\mathbb{N}$ of natural numbers and the type List of lists of natural numbers. We add the following clauses to extend the set of λ-terms:

(nat) $\mathsf{0}$ is a λ-term of type $\mathbb{N}$, and if M is a λ-term of type $\mathbb{N}$ then $\mathsf{S}(M)$ is a λ-term of type $\mathbb{N}$,
(list) nil is a λ-term of type List, and if M is a λ-term of type $\mathbb{N}$ and F, G are λ-terms of type List then $\mathsf{cons}(M, F)$ and $\mathsf{append}(F, G)$ are λ-terms of type List,
(map) if M is a λ-term of type $\mathbb{N} \rightarrow \mathbb{N}$ and N is a closed λ-term of type List then $\mathsf{map}(M, N)$ is a λ-term of type List.

Note that $\mathsf{S}(M), \mathsf{cons}(M, F), \mathsf{append}(F, G)$ and $\mathsf{map}(M, N)$ are constructed not by λ-application but by application of the function symbols $\mathsf{S}, \mathsf{cons}, \mathsf{append}$ and map, respectively. Our set of rewrite rules for the map function consists of the following rules:

1. $\mathsf{append}(\mathsf{nil}, M) \rightarrow M$,
2. $\mathsf{append}(\mathsf{cons}(M, N), L) \rightarrow \mathsf{cons}(M, \mathsf{append}(N, L))$,
3. $\mathsf{append}(\mathsf{append}(M, N), L) \rightarrow \mathsf{append}(M, \mathsf{append}(N, L))$,
4. $\mathsf{map}(M, \mathsf{nil}) \rightarrow \mathsf{nil}$,
5. $\mathsf{map}(M, \mathsf{cons}(N, L)) \rightarrow \mathsf{cons}(MN, \mathsf{map}(M, L))$.

Due to the algebraic rule 3. for append, these rules are not purely recursive ones. By the definition of λ-terms, N and L in the rule 5. are always closed. This restriction is needed to guarantee that a vector of $\mathsf{map}(M, N)$ below belongs to $\boldsymbol{C}$ and so Lemma 6 holds. Then, we add the following axioms and rules of assignment derivations.

$$\frac{}{\mathsf{0} \mapsto \langle 1 \rangle} \qquad \frac{M \mapsto \boldsymbol{a}}{\mathsf{S}(M) \mapsto \langle (\boldsymbol{a})_0 \# 1 \rangle} \qquad \frac{}{\mathsf{nil} \mapsto \langle 1 \rangle} \qquad \frac{M \mapsto \boldsymbol{a} \quad N \mapsto \boldsymbol{b}}{\mathsf{cons}(M, N) \mapsto \langle (\boldsymbol{a})_0 \# (\boldsymbol{b})_0 \rangle}$$

$$\frac{M \mapsto \boldsymbol{a} \quad N \mapsto \boldsymbol{b}}{\mathsf{append}(M, N) \mapsto \langle 2(\boldsymbol{a})_0 \# (\boldsymbol{b})_0 \rangle} \qquad \frac{M \mapsto \boldsymbol{a} \quad N \mapsto \boldsymbol{b}}{\mathsf{map}(M, N) \mapsto \langle ((\boldsymbol{a})_1 \# (\boldsymbol{b})_0, (\boldsymbol{a})_0 \# (\boldsymbol{b})_0) \rangle}$$

Since the rewrite rules 1.–5. decrease the order $\succ_{\mathrm{po}}$ and the monotonicity holds for $\mathsf{S}, \mathsf{cons}, \mathsf{append}$ and map on these assignments, one can prove the termination of the combined system above by the results of the previous section.

Our second example is the combined system of $\lambda_{\rightarrow}$ and rewrite rules for the Ackermann function without recursors. Take the set $\mathcal{S}$ of base types as $\{\mathbb{N}\}$.

In addition to the clause (nat) above, we also consider the following clause: If M, N are λ-terms with M closed, then $\mathsf{ack}(M, N)$ is a λ-term of type $\mathbb{N}$. We call a λ-term of the form $\mathsf{S}(\cdots\mathsf{S}(\mathsf{0})\cdots)$ with n occurrences of S ($n \geq 0$) a *numeral* and denote it by n. We consider the following rewrite rules for the Ackermann function[9]:

1. $\mathsf{ack}(\mathsf{0}, N) \to \mathsf{S}(N)$,
2. $\mathsf{ack}(\mathsf{S}(M), \mathsf{n}) \to$
   $(\lambda X_0.\mathsf{ack}(M, X_0))\Big(\cdots(\lambda X_{n-1}.\mathsf{ack}(M, X_{n-1}))\Big((\lambda X_n.\mathsf{ack}(M, X_n))1\Big)\cdots\Big)$.

These rules are not purely recursive ones in the respect that they are rewrite rules not following the usual primitive recursive calls. By using the following rule of assignment derivations, one can prove the termination of the combined system in this case by the results of the previous section.

$$\frac{M \mapsto \boldsymbol{a} \quad N \mapsto \boldsymbol{b}}{\mathsf{ack}(M, N) \mapsto \langle((1, (\boldsymbol{a})_0), (\boldsymbol{b})_0)\rangle}$$

Next, we introduce another path ordering with an algebra by simplifying Wilken and Weiermann's two step mappings for their termination proof of the system T [16]. Their proof is a refinement of Howard's proof in [9]: A collapsing function was incorporated into Wilken-Weiermann's vector system and they used this machinery to give the strong normalization theorem of T and an optimal derivation lengths classification of T, both of which were not given in Howard's proof. On the other hand, Wilken and Weiermann maintained Howard's two step mappings: The system T is embedded into their vector system $\mathcal{O}^{<\omega}$, and $\mathcal{O}^{<\omega}$ was interpreted in an ordinal notation system up to ε_0. In fact, they used the interpretation into ε_0 not only to guarantee the well foundedness of their ordering but also to define their ordering. Below we note that these two step mappings can be simplified into a single mapping as well.

First of all, we reformulate Wilken and Weiermann's vector system $\mathcal{O}^{<\omega}$ as a subset of a two-kinded Ω-algebra in the sense of [13]. Let $\Omega = (K, \Sigma, \pi)$ be the K-kinded signature which consists of

- the set of kinds: $K = \{\mathtt{Ter}, \mathtt{Vec}, \mathtt{Rel}\}$,
- the $K^* \times K$-indexed family of sets: $\Sigma_{\lambda,\mathtt{Ter}} = \{0\}$, $\Sigma_{\mathtt{Ter},\mathtt{Ter}} = \{\mathsf{exptwo}, \mathsf{omega}, \Psi\}$, $\Sigma_{\mathtt{Ter\,Ter},\mathtt{Ter}} = \{\#, \otimes, \mathsf{exp}, +\}$, $\Sigma_{\lambda,\mathtt{Vec}} = \{\epsilon\}$, $\Sigma_{\mathtt{Ter\,Vec},\mathtt{Vec}} = \{*\}$, $\Sigma_{\mathtt{Ter\,Ter},\mathtt{Rel}} = \mathsf{pair}$,
- the function from sorts to kinds: $S = \{\mathtt{Onf}, \mathtt{Tra}, \mathtt{Nat}, \mathtt{Pos}, \mathtt{Rpo}\}$ and $\pi : S \to K$ is defined as $\pi(\mathtt{X}) := \mathtt{Ter}$ for any $\mathtt{X} \in \{\mathtt{Onf}, \mathtt{Tra}, \mathtt{Nat}, \mathtt{Pos}\}$ and $\pi(\mathtt{Rpo}) := \mathtt{Rel}$.

The function symbol $+$ denotes the usual sum operation on ordinals, which is non-commutative, and the function symbol Ψ denotes the collapsing function ψ defined below. The symbols $+, \mathsf{exp}, \mathsf{pair}$, the kind $\mathtt{Rel}$ and the sort $\mathtt{Rpo}$ will be used only for defining an RPO-style ordering on Wilken and Weiermann's vector

[9] The rule 2. below is a higher-order version of a usual rule $\mathsf{ack}_{m+1}(n) \to \mathsf{ack}_m^{n+1}(1)$ with $f^0(k) := k$ and $f^{n+1}(k) := f(f^n(k))$.

system $\mathcal{O}^{<\omega}$, so these are not included in our formulation of this system. We take the family $\{\mathcal{X}_{\mathtt{Ter}}, \mathcal{X}_{\mathtt{Vec}}\}$ of sets of variables such that $\mathcal{X}_{\mathtt{Ter}}$ is a fixed infinite set and $\mathcal{X}_{\mathtt{Vec}}$ is empty. We put $2^t := \mathsf{exptwo}(t)$, $\omega^t := \mathsf{omega}(t)$, $1 := \omega^0$, $t^s := \mathsf{exp}(t,s)$ and $\langle t, s\rangle := \mathsf{pair}(t,s)$. Terms in $\mathcal{T}(\Omega,\mathcal{X})_{\mathtt{Ter}}$ are called *terms* simply, and terms in $\mathcal{T}(\Omega,\mathcal{X})_{\mathtt{Vec}}$ are called *vectors*. Then, Wilken and Weiermann's vector system consists of the subset $\mathcal{O}$ of $\mathcal{T}(\Omega,\mathcal{X})_{\mathtt{Ter}}$ and the subset $\mathcal{O}^{<\omega}$ of $\mathcal{T}(\Omega,\mathcal{X})_{\mathtt{Vec}}$ defined as follows (cf. [16, Definition 2.1]):[10]

- (i) $\mathcal{X}_{\mathtt{Ter}}$ is a subset of $\mathcal{O}$, (ii) 1 belongs to $\mathcal{O}$ and (iii) if $t, s \in \mathcal{O}$ holds then $t\#s, 2^t \otimes s, \Psi((\omega^1 \otimes t)\#s) \in \mathcal{O}$ holds, and
- all elements of $\mathcal{O}^{<\omega}$ are constructed from ϵ and elements of $\mathcal{O}$ by $*$.

It is not straightforward to define directly an RPO-style ordering compatible with the intended meaning of the symbols in $\mathcal{O}$. Indeed, in [16], the interpretation of $\mathcal{O}$ in the ordinal notation system up to ε_0 was used to define the ordering on $\mathcal{O}$.

To define an RPO-style ordering without such an interpretation, we use membership equational logic in [13]. The subset $\mathcal{O}^{\mathrm{fla}}$ of $\mathcal{T}(\Omega)_{\mathtt{Ter}}$ is defined as the set of all flattened terms of $\mathcal{T}(\Omega)_{\mathtt{Ter}}$ with respect to # which include no occurrence of Ψ. Let $\mathcal{O}^{\mathrm{nf}}$ be the subset of $\mathcal{O}^{\mathrm{fla}}$ all of whose elements are constructed from 1 by $\{\#, \mathsf{omega}\}$, $\mathcal{O}^{\mathbb{Z}^+}$ be the subset of $\mathcal{O}^{\mathrm{nf}}$ all of whose elements are constructed from 1 by # only and $\mathcal{O}^{\mathbb{N}}$ be $\mathcal{O}^{\mathbb{Z}^+} \cup \{0\}$. Note that any $t \in \mathcal{O}^{\mathrm{nf}}$ is of the form $\omega^{t_1}\#\cdots\#\omega^{t_n}$ with $n \geq 1$. We abbreviate $\langle t_1, t_2\rangle : \mathtt{Rpo} \wedge \langle t_2, t_3\rangle : \mathtt{Rpo} \wedge \cdots \wedge \langle t_{n-1}, t_n\rangle : \mathtt{Rpo}$ as $t_1 \geq_{\mathtt{Rpo}} \cdots \geq_{\mathtt{Rpo}} t_n$. Let $\succeq_{\mathrm{rpo}}$ be the recursive path ordering on $\mathcal{O}^{\mathrm{nf}}$ with the precedence relation $\mathsf{omega} > \# > 1$. Later we use the interpretation g of sorts such that

$g(\mathtt{Onf}) = \mathcal{O}^{\mathrm{nf}}$, $g(\mathtt{Tra}) = \mathcal{O}^{\mathrm{nf}} \setminus \mathcal{O}^{\mathbb{Z}^+}$, $g(\mathtt{Nat}) = \mathcal{O}^{\mathbb{N}}$, $g(\mathtt{Pos}) = \mathcal{O}^{\mathbb{Z}^+}$ and $g(\mathtt{Rpo}) = \succeq_{\mathrm{rpo}}$

hold.

Definition 8. *The set E of sentences in membership equational logic consists of the following sentences:*

1.

$$\begin{cases} x + 0 = x \\ 0 + x = x \\ (x+y)+z = x + (y+z) \end{cases}$$

2. $\omega^{x_1}\#\cdots\#\omega^{x_n} = (\cdots(\omega^{x_{p(1)}} + \omega^{x_{p(2)}}) + \cdots) + \omega^{x_{p(n)}}$
$\Leftarrow x_1 : \mathtt{Onf} \wedge \cdots \wedge x_n : \mathtt{Onf} \wedge x_{p(1)} \geq_{\mathtt{Rpo}} \cdots \geq_{\mathtt{Rpo}} x_{p(n)}$
for any $n \geq 2$ and any permutation p of $\{1, \ldots, n\}$.

3. $(\omega^{x_1}\#\cdots\#\omega^{x_n}) \otimes (\omega^{y_1}\#\cdots\#\omega^{y_m}) =$
$\omega^{x_1\#y_1}\#\cdots\#\omega^{x_1\#y_m}\#\cdots\#\omega^{x_n\#y_1}\#\cdots\#\omega^{x_n\#y_m}$ *for any $n, m \geq 1$.*

4.

$$\begin{cases} x^0 = 1 \Leftarrow x : \mathtt{Pos} \\ x^{y+1} = (x^y) \otimes x \Leftarrow x : \mathtt{Pos} \wedge y : \mathtt{Nat} \end{cases}$$

[10] As in the case of Howard's vector system, we omit 0 from $\mathcal{O}$.

5. $2^x = (1\#1)^x \Leftarrow x : \mathtt{Nat}$.
6. $2^{\omega^{x_1}+\cdots+\omega^{x_k}+\omega^{1+y_1}+\cdots+\omega^{1+y_m}+x} = \omega^{\omega^{x_1}+\cdots+\omega^{x_k}+\omega^{y_1}+\cdots+\omega^{y_m}} \otimes (1\#1)^x$
$\Leftarrow x_1 : \mathtt{Tra} \wedge \cdots \wedge x_k : \mathtt{Tra} \wedge y_1 : \mathtt{Nat} \wedge \cdots \wedge y_m : \mathtt{Nat} \wedge x : \mathtt{Pos}$
for any k, m *with* $k + m \geq 1$.

We denote by E' *the set which consists of the sentences 1. and 2. above.*

Intuitively, the sentence 2 corresponds to the definition of the commutative sum $\#$ on $\mathcal{O}^{\mathrm{nf}}$ in terms of the non-commutative sum $+$, and the sentence 3 corresponds to the definition of the commutative product on $\mathcal{O}^{\mathrm{nf}}$ in terms of the commutative sum. The sentences 5 and 6 state the definition of exponentiation of base 2 on $\mathcal{O}^{\mathrm{nf}}$. These sentences are inspired by arithmetical operations on ordinal notations (cf. [15, Chapter V]).

We put W as the oriented set of the sentences 3.–6. on $\mathcal{O}^{\mathrm{fla}}$ which gives to the equations in these sentences the direction from the left-hand side to the right-hand side. We define the W/E'-rewrite relation $\rightarrow_{W/E'}$ on $\mathcal{O}^{\mathrm{fla}}$ as follows: For any $t, s \in \mathcal{O}^{\mathrm{fla}}$, $t \rightarrow_{W/E'} s$ holds if and only if for some $t', s' \in \mathcal{O}^{\mathrm{fla}}$, we have $E' \vdash t = t'$, $t' \rightarrow_W s'$ and $E' \vdash s' = s$ on the interpretation g of sorts, where $\rightarrow_W$ is the W-rewrite relation on $\mathcal{O}^{\mathrm{fla}}$. We fix an interpretation of $\mathcal{O}^{\mathrm{fla}}$ in $\mathbb{N}$ such as the following interpretation τ

$$\tau(0) := 0, \quad \tau(2^t) := 2^{2^{\tau(t)+3}}, \quad \tau(\omega^t) := \tau(t) + 2, \quad \tau(t^s) := \tau(t)^{\tau(s)+2},$$
$$\tau(t + s) := \tau(t) + \tau(s), \quad \tau(t \otimes s) := \tau(t) \cdot \tau(s),$$
$$\tau(t_1 \# \cdots \# t_n) := \tau(t_1) + \cdots + \tau(t_n).$$

One can show that $\tau(t) = \tau(s)$ holds for any equation $t = s$ in E' and that $\tau(t) > \tau(s)$ holds for any rule $t \rightarrow s$ or the conclusion $t \rightarrow s$ of any conditional rule from W. Since we have $\tau(u[t]_p) > \tau(u[s]_p)$ whenever $\tau(t) > \tau(s)$ holds, the rewrite relation $\rightarrow_{W/E'}$ is terminating. This rewrite relation is also convergent, because it is locally confluent and hence it is confluent. For any $t \in \mathcal{O}^{\mathrm{fla}}$, let $\mathrm{nf}(t)$ be a fixed $\rightarrow_{W/E'}$-normal form s of t with $s \in \mathcal{O}^{\mathrm{nf}}$. We define the choice function f_W for the equivalence classes $[t]_{R^E}$ induced by E as $f_W(t) := \mathrm{nf}(t)$, and the ordering $t \succeq_E s$ on $\mathcal{O}^{\mathrm{fla}}$ as $t \succeq_E s$ holds if and only if $f_W([t]_{R^E}) \succeq_{\mathrm{rpo}} f_W([s]_{R^E})$ holds. Then, one can see that the path ordering $(\mathcal{O}^{\mathrm{fla}}, \succeq_E)$ with the algebra E with respect to f_W is a well quasi ordering by an argument similar to the proof of Lemma 1.

To extend this well quasi ordering to the term-set $\mathcal{O}$ in Wilken-Weiermann's vector system, we define the norm function no and the collapsing function ψ, following [16, p. 15]. For any $t \in \mathcal{O}^{\mathrm{nf}}$, the norm function $\mathrm{no} : \mathcal{O}^{\mathrm{nf}} \rightarrow \mathbb{N}$ is defined by induction on the length of t: $\mathrm{no}(1) := 1$ and $\mathrm{no}(\omega^{t_1} \# \cdots \# \omega^{t_n}) := n + \mathrm{no}(t_1) + \cdots + \mathrm{no}(t_n)$ with $n \geq 1$. We define the number theoretic functions $F_n : \mathbb{N} \rightarrow \mathbb{N}$ by $F_0(x) := 2^x$ and $F_{n+1}(x) := F_n^{x+1}(x)$, and fix a fast growing number theoretic function $\varPhi : \mathbb{N} \rightarrow \mathbb{N}$ such that $\varPhi$ is bounded by some suitable F_k. The collapsing function $\psi : \mathcal{O}^{\mathrm{nf}} \rightarrow \mathcal{O}^{\mathbb{Z}^+}$ is defined by recursion on the order type of $(\mathcal{O}^{\mathrm{nf}}, \succ_{\mathrm{rpo}})$:

$$\psi(t) := \max(\{1\} \cup \{\psi(s)\overline{\#}1 \mid t \succ_{\mathrm{rpo}} s,\ \mathrm{no}(s) \leq \varPhi(\mathrm{no}(t))\}).$$

As explained in [16, p. 15], the set $\{t \mid \text{no}(t) \leq m\}$ is finite for any $m \in \mathbb{N}$, hence $\psi(t)$ is always defined.

Definition 9 (Normalization Function). *The function* $[\![\cdot]\!]$ *from closed terms of* $\mathcal{O}$ *to terms of* $\mathcal{O}^{\text{nf}}$ *is defined as follows. We first define the mapping* * *from flattened* $\mathcal{O}$*-terms to* $\mathcal{O}^{\text{nf}}$ *as*

$$1^* := 1, \quad (2^t \otimes s)^* := \text{nf}(2^{(t^*)} \otimes s^*), \quad (t_1 \# \cdots \# t_n)^* := t_1^* \overline{\#} \cdots \overline{\#} t_n^*,$$
$$(\Psi((\omega^1 \otimes t) \# s_1 \# \cdots \# s_n))^* := \psi(\text{nf}((\omega^1 \otimes t^*) \overline{\#} s_1^* \overline{\#} \cdots \overline{\#} s_n^*)).$$

For any closed $t \in \mathcal{O}$*, we define* $[\![t]\!] := \overline{t}^*$*, where* $\overline{t}$ *is the flattened term obtained from* t*.*

This normalization function gives the following well quasi ordering $\succeq$ on closed terms of $\mathcal{O}$: For any closed $t, s \in \mathcal{O}$, $t \succeq s$ holds if and only if $[\![t]\!] \succeq_{\text{rpo}} [\![s]\!]$ holds. For any $t, s \in \mathcal{O}$ such that t, s are not closed, we can define the ordering $t \succeq s$ by using substitutions as in [16, Definition 2.7], and obtain the RPO-style ordering $(\mathcal{O}, \succeq)$. Note that this ordering is formulated by the manner in Sect. 2.1 *plus* the collapsing function ψ. Then, the ordering $\succeq$ can be extended to $\mathcal{O}^{<\omega}$ as in [16, Definition 2.8], and we have the well-founded ordering $(\mathcal{O}^{<\omega}, \succeq)$. By the non-unique assignment method formulated in [16, §§2–3], the system T can be embedded into $(\mathcal{O}^{<\omega}, \succeq)$.

3.2 Comparison with Other Methods

For higher-order termination proofs, which we discussed in the previous subsection, there are some RPO-style orderings such as Jouannaud and Rubio's higher-order recursive path ordering (HORPO) [12] and Blanqui, Jouannaud and Rubio's computability path ordering (CPO) [4]. The ordering HORPO was introduced as an extension of RPO to λ-terms with function symbols: It is an RPO-style ordering defined for these terms directly. Then, CPO was introduced as a syntax-oriented counterpart of the combination of HORPO and the computability closure construction (as to the computability closure construction, see [2]), so the domain of CPO contains λ-terms as well. On the other hand, the domain of our path ordering consists of first-order terms.

By using CPO, one can handle higher-order rewrite rules for several inductive types such as strictly positive inductive types, so the applicability of CPO is wider than our path ordering. Nevertheless, in some case, it is easier to use our ordering in proving termination than to use CPO. To see this, we give an (ad hoc) example: Let $\{P, \bot\}$ be the set of base types and extend λ-terms of $\lambda_{\rightarrow}$ as follows.

- The constant $\mathtt{tt}$ is a λ-term of type P, and the constant $\mathtt{ff}$ is a λ-term of type $P \rightarrow \bot$,
- if M is a λ-term of type P and N is a λ-term of type $P \rightarrow \bot$, then $\neg_i(M)$ and $\mathsf{f}_i(M)$ are λ-terms of type $P \rightarrow \bot$, and $\neg_c(N)$ and $\mathsf{f}_c(N)$ are λ-terms of type P.

We put $\mathcal{F} := \{\mathsf{tt}, \mathsf{ff}, \mathsf{f}_c, \mathsf{f}_i, \neg_c, \neg_i\}$. Intuitively, λ-terms of type P and λ-terms of type $P \to \bot$ are constructed simultaneously from the constants tt, ff and variables by application of the function symbols $\mathsf{f}_c, \mathsf{f}_i, \neg_c, \neg_i$ or λ-abstraction/application. We consider the following set R of rewrite rules.

$$\begin{cases} \mathsf{f}_i(\mathsf{tt}) \to \mathsf{ff} \\ \mathsf{f}_c(\mathsf{ff}) \to \mathsf{tt} \end{cases} \qquad \begin{cases} \mathsf{f}_i(\neg_c(N)) \to \neg_i(\mathsf{f}_c(N)) \\ \mathsf{f}_c(\neg_i(M)) \to \neg_c(\mathsf{f}_i(M)) \end{cases}$$

For example, $\mathsf{f}_i(\neg_c(\neg_i(\mathsf{tt}))) \to \neg_i(\mathsf{f}_c(\neg_i(\mathsf{tt}))) \to \neg_i(\neg_c(\mathsf{f}_i(\mathsf{tt}))) \to \neg_i(\neg_c(\mathsf{ff}))$ holds. We use the terminology of [4] such as *admissible type orderings* [4, Definition 2.2], *accessible terms* [4, Definition 7.5], *structurally smaller terms* [4, Definition 7.8], the relation $\succ^X$ [4, Definition 7.10] and the relation $\succ^X_\tau$ [4, Definition 5.1]. We fix an arbitrary admissible ordering $>$ on types.

Then, one can see that the rules of R cannot be oriented by CPO with accessible subterms on any preference relation $\geq_{\mathcal{F}}$ on $\mathcal{F}$. Indeed, a contradiction follows if we suppose $\mathsf{f}_i(\neg_c(X)) \succ_\tau \neg_i(\mathsf{f}_c(X))$ and $\mathsf{f}_c(\neg_i(Y)) \succ_\tau \neg_c(\mathsf{f}_i(Y))$ for a variable X of type $P \to \bot$ and a variable Y of type P. Roughly speaking, the reason is that λ-terms of type P are constructed by the function symbols f_c and $\neg_c$, the type of whose arguments has a *negative* occurrence of P. This considerably limits the number of accessible terms and structurally smaller terms for the terms in R.[11]

On the other hand, the termination of the combined system of $\lambda_\to$ with the rules above is provable under the assignment derivations in Sect. 2.2 extended by the following axioms and rules.

$$\frac{}{\mathsf{tt} \mapsto \langle 1 \rangle} \qquad \frac{}{\mathsf{ff} \mapsto \langle 1, 1 \rangle} \qquad \frac{M \mapsto \boldsymbol{b}}{\mathsf{f}_i(M) \mapsto \langle 2(\boldsymbol{b})_0, 1 \rangle} \qquad \frac{M \mapsto \boldsymbol{b}}{\neg_i(M) \mapsto \langle (\boldsymbol{b})_0 \# 1, 1 \rangle}$$

$$\frac{N \mapsto \boldsymbol{a}}{\mathsf{f}_c(N) \mapsto \langle 2((\boldsymbol{a})_1, (\boldsymbol{a})_0) \rangle} \qquad \frac{N \mapsto \boldsymbol{a}}{\neg_c(N) \mapsto \langle ((\boldsymbol{a})_1, (\boldsymbol{a})_0) \# 1 \rangle}$$

The path ordering with Howard algebra is not sensitive to the polarity of occurrences of basic types and so one can easily handle this example by using it, while the polarity of occurrences of basic types affects much on the applicability of CPO.

Finally, we briefly compare our termination proof with van de Pol's semantic termination method, following [14] with respect to the notions and terminology. Van de Pol's method is a generalization of semantic termination method of first-order term rewrite systems to higher-order ones. This method includes two key kinds of functionals of finite type, namely, *weakly monotonic functionals* and *strict functionals*, which were introduced to overcome the difficulties in applying Gandy's termination proof to higher-order rewrite systems (cf. [14, Chapters 3–5]). The former functionals of each finite type are equipped with a weakly monotonic ordering, and the latter functionals are the former's special

11 A similar remark can be found in [4, p. 24].

cases which preserve the order in a strict way so that they preserve the order even if they take weakly monotonic functionals as arguments.

There are two major differences between Howard's method, which our termination proof follows, and van de Pol's one: (1) Howard's method does not need functionals of any finite type to interpret λ-terms, and (2) the delta operator in Howard's method is not even weakly monotonic. In Howard's method, all λ-terms are interpreted as vectors, which are finite sequences of terms and so can be considered to be first-order objects. Type level of a λ-term is reflected in the length of its vectors. On the other hand, van de Pol's method interprets λ-terms of each type σ as functionals of type $[\![\sigma]\!]$, where $[\![\sigma]\!]$ is the interpretation of σ defined in this method. The square operator and the delta operator of Howard's method are, roughly speaking, operators from vectors to vectors and so they are higher-order objects as functionals of finite type are. However, as we have mentioned in Sect. 2, the delta operator is not even weakly monotonic, though the square operator is monotonic. Recall that non-unique assignments of vectors in Howard's method were introduced to cope with the non-monotonicity of the delta operator. As to the applicability of van de Pol's method, it is wider than the applicability of Howard's method as the examples in [14, Chapter 5] have shown.

4 Concluding Remark and Future Work

We have introduced the path ordering with Howard algebra, and then we have simplified Howard's two step mappings for his termination proof of $\lambda_{\rightarrow}$ to one mapping. Moreover, we have given some extensions of our ordering and some comparisons with other termination methods such as CPO.

Termination proofs by our ordering could be complementary to ones by HORPO or CPO when an interpretation of λ-abstraction and λ-application is helpful, so we shall investigate such examples. We would also examine how a path ordering with an algebra is related to rewriting modulo equations, although the ways to use a rewrite system for a path ordering with an algebra and the typical rewriting modulo equations are rather different apparently (recall that, in the case of our ordering, a rewrite system was used as a system of oriented equations from an algebra). In addition to it, we would examine whether an application of our ordering to termination proofs of higher-order rewriting can be automated or not. We also plan to investigate the applicability of our ordering modulo an algebra by finding useful examples from the rewriting theoretic view.

As we explained in Sect. 1, our motivation of this work was to view Howard's proof in [9] as a case study towards Lévy's open question. Our work in this paper is still a small step towards clarifying this question. We intend to work further on this topic by investigating other case studies.

References

1. Barbanera, F., Fernández, M., Geuvers, H.: Modularity of strong normalization and confluence in the algebraic-lambda-cube. In: Proceedings of the Ninth Annual Symposium on Logic in Computer Science (LICS 1994), Paris, France, 4–7 July 1994, pp. 406–415 (1994). https://doi.org/10.1109/LICS.1994.316049
2. Blanqui, F., Jouannaud, J.P., Okada, M.: Inductive-data-type systems. Theoret. Comput. Sci. **272**(1), 41–68 (2002). https://doi.org/10.1016/S0304-3975(00)00347-9
3. Blanqui, F., Jouannaud, J., Okada, M.: Corrigendum to "Inductive-data-type systems" [Theoret. Comput. Sci. **272**(1–2) 41–68]. Theor. Comput. Sci. **817**, 81–82 (2020). https://doi.org/10.1016/j.tcs.2018.01.010
4. Blanqui, F., Jouannaud, J., Rubio, A.: The computability path ordering. Logical Methods Comput. Sci. **11**(4) (2015). https://doi.org/10.2168/LMCS-11(4:3)2015
5. Dershowitz, N.: Orderings for term-rewriting systems. Theoret. Comput. Sci. **17**, 279–301 (1982). https://doi.org/10.1016/0304-3975(82)90026-3
6. Dershowitz, N.: Termination of rewriting. J. Symb. Comput. **3**(1), 69–115 (1987). https://doi.org/10.1016/S0747-7171(87)80022-6
7. Dershowitz, N., Jouannaud, J.P.: Rewrite systems. In: van Leeuwen, J. (ed.) Handbook of Theoretical Computer Science, vol. B, pp. 243–320. MIT Press, Cambridge (1990)
8. Dershowitz, N., Okada, M.: Proof-theoretic techniques for term rewriting theory. In: Proceedings of the Third Annual Symposium on Logic in Computer Science (LICS 1988), Edinburgh, Scotland, UK, July 5–8, 1988, pp. 104–111 (1988). https://doi.org/10.1109/LICS.1988.5108
9. Howard, W.A.: Assignment of ordinals to terms for primitive recursive functionals of finite type. In: Kino, A., Myhill, J., Vesley, R.E. (eds.) Intuitionism and Proof Theory: Proceedings of the Summer Conference at Buffalo N.Y. 1968, Studies in Logic and the Foundations of Mathematics, vol. 60, pp. 443–458. Elsevier (1970). https://doi.org/10.1016/S0049-237X(08)70770-5
10. Jouannaud, J., Okada, M.: A computation model for executable higher-order algebraic specification languages. In: Proceedings of the Sixth Annual Symposium on Logic in Computer Science (LICS 1991), Amsterdam, The Netherlands, 15–18 July 1991, pp. 350–361 (1991). https://doi.org/10.1109/LICS.1991.151659
11. Jouannaud, J., Okada, M.: Abstract data type systems. Theoret. Comput. Sci. **173**(2), 349–391 (1997). https://doi.org/10.1016/S0304-3975(96)00161-2
12. Jouannaud, J., Rubio, A.: Polymorphic higher-order recursive path orderings. J. ACM **54**(1), 2:1–2:48 (2007). https://doi.org/10.1145/1206035.1206037
13. Meseguer, J.: Membership algebra as a logical framework for equational specification. In: 12th International Workshop on Recent Trends in Algebraic Development Techniques, WADT 1997, Tarquinia, Italy, June 1997, Selected Papers, pp. 18–61 (1997). https://doi.org/10.1007/3-540-64299-4_26
14. van de Pol, J.: Termination of higher-order rewrite systems. Ph.D. thesis, Universiteit Utrecht (1996)
15. Schütte, K.: Proof Theory, Grundlehren der mathematischen Wissenschaften, vol. 225. Springer, Heidelberg (1977). https://doi.org/10.1007/978-3-642-66473-1
16. Wilken, G., Weiermann, A.: Derivation lengths classification of Gödel's T extending Howard's Assignment. Logical Methods Comput. Sci. **8**(1) (2012). https://doi.org/10.2168/LMCS-8(1:19)2012

Strategies, Model Checking and Branching-Time Properties in Maude

Rubén Rubio(✉), Narciso Martí-Oliet, Isabel Pita, and Alberto Verdejo

Facultad de Informática, Universidad Complutense de Madrid, Madrid, Spain
{rubenrub,narciso,ipandreu,jalberto}@ucm.es

Abstract. Maude 3 includes as a new feature an object-level strategy language. Rewriting strategies can now be used to easily control how rules are applied, restricting the rewriting systems behavior. This new specification layer would not be useful if there were no tools to execute, analyze and verify its creatures. For that reason, we extended the Maude LTL model checker to systems controlled by strategies, after studying their model-checking problem. Now, we widen the range of properties that can be checked in Maude models, both strategy-aware and strategy-free, by implementing a module for the language-independent model checker LTSmin that supports logics like CTL* and μ-calculus.

1 Introduction

The Maude [13] specification language has recently reached its 3.0 version, integrating new features developed during the last years, such as a full implementation of the Maude strategy language [13, §10]. Although rewriting logic owes its natural representation of concurrency to the possibility that different rules can be executed in different positions at each step of the rewriting process, there are situations in which it is convenient to control such nondeterminism. This is the purpose of strategies, which have traditionally been expressed in Maude at the metalevel by means of its reflective features [14,15,34], but since the complexity and learning curve of programming metalevel computations is hard, an object-level strategy language design was proposed [17,27], exercised with different examples [28,33,35,37, ...], and finally added to the Core Maude functionality. Strategies can be described compositionally using strategy modules on top of system modules, and different commands are provided to rewrite a term following a strategy.

However, this new feature would be worthless without convenient tools to analyze the specifications using it. One of the most useful tools for verifying regular Maude modules is its LTL model checker [19]. In a previous work [32], we have studied the model-checking problem for rewriting systems controlled by strategies and presented an extension of the model checker to deal with them.

Research partially supported by MCI Spanish project *TRACES* (TIN2015-67522-C3-3-R). Rubén Rubio is partially supported by MU grant FPU17/02319.

S. Escobar and N. Martí-Oliet (Eds.): WRLA 2020, LNCS 12328, pp. 156–175, 2020.
https://doi.org/10.1007/978-3-030-63595-4_9

However, since the original Maude model checker is limited to LTL properties, these are the only ones that our extension can handle and the discussion was mainly centered on linear-time properties. In this paper, we further discuss branching-time properties and show an implementation of a language plugin for the language-independent model checker LTSmin [23] that extends the repertory of logics in which properties can be expressed to CTL* and μ-calculus, for both the strategy-aware specifications and the regular ones. It can be downloaded from http://maude.ucm.es/strategies.

In the following sections, we briefly introduce the strategy language, the model-checking problem in this context, and the plugin we have developed. But let us first introduce a motivational example: the *river crossing* puzzle. In this classical game, a shepherd needs to cross a river carrying a wolf, a goat, and a cabbage. The only way to cross it is using a boat that only the shepherd can operate and with room for only one more being. The shepherd could ship their companions to the other side one by one, but the wolf would eat the goat and the goat would eat the cabbage as soon as the shepherd is not present to impede it. The Maude signature of the problem is specified in a functional module:

```
fmod RIVER is
  sorts Side Being Group River .
  subsorts Side Being < Group .

  ops left right : -> Side [ctor] .
  ops shepherd wolf goat cabbage : -> Being [ctor] .
  op __ : Group Group -> Group [ctor assoc comm] .
  op _|_ : Group Group -> River [ctor comm] .

  op initial : -> River .
  eq initial = left shepherd wolf goat cabbage | right .
endfm
```

Characters have been defined as constants of sort `Being` and can be put together to form a group. A river is a commutative pair of groups representing its two banks, since most properties and rules of the game are symmetric. However, to distinguish the initial and final states, sides are marked with the constants `left` and `right`. The system module `RIVER-CROSSING` completes the equational specification with rules: `alone`, `wolf`, `goat`, and `cabbage` cause the shepherd to cross the river with the mentioned passenger, while `wolf-eats` and `goat-eats` make such an animal eat its prey, which vanishes from the scene.

```
mod RIVER-CROSSING is
  protecting RIVER .

  vars G G' : Group .

  rl [alone] : shepherd G | G' =>
                        G | G' shepherd .
  rl [wolf] : shepherd wolf G | G' =>
                            G | G' shepherd wolf .
```

```
  rl [goat] : shepherd goat G | G' =>
                                 G | G' shepherd goat .
  rl [cabbage] : shepherd cabbage G | G' =>
                              G | G' shepherd cabbage .

  rl [wolf-eats] : goat wolf G | G' shepherd =>
                              wolf G | G' shepherd .
  rl [goat-eats] : cabbage goat G | G' shepherd =>
                                 goat G | G' shepherd .
endm
```

The rules of the game tell that no character will miss the chance to claim its prey, so the eating rules must be applied if possible before any other crossing. This is not guaranteed in the system module, but expressing this restriction using strategies is easy, and we will see how in the following section.

In a previous specification of this problem in Maude [30], the eating rules were written as equations. While this alternative also ensures the discussed property according to the operational semantics of the Maude rewriting engine, it yields a rewrite theory where rules and equations are not coherent.[1]

2 The Maude Strategy Language

As we have said in the introduction, the Maude strategy language was born to allow expressing rewriting strategies without the difficulties of the metalevel. Its design is based on the experience with reflective computations, and on earlier strategy languages like ELAN [6] and Stratego [8].

A strategy α can be seen, if we look at its results, as a transformation from a term t into a set of terms, since the rewriting process controlled by α may still be nondeterministic. These results can be obtained within the interpreter using the `srewrite` t `using` α command. The most elementary strategy is rule application

$$\textsf{top}(\mathit{label}\,\texttt{[}x_1\texttt{ <- }t_1\texttt{, ... , }x_n\texttt{ <- }t_n\texttt{]}\{\alpha_1\texttt{, ... ,}\alpha_m\}),$$

that executes any available rules with label *label* on any subterm of the subject term. An optional substitution can be specified between brackets to instantiate any occurrence of the variables x_k in the rule and its condition with t_k before matching, and to apply rules with rewriting conditions, strategies α_l must be provided to control each rewriting condition fragment. To restrict the application of the rule to the top of the subject term, it should be surrounded with the **top** modifier. A more powerful tool for selecting to which subterm a strategy is applied is the **matchrew** operator

$$\textbf{matchrew } P \textbf{ s.t. } C \textbf{ by } x_1 \textbf{ using } \alpha_1 \texttt{, ... ,} x_n \textbf{ using } \alpha_n$$

[1] A rewrite theory is *coherent* if for any term t rewritten by a rule to a term t', its canonical form u modulo equations and axioms can be rewritten to a term u' that is equationally equivalent to t', see [13, §5.3]. Coherence is assumed by Maude, which reduces terms to their canonical forms before applying a rule, not to miss any rewrite.

It matches the pattern P on top of the subject term, and for each match satisfying the condition C, the subterms corresponding to the variables $x_1, \ldots, x_n$ are rewritten using the strategies $\alpha_1, \ldots, \alpha_n$ respectively, and reassembled again. The **matchrew** keyword can be prefixed by a to match anywhere or x to match modulo structural axioms. The same variants exist for the tests **match** P **s.t.** C, which check if P matches the subject term and satisfies C. Regular expressions are included in the strategy language by means of the alternation α | β, the concatenation α ; β, the Kleene star α^*, and the constants **idle** and **fail** . A conditional strategy α ? β : γ is also available. It executes α and then β on its results, but if α does not produce any, it applies γ to the initial term. The language includes some other derived operators like α `or-else` β defined as α ? **idle** : β, or **not**(α) defined as α ? **fail** : **idle**.

Using these combinators, we can guarantee that eating happens eagerly before traveling in the river crossing puzzle with the following strategy:

```
((wolf-eats | goat-eats)
 or-else (alone | cabbage | goat | wolf)) *
```

In each step of the iteration, which can stop nondeterministically at any time, the `or-else` combinator ensures that the crossing rules of its second argument are tried only if the eating rules in its first argument do not succeed. However, when strategies become more complex, writing long self-contained strategy expressions is not practical. For example, the previous will be easier to read if we name the first union of the expression as `eating` and the second as `oneCrossing`, writing then `(eating or-else oneCrossing) *`. Strategy modules allow to define strategies, which can take parameters and call themselves recursively, thus extending the expressive power of the language. They are introduced by the **smod** keyword and may contain strategy declarations **strat** `sname : T1 ... Tn @ T` specifying its name and signature, and (possibly conditional) strategy definitions like **sd** `sname(`$t_1, \ldots, t_n$`) :=` α. A strategy call will execute all strategy definitions whose left-hand side matches the call term, instantiating the right-hand side expression with the variables bound in the left-hand side and the optional condition.

The following strategy module gives some strategy definitions for the river crossing problem:

```
smod RIVER-CROSSING-STRAT is
  protecting RIVER-CROSSING .

  var G : Group .

  strats oneCrossing eating @ River .
  sd oneCrossing := alone | wolf | goat | cabbage .
  sd eating := wolf-eats | goat-eats .

  strats solution eagerEating safe @ River .

  sd solution := goat ; alone ; cabbage ; goat ;
                 wolf ; alone ; goat .
```

```
  sd eagerEating := match left | G cabbage goat ? idle
      : ((eating or-else oneCrossing) ; eagerEating) .

  sd safe := match left | G ? idle
      : (oneCrossing ; not(eating) ; safe) .
endsm
```

In addition to the `oneCrossing` and `eating` strategies described before, there is also a deterministic strategy `solution` that simply applies a choice of steps that are known to solve the problem. The `eagerEating` strategy applies any rule in each recursive call respecting their precedence, and continues indefinitely or until a solution is found. Observe that the definition is recursive and nonterminating. This will not pose a problem since the execution engine and the model checker will be able to detect this loop and finish, and it is a useful resource to specify the behavior of reactive systems. The last strategy `safe` discards all rewriting paths where some being can be swallowed by concatenating the `not(eating)` strategy that fails whenever `eating` succeeds. Note that the stop condition only checks whether the left side of the river is empty, which is enough provided no one dies, while in `eagerEating` it is necessary to check that the goat and cabbage are still alive. We can execute the strategy to see how the solution is reached:

```
Maude> srew initial using safe .

Solution 1
rewrites: 33
result River: left | right shepherd wolf goat cabbage

No more solutions.
rewrites: 33
```

More details about the strategy language together with several examples can be found in its chapter in the Maude manual [13], in [16], and in the Maude strategy language website [18].

3 Model Checking

Model checking [11,12] is an automated verification technique based on the exhaustive exploration of a system model to check a property describing aspects of its intended behavior. Multiple variants and algorithms exist, but traditionally the model is represented as a state and transition system, and the property in some temporal logic.

A *transition system* or *abstract reduction system* $\mathcal{A} = (S, \to)$ is a set of states S endowed with a binary transition relation $(\to) \subseteq S \times S$, which is usually required to have a successor for each state to avoid dealing with finite executions. We will write $\Gamma^\omega_\mathcal{A} = \{(s_n)_{n=0}^\infty : s_n \to s_{n+1}\}$ and $\Gamma^*_\mathcal{A}$ for the set of infinite and finite executions, respectively, with an additional subindex $s \in S$ to include only those executions starting at s. In this context [7], a strategy can be seen *extensionally* as a subset $E \subseteq \Gamma_{\mathcal{A}}^{\omega}$ of executions, or *intensionally* as a partial function $\lambda : \Gamma_{\mathcal{A}}^{*} \to \mathcal{P}(S)$ that limits the possible next steps for a given execution prefix. While any intensional strategy λ can be seen extensionally $E(\lambda) := \{(s_n)_{n=0}^{\infty} : s_{n+1} \in \lambda(s_0 \cdots s_n)\}$, the converse is not true [7]. However, most common strategies can be expressed intensionally, and we will generally assume this.

The properties about the system behavior are expressed in terms of some tags declared for each state. This yields a Kripke structure $\mathcal{K} = (S, \to, AP, I, \ell)$ with a finite set of such atomic propositions AP, a finite set of initial states $I \subseteq S$, and a labeling function $\ell : S \to \mathcal{P}(AP)$. Temporal logics combine these properties with operators that describe how they occur in time. Well-known examples of such logics are CTL* and its sublogics LTL (Linear Temporal Logic) and CTL (Computational Tree Logic).

However, some other logics like the μ-calculus do not refer only to state properties but also to the transitions. The abstract setting needs then to be enriched with labels for them: *labeled transition systems* (LTS) are defined as triples (S, A, R) where A is a set of edge labels or actions and $R \subseteq S \times A \times S$ is a tagged relation. Strategies and executions are defined similarly, but in this case interleaving states with edge labels, i.e., $\Gamma_{\mathcal{A},s_0}^{\omega} = \{s_0(a_n s_n)_{n=1}^{\infty} : s_n \to^{a_{n+1}} s_{n+1}\}$.

3.1 The Maude LTL Model Checker

Maude supports on-the-fly LTL model checking since its 2.0 version [19]. The mapping of a rewriting system to the model-checking framework is natural: its states are its terms and its transitions are rule applications. All executions are assumed to be infinite, by repeating the last state of finite executions, adding a loop transition to deadlock states, like in Spin and other verification tools. In order to prepare a Maude module for model checking, users need to extend it including the predefined `SATISFACTION` module, declaring the intended state sort as a subsort of the predefined `State` sort, and the atomic propositions as regular Maude operators of sort `Prop`, and defining them equationally for all terms using the satisfaction relation symbol `_|=_`. Here is an example for the river crossing puzzle:

```
mod RIVER-CROSSING-PREDS is
  protecting RIVER-CROSSING .
  including SATISFACTION .

  subsort River < State .

  ops goal death bad : -> Prop [ctor] .

  var R    : River .
  vars G G' : Group .

  eq left | right shepherd wolf goat cabbage |= goal = true .
  eq R |= goal = false [owise] .

  eq cabbage G | G' goat |= death = false .
  eq cabbage goat G | G' |= death = false .
```

```
  eq R |= death = true [owise] .

  eq wolf goat G | G' shepherd |= bad = true .
  eq goat cabbage G | G' shepherd |= bad = true .
  eq R |= bad = false [owise] .
endm
```

Three propositions are defined: goal that is only satisfied by the puzzle solution, death that tags states where someone has already been eaten, and bad that signals states in which eating is possible but not yet accomplished. Finally, the user should import the predefined MODEL-CHECKER module giving access to a special operator modelCheck that reduces to the verification result, assuming some decidability requirements [19]. An important property of the river crossing puzzle, whether a bad state always leads to a death state, can be checked:

```
Maude> red modelCheck(initial, [] (bad -> <> death)) .
rewrites: 44
result ModelCheckResult: counterexample(
   {right | left shepherd wolf goat cabbage,'alone}
    ...
   {left shepherd cabbage | right wolf goat,'cabbage},
   {left | right shepherd wolf goat cabbage,'alone}
   {left shepherd | right wolf goat cabbage,'alone})
```

In this case, as discussed before, the property is refuted by a counterexample execution, described by a cycle and a path to it, where a bad state is visited but no death state is ever reached.

3.2 Strategy-Aware Model Checking

Recently, we have extended the LTL model checker to rewrite theories controlled by strategies [32]. From an abstract point of view, a system $\mathcal{K}$ controlled by a strategy $E \subseteq \Gamma^\omega_\mathcal{K}$ is said to satisfy a linear property φ if $\mathcal{K}, \pi \models \varphi$ for all $\pi \in E$. This definition is natural and almost unavoidable, since linear-time properties refer to individual executions quantified universally. We just need to know which are the executions $E(\alpha)$ allowed by a Maude strategy language expression α.

This question has been answered by defining a nondeterministic structural operational semantics for the strategy language. Its execution states $q \in \mathcal{XS}$ are terms augmented with a continuation for the strategy execution, and its steps $q \twoheadrightarrow q'$ correspond to single rule rewrites $\mathrm{cterm}(q) \to^1_R \mathrm{cterm}(q')$ on the underlying terms, denoted by $\mathrm{cterm}(q)$. These states are usually of the form $t \,@\, s$ where s is a stack of strategy expressions whose execution is pending and substitutions defining the variable contexts of the active strategy calls, but more complex constructs are required for operators involving subsearches. Projecting the term part of the small-step semantics executions leads to well-defined rewriting paths in the base system, exactly those we denote by

$$E(\alpha, t) := \{(\mathrm{cterm}(q_n))_{n=0}^\infty : q_0 = t \,@\, \alpha,\ q_n \twoheadrightarrow q_{n+1}\} \subseteq \Gamma^\omega_{(T_\Sigma, \to_R)}.$$

Moreover, a property is satisfied for $E(\alpha, t)$ according to the abstract definition iff it is satisfied in the classical sense on the Kripke structure given by the semantics graph

$$\mathcal{B} := (\mathcal{XS}, \twoheadrightarrow, \{t\,@\,\alpha\}, AP, \text{cterm} \circ \ell)$$

under some decidability assumptions [32].

The strategy-aware model checker shares a great part of its infrastructure with the strategy execution engine and the original model checker. Their usage is similar, but in this case the `STRATEGY-MODEL-CHECKER` module should be imported instead of `MODEL-CHECKER` to access the strategy-aware `modelCheck` operator, which receives an additional argument of sort `Qid` to indicate the name of the strategy that controls the system.

```
Maude> red modelCheck(initial, [] ~ bad, 'safe) .
rewrites: 54
result Bool: true

Maude> red modelCheck(initial, [] (bad -> O death),
                      'eagerEating) .
rewrites: 121
result Bool: true
```

A version of Maude including this model checker, its source code, and detailed documentation can be downloaded from [18].

4 Model Checking Branching-Time Properties

While the abstract definition for checking linear-time properties using strategies was very simple, the case of branching-time properties is not so clear. The main difficulty can be observed in the following example of a vending machine, which admits one-euro coins `e` and sells apples `a` and cakes `c` for one and two euros respectively.

```
mod VENDING-MACHINE is
  sorts Thing Soup Machine .
  subsort Thing < Soup .

  ops e a c : -> Thing [ctor] .
  op empty  : -> Soup [ctor] .
  op __     : Soup Soup -> Soup [ctor asoc comm id: empty] .
  op _[_]   : Soup Soup -> Machine [ctor] .

  vars O I : Soup .

  rl [put1]  : O e [I]     => O   [I e] .
  rl [apple] : O   [I e]   => O a [I] .
  rl [cake]  : O   [I e e] => O c [I] .
endm
```

According to the small-step semantics, the execution tree of the strategy $\alpha \equiv$ `(put1 ; apple) | (put1 ; put1 ; cake)` from the term `e e [empty]` is:

```
                      ↠ e [e] @ apple ——↠ e a [empty] @ ε ⟲
e e [empty] @ α <
                      ↠ e [e] @ put1 ; cake
                           └↠ empty [e e] @ cake ——↠ c [empty] @ ε ⟲
```

Looking at this tree, the CTL property $\mathbf{A} \bigcirc \mathbf{E} \Diamond \, \mathit{hasApple}$ would not hold, where *hasApple* is only satisfied if an apple has been bought. The reason is somehow artificial, since only the strategy continuation distinguishes the successors of the initial state. Moreover, the property would hold instead if we consider the tree for the strategy expression $\beta \equiv$ `put1 ; (apple | put1 ; cake)`, which denotes the same abstract strategy as α:

```
                          ┌——————————————————↠ e a [empty] @ ε ⟲
e e [empty] @ β ——↠ e [e] @ apple | put1 ; cake
                          └↠ empty [e e] @ cake ——↠ c [empty] @ ε ⟲
```

This tree coincides with its underlying rewriting tree, where terms are connected by rule rewrites, which should be the reference for a notion of satisfaction that does not depend on the particular representation of the strategy. In practice, this can always be achieved by merging successor states whose terms coincide, like `e [e] @ apple` and `e [e] @ put1 ; cake` in the first tree.

In abstract terms, we suggested in [32] that the satisfaction of a branching-time property φ on a system $\mathcal{A}$ controlled by a strategy can be understood as the satisfaction of φ in its *unwinding*, the transition system whose states are the finite executions $\Gamma^*_{\mathcal{A}}$ of the model and whose transitions are those allowed by the (intensional) strategy.

Definition 1. *Given a Kripke structure $\mathcal{K} = (S, \to, I, AP, \ell)$ and a strategy $E = E(\lambda)$, we define $\mathcal{U}(E) = (S^+, U, I, AP, \ell_{\text{last}})$ where $(w, ws) \in U$ if $s \in \lambda(w)$ for all $w \in S^+$ and $\ell_{\text{last}}(ws) = \ell(s)$ for all $w \in S^*$.*

Definition 2. *$(\mathcal{K}, E) \vDash \varphi$ if $\mathcal{U}(E) \vDash \varphi$, for any $\mathcal{K}$, strategy E and formula φ.*

Similar definitions apply to the labeled case, with an unwinding $\mathcal{U}'(E)$ whose states are $(S \cup A)^+$ executions and where $(w, a, was) \in U'$ if $(a, s) \in \lambda(w)$. However, since these constructs are not finite, the effective usage of these definitions goes through finding a bisimilar finite transition system where algorithms can be applied. For the Maude strategy language, this can be the one derived from its nondeterministic semantics ($\mathcal{B}$ in Sect. 3) after merging successors with a common term, i.e. $\mathcal{M} := (\mathcal{P}(\mathcal{XS}) \backslash \{\emptyset\}, [\twoheadrightarrow], \{\{t_0 \,@\, \alpha\}\}, AP, \ell \circ \text{cterm})$ where[2]

$$Q \, [\twoheadrightarrow] \, Q' \iff \exists t \in T_\Sigma \quad Q' = \{q' : q \twoheadrightarrow q', \text{cterm}(q') = t, q \in Q\}.$$

[2] For simplicity, we are obviating finite and failed executions. More precisely, $\mathcal{M}$ should only include states Q from which a solution or an infinite execution can be reached.

Again, when considering the labeled transition system, a slightly different Kripke structure $\mathcal{M}'$ should be defined, in which the successors Q' are further grouped by the rule label that produce them.

The following proposition states that $\mathcal{M}$ is bisimilar to the strategy unwinding:

Proposition 1. *Given a strategy expression α and a term t_0, the initial state $\{t_0 \mathbin{@} \alpha\}$ of $\mathcal{M}$ is bisimilar to the state t_0 in $\mathcal{U}(E(\alpha, t_0))$.*

Proof. Let $f : T_\Sigma^+ \to \mathcal{P}(\mathcal{XS})$ be $f(t_1 \cdots t_n) = \{q_n \in \mathcal{XS} : t_0 \mathbin{@} \alpha = q_1 \twoheadrightarrow \cdots \twoheadrightarrow q_n, \text{cterm}(q_k) = t_k\}$. For any $w \in S^*$ and $Q \neq \emptyset$, $f(w) [\twoheadrightarrow] Q$ holds if and only if $\exists t \in T_\Sigma \;\; Q = f(wt)$, since:

$$\begin{aligned} f(w) [\twoheadrightarrow] Q &\iff \exists t \in T_\Sigma \;\; Q = \{q' \in \mathcal{XS} : q \in f(v), q \twoheadrightarrow q', \text{cterm}(q') = t\} \\ &\iff \exists t \in T_\Sigma \;\; Q = \{q' \in \mathcal{XS} : t_0 \mathbin{@} \alpha = q_1 \twoheadrightarrow \cdots \twoheadrightarrow q_n \twoheadrightarrow q', \\ &\qquad\qquad \text{cterm}(q') = t, \text{cterm}(q_k) = w_k\} = f(wt) \end{aligned}$$

The relation $R = \{(t_0 w, f(t_0 w)) : w \in S^*, f(t_0 w) \neq \emptyset\}$ is the bisimulation we are looking for. Clearly, $(t_0, \{t_0 \mathbin{@} \alpha\}) \in R$ and $\ell_{\text{last}}(ws) = \ell(s) = \ell(\text{cterm}(Q))$ if $(ws, Q) \in R$. Given two words $v, w \in T_\Sigma^+$, R only relates them to $f(v)$ and $f(w)$, respectively. $(v, w) \in U$ implies $w = vt$ by definition of U, and then $f(v) [\twoheadrightarrow] f(w)$ follows from the previous paragraph. Given two non-empty sets Q and Q' such that $Q [\twoheadrightarrow] Q'$, and a word w with $f(w) = Q$, we must find a w' such that $(w, w') \in R$ and $f(w') = Q'$. However, we already have it thanks to the previous paragraph and $f(w) [\twoheadrightarrow] Q'$, since there is some t such that $f(wt) = Q'$. It remains to prove that $(w, wt) \in U$, i.e. $t \in \lambda(w)$, but since there are no failed states in $\mathcal{M}$, any step of the semantics must be allowed by the strategy.

A similar proposition holds for the labeled variant $\mathcal{M}'$ and $\mathcal{U}'$. In summary, to model check systems controlled by strategies, we propose applying standard algorithms on $\mathcal{M}$ for state-based logics, or $\mathcal{M}'$ for logics that refer to transitions too. In the following sections, we give reasonable generalizations of two specific branching-time logics for strategy-controlled systems, to justify the proposed abstract procedure and show how their notions of satisfaction coincide. CTL* and μ-calculus are chosen because they are well-known and supported by the tool described in Sect. 5, but the procedure is general and can be applied to other logics.

4.1 CTL*

The proposed generalized definition is similar to those we can find in most reference textbooks [11,12] and coincides with a previous definition for trees [36]. We identify abstract strategies with trees since they are in univocal relation as long as trees only branch to distinct children, as it is the case. For an execution $\pi = (\pi_n)_{n=0}^\infty$, we denote the suffix that starts at the position k by $\pi^k = (\pi_{k+n})_{n=0}^\infty$, the prefix that stops at k by $\pi^{-k} = \pi_0 \cdots \pi_k$, and all the executions of a given abstract strategy E continuing a given prefix by $E \upharpoonright ws = \{s\pi : ws\pi \in E\}$ for all $w \in S^*$ and $s \in S$.

- $E \vDash p$ iff $\forall \pi \in E \quad p \in \ell(\pi_0)$
- $E \vDash \neg\Phi$ iff $E \nvDash \Phi$
- $E \vDash \Phi_1 \wedge \Phi_2$ iff $E \vDash \Phi_1$ and $E \vDash \Phi_2$
- $E \vDash \mathbf{A}\,\phi$ iff $\forall \pi \in E \quad E \upharpoonright \pi_0, \pi \vDash \phi$
- $E \vDash \mathbf{E}\,\phi$ iff $\exists \pi \in E \quad E \upharpoonright \pi_0, \pi \vDash \phi$
- $E, \pi \vDash \Phi$ iff $E \vDash \Phi$
- $E, \pi \vDash \neg\varphi$ iff $E, \pi \nvDash \varphi$
- $E, \pi \vDash \varphi_1 \wedge \varphi_2$ iff $E, \pi \vDash \varphi_1$ and $E, \pi \vDash \varphi_2$
- $E, \pi \vDash \bigcirc\varphi$ iff $E \upharpoonright \pi_0\pi_1, \pi^1 \vDash \varphi$
- $E, \pi \vDash \Diamond\varphi$ iff $\exists n \geq 0 \quad E \upharpoonright \pi^{-n}, \pi^n \vDash \varphi$
- $E, \pi \vDash \Box\varphi$ iff $\forall n \geq 0 \quad E \upharpoonright \pi^{-n}, \pi^n \vDash \varphi$
- $E, \pi \vDash \varphi_1 \,\mathbf{U}\, \varphi_2$ iff $\exists n \geq 0 \; E \upharpoonright \pi^{-n}, \pi^n \vDash \varphi_2 \wedge \forall 0 \leq k < n \;\; E \upharpoonright \pi^{-k}, \pi^k \vDash \varphi_1$

Observe that it only differs from the classical definition in the fact that the strategy is carried on. Path formulae φ are understood similarly, but here, a state property Φ does not only depend on the state but on the full state history. The extended and classical relations are linked by the following essential property:

Proposition 2. *Given a CTL* formula φ, $\mathcal{K}, s \vDash \varphi$ iff $\mathcal{K}, \Gamma_s^\omega \vDash \varphi$.*

Proof. Using the fact that $\Gamma_s^\omega \upharpoonright (s \cdots s') = \Gamma_{s'}^\omega$, the definitions coincide almost syntactically, as a mechanical inductive proof can show.

The following proposition justifies that model checking can be solved by the classical procedures applied on $\mathcal{M}$:

Lemma 1. *For every $ws_0 \in S^+$ prefix in E, $E \upharpoonright ws_0 = \{\text{flat}(\pi) : \pi \in \Gamma_{\mathcal{U}(E), ws_0}\}$ where $\text{flat}((ws_0)(ws_0s_1)(ws_0s_1s_2)\cdots) := s_0s_1s_2\cdots$.*

Proof. Notice that executions in $\mathcal{U}(E)$ are of the form $(ws_0)(ws_0s_1)(ws_0s_1s_2)\cdots$ where $s_0s_1\cdots$ is an execution in E. For the $\supseteq$ inclusion, take $\Gamma_{\mathcal{U}(E), ws_0} \ni \pi = (ws_0)(ws_0s_1)(ws_0s_1s_2)\cdots$, whose $\text{flat}(\pi) = s_0s_1s_2\cdots$ and $ws_0s_1s_2\cdots \in E$ since $s_{n+1} \in \lambda(s_n)$. Hence, $\text{flat}(\pi) = s_0s_1\cdots \in E \upharpoonright ws_0$ by definition. For the other $\subseteq$ inclusion, $s_0s_1\cdots \in E \upharpoonright ws_0$ implies $ws_0s_1\cdots \in E$, so $\pi = (ws_0)(ws_0s_1)\cdots \in \Gamma_{\mathcal{U}(E), ws_0}$ and $\text{flat}(\pi) = s_0s_1\cdots$ is in the set.

Proposition 3. *Given any CTL* formula, $\mathcal{K}, E \vDash \Phi$ iff $\mathcal{U}(E), \pi_0 \vDash \Phi$ for all $\pi \in E$. In particular, $E(\alpha, t) \vDash \Phi$ iff $\mathcal{M}, \{t \,@\, \alpha\} \vDash \Phi$.*

Proof. We will follow an inductive proof on the structure of CTL* formulae with the more general property $\mathcal{U}(E), w \vDash \varphi$ iff $\mathcal{K}, E \upharpoonright w \vDash \varphi$ for all $w \in S^+$. Path formulae need to be handled simultaneously, so the inductive property also includes $\mathcal{U}(E), \pi \vDash \varphi$ iff $\mathcal{K}, E \upharpoonright \pi_0, \text{flat}(\pi) \vDash \varphi$ (notice that in the left-hand side executions are successions of growing S^+ words while in the right-hand side they are successions of S states). To facilitate reading, we will omit the $\mathcal{U}(E)$ and $\mathcal{K}$ prefix when writing the satisfaction relations.

- (p, atomic propositions) By definition, $\sqsupseteq s \vDash p$ iff $p \in \ell(s)$, and $E \upharpoonright ws \vDash p$ iff $p \in \ell(s')$ for all $s'w' \in E \upharpoonright ws = \{sw'' : wsw'' \in E\}$. Then, s' can only be s and both conditions coincide.

- ($\Phi_1 \land \Phi_2$) In the standard side, the conjunction is satisfied iff $w \vDash \Phi_i$ for both $i = 1, 2$. In the strategy side, this happens iff $E \restriction w \vDash \Phi_i$. By induction hypothesis on both Φ_i the equivalence holds.
- ($\neg\Phi$) The same inductive argument can be used for negation.
- ($\mathbf{A}\,\varphi$) This formula is satisfied iff $\pi \vDash \varphi$ for all $\pi \in \Gamma^{\omega}_{\mathcal{U}(E),w}$ in the $\mathcal{U}(E)$ side. In the strategy side, this is $E \restriction w, \rho \vDash \varphi$ for all $\rho \in E \restriction w$. Using Lemma 1, all these ρ are exactly those $\mathrm{flat}(\pi)$, and applying the induction hypothesis on φ, both statements are equivalent.

Let π be $(ws_0)(ws_0s_1)\cdots$, we then target the path satisfaction cases:

- ($\circ\varphi$) We should prove that $\pi \vDash \circ\varphi$ is equivalent to $E \restriction ws_0, s_0s_1\cdots \vDash \circ\varphi$. Their definitions translate these to $\pi^1 \vDash \varphi$ and $(E \restriction ws_0) \restriction s_0s_1, (s_0s_1\cdots)^1 \vDash \varphi$. But they are equivalent by induction hypothesis on φ, since $(E \restriction ws_0) \restriction s_0s_1 = E \restriction ws_0s_1 = E \restriction \pi_1 = E \restriction (\pi^1)_0$ and $(s_0s_1\cdots)^1 = s_1s_2\cdots = \mathrm{flat}(\pi^1)$.
- ($\varphi_1\,\mathbf{U}\,\varphi_2$) The formula holds in the standard sense if there is an $n \in \mathbb{N}$ such that $\pi^n \vDash \varphi_2$ and for all k such that $0 \leq k < n$ then $\pi^k \vDash \varphi_1$. In the strategy side, the formula holds if again there is an $n \in \mathbb{N}$ such that $(E \restriction ws_0) \restriction s_0\cdots s_n, s_ns_{n+1}\cdots \vDash \varphi_2$ and $(E \restriction ws_0) \restriction s_0\cdots s_k, s_ks_{k+1}\cdots \vDash \varphi_1$ for all $0 \leq k < n$. Since $(E \restriction ws_0) \restriction s_0\cdots s_k = E \restriction ws_0\cdots s_k = E \restriction (\pi^k)_0$ and $s_ks_{k+1}\cdots = \mathrm{flat}(\pi^k)$ for all $k \in \mathbb{N}$, the induction hypothesis can be applied to φ_1 and φ_2 to conclude the property for $\varphi_1\,\mathbf{U}\,\varphi_2$.
- (Φ) $\pi \vDash \Phi$ is defined as $\pi_0 \vDash \Phi$ in the standard sense, and $E \restriction ws_0, s_0s_1\cdots \vDash \Phi$ is $E \restriction ws_0 \vDash \Phi$ in the strategy case. Since $\pi_0 = ws_0$, both statements are related as in the induction property. The hypothesis on Φ itself can be applied, considering that state satisfaction is below path satisfaction in the induction order (we have never used this argument in reverse), and then they are equivalent.

Only a complete subset of CTL* constructors has been handled in the proof, but simple propositional and first-order properties let us conclude that the following well-know semantic equivalences are also satisfied by the given extended CTL* definition for strategies:

- $\Phi_1 \lor \Phi_2 \equiv \neg(\neg\Phi_1 \land \neg\Phi_2)$ for any state or path formula Φ.
- $\mathbf{E}\,\varphi \equiv \neg(\mathbf{A}\,\neg\varphi)$ for any path formula φ.
- $\Diamond\,\varphi \equiv \top\,\mathbf{U}\,\varphi$ for any path formula φ.
- $\Box\,\varphi \equiv \neg(\Diamond\,\neg\varphi)$ for any path formula φ.

4.2 μ-Calculus

We present a generalized definition of μ-calculus for strategies that mimics the original one. While in the original μ-calculus a valid formula φ is given meaning $[\![\varphi]\!]_\eta$ as the set of states in which it is satisfied, here, a formula will denote instead a set $\langle\!\langle\varphi\rangle\!\rangle_\xi$ of subtrees (in other words, strategies) in which φ is satisfied. The subscripts η and ξ are assignments from the free variables Z in the formula to the denotation values they take, respectively, as subsets of $\mathcal{P}(\Gamma_{\mathcal{K}})$ and S.

- $\langle\!\langle p \rangle\!\rangle_\xi \quad = \{T \subseteq \Gamma_\mathcal{K}^\omega : \forall sa\pi \in T \quad p \in \ell(s)\}$
- $\langle\!\langle \neg\varphi \rangle\!\rangle_\xi \quad = \mathcal{P}(\Gamma_\mathcal{K}^\omega) \setminus \langle\!\langle \varphi \rangle\!\rangle_\xi$
- $\langle\!\langle \varphi_1 \wedge \varphi_2 \rangle\!\rangle_\xi \quad = \langle\!\langle \varphi_1 \rangle\!\rangle_\xi \cap \langle\!\langle \varphi_2 \rangle\!\rangle_\xi$
- $\langle\!\langle Z \rangle\!\rangle_\xi \quad = \xi(Z)$
- $\langle\!\langle \langle a \rangle \varphi \rangle\!\rangle_\xi \quad = \{T \subseteq \Gamma_\mathcal{A}^\omega : \exists\, sa\pi \in T \quad T \restriction sa\pi_0 \in \langle\!\langle \varphi \rangle\!\rangle_\xi\}$
- $\langle\!\langle \nu Z.\varphi \rangle\!\rangle_\xi \quad = \bigcup \{F \subseteq \mathcal{P}(\Gamma_\mathcal{A}^\omega) : F \subseteq \langle\!\langle \varphi \rangle\!\rangle_{\xi[Z/F]}\}$

Other constructors like $[a]\varphi$ and $\mu Z.\varphi$ are defined by their usual equivalences to these. Provided that every variable is under an even number of negations, the definition is monotone and the fixpoints are well-defined. When the formula φ is ground, i.e. it does not have free variables, we omit the valuation subscript ξ. This generalization is connected with the original definition by the property:

Proposition 4. $[\![\varphi]\!] \ni s$ *iff* $\Gamma_{\mathcal{K},s} \in \langle\!\langle \varphi \rangle\!\rangle$ *for any ground* μ*-calculus formula.*

Proof. This property can be proven inductively, adding the variable valuations to the inductive property and the premise that $\eta(Z) \ni s$ iff $\Gamma_s \in \xi(Z)$ for all variables Z. For the initial φ, this premise is trivially satisfied since we can take $\eta(Z) = \emptyset = \xi(Z)$ regardless of the given two, since the formula is closed. We will not detail some trivial cases:

- (p) By definition, $s \in [\![p]\!]_\eta$ is $p \in \ell(s)$ and $\Gamma_s \in \langle\!\langle p \rangle\!\rangle_\xi$ is $\forall \pi \in \Gamma_s\ p \in \ell(\pi_0)$. Since Γ_s are the executions of $\mathcal{K}$ starting at s, $\pi_0 = s$ and both statements are equivalent.
- $(\langle a \rangle \varphi)$ $s \in [\![\langle a \rangle \varphi]\!]_\eta$ if there is an $s' \in S$ such that $s \to^a s'$ and $s' \in [\![\varphi]\!]_\eta$. On the other side, $\Gamma_s \in \langle\!\langle \langle a \rangle \varphi \rangle\!\rangle_\xi$ holds iff there is $saw \in \Gamma_s$ such that $\Gamma_s \restriction saw_0 = \Gamma_{w_0} \in \langle\!\langle \varphi \rangle\!\rangle_\xi$. The induction hypothesis with $s' = w_0$ lets us conclude the property.
- $(\nu Z.\varphi)$ $s \in [\![\nu Z.\varphi]\!]_\eta$ iff there is a set V such that $s \in V$ and $V \subseteq [\![\varphi]\!]_{\eta[Z/V]}$. In the strategy side, $\Gamma_s \in \langle\!\langle \nu Z.\varphi \rangle\!\rangle_\xi$ iff there is an F such that $\Gamma_s \in F$ and $F \subseteq \langle\!\langle \varphi \rangle\!\rangle_{\xi[Z/F]}$. Both implications can be proven like in the previous case, but taking $F = \{\Gamma_s : s \in V\}$ for a given V, and $V = \{s \in S : \Gamma_s \in F\}$ for a given F.

As for CTL*, the following proposition claims that a formula is satisfied for a strategy in the generalized sense iff it is satisfied in the merged labeled transition system generated by the nondeterministic semantics:

Proposition 5. *For any ground formula* φ*,* $E \in \langle\!\langle \varphi \rangle\!\rangle_\mathcal{K}$ *iff* $\pi_0 \in [\![\varphi]\!]_{\mathcal{U}(E)}$ *for all* $\pi \in E$*. In particular,* $E_{labeled}(\alpha, t) \in \langle\!\langle \varphi \rangle\!\rangle_{(T_\Sigma, \to_R)}$ *iff* $t \in [\![\varphi]\!]_{\mathcal{M}'}$*.*

Proof. Let us inductively prove the more general property that $[\![\varphi]\!]_\eta \ni w$ iff $E \restriction w \in \langle\!\langle \varphi \rangle\!\rangle_\xi$ provided that $\eta(Z) \ni w$ iff $E \restriction w \in \xi(Z)$ for all variables Z.

- (p) By definition, $ws \in [\![\varphi]\!]_\eta$ iff $p \in \ell(s)$, and $E \restriction ws \in \langle\!\langle \varphi \rangle\!\rangle_\xi$ iff $p \in \ell(\pi_0)$ for all $\pi \in E \restriction ws$. However, π_0 must be s since $E \restriction ws = \{sw' : wsw' \in E\}$, so both sides are equivalent.

- (Z) The value of Z in both contexts is respectively $\eta(Z)$ and $\xi(Z)$, so the property directly follows from the assumption over these two functions.
- ($\varphi_1 \wedge \varphi_2$) The standard definition says $[\![\varphi_1 \wedge \varphi_2]\!]_\eta = [\![\varphi_1]\!]_\eta \cap [\![\varphi_2]\!]_\eta$ and the strategy one is $\langle\!\langle \varphi_1 \wedge \varphi_2 \rangle\!\rangle_\xi = \langle\!\langle \varphi_1 \rangle\!\rangle_\xi \cap \langle\!\langle \varphi_2 \rangle\!\rangle_\xi$. Hence, the property holds by induction hypothesis on φ_1 and φ_2.
- ($\neg\varphi$) By definition, $[\![\neg\varphi]\!]_\eta = S^+ \backslash [\![\varphi]\!]_\eta$ and $\langle\!\langle \neg\varphi \rangle\!\rangle_\xi = \mathcal{P}(\Gamma_{\mathcal{K}}) \backslash \langle\!\langle \varphi \rangle\!\rangle_\xi$, so the property holds by induction hypothesis on φ.
- ($\langle a \rangle \varphi$) $ws \in [\![\langle a \rangle \varphi]\!]_\eta$ iff there is an $(a, s') \in \lambda(ws)$ such that $wsas' \in [\![\varphi]\!]_\eta$ according to the standard definition of μ-calculus and the transition relation on $\mathcal{U}'(E)$. On the other side, $E \upharpoonright ws \in \langle\!\langle \langle a \rangle \varphi \rangle\!\rangle_\xi$ iff there is a $w' \in (S \cup A)^\infty$ such that $saw' \in E \upharpoonright ws$ and $(E \upharpoonright ws) \upharpoonright saw_0' = E \upharpoonright wsaw_0' \in \langle\!\langle \varphi \rangle\!\rangle_\xi$.
By definition of $E(\lambda)$, there is a $w' \in (S \cup A)^\infty$ such that $wsaw' \in E$ iff $(a, w_0') \in \lambda(ws)$. Hence, by induction hypothesis on φ and taking $w_0' = s'$, we conclude that the property holds.
- ($\nu Z.\varphi$) According to the standard definition, $ws \in [\![\nu Z.\varphi]\!]_\eta$ iff there is a $V \subseteq S^+$ such that $V \subseteq [\![\varphi]\!]_{\eta[Z/V]}$ and $ws \in V$. According to our definition for strategies, $E \upharpoonright ws \in \langle\!\langle \nu Z.\varphi \rangle\!\rangle_\xi$ iff there is an $F \subseteq \mathcal{P}(\Gamma_{\mathcal{K}})$ such that $F \subseteq \langle\!\langle \varphi \rangle\!\rangle_{\xi[Z/F]}$ and $E \upharpoonright ws \in F$. Assuming there exists a V with these properties ($\Rightarrow$), consider $F = \{E \upharpoonright w : w \in V\}$. In other words, $w \in V$ iff $E \upharpoonright w \in F$, so $\eta[Z/V]$ and $\xi[Z/F]$ are properly related. Hence, by induction hypothesis on φ, $E \upharpoonright w \in \langle\!\langle \varphi \rangle\!\rangle_{\xi[Z/F]}$ iff $w \in [\![\varphi]\!]_{\eta[Z/V]}$, so $F \subseteq \langle\!\langle \varphi \rangle\!\rangle_{\xi[Z/F]}$ as we wanted to prove. In the opposite direction ($\Leftarrow$), assuming the existence of an F with the mentioned properties, consider $V = \{w \in S^+ : E \upharpoonright w \in F\}$ and the proof is the same.

5 The Maude Language Module for LTSmin

According to the previous section, to check CTL* or μ-calculus properties on Maude specifications we should take the Kripke structure $\mathcal{B}$, already generated for the LTL model checker, merge its states as in $\mathcal{M}$ or $\mathcal{M}'$ and apply standard algorithms on them. To avoid programming these algorithms from scratch, we have developed instead a language module for the language-independent model checker LTSmin [23]. Oversimplifying, this software allows defining *language frontends* that expose programs in a specification language like Maude as labeled transition systems to some builtin *algorithmic backends*, including model checkers for different logics. A Kripke-like C interface called PINS (Partitioned Next State Interface) is used, which promotes sharing additional information about the internal structure of the models to speed up algorithms. Frontends are included for various modeling formalisms like Promela [22], PNML [5], DIVINE [31], UPPAAL [25], etc., and custom language modules, like ours, can also be loaded by the LTSmin tools using the POSIX's `dlopen` API.

The language module is the C library `libmaudemc.so` illustrated in Fig. 1. On the one hand, the module is linked with the C++ implementation of Maude 3 including the extended LTL model checker for strategy-controlled systems, which processes the Maude files and gives access to the transition system used for LTL

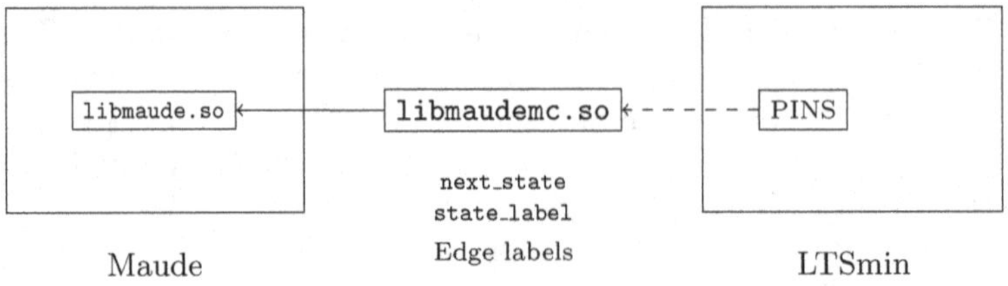

Fig. 1. Architecture of the Maude LTSmin plugin

model checking. On the other hand, the plugin implements the PINS interface by exporting some C functions that the LTSmin model-checking algorithms will call to introspect the model:[3] the `next_state` function provides the successors of a given state, including their edge labels, and `state_label` tests whether an atomic proposition holds in a state. The module itself takes care of merging states as explained in Sect. 4 and removing those in which the strategy has failed, since they are not considered valid executions[4]. LTSmin lets frontend designers represent states as vectors of integers, whose mutual dependencies can be declared as matrices that the algorithms may use to improve their efficiency and allow distributed implementations. However, in our case the state is a single integer that indexes an internal state of the Maude model checker, since partitioning and inferring relations about arbitrary Maude specifications seems unpractical.

LTSmin is a collection of commands like `pins2lts-seq` for explicit-state and `pins2lts-sym` for symbolic model-checking, which are able to handle Maude specifications when the `--loader=libmaudemc.so` option is passed. The Maude source file, the initial term, and an optional strategy expression should also be passed to the program as arguments, along with the temporal formula to be checked using LTSmin's syntax. A helper utility `umaudemc` has been written to facilitate its usage, as it selects the appropriate tool and configuration for the given formula. Moreover, it allows expressing the temporal formulae using Maude's LTL syntax extended with the quantifiers `A_` and `E_` for CTL*, and the operators `<_>_`, `[_]_`, `mu_._` and `nu_._` for μ-calculus.

After downloading the plugin from http://maude.ucm.es/strategies and LTSmin from https://ltsmin.utwente.nl, we come back to the river crossing puzzle and check whether every execution can be continued to a solution with the CTL property $\mathbf{A} \Box \mathbf{E} \Diamond \mathit{goal}$. This formula is satisfied when the system is controlled by the `safe` strategy, but neither when using the `eagerEating` strategy nor when the system runs uncontrolled.

[3] LTSmin uses the `dlopen` API to load `libmaudemc.so` into memory, and then the function `dlsym` to obtain pointers to its symbols (global variables, functions..., namely those required by the PINS interface) so that they can be read and called.

[4] It could be necessary to execute one or more rewrites until realizing that an execution path should be abandoned (by an explicit `fail`, a failed test...) These are implicitly ignored by the nested depth-first search of the LTL algorithm, since no cycles can be found through them, but they must be explicitly purged for other algorithms.

```
$ umaudemc check river.maude initial 'A [] E <> goal' safe
The property is satisfied in the initial state
(16 system states, 264 rewrites).

$ umaudemc check river initial 'A [] E <> goal' eagerEating
The property is not satisfied in the initial state
(43 system states, 4012 rewrites).

$ umaudemc check river.maude initial 'A [] E <> goal'
The property is not satisfied in the initial state
(36 system states, 3058 rewrites).
```

The reason is that no solution can be reached once a character has been eaten, which may happen in the last two cases. However, the property $\mathbf{A}\,\Box\,(bad \vee death \vee \mathbf{E}\,\Diamond\,goal)$ holds under the eagerEating strategy too:

```
$ umaudemc check river.maude initial \
    'A [] (bad \/ death \/ E <> goal)' eagerEating
The property is satisfied in the initial state
(43 system states, 1088 rewrites).
```

We can also check μ-calculus properties, like the fact that the only initial movement not leading to a bad state is goat:

```
$ umaudemc check river.maude initial \
    '[ alone wolf cabbage ] bad /\ < goat > ~ bad'
The property is satisfied in the initial state
(5 system states, 18 rewrites, 15 game states).
```

Then, we wonder if reaching the goal without crossing the goat again is possible: this is the property $[\text{goat}]\,(\mu Z.\,goal \vee \langle \texttt{alone wolf cabbage} \rangle\, Z)$ where the fixed-point subformula describes the states where the goal can be reached using any sequence of moves other that goat. The answer is no if the rules of the game are respected as in the eagerEating strategy:[5]

```
$ umaudemc check river.maude initial \
    '[ goat ] (mu Z . goal \/ < ~ goat > Z)' eagerEating
The property is not satisfied in the initial state
(43 system states, 192 rewrites, 364 game states).
```

However, the uncontrolled system satisfies the formula, since it can pass by forbidden states:

```
$ umaudemc check river.maude initial \
    '[ goat ] (mu Z . goal \/ < ~ goat > Z)'
The property is satisfied in the initial state
(33 system states, 168 rewrites, 362 game states).
```

[5] Our syntax for μ-calculus lets modalities take a list of rule labels, where $\langle C \rangle\, \varphi = \bigvee_{a \in C} \langle a \rangle\, \varphi$, which can be preceded by a negation symbol ~ to indicate its complement.

LTL properties can be checked both directly in Maude or using the LTSmin plugin. Against the model-checking examples available in our web page [18], LTSmin is 10,73% slower in average (or 11,21% using its builtin caching) and requires more memory. However, the communication costs and the partially redundant representation of the state can explain this difference. Moreover, since the PINS interface asks for all the successors of a state at once, the on-the-fly state space expansion is lazier in Maude and the order in which children are processed is reversed. The size of the property automata generated from the formulae by both tools coincide, except in one case when Maude's is one state smaller, since it uses an optimized implementation of the same LTL2BA [21] algorithm.

Other alternatives to bring CTL* and μ-calculus model checking to Maude have been considered like generating an equivalent model for a specific tool or exporting it to a somehow standard representation. For example, the Model Checking Contest [2] uses the Petri Net Markup Language (PNML) to state the problems for all the competitor tools. In fact, the `umaudemc` utility can use `pyModelChecking` [9] and NuSMV [10] as alternative model-checking backends. However, we have prioritized LTSmin because it efficiently supports a wide range of logics, its interface is closer to our description of the transition system, and because of its live connection that allows generating the state space and checking propositions on the fly. While only the already-covered LTL model checking can benefit from the first advantage, the second is always convenient since testing atomic properties can be arbitrarily expensive.

6 Related Work

Each section includes references to related work for its topic, but we should also mention that other model checkers have been developed for Maude. A timed CTL model checker is included as part of Real-Time Maude [26], and the builtin one was also extended to support the more expressive Linear Temporal Logic of Rewriting (LTLR) [4], as well as models based on narrowing instead of rewriting in the abstract logical model checker [3].

The combination of strategies and model checking is not original. In the field of multiplayer games, various logics like ATL* [1] and *strategy logic* [29] have been proposed to reason about player strategies. Other logics like mCTL* [24] are extended to take past actions into account. However, our approach is different, since strategies are part of the specification of the model, keeping the property specification unaltered.

7 Conclusions

In this paper, the study of model checking for systems controlled by strategies is extended to branching-time properties, and a tool is presented that allows CTL* and μ-calculus properties to be checked on both strategy-controlled and standard Maude specifications. In a wider sense, this work aims to make strategies a more useful and convenient choice to specify and verify systems. While strategy-free models can be fully explored at the metalevel using the `metaXApply` function, there were no resources in the current metalevel to follow step by step the execution of a strategy, without implementing them from scratch. Our plugin exposes these Maude models to external tools for verification, visualization, and other types of analysis. This effort has been continued in the Maude language bindings [20], giving access to Maude entities and operations from other programming languages, which have been used to implement the `umaudemc` utility.

References

1. Alur, R., Henzinger, T.A., Kupferman, O.: Alternating-time temporal logic. J. ACM **49**(5), 672–713 (2002). https://doi.org/10.1145/585265.585270
2. Amparore, E., et al.: Presentation of the 9th edition of the model checking contest. In: Beyer, D., Huisman, M., Kordon, F., Steffen, B. (eds.) TACAS 2019. LNCS, vol. 11429, pp. 50–68. Springer, Cham (2019). https://doi.org/10.1007/978-3-030-17502-3_4
3. Bae, K., Escobar, S., Meseguer, J.: Abstract logical model checking of infinite-state systems using narrowing. In: van Raamsdonk, F. (ed.) 24th International Conference on Rewriting Techniques and Applications, RTA 2013, June 24–26, 2013, Eindhoven, The Netherlands. LIPIcs, vol. 21, pp. 81–96. Schloss Dagstuhl - Leibniz-Zentrum fuer Informatik (2013). https://doi.org/10.4230/LIPIcs.RTA.2013.81
4. Bae, K., Meseguer, J.: Model checking linear temporal logic of rewriting formulas under localized fairness. Sci. Comput. Program. **99**, 193–234 (2015). https://doi.org/10.1016/j.scico.2014.02.006
5. Billington, J., et al.: PNML reference site. http://www.pnml.org/
6. Borovanský, P., Kirchner, C., Kirchner, H., Ringeissen, C.: Rewriting with strategies in ELAN: a functional semantics. Int. J. Found. Comput. Sci. **12**(1), 69–95 (2001). https://doi.org/10.1142/S0129054101000412
7. Bourdier, T., Cirstea, H., Dougherty, D.J., Kirchner, H.: Extensional and intensional strategies. In: Fernández, M. (ed.) Proceedings Ninth International Workshop on Reduction Strategies in Rewriting and Programming, WRS 2009, Brasilia, Brazil, 28th June 2009. EPTCS, vol. 15, pp. 1–19 (2009). https://doi.org/10.4204/EPTCS.15.1
8. Bravenboer, M., Kalleberg, K.T., Vermaas, R., Visser, E.: Stratego/XT 0.17. A language and toolset for program transformation. Sci. Comput. Program. **72**(1–2), 52–70 (2008). https://doi.org/10.1016/j.scico.2007.11.003
9. Casagrande, A.: pyModelChecking. A simple Python model-checking package. https://pypi.org/project/pyModelChecking/
10. Cimatti, A.A., et al.: NuSMV 2: an OpenSource tool for symbolic model checking. In: Brinksma, E., Larsen, K.G. (eds.) CAV 2002. LNCS, vol. 2404, pp. 359–364. Springer, Heidelberg (2002). https://doi.org/10.1007/3-540-45657-0_29
11. Clarke, E.M., Grumberg, O., Peled, D.A.: Model Checking. The MIT Press, Cambridge (1999)
12. Clarke, E.M., Henzinger, T.A., Veith, H., Bloem, R. (eds.): Handbook of Model Checking. Springer, Cham (2018). https://doi.org/10.1007/978-3-319-10575-8

13. Clavel, M., et al.: Maude Manual v3.1 (2020–10). http://maude.lcc.uma.es/maude31-manual-html/maude-manual.html
14. Clavel, M., Meseguer, J.: Reflection and strategies in rewriting logic. In: Meseguer, J. (ed.) Proceedings of the First International Workshop on Rewriting Logic and its Applications, WRLA 1996, Asilomar, California, 3–6 September 1996. Electronic Notes in Theoretical Computer Science, vol. 4, pp. 126–148. Elsevier (1996). https://doi.org/10.1016/S1571-0661(04)00037-4
15. Clavel, M., Meseguer, J.: Internal strategies in a reflective logic. In: Gramlich, B., Kirchner, H. (eds.) Proceedings of the CADE 2014 Workshop on Strategies in Automated Deduction, pp. 1–12 (1997)
16. Durán, F., et al.: Programming and symbolic computation in Maude. J. Log. Algebr. Methods Comput. Program. **110**, 1–58 (2020). https://doi.org/10.1016/j.jlamp.2019.100497
17. Eker, S., Martí-Oliet, N., Meseguer, J., Verdejo, A.: Deduction, strategies, and rewriting. In: Archer, M., de la Tour, T.B., Muñoz, C. (eds.) Proceedings of the 6th International Workshop on Strategies in Automated Deduction, STRATEGIES 2006, Seattle, WA, USA, 16 August 2006. Electronic Notes in Theoretical Computer Science, vol. 174(11), pp. 3–25. Elsevier (2007). https://doi.org/10.1016/j.entcs.2006.03.017
18. Eker, S., Martí-Oliet, N., Meseguer, J., Pita, I., Rubio, R., Verdejo, A.: Strategy language for Maude. http://maude.ucm.es/strategies
19. Eker, S., Meseguer, J., Sridharanarayanan, A.: The Maude LTL model checker. In: Gadducci, F., Montanari, U. (eds.) Proceedings of the Fourth International Workshop on Rewriting Logic and its Applications, WRLA 2002, Pisa, Italy, 19–21 September 2002. Electronic Notes in Theoretical Computer Science, vol. 71, pp. 162–187. Elsevier (2004). https://doi.org/10.1016/S1571-0661(05)82534-4
20. FADoSS: Experimental language bindings for Maude. https://github.com/fadoss/maude-bindings
21. Gastin, P., Oddoux, D.: Fast LTL to Büchi automata translation. In: Berry, G., Comon, H., Finkel, A. (eds.) CAV 2001. LNCS, vol. 2102, pp. 53–65. Springer, Heidelberg (2001). https://doi.org/10.1007/3-540-44585-4_6
22. Holzmann, G., et al.: Spin - Formal verification. https://spinroot.com
23. Kant, G., Laarman, A., Meijer, J., van de Pol, J., Blom, S., van Dijk, T.: LTSmin: high-performance language-independent model checking. In: Baier, C., Tinelli, C. (eds.) TACAS 2015. LNCS, vol. 9035, pp. 692–707. Springer, Heidelberg (2015). https://doi.org/10.1007/978-3-662-46681-0_61
24. Kupferman, O., Vardi, M.Y.: Memoryful branching-time logic. In: Alur, R. (ed.) 21th IEEE Symposium on Logic in Computer Science (LICS 2006), Seattle, WA, USA, 12–15 August 2006. Proceedings, pp. 265–274. IEEE Computer Society (2006). https://doi.org/10.1109/LICS.2006.34
25. Larsen, K.G., et al.: UPPAAL. http://www.uppaal.org/
26. Lepri, D., Ábrahám, E., Ölveczky, P.C.: Sound and complete timed CTL model checking of timed Kripke structures and real-time rewrite theories. Sci. Comput. Program. **99**, 128–192 (2015). https://doi.org/10.1016/j.scico.2014.06.006
27. Martí-Oliet, N., Meseguer, J., Verdejo, A.: Towards a strategy language for Maude. In: Martí-Oliet, N. (ed.) Proceedings of the Fifth International Workshop on Rewriting Logic and its Applications, WRLA 2004, Barcelona, Spain, 27 March–4 April 2004. Electronic Notes in Theoretical Computer Science, vol. 117, pp. 417–441. Elsevier (2004). https://doi.org/10.1016/j.entcs.2004.06.020

28. Martí-Oliet, N., Palomino, M., Verdejo, A.: Strategies and simulations in a semantic framework. J. Algorithms **62**(3–4), 95–116 (2007). https://doi.org/10.1016/j.jalgor.2007.04.002
29. Mogavero, F., Murano, A., Perelli, G., Vardi, M.Y.: Reasoning about strategies: on the model-checking problem. ACM Trans. Comput. Log. **15**(4), 34:1–34:47 (2014). https://doi.org/10.1145/2631917
30. Palomino, M., Martí-Oliet, N., Verdejo, A.: Playing with Maude. In: Abdennadher, S., Ringeissen, C. (eds.) Proceedings of the 5th International Workshop on Rule-Based Programming, RULE 2004, Aachen, Germany, 1 June 2004. Electronic Notes in Theoretical Computer Science, vol. 124(1), pp. 3–23. Elsevier (2005). https://doi.org/10.1016/j.entcs.2004.07.012
31. Ročkai, P., Barnat, J., Štill, V., et al.: DIVINE. https://divine.fi.muni.cz/
32. Rubio, R., Martí-Oliet, N., Pita, I., Verdejo, A.: Model checking strategy-controlled rewriting systems. In: Geuvers, H. (ed.) 4th International Conference on Formal Structures for Computation and Deduction, FSCD 2019, 24–30 June 2019, Dortmund, Germany. LIPIcs, vol. 131, pp. 34:1–34:18. Schloss Dagstuhl - Leibniz-Zentrum für Informatik (2019). https://doi.org/10.4230/LIPIcs.FSCD.2019.31
33. Rubio, R., Martí-Oliet, N., Pita, I., Verdejo, A.: Parameterized strategies specification in Maude. In: Fiadeiro, J.L., Ţuţu, I.I., et al. (eds.) WADT 2018. LNCS, vol. 11563, pp. 27–44. Springer, Cham (2019). https://doi.org/10.1007/978-3-030-23220-7_2
34. Santos-Buitrago, B., Riesco, A., Knapp, M., Alcantud, J.C.R., Santos-García, G., Talcott, C.L.: Soft set theory for decision making in computational biology under incomplete information. IEEE Access **7**, 18183–18193 (2019). https://doi.org/10.1109/ACCESS.2019.2896947
35. Santos-García, G., Palomino, M.: Solving Sudoku puzzles with rewriting rules. In: Denker, G., Talcott, C. (eds.) Proceedings of the 6th International Workshop on Rewriting Logic and its Applications, WRLA 2006, Vienna, Austria, 1–2 April 2006. Electronic Notes in Theoretical Computer Science, vol. 176(4), pp. 79–93. Elsevier (2007). https://doi.org/10.1016/j.entcs.2007.06.009
36. Thomas, W.: Computation tree logic and regular ω-languages. In: de Bakker, J.W., de Roever, W.-P., Rozenberg, G. (eds.) REX 1988. LNCS, vol. 354, pp. 690–713. Springer, Heidelberg (1989). https://doi.org/10.1007/BFb0013041
37. Verdejo, A., Martí-Oliet, N.: Basic completion strategies as another application of the Maude strategy language. In: Escobar, S. (ed.) Proceedings 10th International Workshop on Reduction Strategies in Rewriting and Programming, WRS 2011, Novi Sad, Serbia, 29 May 2011. EPTCS, vol. 82, pp. 17–36 (2011). https://doi.org/10.4204/EPTCS.82.2

Verification of the IBOS Browser Security Properties in Reachability Logic

Stephen Skeirik[1], José Meseguer[1], and Camilo Rocha[2(✉)]

[1] University of Illinois at Urbana-Champaign, Champaign, USA
{skeirik2,meseguer}@illinois.edu
[2] Pontificia Universidad Javeriana Cali, Cali, Colombia
camilo.rocha@javerianacali.edu.co

Abstract. This paper presents a rewriting logic specification of the Illinois Browser Operating System (IBOS) and defines several security properties, including the *same-origin policy* (SOP) in reachability logic. It shows how these properties can be deductively verified using our constructor-based reachability logic theorem prover. This paper also highlights the reasoning techniques used in the proof and three modularity principles that have been crucial to scale up and complete the verification effort.

1 Introduction

Rationale and Origins. Web browsers have in fact become operating systems for a myriad of web-based applications. Given the enormous user base and the massive increase in web-based application areas, browsers have for a long time been a prime target for security attacks, with a seemingly unending sequence of browser security violations. One key reason for this problematic state of affairs is the enormous size (millions of lines of code) and sheer complexity of conventional browsers, which make their formal verification a daunting task. An early effort to substantially improve browser security by formal methods was jointly carried out by researchers at Microsoft Research and the University of Illinois at Urbana-Champaign (UIUC), who formally specified Internet Explorer (IE) in Maude [11], and model checked that formalization finding 13 new types of unknown address bar or status bar spoofing attacks in it [8]. To avoid attacks on those newly found vulnerabilities, they were all corrected in IE *before* [8] was published. But the research in [8] just uncovered *some* kinds of possible attacks, and the sheer size and complexity of IE made full verification unfeasible. This stimulated a team of systems and formal methods researchers at UIUC to ask the following question: *could formal methods be used from the very beginning in the design of a secure browser with a very small trusted code base (TCB) whose design could be verified?* The answer given to this question was the Maude-based design, model checking verification, and implementation of the IBOS Browser cum operating system [39,40,49,50], with a 42K line trusted code base (TCB), several orders of magnitude smaller than the TCBs of commodity browsers.

Why This Work. As further explained in Sect. 6, only a model checking verification of the IBOS security properties relying on a hand-proof abstraction argument for its full

S. Escobar and N. Martí-Oliet (Eds.): WRLA 2020, LNCS 12328, pp. 176–196, 2020.
https://doi.org/10.1007/978-3-030-63595-4_10

applicability was possible at the time IBOS was developed [36,39,40]. A subsequent attempt at a full deductive verification of IBOS in [36] had to be abandoned due to the generation of thousands of proof obligations. In retrospect, this is not surprising for two reasons. (1) Many of the symbolic techniques needed to scale up the IBOS deductive verification effort, including variant unification and narrowing [14], order-sorted congruence closure module axioms [32], and variant-based satisfiability [34,43], did not exist at the time. In the meantime, those symbolic techniques have been developed and implemented in Maude. (2) Also missing was a *program logic* generalizing Hoare logic for Maude specifications in which properties of concurrent systems specified in Maude could be specified and verified. This has been recently addressed with the development of a *constructor-based reachability logic* for rewrite theories in [44,45], which extends prior reachability logic research on verification of conventional programs using K in [37,38,47,48]. In fact, what has made possible the deductive proof of the IBOS security properties presented in this paper is precisely the combination of the strengths from (1) and (2) within the reachability logic theorem prover that we have developed for carrying out such a proof. Implicit in both (1) and (2) are two important proof obligations. First, both our symbolic reasoning and reachability logic engines take as input a rewrite theory $\mathcal{R}$. However, the correctness of the associated deductions depends on the theory being *suitable* for symbolic reachability analysis, i.e., its equations should be ground convergent and sufficiently complete; therefore, these properties are proof obligations that must be discharged. Second, the previous model-checking-based verification that the IBOS design satisfies certain security properties [39,40] was based on an invariant I_0. Our deductive verification uses a slightly different invariant I that is also *inductive* (as explained in Sect. 3). Thus, we require that I is *at least* as strong as or stronger than I_0 to ensure that our specification of the IBOS security properties does not miss any cases covered by the prior work. Both of these important proof obligations have been fully checked as explained in [42]. Last, but not least, as we further explain in Sect. 6, the IBOS browser security goals remain as relevant and promising today as when IBOS was first developed, and this work bring us closer to achieving those goals.

Main Contributions. They include:

- The first full *deductive verification of the IBOS browser* as explained above.
- A general *modular proof methodology* for scaling up reachability logic proofs of object-based distributed systems that has been invaluable for verifying IBOS, but has a much wider applicability to general distributed system verification.
- A substantial and useful *case study* that can be of help to other researchers interested in both browser verification and distributed system verification.
- New capabilities of the *reachability logic prover*, which in the course of this research has evolved from the original prototype reported in [44] to a first prover version to be released in the near future.

Plan of the Paper. Preliminaries are gathered in Sect. 2. Reachability Logic and invariant verification are presented in Sect. 3. IBOS, its rewriting logic Maude specification, and the specification of its security properties are explained in Sect. 4. The deductive proof of those IBOS properties and the modular proof methodology used are described in Sect. 5. Section 6 discusses related work and concludes the paper.

2 Preliminaries on Equational and Rewriting Logic

We present some preliminaries on order-sorted equational logic and rewriting logic. The material is adapted from [15,30,31].

Order-Sorted Equational Logic. We assume the basic notions of order-sorted (abbreviated OS) signature Σ, Σ-term t, Σ-algebra A, and Σ-homomorphism $f : A \to B$ [15,30]. Intuitively, Σ defines a partially ordered set of sorts $(S, \leqslant)$, which are interpreted in a Σ-algebra A with carrier family of sets $A = \{A_s\}_{s \in S}$ as sort containments. For example, if we have a sort inclusion $Nat < Int$, then we must have $A_{Nat} \subseteq A_{Int}$. An operator, say $+$, in Σ may have several related typings, e.g., $+ : Nat\ Nat \to Nat$ and $+ : Int\ Int \to Int$, whose interpretations in an algebra A must agree when restricted to subsorts. The OS algebras over signature Σ and their homomorphisms form a category $\mathbf{OSAlg}_\Sigma$. Furthermore, under mild syntactic conditions on Σ, the term algebra T_Σ is initial [30]; all signatures are assumed to satisfy these conditions.

An S-sorted set $X = \{X_s\}_{s \in S}$ of *variables*, satisfies $s \neq s' \Rightarrow X_s \cap X_{s'} = \emptyset$, and the variables in X are always assumed disjoint from all constants in Σ. The *Σ-term algebra* on variables X, $T_\Sigma(X)$, is the *initial algebra* for the signature $\Sigma(X)$ obtained by adding to Σ the variables X *as extra constants*. Given a Σ-algebra A, an *assignment* a is an S-sorted function $a \in [X \to A]$ mapping each variable $x \in X_s$ to a value $a(x) \in A_s$ for each $s \in S$. Each such assignment uniquely extends to a Σ-homomorphism $\_a : T_\Sigma(X) \to A$, so that if $x \in X_s$, then $x a = a(x)$. In particular, for $A = T_\Sigma(X)$, an assignment $\sigma \in [X \to T_\Sigma(X)]$ is called a *substitution* and uniquely extends to a Σ-homomorphism $\_\sigma : T_\Sigma(X) \to T_\Sigma(X)$. Define $dom(\sigma) = \{x \in X \mid x \neq x\sigma\}$ and $ran(\sigma) = \bigcup_{x \in dom(\sigma)} vars(x\sigma)$.

We assume familiarity with the language of first-order logic with equality. In particular, given a Σ-formula φ, we assume familiarity with the satisfaction relation $A, a \models \varphi$ for a Σ-algebra A and assignment $a \in [fvars(\varphi) \to A]$ for the *free variables* $fvars(\varphi)$ of φ. Then, φ is *valid* in A, denoted $A \models \varphi$, iff $\forall\, a \in [fvars(\varphi) \to A]\ A, a \models \varphi$, and is *satisfiable* in A iff $\exists\, a \in [fvars(\varphi) \to A]\ A, a \models \varphi$. Let $Form(\Sigma)$ (resp. $QFForm(\Sigma)$) denote the set of Σ-formulas (resp. quantifier free Σ-formulas).

An OS *equational theory* is a pair $T = (\Sigma, E)$, with E a set of (possibly conditional) Σ-equations. $\mathbf{OSAlg}_{(\Sigma,E)}$ denotes the full subcategory of $\mathbf{OSAlg}_\Sigma$ with objects those $A \in \mathbf{OSAlg}_\Sigma$ such that $A \models E$, called the *(Σ, E)-algebras*. The inference system in [30] is *sound and complete* for OS equational deduction. *E-equality*, i.e., provability $E \vdash u = v$, is written $u =_E v$. $\mathbf{OSAlg}_{(\Sigma,E)}$ has an *initial algebra* $T_{\Sigma/E}$ [30]. Given a system of Σ equations $\phi = u_1 = v_1 \wedge \ldots \wedge u_n = v_n$, an *E-unifier* for ϕ is a substitution σ such that $u_i\sigma =_E v_i\sigma$, $1 \leqslant i \leqslant n$; an *E-unification algorithm* for (Σ, E) generates a *complete set* of E-unifiers $Unif_E(\phi)$ for any system ϕ in the sense that, up to E-equality, any E-unifier σ of ϕ is a substitution instance of some unifier $\theta \in Unif_E(\phi)$.

Rewriting Logic. A *rewrite theory* $\mathcal{R} = (\Sigma, E \cup B, R)$, with $(\Sigma, E \cup B)$ an OS-equational theory with equations E and structural axioms B (typically any combination of associativity, commutativity, and identity), and R a collection of rewrite rules, specifies a *concurrent system* whose states are elements of the initial algebra $T_{\Sigma/E \cup B}$ and whose *concurrent transitions* are specified by the rewrite rules R. The concurrent system thus specified is the *initial reachability model* $\mathcal{T}_\mathcal{R}$ associated to $\mathcal{R}$ [6,31].

Maude [11] is a declarative programming language whose programs are exactly rewrite theories. To be executable in Maude, a rewrite theory $\mathcal{R} = (\Sigma, E \cup B, R)$ should satisfy some *executability conditions* spelled out below. Recall the notation for term positions, subterms, and replacement from [12]: (i) positions in a term are marked by strings $p \in \mathbb{N}^*$ specifying a path from the root, (ii) $t|_p$ denotes the subterm of term t at position p, and (iii) $t[u]_p$ denotes the result of *replacing* subterm $t|_p$ at position p by u.

Definition 1. *An* executable rewrite theory *is a 3-tuple* $\mathcal{R} = (\Sigma, E \cup B, R)$ *with* $(\Sigma, E \cup B)$ *an OS equational theory with E possibly conditional and R a set of possibly conditional* Σ-rewrite rules, *i.e.*, *sequents* $l \rightarrow r$ *if* ϕ, *with* $l, r \in T_\Sigma(X)_s$ *for some* $s \in S$, *and* ϕ *a quantifier-free* Σ*-formula. We further assume that:*

1. *B is a collection of associativity and/or commutativity and/or identity axioms and* Σ *is B-*preregular *[11].*
2. *Equations E, oriented as rewrite rules* $\vec{E}$, *are* convergent *modulo B [28].*
3. *Rules R are* ground coherent *with the equations E modulo B [13].*

The one-step R, B-rewrite relation $t \rightarrow_{R,B} t'$ *holds iff there is a rule* $l \rightarrow r$ *if* $\phi \in R$, *a ground substitution* $\sigma \in [Y \rightarrow T_\Sigma]$ *with Y the rule's variables, and position p where* $t|_p =_B l\sigma$, $t' = t[r\sigma]_p$, *and* $T_{\Sigma/E \cup B} \models \phi\sigma$. *Let* $\rightarrow^*_{R,B}$ *denote the reflexive-transitive closure of the rewrite relation* $\rightarrow_{R,B}$.

Intuitively, conditions (1)–(2) ensure that the initial algebra $T_{\Sigma/E \cup B}$ is isomorphic to the *canonical term algebra* $C_{\Sigma/E,B}$, whose elements are B-equivalence classes of $\vec{E}, B$-*canonical* ground Σ-terms, where v is the $\vec{E}, B$-*canonical form* of a term t, denoted $u = t!_{\vec{E},B}$, iff: (i) $t \rightarrow^*_{\vec{E},B} u$, and (ii) $(\nexists v \in T_\Sigma)\ u \rightarrow_{\vec{E},B} v$. By $\vec{E}$ convergent modulo B, $t!_{\vec{E},B}$ is unique up to B-equality [28]. Adding (3) ensures that "computing $\vec{E}, B$-canonical forms before performing R, B-rewriting" is a *complete* strategy for rewriting with the rules R module equations E. That is, if $t \rightarrow_{R,B} t'$ and $t!_{\vec{E},B} = u$, then there exists a u' such that $u \rightarrow_{R,B} u'$ and $t'!_{\vec{E},B} =_B u'!_{\vec{E},B}$. We refer to [13,28,31] for more details.

Conditions (1)–(3) allow a simple and intuitive description of the *initial reachability model* $\mathcal{T}_\mathcal{R}$ [6] of $\mathcal{R}$ as the *canonical reachability model* $C_\mathcal{R}$ whose states are the elements of the *canonical term algebra* $C_{\Sigma/E,B}$, and where the one-step transition relation $[u] \rightarrow_\mathcal{R} [v]$ holds iff $u \rightarrow_{R,B} u'$ and $[u'!_{\vec{E},B}] = [v]$. Finally, if $u \rightarrow_{R,B} u'$ via rule $(l \rightarrow r \text{ if } \phi) \in R$ and a ground substitution $\sigma \in [Y \rightarrow T_\Sigma]$, then checking if condition $T_{\Sigma/E \cup B} \models \phi\sigma$ holds is *decidable* by reducing terms in $\phi\sigma$ to $\vec{E}, B$-canonical form.

An OS-subsignature $\Omega \subseteq \Sigma$ is called a *constructor subsignature* for an OS equational theory $(\Sigma, E \cup B)$ where $\vec{E}$ is convergent modulo B iff $\forall t \in T_\Sigma\ t!_{\vec{E},B} \in T_\Omega$. Furthermore, the constructors Ω are then called *free* modulo axioms $B_\Omega \subseteq B$ iff, as S-sorted sets, $C_{\Sigma/E,B} = T_{\Omega/B_\Omega}$. This assumption gives a particularly simple description of the states of the canonical reachability model $C_\mathcal{R}$ as B_Ω-equivalence classes of ground Ω-terms. As explained in Sect. 3, this simple *constructor-based* description is systematically exploited in reachability logic.

An executable rewrite theory $\mathcal{R} = (\Sigma, E \cup B, R)$ with constructor subsignature Ω is called *topmost* iff the poset of sorts $(S, \leqslant)$ has a maximal element, call it *State*, such that: (i) for all rules $(l \rightarrow r \text{ if } \phi) \in R$, $l, r \in T_\Omega(X)_{State}$; and (ii) for any $f : s_1 \ldots s_n \rightarrow s$

in Ω with $s \leqslant State$ we have $s_i \nleqslant State$, $1 \leqslant i \leqslant n$. This ensures that if $[u] \in C_{\mathcal{R}} = T_{\Omega/B_{\Omega}}$, and $[u] \in C_{\mathcal{R},State}$, then all rewrites $u \rightarrow_{R,B} u'$ happen at the top position ϵ. This topmost requirement is easy to achieve in practice. In particular, it can *always* be achieved for *object-based rewrite theories*, which we explain next.

Object-Based Rewrite Theories. Most distributed systems, including the IBOS browser, can be naturally modeled by *object-based rewrite theories*. We give here a brief introduction and refer to [11,29] for more details. The *distributed state* of an object-based system, called a *configuration*, is modeled as a *multiset* or "soup" of objects and messages built up by an *associative-commutative* binary multiset union operator (with juxtaposition syntax) $\_\,\_ : Conf\ Conf \rightarrow Conf$ with identity *null*. The sort *Conf* has two subsorts: a sort *Object* of *objects* and a sort *Msg* of *messages* "traveling" in the configuration from a sender object to a receiver object. The syntax for messages is user-definable, but it is convenient to adopt a conventional syntax for objects as record-like structures of the form: $\langle o \mid a_1(v_1), \ldots, a_n(v_n)\rangle$, where o is the object's name or *object identifier*, belonging to a subsort of a general sort *Oid*, and $a_1(v_1), \ldots, a_n(v_n)$ is a *set* of object *atributes* of sort *Att* built with an associative-commutative union operator $\_\,,\_ : Atts\ Atts \rightarrow Atts$, with *null* as identity element and with $Att < Atts$. Each a_i is a constructor operator $a_i : s_i \rightarrow Att$ so that the *data value* v_i has sort s_i. Objects can be classified in *object classes*, so that a class C has an associated subsort $C.Oid < Oid$ for its object identifiers and associated attribute constructors $a_i : s_i \rightarrow Att$, $1 \leqslant i \leqslant n$. Usually, a configuration may have many objects of the same class, each with a different object identifier; but some classes (e.g., the *Kernel* class in IBOS) are *singleton classes*, so that only one object of that class, with a fixed name, will apear in a configuration. Another example in the IBOS specification is the singleton class *Display*. The single display object represents the rendering of the web page shown to the user and has the form: *<display | displayContent(D), activeTab(WA)>*, where the *activeTab* attribute constructor contains a reference to the web process that the user has selected (each tab corresponds to a different web process) and the *displayContent* constructor encapsulates the web page content currently shown on the display. Not all configurations of objects and messages are sensible. A configuration is *well-formed* iff it satisfies the following two requirements: (i) *unique object identifiers*: each object has a unique name different from all other object names; and (ii) *uniqueness of object attributes*: within an object, each object attribute *appears only once*; for example, an object like *<display | displayContent(D), activeTab(WA), activeTab(WA′)>* is nonsensical.

The *rewrite rules* R of an object-based rewrite theory $\mathcal{R} = (\Sigma, E \cup B, R)$ have the general form $l \rightarrow r\ if\ \phi$, where l and r are terms of sort *Conf*. Intuitively, l is a pattern describing a *local fragment* of the overall configuration, so that a substitution instance $l\sigma$ describing a concrete such fragment (e.g., two objects, or an object and a message) can be rewritten to a new subfragment $r\sigma$, provided the rule's condition $\phi\sigma$ holds (see Sect. 4.1 for an example rule). Classes can be structured in *multiple inheritance hierarchies*, where a subclass C' of class C, denoted $C' < C$, may have additional attributes and has a subsort $C'.Oid < C.Oid$ for its object identifiers. By using extra variables $Attrs_j$ of sort *Atts* for "any extra attributes" that may appear in a subclass of any object o_j in the left-hand side patterns l of a rule, rewrite rules can be *automatically inherited by subclasses* [29]. Furthermore, a subclass $C' < C$ may have *extra rules*, which may modify both its superclass attributes and its additional attributes.

An object-based rewrite theory $\mathcal{R} = (\Sigma, E \cup B, R)$ *can easily be made topmost* as follows: (i) we add a fresh now sort *State* and an "encapsulation operator," say, $\{\_\} : Conf \rightarrow State$, and (ii) we trasform each rule $l \rightarrow r$ *if* ϕ into the rule $\{l\ C\} \rightarrow \{r\ C\}$ *if* ϕ, where C is a fresh variable of sort *Conf* modeling "the rest of the configuration," which could be empty by the identity axiom for *null*.

3 Constructor-Based Reachability Logic

Constructor-based reachability logic [44,45] is a partial correctness logic generalizing Hoare logic in the following sense. In Hoare logic we have state predicates $A, B, C, \ldots$ and formulas are Hoare triples $\{A\}\, p\, \{B\}$ where A is the *precondition*, B is the *postcondition*, and p is the *program* we are reasoning about. Since a Maude program is a rewrite theory $\mathcal{R}$, a Hoare triple in Maude has the form $\{A\}\, \mathcal{R}\, \{B\}$, with the expected *partial correctness semantics*. But we can be more general and consider *reachability logic formulas* of the form: $A \rightarrow^{\circledast} B$, with A the *precondition* (as in Hoare logic) but with B what we call the formula's *midcondition*. That is, B need not hold *at the end* of a terminating computation, as in Hoare logic, but just *somewhere in the middle* of such a computation. A topmost rewrite theory $\mathcal{R}$ *satisfies* $A \rightarrow^{\circledast} B$, written $\mathcal{R} \models A \rightarrow^{\circledast} B$, iff along any terminating computation from an initial state $[u]$ satisfying A there is some intermediate state satisfying B. More precisely:

Definition 2. *Let $\mathcal{R} = (\Sigma, E \cup B, R)$ be topmost with top sort State and with free constructors Ω modulo B_Ω, and let A and B be state predicates for states of sort State, so that $[\![A]\!]$ and $[\![B]\!]$ denote the respective subsets of $T_{\Omega/B_\Omega,State}$ defined by A and B. Furthermore, let T be a state predicate of* terminating states *so that $[\![T]\!] \subseteq Term_{\mathcal{R}}$, where $Term_{\mathcal{R}} = \{[u] \in T_{\Omega/B_\Omega,State} \mid (\nexists [v])\ [u] \rightarrow_{\mathcal{R}} [v]\}$. Then, a reachability formula $A \rightarrow^{\circledast} B$ such that $vars(A) \cap vars(B) = \varnothing$ holds for the canonical reachability model $C_{\mathcal{R}}$ of $\mathcal{R}$ relative to T in the* all paths satisfaction relation, *denoted $\mathcal{R} \models^{\forall}_{T} A \rightarrow^{\circledast} B$, iff for every sequence $[u_0] \rightarrow_{\mathcal{R}} [u_1] \ldots [u_{n-1}] \rightarrow_{\mathcal{R}} [u_n]$ with $[u_0] \in [\![A]\!]$ and $[u_n] \in [\![T]\!]$ there exists k, $0 \leqslant k \leqslant n$ such that $[u_k] \in [\![B]\!]$. When $vars(A) \cap vars(B) = Y \neq \varnothing$, $\mathcal{R} \models^{\forall}_{T} A \rightarrow^{\circledast} B$ holds iff $\mathcal{R} \models^{\forall}_{T} A\rho \rightarrow^{\circledast} B\rho$ for each $\rho \in [Y \rightarrow T_\Omega]$. Call Y the* parameters *of $\mathcal{R} \models^{\forall}_{T} A \rightarrow^{\circledast} B$.*

When $[\![T]\!] = Term_{\mathcal{R}}$, we abbreviate the relation $\models^{\forall}_{T}$ to just $\models$.

We can define the satisfaction of a Hoare triple $\{A\}\, \mathcal{R}\, \{B\}$ as syntactic sugar for the satisfaction relation $\mathcal{R} \models A \rightarrow^{\circledast} (B \wedge Term_{\mathcal{R}})$. As explained in [45], the case of a Hoare logic for an *imperative* programming language $\mathcal{L}$ is obtained as syntactic sugar for a special class of reachability logic formulas for a rewrite theory $\mathcal{R}_{\mathcal{L}}$ giving a rewriting logic semantics to the programming language $\mathcal{L}$.

But in what sense is such a reachability logic *constructor-based*? In the precise sense that the state predicates $A, B, C, \ldots$ used in the logic are *constrained constructor pattern predicates* that exploit for symbolic purposes the extreme simplicity of the constructor theory (Ω, B_Ω), which is much simpler than the equational theory $(\Sigma, E \cup B)$.

Definition 3. *Let* $(\Sigma, E \cup B)$ *be convergent modulo* B *and sufficiently complete with respect to* (Ω, B_Ω)*, i.e.,* $C_{\Sigma/E,B} = T_{\Omega/B_\Omega}$*. A* constrained constructor pattern *is an expression* $(u \mid \phi)$ *such that* $(u, \phi) \in T_\Omega(X) \times QFForm(\Sigma)$*. The set of* constrained constructor pattern predicates $PatPred(\Omega, \Sigma)$ *is defined inductively over* $T_\Omega(X) \times QFForm(\Sigma)$ *by adding* $\bot$ *and closing under* $(\vee)$ *and* $(\wedge)$*. We let capital letters* $A, B, \ldots, P, Q, \ldots$ *range over* $PatPred(\Omega, \Sigma)$*. The* semantics *of* $A \in PatPred(\Omega, \Sigma)$ *is the subset* $[\![A]\!] \subseteq C_{\Sigma/E,B}$ *such that:*

(i) $[\![\bot]\!] = \emptyset$,
(ii) $[\![u \mid \varphi]\!] = \{[(u\rho)!]_{B_\Omega} \in C_{\Sigma/E,B} \mid \rho \in [X \to T_\Omega] \ \wedge\ C_{\Sigma/E,B} \models \varphi\rho\}$,
(iii) $[\![A \vee B]\!] = [\![A]\!] \cup [\![B]\!]$*, and*
(iv) $[\![A \wedge B]\!] = [\![A]\!] \cap [\![B]\!]$.

For any sort s*, let* $PatPred(\Omega, \Sigma)_s \subseteq PatPred(\Omega, \Sigma)$ *where* $A \in PatPred(\Omega, \Sigma)_s$ *iff each subpattern* $(u \mid \phi)$ *of* A *has* $u \in T_\Omega(X)_s$*.* $A \in PatPred(\Omega, \Sigma)$ *is* normal *if it has no subpattern of the form* $P \wedge Q$*. If* B_Ω *has a finitary unification algorithm, normalization is effectively computable by (disjoint)* B_Ω *unification [44, 45].*

We can now fully specify our constructor-based reachability logic: it is a reachability logic for topmost rewrite theories $\mathcal{R} = (\Sigma, E \cup B, R)$ with top sort *State* and with free constructors Ω modulo B_Ω whose set of state predicate formulas is $PatPred(\Omega, \Sigma)_{State}$.

Reachability Logic Proof Rules [44,45]**.** We review our proof system for reachability logic that was proved sound with respect to the all-paths satisfaction relation in [44,45]. The proof rules derive sequents of the form $[\mathcal{A}, C] \vdash_T A \to^{\circledast} B$, where $\mathcal{A}$ and C are finite sets of reachability formulas, $T \subseteq Term_{\mathcal{R}}$, and reachability formula $A \to^{\circledast} B$ is normalized. Formulas in $\mathcal{A}$ are called *axioms*; those in C are called *circularities*. The proof system has three rules: Step, Axiom, and Subsumption. See the brief overview in Table 1. For simplicity we treat the non-parametric case. See [45] for details. E.g., when $vars(A) \cap vars(B) = Y \neq \emptyset$, $[\![A]\!] \subseteq [\![B]\!]$ becomes $[\![A]\!] \subseteq_Y [\![B]\!]$.

Table 1. Overview of proof rules

Assumptions:
1. $\mathcal{R} = (\Sigma, E \cup B, R)$ is suff. comp. w.r.t. (Ω, B_Ω) with $R = \{l_i \to r_i \text{ if } \phi_i\}_{i \in I}$
2. $P \to^{\circledast} (\bigvee_j v_j \mid \psi_j) \in \mathcal{A}$

Name	Rule	Condition
Step*	$\dfrac{\bigwedge_{i \in I, \alpha \in Y(i)} [\mathcal{A} \cup C,\ \emptyset] \vdash_T (r_i \mid \varphi' \wedge \phi_i)\alpha \to^{\circledast} B\alpha}{[\mathcal{A},\ C] \vdash_T u \mid \varphi \to^{\circledast} B}$	
Axiom	$\dfrac{\bigwedge_j [\mathcal{A},\ C] \vdash_T (v_j\alpha \mid \varphi \wedge \psi_j\alpha) \to^{\circledast} B}{[\mathcal{A},\ C] \vdash_T (u \mid \varphi) \to^{\circledast} B}$	$[\![u \mid \varphi]\!] \subseteq [\![P\alpha]\!]$
Sub.	$\dfrac{}{[\mathcal{A},\ C] \vdash_T A \to^{\circledast} B}$	$[\![A]\!] \subseteq [\![B]\!]$

*$\varphi' = \varphi \wedge \bigwedge\{\neg\psi\beta \mid (w \mid \psi) \in B \wedge \exists\beta\ w\beta = u\}$, $Y(i) = Unif_{B_\Omega}(u, l_i)$

This inference system has been mechanized using the Maude rewriting engine [44,45]. Let us say a few words about its *automation*. The STEP rule can be automated by *narrowing*, i.e., symbolic rewriting where the lefthand side of a rewrite rule $l \to r$ if ϕ, instead of being *matched* by a term t to be rewritten, only *B_Ω-unifies* with it. Assuming B_Ω has a finitary unification algorithm, the narrowing relation lifted to constrained constructor patterns is *decidable*. The AXIOM and SUBSUMPTION rules require automating a constrained constructor pattern subsumption check of the form $[\![u \mid \varphi]\!] \subseteq [\![v \mid \phi]\!]$; this can be shown to hold by B_Ω-matching $v\alpha =_{B_\Omega} u$ and checking whether $T_{\Sigma/E \cup B} \models \varphi \Rightarrow \phi\alpha$. Since B_Ω-matching is decidable, the only undecidable check is the implication's validity. Our tool employs multiple heuristics to check whether $T_{\Sigma/E \cup B} \models \varphi \Rightarrow \phi\alpha$. Given a goal $G = [\mathcal{A}, C] \vdash_T A \to^{\circledast} B$, there are two final operations needed: (i) checking whether the proof failed, i.e., whether $[\![A]\!] \cap [\![T]\!] \neq \varnothing$ but not $[\![A]\!] \subseteq [\![B]\!]$, (ii) as an optimization, discarding a goal G where A's constraint is unsatisfiable. These two checks are also undecidable in general, so we rely on best-effort heuristics. Interestingly, thanks to their use of the symbolic techniques for variant unification and satisfiability [14,34,43], and for order-sorted congruence closure module axioms [32] mentioned in the Introduction, these heuristics were sufficient to complete all reachability logic proofs of the IBOS properties without relying on an external prover. In general, the heuristics are implemented in such a way that they will stop after a given number of steps, thus failing if they do not succeed in finding a proof.

Reachability Logic Derived Proof Rules. We document the three derived rules CASE, SPLIT, and SUBSTITUTION in our proof system in Table 2.

Table 2. Overview of derived proof rules

Assumption: $\mathcal{R} = (\Sigma, E \cup B, R)$ is suff. comp. w.r.t. (Ω, B_Ω)

Name	Rule	Condition
CASE*	$\dfrac{\bigwedge_{a \in M} [\mathcal{A}, C] \vdash_T A[x/a] \to^{\circledast} B[x/a]}{[\mathcal{A}, C] \vdash_T A \to^{\circledast} B}$	$x{:}s \in V \wedge cover(M, s)$
SPLIT†	$\dfrac{\bigwedge_{\phi \in \Phi} [\mathcal{A}, C] \vdash_T (u \mid \varphi \wedge \phi) \to^{\circledast} B}{[\mathcal{A}, C] \vdash_T (u \mid \varphi) \to^{\circledast} B}$	$(\bigvee \Phi = \top) \wedge away(\Phi, A, B)$
SUBST.‡	$\dfrac{\bigwedge_{\alpha \in Unif_E(\psi)} [\mathcal{A}, C] \vdash_T (u \mid \rho)\alpha \to^{\circledast} B\alpha}{[\mathcal{A}, C] \vdash_T (u \mid \varphi) \to^{\circledast} B}$	$\varphi = \psi \wedge \rho$

* $cover(M, s) \equiv M \subseteq T_\Omega(Y)_s \wedge Y \cap vars(A, B) = \varnothing \wedge [\![M]\!] = T_{\Omega,s} \wedge |M|$ finite
† $away(\Phi, A, B) \equiv vars(\Phi) \cap (vars(B)/vars(A)) = \varnothing$.
‡ Usable only when $Unif_E(\psi)$ is decidable.

In some sense, the Case and Split rules are performing the exact same operation. In the former, we are considering how to decompose a variable into multiple patterns which entirely *cover* the sort of the given variable; in the later, we are considering how we can decompose the true formula $\top$ into a set of quantifier-free formulas whose disjunction is equivalent to $\top$. In either case, what we want is to make use of the extra information available after case analysis or formula splitting to help us discharge pattern subsumption proofs in the side-condition of Axiom. These rules are both essential for our proofs of both SOP and ABC (see Sect. 4.1), since they allow us to infer additional information in a sound way that is implied by application of the system rewrite rules but not directly stated. The Substitution rule has a slightly different flavor from Case or Split; essentially, it encodes a commonly applicable sequent simplification technique when a fragment of the sequent constraint is a *unifiable* conjunction of equalities. Its usefulness primarily comes from the fact that such unifications often *fail*, which can lead to a huge reduction in the number of goals to be proved.

As for automation, these rules present no special difficulties. Substitution is implementable directly by Maude's built-in unification modulo axioms and variant unification algorithms. The Case and Split rules are also easy to apply. Regarding the checking of their side conditions, checking in Case that M is a cover set for sort s is easy to automate by tree automata modulo axioms B techniques supported by Maude's Sufficient Completeness Checker [17,18]. In the case of Split, although proving that an *arbitrary* disjunction $\bigvee \Phi$ of formulas is inductively equivalent to $\top$ in the initial algebra $T_{\Sigma/E \cup B}$ is in general undecidable, in practice $\bigvee \Phi$ is *not arbitrary at all*, since $\bigvee \Phi$ typically has the form $p = true \vee p = false$, where p is a Boolean expression, or the form $F \vee \neg F$, for F a QF-formula; so many such checks are trivial in practice.

Proving Inductive Invariants. [33,45]. For a transition system $\mathcal{Q} = (Q, \to_Q)$ and a subset $Q_0 \subseteq Q$ of *initial states*, a subset $I \subseteq Q$ is called an *invariant* for $\mathcal{Q}$ from Q_0 iff for each $a \in Q_0$ and $b \in Q$, $a \to_Q^* b$ implies $b \in I$, where $\to_Q^*$ denotes the reflexive-transitive closure of $\to_Q$. A subset $A \subseteq Q$ is called *stable* in $\mathcal{Q}$ iff for each $a \in A$ and $b \in Q$, $a \to_Q b$ implies $b \in A$. An invariant I for $\mathcal{Q}$ from Q_0 is called *inductive* iff I is stable. We instantiate this generic framework to prove invariants over a topmost rewrite theory $\mathcal{R} = (\Sigma, E \cup B, R)$ with $(\Sigma, B, \vec{E})$ convergent and sufficiently complete with respect to (Ω, B_Ω) and consider the transition system induced by $\mathcal{R}$ over sort *State*, i.e., $(C_{\Sigma/E \cup B, State}, \to_{\mathcal{R}})$.

To prove an invariant I from Q_0 over $\mathcal{R}$, we use a simple theory transformation mapping topmost theory $\mathcal{R}$ to a theory $\mathcal{R}_{stop}$ having a fresh operator [_] and a rule $stop$: $c(\vec{x}) \to [c(\vec{x})]$ for each constructor c of sort *State*. Then, by Corollary 1 in [44], to prove I is an invariant from Q_0 over $\mathcal{R}$ we prove $Q_0 \subseteq I$ and that the reachability formula $I\sigma \to^{\circledast} [I]$ holds over $\mathcal{R}$, where: (i) $I\sigma$ is a renaming of I with $vars(I) \cap vars(I\sigma) = \emptyset$ and (ii) if $I = (u \mid \varphi)$ then $[I] = ([u] \mid \varphi)$. If I is inductive and $I = u \mid \varphi$, the proof of $I\sigma \to^{\circledast} [I]$ proceeds as follows:

1. The initial sequent is $[\emptyset, I\sigma \to^{\circledast} [I]] \vdash_{[]} I\sigma \to^{\circledast} [I]$.
2. Apply the Step rule; based on which rule $\zeta : l \to r$ if ϕ was used, obtain:
   (a) if ζ is $stop$, $[I\sigma \to^{\circledast} [I], \emptyset] \vdash_{[]} [I\sigma] \to^{\circledast} [I]$;
   (b) otherwise, $\bigwedge_{\alpha \in Unif_{B_\Omega}(u,l)} [I\sigma \to^{\circledast} [I], \emptyset] \vdash_{[]} (r \mid \varphi \wedge \phi)\alpha \to^{\circledast} [I]$.

3. For case (2a), apply Subsumption. For case (2b), apply zero or more derived rules to obtain sequents of the form: $[I\sigma \to^{\circledast} [I], \varnothing] \vdash_{[]} A \to^{\circledast} [I]$.
4. Since I is assumed inductive, we have $[\![A]\!] \subseteq [\![I\sigma]\!]$. Thus, apply Axiom to derive $[I\sigma \to^{\circledast} [I], \varnothing] \vdash_{[]} [I] \to^{\circledast} [I]$.
5. Finally, apply Subsumption.

Since all the IBOS security properties *are invariants*, all our proofs follow steps (1)–(5) above.

4 IBOS and Its Security Properties

One important security principle adopted by all modern browsers is the same-origin policy (SOP): it isolates web apps from different origins, where an origin is represented as a tuple of a protocol, a domain name, and a port number. For example, if a user loads a web page from origin (`https`,`mybank.com`,`80`) in one tab and in a separate tab loads a web page from origin (`https`,`mybnk.com`,`80`), i.e., a spoofed domain that omits the 'a' in 'mybank,' any code originating from the spoofed domain in the latter tab will not be able to interact with the former tab. SOP also ensures that asynchronous JavaScript and XML (AJAX) network requests from a web app are routed to its origin. Unfortunately, browser vendors often fail to correctly implement the SOP policy [9,41].

The Illinois Browser Operating System (IBOS) is an operating system and web browser that was designed and modeled in Maude with security and compatibility as primary goals [40,49,50]. Unlike commodity browsers, where security checks are implemented across millions of lines of code, in IBOS a small trusted computing base of only 42K code lines is established in the *kernel* through which all network interaction is filtered. What this means in practice is that, even if highly complex HTML rendering or JavaScript interpretation code is compromised, the browser *still* cannot violate SOP (and several other security properties besides). The threat model considered here allows for much of the browser code itself to be compromised while still upholding the security invariants we describe below.

In the following subsections we survey the IBOS browser and SOP, how the IBOS browser can be formally specified as a rewriting logic theory, and how the SOP and other IBOS security properties can be formally specified as invariants.

4.1 IBOS System Specification

IBOS System Design. The Illinois Browser Operating System is an operating system and web browser designed to be highly secure as a browser while maintaining compatibility with modern web apps. It was built on top of the micro-kernel L4Ka::Pistachio [24,25], which embraces the principles of least privilege and privilege separation by isolating operating subsystems into different daemons that communicate through the kernel via checked inter-process communication (IPC). IBOS directly piggybacks on top of this micro-kernel design by implementing various browser abstractions, such as the browser chrome and network connections, as separate components that communicate using L4ka kernel message passing infrastructure. Figure 1 gives an overview of the IBOS architecture; as an explanatory aid we highlight a few key objects:

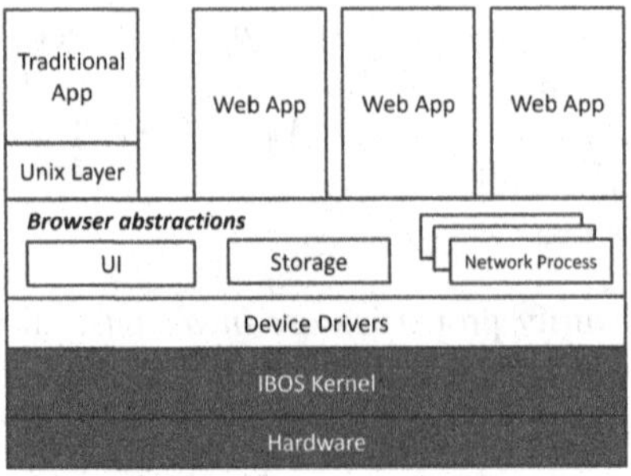

Fig. 1. IBOS system architecture [40].

- **Kernel.** The IBOS kernel is built on top of the L4Ka::Pistachio micro-kernel which, as noted previously, can check IPC messages against security policies.
- **Network Process.** A network process is responsible for managing a network connection (e.g., HTTP connections) to a specific origin. It understands how to encode and decode TCP datagrams and Ethernet frames and can send and receive frames from the network interface card (NIC).
- **Web Application.** A web application represents a specific instance of a web page loaded in a particular browser tab (e.g., when a link is clicked or a URL is entered into the address bar). Web applications know how to render HTML documents. As per SOP, each web page is labeled by its origin.
- **Browser UI.** The browser user inferface (UI) minimally includes the address bar and the mouse pointer and extends to any input mechanism.
- **Display.** The display represents the rendered web app shown to the user; it is blank when no web app has loaded. For security, it cannot modify the UI.

IBOS System Specification in Maude. We present an overview of the IBOS formal executable specification as a Maude rewrite theory, which closely follows previous work [36,39,40]. We model IBOS as an object-based rewrite theory (see Sect. 2). We use *italics* to write Maude rewrite rules and *CamelCase* for variable or sort names. Some objects of interest include the singleton objects *kernel*, *ui*, and *display* (in classes *Kernel*, *UI*, and *Display*, respectively). We also have non-singleton classes *WebApp* and *NetProc* representing web apps and network processes in IBOS, respectively.

As a further aid to the reader and a complement to the graphical overview of IBOS in Fig. 1, we rewrite this graphical figure using our formal specification. Said another way, we provide in Fig. 2 a representative state (e.g., a ground term) of the transition system $(C_{\Sigma/E\cup B,State}, \rightarrow_{\mathcal{R}})$ where $\mathcal{R}$ is the Maude rewrite theory specifying IBOS. To improve readability, we write each object attribute on a separate line.

Let us make a few high-level remarks about the figure. In our specification, urls are encoded as numbers wrapped by constructor *url*(...). In IBOS, to enforce SOP as well as other security policies, both browser frames and network connections must be tracked. Each browser frame is represented by an object of class *WebApp*, while each network connection is represented by an object of class *NetProc*. The *kernel* manages process state by internal metadata tables *webAppInfo* where each web app is tagged by its origin and *netProcInfo* where each network connection is tagged by its origin web app and destination server. When a new web app is created, the kernel automatically creates a corresponding network process between the webapp and its origin server. Since the *kernel* is responsible for creating network connections, it records the next fresh network process identifier in *nextNetProc*.

The *kernel*'s *secPolicy* attribute stores its security policy. Each policy consists of a sender, a receiver, and a message type. Any message not explicitly allowed by the policy is dropped. In the policy, the special *Oid*s *network* and *webapp* represent a policy allowing any network process or webapp to send a particular kind of message to its corresponding webapp or network process, respectively. In the figure, the *kernel* is preparing to forward a message from *webapp(0)* to its corresponding network process *network(0)* asking to fetch an item from the web app's origin *url(15)*.

Aside from the *kernel*, the system has a few other distinguished objects. The *display* object tracks the content currently shown on the screen in *displayContent*; to do that, it should know which web app is the *activeTab*. The *ui* (user interface) contains the list of commands given by the user during some usage session in its *toKernel* attribute. The *webappmgr* (web app manager) is responsible for spawning new web apps; in our model, it just records the next fresh web app identifier in attribute *nextWebApp*. Finally, the *nic* (network interface card) has two attributes for ingoing and outgoing data. In our model, we identify urls and their loaded content. To model network latency, outgoing messages in *nic-out* are queued up in *nic-in* in a random order.

Of course, we also have objects representing web apps and network connections. In the figure, *webapp(0)*'s *rendered* content is blank. However, it is currently *loading* its content from its origin *url(15)*; its request to fetch data from its corresponding network process is currently being handled by the kernel. Currently, its *toKernel* and *fromKernel* IPC message queues are blank because it is not performing any other communication at this time. There is also a corresponding network process *network(0)*; it has two direct-memory access (DMA) buffers *mem-in* and *mem-out* that are used as I/O channels between itself and the network card driver. Like web apps, network processes also have two IPC message queues. Finally, a network process also stores which web app its received data should be sent back to.

As an example, let us consider the specification of the *change-display* rewrite rule shown next:

$$
\begin{aligned}
& \{\langle display \mid displayContent(D), activeTab(WA), Atts\rangle\ \langle WA \mid rendered(D'), Atts'\rangle\ Conf\} \\
\rightarrow\ & \{\langle display \mid displayContent(D'), activeTab(WA), Atts\rangle\ \langle WA \mid rendered(D'), Atts'\rangle\ Conf\} \\
\text{if }\ & D \neq D'
\end{aligned}
$$

This rule involves the *display* object and the *WebApp* designated as the display's *activeTab*. In our model, the *rendered* attribute of a web app represents its current rendering of the HTML document located at its origin. When the web app is first created, its *rendered* attribute has the value *about-blank*, i.e., nothing has yet been rendered. Thus, this rule essentially states that, at any time, the displayed content can be replaced by currently rendered HTML document of the active tab, *only if* it is different from the currently displayed content.

```
< kernel | addrBar(url(15)),
           handling(msg(webapp(0), network(0), FETCH-URL, url(15)))
           nextNetProc(1),
           webAppInfo(pi(webapp(0), url(15))),
           netProcInfo(pi(network(0), url(15), url(15))),
           secPolicy(policy(webapp, network, FETCH-URL),
             policy(network, webapp, RETURN-URL),
             policy(ui, webapp, NEW-URL),
             policy(ui, webapp, SWITCH-TAB)) >
< display | displayContent(about-blank),
            activeTab(webapp(0)) >
< ui | toKernel(msg(ui, webapp, NEW-URL, url(25))) >
< webappmgr | nextWebApp(1) >
< nic | nic-in(emtpy),
        nic-out(empty) >
< webapp(0) | URL(url(15)),
              rendered(about-blank),
              loading(true),
              toKernel(empty),
              fromKernel(empty) >
< network(0) | mem-in(empty),
               mem-out(empty),
               returnTo(webapp(0)),
               toKernel(empty),
               fromKernel(empty) >
```

Fig. 2. Representative IBOS system state

Our IBOS browser specification contains 23 rewrite rules and is about 850 lines of Maude code; it is available at https://github.com/sskeirik/ibos-case-study.

4.2 Specification of the IBOS Security Properties

We first describe at a high level the security properties that we will formally specify and verify. The key property that we verify is the *same-origin policy* (SOP), but we also specify and verify the *address bar correctness* (ABC) property. Our discussion follows that of [39,40], based on invariants P_1–P_{11}:

- P_1 Network requests from web page instances must be handled by the proper network process.
- P_2 Ethernet frames from the network interface card (NIC) must be routed to the proper network process.
- P_3 Ethernet frames from network processes to the NIC must have an IP address and TCP port that matches the origin of the network process.
- P_4 Data from network processes to web page instances must be from a valid origin.
- P_5 Network processes for different web page instances must remain isolated.
- P_6 The browser chrome and web page content displays are isolated.

P_7 Only the current tab can access the screen, mouse, and keyboard.
P_8 All components can only perform their designated functions.
P_9 The URL of the active tab is displayed to the user.
P_{10} The displayed web page content is from the URL shown in the address bar.
P_{11} All configurations are well-formed, i.e., non-duplication of *Oids* and *Atts*.

We define same-origin policy as SOP $= \bigwedge_{1 \leqslant i \leqslant 7} P_i$; address-bar correctness is specified as ABC $= P_{10}$. Note that $P_9 \wedge P_{10} \Rightarrow P_7$. Since P_5, P_6, and P_8 follow directly from the model design, it is sufficient to prove $\bigwedge_{i \in I} P_i$ for $I = \{1, 2, 3, 4, 9, 10\}$. Invariant P_{11} is new to our current formalization, but is implicitly used in prior work; it forbids absurd configurations, e.g., having two *kernels* or a *WebApp* that has two *URLs* (see Sect. 2). Due to its fundamental relation to how object-based rewrite theories are defined, we need P_{11} in the proof of *all* other invariants. As an example of how these invariant properties can be formalized in our model as constrained pattern predicates, we show how the address bar correctness invariant can be specified in our system below:

$$\{\langle kernel \mid addrBar(U), Atts\rangle \\ \langle display \mid displayContent(U'), Atts'\rangle \; Conf\} \mid U' \trianglelefteq U \qquad \text{(ABC)}$$

where $U' \trianglelefteq U \Leftrightarrow_{\text{def}} (U' \neq \textit{about-blank} \Rightarrow U = U')$, i.e., the *display* is either blank *or* its contents' origin matches the address bar. Note that, for simplicity, in our model, we identify displayed content with its origin URL. As a second example, consider how to formalize invariant P_9:

$$\{\langle kernel \mid addrBar(U), Atts\rangle \\ \langle display \mid activeTab(WA), Atts'\rangle \\ \langle WA \mid URL(U''), Atts''\rangle \; Conf\} \mid U \trianglelefteq U'' \qquad (\text{P}_9)$$

i.e., the address bar must match the URL of the active tab, unless the address shown is *about-blank*, i.e., nothing is shown. Finally, P_{11} has a trivial encoding: $\{Conf\} \mid WF(Conf)$, where $WF : Conf \rightarrow Bool$ is the well-formedness predicate. Our specification has 200 lines of Maude code to specify the pattern predicates used in our invariants and another 900 lines of code specifying all of the auxiliary functions and predicates. As stated in the Introduction, we additionally must prove that: (a) the IBOS system specification extended by our security property specification is *suitable* for symbolic reachability analysis; and (b) our ABC and SOP invariants are at least as strong as the corresponding invariants in prior work [39,40] ABC_0 and SOP_0. Proof obligation (a) can be met by using techniques for proving *ground convergence* and *sufficient completeness* of conditional equational theories, while proof obligation (b) can be reduced to proving associated implications, e.g., SOP $\Rightarrow \text{SOP}_0$. We have carried out full proofs of (a) and (b); due to space limitations, the full details are available at [42].

5 Proof of IBOS Security Properties

In this section, due to space limitations, we give a high-level overview of our proof methodology for verifying the SOP and ABC properties for IBOS, and show a subproof used in deductively verifying ABC. Each proof script has roughly 200 lines of code and another 20 to specify the reachability logic sequent being proved.

Modular Proof Methodology. In this subsection we survey our modular proof methodology for proving invariants using reachability logic and comment on how we exploit modularity in three key ways, i.e., we show how we efficiently structured and carried out our proofs by decomposing them into composable, independent, and reusable pieces.

Most of the IBOS proof effort was spent strengthening an invariant I into an inductive invariant I_{ind}, where I is either SOP or ABC. Typically, I_{ind} is obtained by iteratively applying the proof strategy given in Sect. 2. In each round, assume candidate I' is inductive and attempt to complete the proof. If, after applying the STEP rule (and possibly some derived rules), an application of AXIOM is impossible, examine the proof of failed pattern subsumption $[\![A]\!] \subseteq [\![I']\!]$ in the side-condition of AXIOM. If pattern formula C (possibly using new functions and predicates defined in theory Δ) can be found that might enable the subsumption proof to succeed, try again with candidate $I' \wedge C$. In parallel, our system specification $\mathcal{R}$ is enriched by extending the underlying *convergent* equational theory $\mathcal{E}$ to $\mathcal{E} \cup \Delta$ to obtain the enriched rewrite theory $\mathcal{R}_\Delta$.

The first kind of modularity we exploit is *rule modularity*. Recall that any reachability logic proof begins with an application of the STEP rule. Since STEP must consider the result of symbolically rewriting the initial sequent with all possible rewrite rules, we can equivalently construct our proof on a "rule-by-rule" basis, i.e., if $\mathcal{R} = (\Sigma, E \cup B, \{l_j \to r_j \text{ if } \phi_j\}_{j \in J})$, we can consider $|J|$ separate reachability proofs using respective theories $\mathcal{R}_j = (\Sigma, E \cup B, \{l_j \to r_j \text{ if } \phi_j\})$ for $j \in J$. Thus, we can focus on strengthening invariant I' for each rule $j \in J$ separately.

Another kind of modularity that we can exploit is *subclass modularity*. Because we are reasoning in an object-based rewrite theory, each rule mentions one or more objects in one or more classes, and describes how they evolve. Recall from Sect. 2 that subclasses must contain all of the attributes of their superclass, but may define additional attributes and have additional rewrite rules which affect them. The upshot of all this is that if we *refine* our specification by instantiating objects in one class into some subclass, any invariants proved for the original rules immediately hold for the same rules in the refined specification. Because of rule modularity, we need only prove our invariants hold for the newly defined rules. Even among newly defined rules, all *non-interfering* rules trivially satisfy any already proved invariants, where non-interfering rules do not directly or indirectly influence the state of previously defined attributes.

Lastly, we exploit what we call *structural modularity*. Since our logic is constructor-based and we assume that B_Ω-matching is decidable, by pattern matching we can easily specify a set S of sequents to which we can apply the *same* combination of derived proof rules. This is based on the intuition that syntactically similar goals typically can be proved in a similar way. More concretely, given a set of reachability formulas S and pattern $p \in T_\Omega(X)$, we can define the subset of formulas $S_p = \{(u \mid \varphi) \to^{\circledast} B \in S \mid \exists \alpha \in [X \to T_\Omega(X)]\, p\alpha =_{B_\Omega} u\}$. Although the simplified example below does not illustrate structural modularity, we have heavily exploited this principle in our formal verification of IBOS.

Address Bar Correctness Proof Example. Here we show a snippet of the ABC invariant verification, namely, we prove that the invariant holds for the *change-display* rule by exploiting rule modularity as noted above. As mentioned in our description of invariant P_{11}, well-formedness is required for all invariants. Therefore, we begin with ABC $\wedge P_{11}$ as our candidate inductive invariant, which, as mentioned in Sect. 2, normalizes by disjoint B_{Ω}-unification to the invariant:

$$\{\langle kernel \mid addrBar(U), Atts\rangle \\ \langle display \mid displayContent(U'), Atts'\rangle\ Conf\} \mid U' \trianglelefteq U \wedge WF(\ldots)$$

where for brevity ... expands to the entire term of sort *Conf* wrapped inside operator {_}, i.e., the entire configuration is *well-formed.* Recall the definition of the *change-display* rule in Sect. 4.1. We can see that our invariant only mentions the *kernel* and *display* processes, whereas in rule *change-display* the value of *displayContent* depends on the *rendered* attribute of a *WebApp*, i.e., the one selected as the *activeTab*. Clearly, our invariant seems too weak. How can we strengthen it? The reader may recall P_9, which states "the URL of the active tab is displayed to the user." Thus, by further disjoint B_{Ω}-unification, the strengthened invariant ABC $\wedge P_{11} \wedge P_9$ normalizes to:

$$\{\langle kernel \mid addrBar(U), Atts\rangle\ \langle display \mid displayContent(U'), activeTab(WA), Atts'\rangle \\ \langle WA \mid URL(U''), Atts''\rangle\ Conf\} \mid U' \trianglelefteq U \wedge U \trianglelefteq U'' \wedge WF(\ldots)$$

This new invariant is closer to what we need, since the pattern now mentions the particular web app we want. Unfortunately, since our invariant still knows nothing about the *rendered* attribute, at least one further strengthening is needed.

At this point, we can enrich our theory with a new predicate stating that the *rendered* and *URL* attributes of any *WebApp* always agree[1]. Let us declare it as $R : Conf \to Bool$. We can define it inductively over configurations by:

$$R(\langle WA \mid rendered(U), URL(U'), Atts\rangle\ Conf) = U \trianglelefteq U' \wedge R(Conf) \quad (R_1)$$

$$R(\langle P \mid Atts\rangle\ Conf) = R(Conf)\ if\ \neg WA(P) \quad (R_2)$$

$$R(none) = \top \quad (R_3)$$

where $WA : Oid \to Bool$ ambiguously denotes a predicate that holds iff an *Oid* refers to a web app. Intuitively, it says that whatever a *WebApp* has *rendered* is either blank or has been loaded from its *URL*. The strengthened invariant becomes:

$$\{\langle kernel \mid addrBar(U), Atts\rangle\ \langle display \mid displayContent(U'), activeTab(WA), Atts'\rangle \\ \langle WA \mid URL(U''), Atts''\rangle\ Conf\} \mid \\ U' \trianglelefteq U \wedge U \trianglelefteq U'' \wedge WF(\ldots) \wedge R(\ldots)$$

[1] Note that, in a very real sense, this requirement is at the heart of the SOP, since it means that any *WebApp* has indeed obtained content from its claimed origin.

where, as before, the ... represents the entire term of sort *Conf* enclosed in {_}. Now, all of the required relationships between variables in the rewrite rule seem to be accounted for. Uneventfully, with the strengthened invariant $ABC \wedge P_{11} \wedge P_9 \wedge R$, the subproof for the *change-display* rule now succeeds.

6 Related Work and Conclusions

Related Work on IBOS Verification. In this paper, we have presented the first full deductive verification of SOP and ABC for IBOS. Note that in [39,40], SOP and ABC were also verified. Their approach consisted of a hand-written proof that any counterexample must appear on some trace of length n plus bounded model checking showing that such counterexamples are unreachable on all traces of length n. In [36], an attempt was made to deductively verify these same invariants via the Maude invariant analyzer. Though a few basic invariants were proved, due to thousands of generated proof obligations, none of the properties listed in Sect. 4.2 were verified. Compared to previous work, this paper presents the first full deductive verification of IBOS security properties.

Related Work on Browser Security. In terms of computer technology, the same-origin policy is quite old: it was first referenced in Netscape Navigator 2 released in 1996 [1]. As [41] points out, different browser vendors have different notions of SOP. Here, we situate IBOS and our work into this larger context. Many papers have been written on policies for enforcing SOP with regards to frames [2], third-party scripts [20,23], cached content [21], CSS [19], and mobile OSes [51]. Typically, these discussions assume that browser code is working as intended and then show existing policies are insufficient. Instead, IBOS attacks the problem taking a different tack: even if the browser itself is compromised, can SOP still be ensured? What the IBOS verification demonstrates is that—by using a minimal trusted computing base in the kernel, implementing separate web frames as separate processes, and requiring all IPC to be kernel-checked—one can in fact enforce the standard SOP notions, *even if* the complex browser code for rendering HTML or executing JavaScript is *compromised.* Although our model does not treat JavaScript, HTML, or cookies, explicitly, since it models system calls which are used for process creation, network access, and inter-process communication, code execution and resource references can be abstracted away into the communication primitives they ultimately cause to be invoked, allowing us to perform strong verification in a high-level fashion. [7] surveys many promising lines of research in the formal methods web security landscape. Prior work on formal and declarative models of web browsers includes [3] as well as the *executable* models [4,5]. Our work complements the Quark browser design and implementation of [22]: Quark, like IBOS, has a small trusted kernel (specified in Coq). In addition to proving tab non-interference and address bar correctness theorems, the authors use Coq code extraction to produce a verified, functional browser.

Related Work on Reachability Logic. Our work on *constructor-based* reachability logic [44,45] builds upon previous work on reachability logic [37,38,47,48] as a language-generic approach to program verification, parametric on the operational semantics of a programming language. Our work extends in a non-trivial manner reachability logic from a programming-language-generic logic of programs to a rewrite-theory-generic logic to reason about *both* distributed system designs and programs based on rewriting logic semantics. Our work in [44,45] was also inspired by the work in [27], which for the first time considered reachability logic for rewrite theories, but went beyond [27] in several ways, including more expressive input theories and state predicates, and a simple inference system as opposed to an algorithm. Also related to our work in [44,45], but focusing on *coinductive reasoning*, we have the recent work in [10,26,35], of which, in spite of various substantial differences, the closest to our work regarding the models assumed, the kinds of reachability properties proved, and the state predicates and inference systems proposed is the work in [10].

Conclusion and Future Work. We have presented a full deductive proof of the SOP and ABC properties of the IBOS browser design, as well as a prover and a modular reachability logic verification methodology making proofs scalable to substantial proof efforts like that of IBOS. Besides offering a case study that can help other distributed system verification efforts, this work should also be seen as a useful step towards incorporating the IBOS design ideas into future fully verified browsers. The web is alive and evolving; these evolution necessitates that formal approaches evolve as well. Looking towards the future of IBOS, two goals stand out: (i) extending the design of IBOS to handle some recent extensions of the SOP, e.g., cross-origin resource sharing (CORS) to analyze potential cross-site scripting (XSS) and cross-site request forgery attacks (XSRF) [16], and to check for incompatible content security policies (CSP) [46] in relation to SOP; by exploiting subclass and rule modularity, the verification of an IBOS extension with such new functionality could reuse most of the current IBOS proofs, since extra proofs would only be needed for the new, functionality-adding rules; and (ii) exploiting the intrinsic concurrency of Maude rewrite theories to transform them into correct-by-construction, deployable Maude-based distributed system implementations, closing the gap between verified designs and correct implementations. Our work on IBOS takes one more step towards demonstrating that a formally secure web is possible in a connected world where security is needed more than ever before.

Acknowledgments. The first two authors were partially supported by NRL under contract N00173-17-1-G002. The third author was partially supported by the ECOS-NORD project FACTS (C19M03).

References

1. JavaScript Guide (1.2). Netscape Communications Corporation (1997). Originally http://developer.netscape.com/docs/manuals/communicator/jsguide4/index.htm. https://www.cs.rit.edu/~atk/JavaScript/manuals/jsguide/
2. Barth, A., Jackson, C., Mitchell, J.C.: Securing frame communication in browsers. Commun. ACM **52**(6), 83–91 (2009)
3. Bauer, L., Cai, S., Jia, L., Passaro, T., Stroucken, M., Tian, Y.: Run-time monitoring and formal analysis of information flows in chromium. In: NDSS (2015)
4. Bohannon, A.: Foundations of web script security. Citeseer (2012)

5. Bohannon, A., Pierce, B.C.: Featherweight Firefox: formalizing the core of a web browser. In: Proceedings of the 2010 USENIX Conference on Web Application Development, p. 11. Usenix Association (2010)
6. Bruni, R., Meseguer, J.: Semantic foundations for generalized rewrite theories. Theoret. Comput. Sci. **360**(1–3), 386–414 (2006)
7. Bugliesi, M., Calzavara, S., Focardi, R.: Formal methods for web security. J. Log. Algebr. Methods Program. **87**, 110–126 (2017)
8. Chen, S., Meseguer, J., Sasse, R., Wang, H.J., Wang, Y.M.: A systematic approach to uncover security flaws in GUI logic. In: IEEE Symposium on Security and Privacy, pp. 71–85. IEEE (2007)
9. Chen, S., Ross, D., Wang, Y.M.: An analysis of browser domain-isolation bugs and a light-weight transparent defense mechanism. In: ACM Conference on Computer and Communications Security, pp. 2–11. ACM (2007)
10. Ciobâcă, Ş., Lucanu, D.: A coinductive approach to proving reachability properties in logically constrained term rewriting systems. In: Galmiche, D., Schulz, S., Sebastiani, R. (eds.) IJCAR 2018. LNCS (LNAI), vol. 10900, pp. 295–311. Springer, Cham (2018). https://doi.org/10.1007/978-3-319-94205-6_20
11. Clavel, M., et al.: All About Maude - A High-Performance Logical Framework. LNCS, vol. 4350. Springer, Heidelberg (2007). https://doi.org/10.1007/978-3-540-71999-1
12. Dershowitz, N., Jouannaud, J.P.: Rewrite systems. In: van Leeuwen, J. (ed.) Handbook of Theoretical Computer Science, vol. B, pp. 243–320. North-Holland (1990)
13. Durán, F., Meseguer, J.: On the Church-Rosser and coherence properties of conditional order-sorted rewrite theories. J. Logic Algebraic Program. **81**(7–8), 816–850 (2012)
14. Escobar, S., Sasse, R., Meseguer, J.: Folding variant narrowing and optimal variant termination. J. Logic Algebraic Program. **81**, 898–928 (2012)
15. Goguen, J., Meseguer, J.: Order-sorted algebra I: equational deduction for multiple inheritance, overloading, exceptions and partial operations. Theoret. Comput. Sci. **105**, 217–273 (1992)
16. Gollmann, D.: Problems with same origin policy. In: Christianson, B., Malcolm, J.A., Matyas, V., Roe, M. (eds.) Security Protocols 2008. LNCS, vol. 6615, pp. 84–85. Springer, Heidelberg (2011). https://doi.org/10.1007/978-3-642-22137-8_11
17. Hendrix, J., Meseguer, J., Ohsaki, H.: A sufficient completeness checker for linear order-sorted specifications modulo axioms. In: Third International Joint Conference on Automated Reasoning, IJCAR 2006, pp. 151–155 (2006)
18. Hendrix, J.D.: Decision procedures for equationally based reasoning. Ph.D. thesis, University of Illinois at Urbana-Champaign (2008). http://hdl.handle.net/2142/10967
19. Huang, L.S., Weinberg, Z., Evans, C., Jackson, C.: Protecting browsers from cross-origin CSS attacks. In: CCS 2010, pp. 619–629. ACM, New York (2010)
20. Jackson, C., Barth, A.: Beware of finer-grained origins. Web (2008)
21. Jackson, C., Bortz, A., Boneh, D., Mitchell, J.C.: Protecting browser state from web privacy attacks. In: Proceedings of the 15th International Conference on World Wide Web, pp. 737–744. ACM (2006)
22. Jang, D., Tatlock, Z., Lerner, S.: Establishing browser security guarantees through formal shim verification. In: Presented as part of the 21st {USENIX} Security Symposium ({USENIX} Security 2012), pp. 113–128 (2012)
23. Karlof, C., Shankar, U., Tygar, J.D., Wagner, D.: Dynamic pharming attacks and locked same-origin policies for web browsers. In: Proceedings of the 14th ACM Conference on Computer and Communications Security, pp. 58–71. ACM (2007)
24. Klein, G., Tuch, H.: Towards verified virtual memory in L4. TPHOLs Emerg. Trends **4**, 16 (2004)

25. Kolanski, R., Klein, G.: Formalising the L4 microkernel API. In: Proceedings of the 12th Computing: The Australasian Theory Symposium, vol. 51, pp. 53–68. Australian Computer Society, Inc. (2006)
26. Lucanu, D., Rusu, V., Arusoaie, A.: A generic framework for symbolic execution: a coinductive approach. J. Symb. Comput. **80**, 125–163 (2017)
27. Lucanu, D., Rusu, V., Arusoaie, A., Nowak, D.: Verifying reachability-logic properties on rewriting-logic specifications. In: Martí-Oliet, N., Ölveczky, P.C., Talcott, C. (eds.) Logic, Rewriting, and Concurrency. LNCS, vol. 9200, pp. 451–474. Springer, Cham (2015). https://doi.org/10.1007/978-3-319-23165-5_21
28. Lucas, S., Meseguer, J.: Normal forms and normal theories in conditional rewriting. J. Log. Algebr. Methods Program. **85**(1), 67–97 (2016)
29. Meseguer, J.: A logical theory of concurrent objects and its realization in the Maude language. In: Agha, G., Wegner, P., Yonezawa, A. (eds.) Research Directions in Concurrent Object-Oriented Programming, pp. 314–390. MIT Press (1993)
30. Meseguer, J.: Membership algebra as a logical framework for equational specification. In: Presicce, F.P. (ed.) WADT 1997. LNCS, vol. 1376, pp. 18–61. Springer, Heidelberg (1998). https://doi.org/10.1007/3-540-64299-4_26
31. Meseguer, J.: Twenty years of rewriting logic. J. Algebr. Log. Program. **81**, 721–781 (2012)
32. Meseguer, J.: Order-sorted rewriting and congruence closure. In: Jacobs, B., Löding, C. (eds.) FoSSaCS 2016. LNCS, vol. 9634, pp. 493–509. Springer, Heidelberg (2016). https://doi.org/10.1007/978-3-662-49630-5_29
33. Meseguer, J.: Generalized rewrite theories, coherence completion and symbolic methods. Technical report, Computer Science Department, University of Illinois, December 2018. http://hdl.handle.net/2142/102183
34. Meseguer, J.: Variant-based satisfiability in initial algebras. Sci. Comput. Program. **154**, 3–41 (2018)
35. Moore, B.: Coinductive program verification. Ph.D. thesis, University of Illinois at Urbana-Champaign (2016). http://hdl.handle.net/2142/95372
36. Rocha, C.: Symbolic reachability analysis for rewrite theories. Ph.D. thesis, University of Illinois at Urbana-Champaign (2012)
37. Rosu, G., Stefanescu, A.: Checking reachability using matching logic. In: Proceedings of OOPSLA 2012, pp. 555–574. ACM (2012)
38. Roşu, G., Ştefănescu, A.: From Hoare logic to matching logic reachability. In: Giannakopoulou, D., Méry, D. (eds.) FM 2012. LNCS, vol. 7436, pp. 387–402. Springer, Heidelberg (2012). https://doi.org/10.1007/978-3-642-32759-9_32
39. Sasse, R.: Security models in rewriting logic for cryptographic protocols and browsers. Ph.D. thesis, University of Illinois at Urbana-Champaign (2012). http://hdl.handle.net/2142/34373
40. Sasse, R., King, S.T., Meseguer, J., Tang, S.: IBOS: a correct-by-construction modular browser. In: Păsăreanu, C.S., Salaün, G. (eds.) FACS 2012. LNCS, vol. 7684, pp. 224–241. Springer, Heidelberg (2013). https://doi.org/10.1007/978-3-642-35861-6_14
41. Schwenk, J., Niemietz, M., Mainka, C.: Same-origin policy: evaluation in modern browsers. In: 26th USENIX Security Symposium (USENIX Security 2017), Vancouver, BC, pp. 713–727. USENIX Association (2017)
42. Skeirik, S.: Rewriting-based symbolic methods for distributed system analysis. Ph.D. thesis, University of Illinois at Urbana-Champaign (2019)
43. Skeirik, S., Meseguer, J.: Metalevel algorithms for variant satisfiability. J. Log. Algebr. Methods Program. **96**, 81–110 (2018)
44. Skeirik, S., Stefanescu, A., Meseguer, J.: A constructor-based reachability logic for rewrite theories. In: Fioravanti, F., Gallagher, J.P. (eds.) LOPSTR 2017. LNCS, vol. 10855, pp. 201–217. Springer, Cham (2018). https://doi.org/10.1007/978-3-319-94460-9_12

45. Skeirik, S., Stefanescu, A., Meseguer, J.: A constructor-based reachability logic for rewrite theories. Fundam. Inform. **173**(4), 315–382 (2020)
46. Some, D.F., Bielova, N., Rezk, T.: On the content security policy violations due to the same-origin policy. In: WWW 2017, Republic and Canton of Geneva, Switzerland, pp. 877–886 (2017)
47. Ştefănescu, A., Ciobâcă, Ş., Mereuta, R., Moore, B.M., Şerbănută, T.F., Roşu, G.: All-path reachability logic. In: Dowek, G. (ed.) RTA 2014. LNCS, vol. 8560, pp. 425–440. Springer, Cham (2014). https://doi.org/10.1007/978-3-319-08918-8_29
48. Stefanescu, A., Park, D., Yuwen, S., Li, Y., Rosu, G.: Semantics-based program verifiers for all languages. In: Proceedings of OOPSLA 2016, pp. 74–91. ACM (2016)
49. Tang, S.: Towards secure web browsing. Ph.D. thesis, University of Illinois at Urbana-Champaign, 25 May 2011. http://hdl.handle.net/2142/24307
50. Tang, S., Mai, H., King, S.T.: Trust and protection in the Illinois Browser Operating System. In: 9th USENIX Symposium on Operating Systems Design and Implementation, OSDI 2010, Proceedings, Vancouver, BC, Canada, 4–6 October 2010, pp. 17–32. USENIX Association (2010)
51. Wang, R., Xing, L., Wang, X., Chen, S.: Unauthorized origin crossing on mobile platforms: threats and mitigation. In: Proceedings of the 2013 ACM SIGSAC Conference on Computer Communications Security, CCS 2013, pp. 635–646. ACM, New York (2013)

Automated Construction of Security Integrity Wrappers for Industry 4.0 Applications

Vivek Nigam[1,3](✉) and Carolyn Talcott[2]

[1] fortiss, Munich, Germany
nigam@fortiss.org
[2] SRI International, Melno Park, USA
clt@csl.sri.com
[3] Federal University of Paraíba, João Pessoa, Brazil

Abstract. Industry 4.0 (I4.0) refers to the trend towards automation and data exchange in manufacturing technologies and processes which include cyber-physical systems, where the internet of things connect with each other and the environment via networking. This new connectivity opens systems to attacks, by, *e.g.*, injecting or tampering with messages. The solution supported by standards such as OPC-UA is to sign and/or encrypt messages. However, given the limited resources of devices, instead of applying crypto algorithms to all messages in the network, it is better to focus on the messages that if tampered with or injected, could lead to undesired configurations.

This paper describes a framework for developing and analyzing formal executable specifications of I4.0 applications in Maude. The framework supports the engineering design workflow using theory transformations that include algorithms to enumerate network attacks leading to undesired states, and to determine wrappers preventing these attacks. In particular, given a deployment map from application components to devices we define a theory transformation that models execution of the application on the given set of (networked) devices. Given an enumeration of attacks (message flows) we define a further theory transformation that wraps each device with policies for signing/signature checking for just those messages needed to prevent the attacks.

1 Introduction

Manufacturing technologies and processes are increasingly automated with highly interconnected components that may include simple sensors and controllers as well as cyber-physical systems and the Internet of Things (IoT) components. This trend is sometimes referred to Industry 4.0 (I4.0). Among other benefits, I4.0 enables process agility and product specialization. This increase of interconnectivity has also enabled cyber-attacks. These attacks can lead to catastrophic events possibly leading to material and human damages. For example, after an attack on a steel mill, the factory had to stop its production leading to great financial loss [1].

A recent BSI report on the security of OPC-UA (machine to machine communication protocol for industrial automation) [7], points out that the lack of signed and encrypted messages on sensitive parts of the factory network can lead to high risk

S. Escobar and N. Martí-Oliet (Eds.): WRLA 2020, LNCS 12328, pp. 197–215, 2020.
https://doi.org/10.1007/978-3-030-63595-4_11

attacks. For example, attackers can inject or tamper with messages, confusing factory controllers and ultimately leading to a stalled or fatal state. Given the limited bandwidth and processing power of I4.0 elements, instead of signing all messages, it is much better to only sign the messages that when not protected could be modified or injected by an intruder to lead to an undesirable situation. This leads to the question of how to determine critical communications.

This paper presents a formal framework for specifying I4.0 applications and analyzing safety and security properties using Maude [4]. The engineering development process from application design and testing to systems deployment is captured by theory transformations with associated theorems showing that results of analysis carried out at the abstract application level hold for models of deployed systems.

Our key contributions are as follows:

- **I4.0 Application Behavior:** We present a formal executable model of the behavior of I4.0 applications in the rewriting logic system Maude [4]. An application is composed of interacting state transition machines which, following the IEC 61499 standard [19], we call function blocks. Maude's search capability is used to formally check such applications for logical defects, which may lead to unsafe conditions.
- **Bounded Symbolic Intruder Model:** To evaluate the security of an application, we formalize a family of bounded intruders parameterized by the number of messages the intruder can inject. Our intruder can generate any clear text message, but can not generate (or read) messages signed by honest devices. To reduce state space complexity the intruder model is converted to one in which messages are symbolic and are instantiated opportunistically according to what can be received at a given time. Using search in the symbolic model all intruder message sets that can lead to a bad state can be enumerated. Each such message defines a flow between two function blocks that must be protected. Proof of the *Intruder Theorem* shows that the concrete and symbolic intruder models yield the same attacks.
- **Deployment transformation:** The application model is suited to reason about functionality and message flows, but does not support reasoning about resources and communication issues that arise when function blocks run on different devices. We define a theory transformation from an application executable specification to a specification of a deployment of that application using a map from application function blocks to a given set of devices. Proof of the *Deployment Theorem* shows that in the absence of intruders, applications and their deployments satisfy the same function block based properties. Proof of the *Deployment Intruder Theorem* shows that any bounded intruder attack at the system level can be found at already at the application level. Thus one can carry out security verification at the application level as the results can be transferred to deployed applications.
- **Security Integrity Wrappers:** Use of security wrappers is a mechanism to protect communications [3]. Here it is used to secure message integrity between devices using signing. Since signing is expensive, it is important to minimize message signing. We define a transformation from a specification of a deployed application to one in which devices are wrapped with a policy enforcement layer where the policies are computed from a set of message flows that must be protected as determined by the enumeration of possible attacks. The proof of the *Wrapping theorem* shows that the wrapping transformation protects the deployed system against identified attacks.

We have implemented the framework and carried out a number of experiments demonstrating analysis, deployment, and wrapping for variations of a PickNPlace application. The Maude code along with documentation, scenarios, sample runs and a technical report with details and proofs can be found at https://github.com/SRI-CSL/WrapPat.git. An early version of the framework was presented in [14] where we demonstrated the use of the search command to find logical defects and enumerate attacks, and proposed the idea of device wrappers. That paper contains a number of experiments, including scalability results. The new contributions include the theorems and proofs, implementation of the deployment and wrapping functions, and a simplified version of the symbolic intruder model.

Plan: Section 2 gives an overview of technical ideas and theorems, and describes a motivating example, which will be used as a running example in the paper. Section 3 presents the formalization of our I4.0 framework and bounded attack model in Maude: the application level, the deployment and security wrapper transformations, and theorems characterizing the guarantees of the transformations. Sect. 4 discusses related work, and Sect. 5 concludes with ideas for future work.

2 Overview

Threat Model. We assume that devices have their pair of secret and public key. Moreover, that devices can be trusted and that a secret key is only known by its corresponding device. However, the communication channels shared by devices are not trusted. An intruder can, for example, inject and tamper with (unsigned) messages in any communication channel. This intruder model reflects the critical types of attacks in Industry 4.0 applications as per the BSI report [7].

To protect communications between function blocks on different devices we use the idea of formal wrapper [3] to transform a system `S` into a system, `wrap(S,emsgs)`, in which system devices are wrapped in a policy layer protecting communications between devices by signing messages and checking signatures on flows. Intuitively, a security integrity wrapper enforces a policy that specifies which incoming events a device will accept only if they are correctly signed and which outgoing events should be signed. By using security integrity wrappers it is possible to prevent injection attacks. For example, if all possible incoming events expected in a device are to be signed, then any message injected by an intruder would be rejected by the device. However, more messages in security integrity wrappers means greater computational and network overhead. One goal of our work is to derive security integrity wrappers, $WR_1, \ldots, WR_n$, for devices, $Dev_1, \ldots, Dev_n$ in which software, called function blocks, are to be executed, to ensure the security of an application while minimizing the number of events that must be signed.

Figure 1 depicts the key components in achieving this goal with the inputs:

- **Application (App):** a set, $\{FB_1, \ldots, FB_n\}$, of function blocks (FBs) and links, $Links$ between output and target input ports. An FB is a finite state machine similar to a Mealy Machine. An App executes its function blocks in cycles. In each cycle, the input pool is delivered to function block inputs and each function block fires one

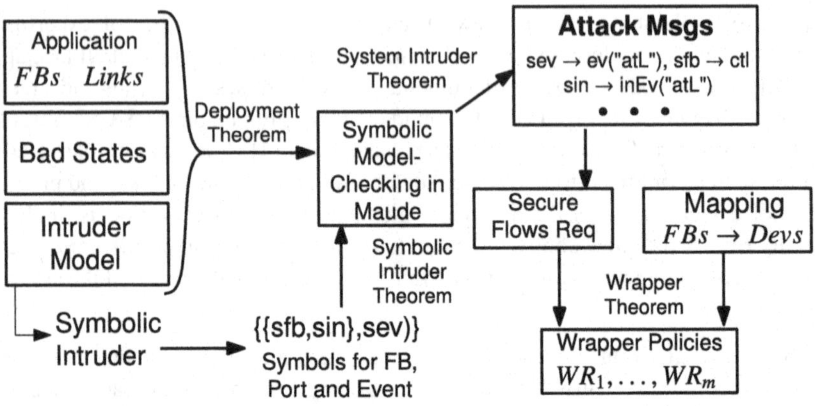

Fig. 1. Methodology overview

transition if possible. The remaining inputs are cleared, the function block outputs are collected, routed along the application links, and stored in the application input pool.

- **Bad State:** a predicate (`badstate`) specifying which combined FB states should be avoided, for example, states that correspond to catastrophic situations.
- **Intruder Capabilities:** The intruder is given a set of all possible messages deliverable in the given application. For up to n times the intruder can pick a message from this set and inject it into the application input pool at any moment of execution.

We use a symbolic representation of intruder messages and Maude's search capability to determine which messages, called *attack messages*, that an intruder can inject to drive the system to a bad state. Due to the finiteness of the FBs, applications either get stuck or are periodic. Thus, due to Maude's loop detection, the search is finite, as a search path is interrupted whenever a state that has been visited is re-visited. Using reflection and the search descent functions, we enumerate the critical events, *i.e.*, injected message sets leading to a bad state, given an application in a symbolic intruder environment.

Deploying an application is a theory transformation [13]. The function `deployApp` takes an application and a deployment mapping from FBs to devices and returns a system model that is the deployed version of the application corresponding to the mapping.

From the enumerated attack messages, we derive which flows between function blocks on different devices need to have their events signed. Finally, from these flows, we are able to derive the security integrity wrapper policies for a given mapping of function blocks to devices.

Notice that we are able to capture multi-stage attacks, where the system is moved to multiple states before reaching a bad state. This is done by using stronger intruders that can use a greater number of messages.

Challenges. To achieve our goal, we encounter a number of challenges.

- **Challenge 1 (Deployment Agnostic):** As pointed out above, the deployment of FBs on devices can affect the security requirements of flows. Analysis at the system level is more complex than at the application level. Thus it is important to understand how analysis on the application level can be transferred to the system level.
- **Challenge 2 (Symbolic Intruder):** Our intruder possess a set of concrete messages and a bound n on the number of injections. The search space grows rapidly with the bound. To reduce the search space, the concrete messages and bound n is replaced by n distinct symbolic messages. The symbols are instantiated only when required. It is important to understand the realtion of the symbolic model to the concrete model.
- **Challenge 3 (Complete Set of Attack Messages):** Given an intruder, how do we know that at the end the set of attack messages found is a complete set for any deployment?
- **Challenge 4 (System Security by Wrapping):** How do we know that the wrappers constructed from identified flows and deployment mapping ensure the security of the system assuming our threat model?

To address these challenges, we prove the following theorems:

Symbolic Intruder Theorem (Theorem 1) states that each execution of an application `A` in a symbolic intruder environment has a corresponding execution of `A` in the concrete intruder environment with the same bound, and conversely. Thus, using the symbolic intruder is sound and complete with respect to the concrete intruder–enumeration of attacks gives the same result in both cases. The key to this result is the soundness and completeness of the symbolic match generation.

Deployment Theorem (Theorem 2) states that executions of an application `A` and a deployment `S` of `A` are in close correspondence. In particular the underlying function block transitions are the same and thus properties that depend only on function block states are preserved.

System Intruder Theorem (Theorem 3) states that, letting `A`, `S` be as in the Deployment Theorem, (1) for any execution of `S` in an intruder environment there is a corresponding execution of `A` in that environment; and (2) for any execution of `A` in an intruder environment that does not deliver any intruder messages that should flow on links internal to some device, has a corresponding execution from `S` in that environment. Corresponding executions preserve attacks and FB properties. The condition in part (2) is because internal messages are protected by the device execution semantics.

Wrapper Theorem (Theorem 4**).** Let `A` be an application, `S` a deployment of `A`, and `emsgs` a set of messages containing the attack messages enumerated by symbolic search with an n bounded intruder. The wrapper theorem says that the wrapped system `wrap(S,emsgs)` is resistant to attacks by an n bounded intruder.

2.1 Example

Consider an I4.0 unit, called Pick and Place (PnP),[1] used to place a cap on a cylinder. The cylinder moving on the conveyor belt is stopped by the PnP at the correct location.

---

[1] See https://www.youtube.com/watch?v=Tkcv-mbhYqk starting at time 55 s for a very small scale version of the PnP.

Then an arm picks a cap from the cap repository, by using a suction mechanism that generates a vacuum between the arm gripper and the cap. The arm is then moved, so that the cap is over the cylinder and then placed on the cylinder. Finally, the cylinder with the cap moves to the next factory element, e.g., storage element.

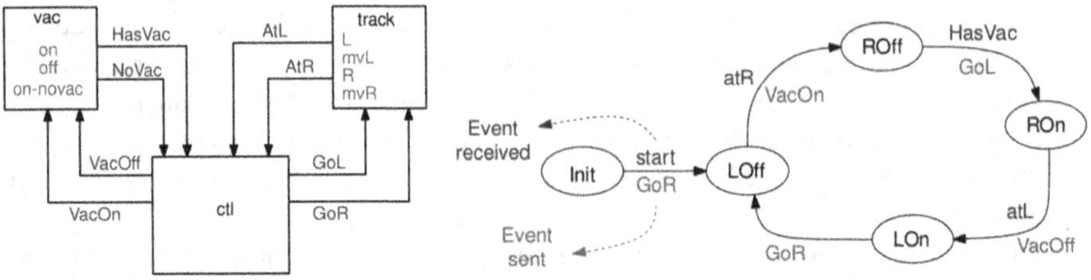

Fig. 2. PnP Function Blocks, ctl, vac, and track. The internal states of vac and track are shown in their corresponding boxes and their transitions are elided. The complete specification is shown in the finite machine to the right.

An application implementing the PnP logic has three function blocks that communicate using the channels as shown in Fig. 2. The controller, ctl, coordinates with the vac and track function blocks as specified by the finite machine in Fig. 2. For example, after starting, it sends the message GoR to the Arm that then moves to the right-most position where the caps are to be picked. When the Arm reaches this position, it informs the controller by sending the message atR. The controller then sends the message VacOn to the vac function block that starts its vacuum mechanism. If a vacuum is formed indicating that a cap has been picked, vac sends the message on-hasVac to the ctl. The controller then sends GoL to the track that then moves to the left-most position where the cylinder is located on which the cap has to be placed. The track sends the message atL. The controller then sends the message VacO to the vac to turn off the vacuum mechanism causing the cap to be placed over the cylinder.

For larger scale PnP, the hazard "Unintended Release of Cap" is catastrophic, for example picking bricks rather than caps, as dropping a brick can hurt someone that is near the PnP. By performing analysis, such as STPA (Systems-Theoretic Process Analysis), one can determine that this event can occur when *The track function block is at state mvL and the vac function block is in state on-noVac or in state off.* This is because when starting to move to the position to the left, the gripper may have succeeded to grab a cap. However, while the arm is moving, the vacuum may have been lost causing the cap to be released, *i.e.*, the vac function block is in state on-noVac or off. An intruder can cause such an event by injecting the message VacO to the vac when the arm is moving left, that is, in state mvL, while the gripper is holding something.

Following our methodology, shown in Fig. 1, we feed to our Symbolic Model-Checker the PnP function blocks, its bad state above, and a symbolic intruder that can inject at most one message. One can specify stronger intruders, but this weak intruder is already able to lead the system into a bad state. Indeed, from the model-checker's output, we find that there are four different attack messages. One of them is shown in

Fig. 1, where the intruder impersonates the track and sends to the ctl a message atL while the track is still moving.

From the identified attack messages we can see that messages in the flow from the track to the ctl involving the message atL should be protected.

Finally, suppose track and ctl are deployed in dev_1 and dev_2, respectively, then the computed security integrity wrapper on dev_1 will sign atL messages, and the security integrity wrapper on dev_2 will check whether atL messages are signed by dev_1. If track and ctl are deployed on the same device, there is no need to sign atL messages as we trust devices to protect internal communications.

3 Formalization of the I4.0 Framework in Maude

We now describe the formal representation of applications, and the deployment and wrapping transformations. We formalize theorems. We describe the main structures, operations, and rules using snippets from the Maude specification. Examples come from the Maude formalization of the PnP application of Sect. 2.

3.1 Function Blocks

An I4.0 application is composed of a set of interconnected interactive finite state machines called function blocks. A function block is characterized by its finite set of states, finite sets of inputs and outputs, a finite set of possible events at each input or output, and a finite set of transitions. We call this a class and we give FBs both an instance and a class identifier to allow for multiple occurrences of a given class.

The Maude representation of a function block (FB) is a term of the form `[fbId : fbCid | fbAttrs]`, where `fbId` is the FB identifier, `fbCid` its class identifier and `fbAttrs` is a set of attribute-value pairs, including `(state : st)`, `(oEvEffs : oeffs)`, and `(ticked : b)`, with `state`, `oEvEffs`, `ticked` being the attribute tags, `st` the current state, `oeffs` a set of signals/events to be transmitted (out effects), and `b` a boolean indicating whether the FB has fired a transition in the current cycle.

A transition is a term of the form `tr(st0,st1,cond,oeffs)` where `st0` is the initial state and `st1` the final state, `cond` is the condition, and `oeffs` is the set of outputs. A condition is a boolean combination of primitive conditions `(in is ev)` specifying a particular event (`ev`) at input `in`. A transition `tr(st0,st1,cond,oeffs)` is enabled by a set of inputs if they satisfy `cond` and the current state of the function block state `st0`. In this case, the transition can fire, changing the function block state to `st1` and emitting `oeffs`.

Example FB. The FB with class id `vac` has states

```
st("off"), {st("on"), st("on-novac");
```

inputs

```
inEv("VacOn"), inEv("VacOff");
```

outputs

```
outEv("NoVac"), outEv("HasVac").
```

The initial state, `vacInit(id("vac"))`, of an FB with class `vac` and identifier `id("vac")` is

```
[id("vac") : vac | state : st("off") ; ticked : false ;
                   iEvEffs : none ; oEvEffs : none]
```

The function `trsFB(fbCid)` returns the set of transitions for function blocks of class `fbCid`. `trsFB(fbCid,st)` selects the transitions in `trs(fbCid)` with initial state `st`. For example `trsFB(vac, st("off"))` returns three transitions

```
tr(st("on"), st("off"), inEv("VacOff") is ev("VacOff"),
   outEv("NoVac") :~ ev("NoVac"))
tr(st("off"), st("on-novac"), inEv("VacOn") is ev("VacOn"),
   outEv("NoVac") :~ ev("NoVac"))
tr(st("off"), st("on"), inEv("VacOn") is ev("VacOn"),
   outEv("HasVac") :~ ev("HasVac"))
```

We compile a transition condition into a representation as a set of constraint sets which simplifies satisfaction checking, and matching when messages are symbolic. We can think of a constraint set (CSet) as a finite map from function block inputs to finite sets of events. A set of inputs $\texttt{ieffs} = \{(\texttt{in}_i \rhd \texttt{ev}_i) | 1 \leq i \leq k\}$ satisfies a CSet, `css`, just if `css` has size k, the $\texttt{in}_i$ form a set equal to the domain of `css`, and $\texttt{ev}_i$ is in $\texttt{css}(in_i)$ for $1 \leq i \leq k$. The function `condToCSet(cond)` returns the set of CSets such that an input set satisfies some CSet in the result just if it satisfies `cond`. This is lifted to transitions by the function

```
tr2symtr(tr(st1,st2,cond,oeffs) =
         symtr(st1,st2,condToCSet(cond),oeffs) .
```

For the `vac` example, the CSet

```
condToCSet( inEv("VacOn") is ev("VacOn"))
```

maps `inEv("VacOn")` to the singleton `ev("VacOn")`.

3.2 Application Structure and Semantics

An application term has the form `[appId | appAttrs]`. Here `appAttrs` is a set of attribute-value pairs including `(fbs : funBs)` and `(iEMsgs : emsgs)`, where `funBs` is a set of function blocks (with unique identifiers), and `emsgs` is the set of incoming messages of the form `{{fbId,in},ev}`.

We use `fbId`, `fbId0` ...for FB identifiers, `in/out` for FB input/output connections, and `ev` for the event transmitted by a message. Terms of the form `{fbId,in/out}` are called Ports. For entities X with attributes, we write X.tag for the value of the attribute of X with name ‘tag’.

The initial state of the PickNPlace (PnP) application described in Sect. 2 is

```
[id("pnp") | fbs : (ctlInit(id("ctl")
                  trackInit(id("track")) vacInit(id("vac"))) ;
  iEMsgs : {{id("ctl"),inEv("start")},ev("start")} ;
  oEMsgs : none ; ssbs : none]
```

where the message `{{id("ctl"),inEv("start")},ev("start")}` starts the application controller.

Links of the form `{{fbId0,out},{fbId1,in}}` connect output ports of one FB to inputs of another possibly the same FB. They also connect application level inputs to FB inputs and FB external outputs to application level outputs. In a well formed application, each FB input has exactly one incoming link. In principle the link set is an attribute of the application structure. In practice, since it models fixed 'wires' connecting function block outputs and inputs and does not change, to avoid redundant information in traces, we specify a function `appLinks(appId)` which is defined in application specific scenario modules.

As an example, here are the two links that connect `vac` outputs to controller inputs.

```
{{id("vac"),outEv("NoVac")}, {id("ctl"),inEv("NoVac")}}
{{id("vac"),outEv("HasVac")},{id("ctl"),inEv("HasVac")}}
```

Application Execution Rules. There are two execution rules for application behavior and two rules modeling bounded intruder actions, one for the concrete case and one for the symbolic case. To ensure that an FB fires at most one transition per cycle, each FB is given a boolean `ticked` attribute, initially `false`, which is set to `true` when a transition fires, and reset to `false` when the outputs are collected.

The rule `[app-exe1]` fires an enabled function block transition and sets the ticked attribute to `true`.

```
crl[app-exe1]:
  [appId | fbs : ([fbId : fbCid | (state : st) ;
     (ticked : false) ; oEvEffs : none ;  fbAttrs] fbs1) ;
     iEMsgs : (emsgs0 iemsgs) ; ssbs : ssbs0 ;  appAttrs ]
=>
  [appId | fbs : ([fbId : fbCid | (state : st1) ;
     (ticked : true) ; oEvEffs : oeffs ;  fbAttrs] fbs1) ;
     iEMsgs : iemsgs) ; ssbs : (ssbs0 ssbs1) ;  appAttrs ]
 if symtr(st,st1,[css] csss,oeffs) symtrs := symtrsFB(fbCid,st)
 /\ size(emsgs0) = size(css)
 /\({ssbs1} ssbss) := genSol1(fbId,emsgs0,css) .
```

The function `genSol1(fbId,emsgs0,css)` returns a set of substitutions, consisting of all and only substitutions that match `emsgs0` to a solution of the CSet, `css`. In the case of concrete messages, *i.e.*, not containing symbols, the function `genSol1` just returns an empty substitution if `emsgs0` satisfies `css`. When rewriting, just one partition of `iemsgs`, one choice of (symbolic) transition, and one satisfying substitution is selected. Search will explore all possible choices.

When [app-exe1] is no longer applicable (hasSol(fbs,iemsgs) is false), [app-exe2] collects and routes generated output and prepares for the next cycle.

```
crl[app-exe2]: [appId | fbs : fbs ; iEMsgs : iemsgs ;
                       oEMsgs : oemsgs ; ssbs : ssbs ; attrs]
=> [appId | fbs : fbs2 ; iEMsgs : emsgs0 ;
            oEMsgs : (oemsgs emsgs1) ; ssbs : ssbs  ; attrs1]
 if not hasSol(fbs,iemsgs)
 /\ tick := notApp(attrs)
 /\ not getTicked(attrs)  --- avoid extracting when no trans
 /\ attrs1 := setTicked(attrs, true)
 /\ {fbs2,emsgs0,emsgs1} :=
    extractOutMsgs(tick,fbs,none, none,none,appLinks(appId)) .
```

The function extractOutMsgs removes outputs from the function blocks that fired and routes them using appLinks(appId) to the linked FB input or application output. Application level inputs are accumulated in emsgs0 and outputs are accumulated in emsgs1. The ticked attribute of each FB is set to the value of tick. In the case of a basic application, this will be false indicating the FB is ready for the next cycle. When the application level execution rules are used in a larger context, (notApp(attrs) is true), extractOutMsgs ensures that each FBs ticked attribute is true, allowing further message processing before repeating the execution cycle. If the application has a ticked attribute, it is set to true, to indicate it has completed the current cycle. fbs2 collects the updated function blocks.

3.3 Intruders

An application A in the context of an intruder is represented in the concrete case by a term of the form [A, emsgs, n] where emsgs is a set of specific messages (typically all the messages that could be delivered) and n is the number of injection actions remaining. The rule [app-intruder-c] (omitted) selects one of the candidate messages, injects it, and decrements the counter.

An application A in the context of a symbolic intruder is represented by a structure of the form [A, smsgs] where smsgs are symbolic intruder messages of the form {{idSym,inSym},evSym} (idSym, inSym, evSym are symbols standing for function block identifiers, inputs, and events respectively). We require different messages to have distinct symbols. The rule [app-intruder] selects one of the intruder messages, and moves it from the intruder message set to the incoming messages iEMsgs.

```
rl[app-intruder]:
[[appId | fbs : fbs ; iEMsgs : emsgs0 ;  attrs], emsg emsgs]
=>
[[appId | fbs : fbs ; iEMsgs : (emsgs0 emsg) ; attrs], emsgs] .
```

We note that this rule works equally well with concrete or symbolic messages, allowing one to explore consequences of injecting specific messages. Using `genSol1`, a symbolic message can be instantiated to any deliverable message. Also, if a message is injected after all function blocks have been ticked and before `[app-exe2]` is applied, it will be dropped by `[app-exe2]`, since function block inputs are cleared before collecting the next round of inputs.

3.4 The Intruder Theorem

We define the following correspondence between symbolic and concrete intruder states:
`[A,smsgs]` $\sim$ `[A,cmsgs,n]` holds only if

- `size(smsgs)` $= n$,
- `As.fbs` $=$ `Ac.fbs`, and
- `(As.iEMsgs)[ssbs]` $=$ `Ac.iEMsgs`

for some symbol substitution `ssbs`.[2] Two rule instances correspond if they are instances of the same rule. Also, in the `[app-exe1]` case the instances are the same transition of FBs with the same identifier, and in the `[app-exe2]` case the instances collect the same outputs.

An execution trace is an alternating sequence of (application) states and rule instances connecting adjacent states as usual. A symbolic trace TrS from `[A,smsgs]` and a concrete trace TrC from `[A,emsgs,n]` correspond just if they have the same length and the ith elements correspond as defined above.

Theorem 1. Let `[A,smsgs]` $\sim$ `[A,cmsgs,n]` be corresponding initial application states in symbolic and concrete intruder environments respectively, where no intruder messages have been injected.

If TrS is an execution trace from `[A,smsgs]` then there is a corresponding execution trace TrC starting with `[A,cmsgs,n]` and conversely.

Proof. By induction on trace length. The base case is simple in either direction, since an intruder message is only involved if the rule is an `app-intruder` rule. Let

$$TrS = TrS_0 \rightarrow [\texttt{As}_k, \texttt{smsgs}_k] - rl_k \rightarrow [\texttt{As}_k + 1, \texttt{smsgs}_{k+1}]$$

be an execution trace from `[A,smsgs]`. By induction, let

$$TrC_0(\texttt{pmsgs}) \rightarrow [\texttt{Ac}_k, \texttt{cmsgs}, n_k]$$

be the set of corresponding concrete traces from `[A,cmsgs,n]` where `pmsgs` are parameters for delayed choices of injected concrete messages that remain in `iEMsgs` (have been injected and not delivered or cleared), thus were injected since the last `[app-exe2]` rule. If rl_k is an instance of `[app-exe1]` then

$$\texttt{As}_k\texttt{.iEMsgs} = \texttt{iemsgs} = \texttt{iemsgs0 emsgs0}$$

[2] Note that the attributes `ssbs` and `oEMsgs` do not affect rule application.

and the function block with identifier fbId has a transition delivering emsgs0[ssbs]. Let iemsgs0 = iemsgs00iemsgs01 and emsgs0 = emsgs00 emsgs01 where iemsgs00, emsgs00 are concrete and iemsgs01, emsgs01 are symbolic. By the correspondence

$$\mathtt{Ac}_k.\mathtt{iEMsgs} = \mathtt{iemsgs00\ ipmsgs01\ emsgs00\ pmsgs01}$$

where ipmsgs01 pmsgs01 are the injection message parameters such that the following equations are satisfied:

$$\mathtt{size(pmsgs01)} = \mathtt{size(emsgs01)} \quad \mathtt{size(ipmsgs01)} = \mathtt{size(iemsgs01)}$$

$\mathtt{Ac}_k$ can deliver the same messages to the same function block. Let pmsgs01 = emsgs01[ssbs]. We extend TrC by a applying of [app-exe1] to

$$[\mathtt{A}_{k+1}, \mathtt{pmsgs00}] = [Ac_k[\mathtt{pmsgs01} = \mathtt{emsgs01[ssbs]}], \mathtt{cmsgs}, n_k].$$

For rl_k an instance of [app-exe2] or the intruder rule it is easy to see that TrC extends to a corresponding trace.

Conversely, let

$$TrC = TrC_0 \rightarrow [\mathtt{Ac}_k, \mathtt{cmsgs}_k, n_k] - rl_k \rightarrow [\mathtt{Ac}_{k+1}, \mathtt{cmsgs}_{k+1}, n_{k+1}]$$

be a concrete trace. By induction let $TrS_0 \rightarrow [\mathtt{As}_k, \mathtt{smsgs}_k]$ be a corresponding symbolic trace. If rl_k is an instance of crl[app-exe1] then

$$\mathtt{Ac}_k.\mathtt{iEMsgs} = \mathtt{iemsgs} = \mathtt{iemsgs0\ emsgs0}$$

and function block with identifier fbId has a transition delivering emsgs0. Let ssbs be a substitution such that $\mathtt{As}_k.\mathtt{iEMsgs} = \mathtt{iemsgs'} = \mathtt{iemsgs0'\ emsgs0'}$ and emsgs0'[ssbs] = emsgs0. By 'completeness' of genSol1, ssbs will be a solution generated by genSol1 and

$$[\mathtt{As}_k, \mathtt{smsgs}_k] - rl_k \rightarrow [\mathtt{As}_{k+1}, \mathtt{smsgs}_k]\ [\mathtt{Ac}_{k+1}, \mathtt{cmsgs}_{k+1}, n_{k+1}]$$

extending TrS_0 to TrS corresponding to TrC. If rl_k is an instance of [app-exe2] or an intruder rule it is easy to see that TrS_0 extends as desired.

Corollary 1. Search using the symbolic intruder model for paths reaching a badState finds all successful (bounded intruder) attacks.

We define the function getBadEMsgs([A,smsgs]) that returns the set of injected message sets that lead to badState. This function uses reflection to enumerate search paths reflecting the command

```
search [A,smsgs] =>+ appInt:AppIntruder
        such that badState(appInt:AppIntruder) .
```

Injected symbolic messages are determined by looking for adjacent states where the symbolic message set decreases. The symbols of injected messages that were actually delivered are in the domain of the value of the `sbss` attribute of the final state.

In the PnP application for an intruder with a single message, `getBadEMsgs` returns four attack message sets

```
{{{id("ctl"),inEv("HasVac")},ev("HasVac")}}
{{{id("ctl"),inEv("atL")},ev("atL")}}
{{{id("track"),inEv("GoL")},ev("GoL")}}
{{{id("vac"),inEv("VacOff")},ev("VacOff")}}
```

Recall from Sect. 2 that the PnP application state satisfies `badState` if the `track` FB is in state `st("mvL")`, presumably carrying something from right to left, and the `vac` FB is in an *off* state (`st("on-novac")` or `st("off")`).

3.5 Deploying an Application

Once an application is designed, the next step is determining how to deploy FBs on devices. We model deployment as a theory transformation, introducing a data structure to represent deployed applications, called *Systems*, extending the application module with rules to model system level communication elements, and defining a function mapping applications to their deployment given an assignment of FBs to host devices.

A deployed application is represented in Maude by terms of the form: `[sysId | appId | sysAttrs]` where `sysAttrs` is a set of attribute-value pairs including `(devs : devs)` and `(iMsgs : msgs)`. `devs` is a set of devices, and `msgs` is a set of system level messages of the form `{srcPort,tgtPort,ev}` where `srcPort/tgtPort` are terms of the form `{devId, {fbId, out/in}}`.

A device is represented as an application term with additional attributes including `(ticked : b)` which indicates whether all FBs have had a chance to execute. The function blocks of the application named by `appId` are distributed amongst the devices. The function `sysMap(sysId)` maps each FB identifier to the identifier of the device where the FB is hosted. Each device has incoming/outgoing ports corresponding to links between its function blocks and function blocks on other devices.

The function `deployApp(sysId,A,sysMap(sysId))` produces the deployment of application `A` as a system with identifier `sysId` and FBs distributed to devices according to `sysMap(sysId)`.

```
ceq deployApp(sysId,app,idmap) =
      mkSys(sysId,getId(app),devs,msgs)
if emsgs := getIEMsgs(app)
/\ devs := deployFBs(getFBs(app),none,idmap)
/\ msgs := emsgs2imsgs(sysId,emsgs,idmap,none) .
```

The real work is done by the function `deployFBs(fbs,none,idmap)` which creates an empty device for each device identifier in the range of `idmap` (setting `iMsgs` to `none` and `ticked` to `true`). Then each FB (identifier `fbId`) of `app` is added to the `fbs` attribute of the device identified by `idmap[fbId]`.

Note that the deployApp function can be applied to any state A_k in an execution trace from A. A system S_k can be abstracted to an application by collecting all the device FBs in the application fbs attribute, collecting the iEMsgs attributes of devices into the iEMsgs attribute of the application and adding system level input messages to the iEMsgs attribute of the application (after conversion to application level).

The execution rules for applications apply to devices in a system. There are two additional rules for system execution: [sys-deliver] and [sys-collect].

The rule [sys-deliver] delivers messages associated to the iMsgs attribute. The rule requires isDone to hold of the system devices, which means all the devices have their ticked attribute set to true. The target port of a system level message identifies the device and function block for delivery.

The rule [sys-collect] collects and distributes messages produced by the application level execution rules. It collects application level output messages from each device and converts them to system level output messages. Messages from device iEMsgs attributes are split into local and external. The local messages are left on the device, the external messages are converted to system level input messages.

We define a correspondence between execution traces from an application A, and a deployment S = deployApp(sysId,A,idmap) of that application. An application state A1 corresponds to a system state S1 just if they have the same function blocks and the same undelivered messages. (Note that the deployment and abstraction operations are subsets of this correspondence relation.) An instance of the [app-exe1] rule in an application trace corresponds to the same instance of that rule in a system trace (fires the same transition for the same function block). An instance of [app-exe2] in an application trace corresponds to a sequence

```
app-exe2+;sys-collect;sys-deliver
```

in a system trace collecting and delivering corresponding messages.

Theorem 2. Let A be an application and S = deployApp(sysid,A,idmap) be a deployment of A. Then A and S have corresponding executions.

Proof. This is a direct consequence of the definition of corresponding traces.

Corollary 2. A and S as above satisfy the same properties that are based only on FB states and transitions. This is because corresponding traces have the same underlying function block transitions.

Intruders at the System Level. Deployed applications are embedded in an intruder environment analogously to applications. We consider a simple case where the intruder has a finite set of concrete messages to inject, using it to show that any attack at the system level can already be found at the application level. A system in a bounded intruder environment is a term of the form [sys,msgs] where sys is a system as above, and msgs is a finite set of system level messages. The deployment function is lifted by

```
deployAppI(sysId,[A,emsgs],idmap) =
  [deployApp[sysId,A,idmap],deployMsgs(emsgs,appLinks(A),idmap)]
```

where `deployMsgs` transforms application level messages `{fbport,ev}` to system level, `{srcdevport,tgtdevport,ev}` using the link and deployment maps.

The intruder injection rule, `[app-intruder]`, is lifted to `[sys-intruder]` and the correspondence relation of the deployment theorem is lifted in the natural way to the intruder case.

Theorem 3. Assume `Ai` = `[A,emsgs]` where `A` is an application in its initial state (no intruder messages injected) and `Si` = `deployAppI(sysId,Ai,idmap)`.

1. If TrS is a trace from `Si` then there is a corresponding trace from `Ai`.
2. If `TrA` is a trace from `Ai` that delivers no intruder messages that flow on links internal to a device, then there is a corresponding trace from `Si`.

Proof. The proof is the same as for the correspondence of an application and its deployment. The additional condition in part 2 is needed because a device protects communications between FBs it hosts by having no port for delivery of such messages. In particular, if all the FBs are hosted on a single device then no intruder messages can be delivered.

Corollary 3. If a `badState` is reachable from `Si` then `sys2app(msgs)` is an element of `getBadEMsgs([A,smsgs])` where `size(smsgs)` = `size(msgs)`.

3.6 Wrapping

Towards the goal of signing only when necessary (Sect. 2) we define the transformation `wrapApp(A,smsgs,idmap)` of deployed applications as:

```
wrapSys(deployApp(sysId,A,idmap),flatten(getBadEMsgs([A,smsgs])))
```

where flatten unions the sets in a set of sets. `wrapSys(S,emsgs)` wraps the devices in `S` with policies for signing and checking signatures of messages on flows defined by `emsgs` as described below.

A wrapped device has input/output policy attributes `iPol`/`oPol` used to control the flow of messages in and out of the device. An input/output policy is an `iFact`/`oFact` set where an `iFact` has the form `[i : fbId ; in, devId]` and an `oFact` has the form `[o : fbId ; out]`. If `[i : fbId ; in, devId]` is in the input policy of a device then a message `{{fbId,in}, ev}` is accepted by that device only if `ev` is signed by `devId`, otherwise the message is dropped. Dually, if `[o : fbId ; out]` is in the output policy of a device, then when a message `{{fbId,out}, ev}` is transmitted `ev` is signed by the device. Following the usual logical representation of crypto functions, we represent a signed event by a term `sg(ev,devId)`, assuming that only the device with identifier `devId` can produce such a signature, and any device that knows the device identifier can check the signature.

The function `wrapSys(S,emsgs)` invokes the function `wrap-dev` to wrap each of its devices, `S.devs`. In addition to the device, the arguments of this function include the set of messages, `emsgs`, to protect, the application links and the deployment map. The links determine the sending FB, and the deployment determines the sending/receiving devices. If these are the same, no policy facts are added. Otherwise, policy facts are added so the sending device signs the message event and the receiving device checks for a signature according to the rules above.

```
ceq wrap-dev(dev,{{fbId,in},ev} emsgs,links,idmap,ipol,opol)
  = wrap-dev(dev,emsgs,links,idmap,(ipol ipol1), (opol opol1))
if {{fbId0,out},{fbId,in}} links0 := links
/\ devId1 := idmap[fbId]
/\ devId0 := idmap[fbId0]
/\ devId1 =/= devId0     ---- not an internal link
/\ devId := getId(dev)
**** if emsg sent from dev add opol to sign outgoing
/\ opol1 := (if devId == devId0
             then [o : fbId0 ; out ]
             else none
             fi)
**** if emsg rcvd by dev, require signed by sender devId0
/\ ipol1 := (if devId == devId1
             then [i : fbId ; in, devId0]
             else none
             fi) .

eq wrap-dev(dev,emsgs,links,idmap,ipol,opol) =
    addAttr(dev,(iPol : ipol ; oPol : opol)) [owise] .
```

Theorem 4. Assume A is an application, allEMsgs is the set of all messages deliverable in some execution of A, and smsgs is a set of symbolic messages of size n. Assume badState is not reachable in an execution of A, and emsgs contains flatten(getBadEMsgs([A,smsgs])).

1. Let wA = [wrapSys(deployApp(sysId,A,idmap),emsgs]. Every execution from wA has a corresponding execution from A and conversely. In particular badState is not reachable from wA.
2. badState is not reachable from

$$\texttt{wAC} = \texttt{[wrap(deploy(A,idmap),emsgs),allEMsgs,n]}$$

Proof 1. The proof is similar to the proof of the deployment theorem part 1, noting that by definition of the wrap function, any message in emsg will be signed by the sending device and thus will satisfy the receiving device input policy and be delivered in the wA trace as it will in the A trace.

Proof 2. Assume badState is reachable from wAC. Let wAC $rl_0 \ldots rl_k$ $\texttt{wAC}_{k+1}$ be a witness execution where badState holds of $\texttt{wAC}_{k+1}$. By the assumption on A from part 1, at least one intruder message must have been delivered.

Let $\{\texttt{emsg}_1 \ldots \texttt{emsg}_l\}$ be the intruder messages delivered in the trace, say by rules $rl_{j_1} \ldots rl_{j_l}$. None of these messages are in emsgs since their events cannot be signed by one of the devices, and thus would not satisfy the relevant input policy. Thus there is a corresponding trace from the unwrapped system

$$\texttt{AC} = \texttt{[deploy(A,idmap),allEMsgs,n]}$$

and by the *Deploy Intruder Theorem* there is a corresponding trace from `[A,allEMsgs,n]` reaching a `badState`. But `emsgs` contains all messages that are part of an intruder message set which if injected can cause `badState` to be reached. A contradiction.

4 Related Work

There are a number of recent reports concerning the importance of cybersecurity for Industry 4.0. Two examples are the German Federal Office for Information Security (BSI) commissioned report on OPC UA security [7], and the ENISA study on good practices for IoT security [6]. OPC Unified Architecture (OPC UA) is a standard for networking for Industry 4.0 and includes functionality to secure communication. The BSI commissioned report describes a comprehensive analysis of security objectives and threats, and a detailed analysis of the OPC UA Specification. The analyses are informal but systematic, following established methods. A number of ambiguities and issues were found in this process. The ENISA report provides guidelines and security measures especially aimed at secure integration of IoT devices into systems. It includes a comprehensive review of resources on Industry 4.0 and IoT security, defines concepts, threat taxonomies and attack scenarios. Again, systematic but informal.

Although there is much work on modeling cyber physical systems and cyber-physical security (see [12] for recent review), much of it is based on simulation and testing. The formal modeling work focuses on general CPS and IoT not on the issues specific to I4.0 type situations. Lanotte *et al.* [10] propose a hybrid model of cyber and physical systems and associated models of cyber-physical attacks. Attacks are classified according to target device(s) and timing characteristics. Vulnerability to a given class is assessed based on the trace semantics. A measure of attack impact is proposed along with a means to quantify the chances of success. The proposed model is much more detailed than our model, considering device dynamics, and is focussed on traditional control systems rather than IoT in an Industry 4.0 setting. The attacks on devices modeled include our injection attacks. The Lanotte et al. work is complementary to ours, while being more detailed we suspect our more abstract model combined with symbolic analysis is more scalable. The work in [16] relates to our work in proposing a method using model-checking to find all attacks on a system given possible attacker actions. The authors do not propose mitigations. SOTERIA [2] is a tool for evaluating safety and security of individual or collections of IoT applications. It uses model-checking to verify properties of abstract models of applications derived automatically from code (of suitable form). It requires access to the application source code.

The idea of using theory transformations to relate the application, system level specifications and reduce many reasoning problems to reasoning at the application level is based on the notion of formal patterns reviewed in [13]. An early example of wrapping to achieve security guarantees is presented in [3] to mitigate DoS attacks.

5 Conclusions and Future Work

This paper presents a formal framework in rewriting logic for exploring I4.0 (smart factory) application designs and a bounded intruder model for security analysis. The framework provides functions for enumerating message injection attacks, and generating policies mitigating such attacks. It provides theory transformations from application specifications to specifications of systems with application components executing on devices, and for wrapping devices to protect against attacks using the generated policies. Theorems relating different specifications and showing preservation of key properties are given. We believe that formal executable models can be valuable to system designers to find corner cases and to explore tradeoffs in design options concerning the cost and benefits of security elements.

Future work includes theory transformations to refine the system level model to a network model with multiple subnets and switches, adding timing and modeling constraints induced by use of the TSN network protocol. As in our previous work [8], we are investigating the complexity of security properties given intruder models weaker than the traditional Dolev-Yao intruder [5]. We are also considering increasing the expressiveness of function block specifications to include time constraints as in [9] to automate the verification of properties based on time trace equivalence [15], such as privacy attacks. Finally, since these devices have limited resources, they may be subject to DDoS attacks. Symbolic verification can be used to check for such vulnerabilities [18].

Another important direction is developing theory transformations for correct-by-construction distributed execution [11]. This means accounting for real timing considerations and network protocols, and identifying conditions under which application and system level properties are preserved. An important use of the framework that we intend to investigate is relating safety and security analyses and connecting formal analyses to the engineering notations used for safety and security.

We are also currently extending our implementation to support the automated exploration of mappings of function blocks to devices. In particular, we are investigating the extension of [17] to take into account security objectives in addition to device performance limitations, device capabilities, and deadlines.

Acknowledgements. This project has received funding from the European Union's Horizon 2020 research and innovation programme under grant agreement No 830892. Talcott is partly supported by ONR grant N00014-15-1-2202 and NRL grant N0017317-1-G002. Nigam is partially supported by NRL grant N0017317-1-G002, and CNPq grant 303909/2018-8.

References

1. Cyberattack on a German steel-mill (2016). https://www.sentryo.net/cyberattack-on-a-german-steel-mill/
2. Celik, Z.B., McDaniel, P., Tan, G.: SOTERIA: automated IoT safety and security analysis (2018). https://arxiv.org/pdf/1805.08876
3. Chadha, R., Gunter, C.A., Meseguer, J., Shankesi, R., Viswanathan, M.: Modular preservation of safety properties by cookie-based DoS-protection wrappers. In: Barthe, G., de Boer, F.S. (eds.) FMOODS 2008. LNCS, vol. 5051, pp. 39–58. Springer, Heidelberg (2008). https://doi.org/10.1007/978-3-540-68863-1_4

4. Clavel, M., et al.: All About Maude - A High-Performance Logical Framework. LNCS, vol. 4350. Springer, Heidelberg (2007). https://doi.org/10.1007/978-3-540-71999-1
5. Dolev, D., Yao, A.: On the security of public key protocols. IEEE Trans. Inf. Theory **29**(2), 198–208 (1983)
6. ENSIA: Good practices for security of internet of things in the context of smart manufacturing (2018)
7. Fiat, M., et al.: OPC UA security analysis (2017)
8. Kanovich, M.I., Kirigin, T.B., Nigam, V., Scedrov, A.: Bounded memory Dolev-Yao adversaries in collaborative systems. Inf. Comput. **238**, 233–261 (2014)
9. Kanovich, M.I., Kirigin, T.B., Nigam, V., Scedrov, A., Talcott, C.L.: Time, computational complexity, and probability in the analysis of distance-bounding protocols. J. Comput. Secur. **25**(6), 585–630 (2017)
10. Lanotte, R., Merro, M., Muradore, R., Vigano, L.: Time, computational complexity, and probability in the analysis of distance-bounding protocols. J. Comput. Secur. **25**(6), 585–630 (2017)
11. Liu, S., Sandur, A., Meseguer, J., Ölveczky, P.C., Wang, Q.: Generating correct-by-construction distributed implementations from formal Maude designs. In: NFM20 (2020)
12. Lun, Y.Z., D'Innocenzo, A., Malavolta, I., Di Benedetto, M.D.: Cyber-physical systems security: a systematic mapping study. CoRR, abs/1605.09641 (2016)
13. Meseguer, J.: Taming distributed system complexity through formal patterns. Sci. Comput. Program. **83**, 3–34 (2014)
14. Nigam, V., Talcott, C.: Formal security verification of industry 4.0 applications. In: ETFA, Special Track on Cybersecurity in Industrial Control Systems (2019)
15. Nigam, V., Talcott, C., Urquiza, A.A.: Symbolic timed trace equivalence. In: Catherine Meadow's Festschirft (2019)
16. Tabrizi, F.M., Pattabiraman, K.: IOT: formal security analysis of smart embedded systems. In: Proceedings of the 32nd Annual Conference on Computer Security Applications, pp. 1–15. ACM, New York (2016)
17. Terzimehic, T., Voss, S., Wenger, M.: Using design space exploration to calculate deployment configurations of IEC 61499-based systems. In: 14th IEEE International Conference on Automation Science and Engineering, pp. 881–886 (2018)
18. Urquiza, A.A., et al.: Resource-bounded intruders in denial of service attacks. In: CSF, pp. 382–396 (2019)
19. Yoong, L.H., Roop, P.S., Bhatti, Z.E., Kuo, M.M.Y.: Model-Driven Design Using IEC 61499. Springer, Cham (2015). https://doi.org/10.1007/978-3-319-10521-5

Author Index

Printed in the United States
By Bookmasters